A note about this combined book

Thank you for purchasing the *Adobe Photoshop Elements 7 and Adobe Premiere Elements 7 Classroom in a Book Collection*. By combining two books in one, you'll get the opportunity to learn two exciting applications in the same book.

The *Adobe Photoshop Elements 7 Classroom in a Book* is in the front of this combined volume. The index for the *Adobe Photoshop Elements 7 Classroom in a Book* immediately follows the text, and begins on page 373.

Immediately following is the *Adobe Premiere Elements 7 Classroom in a Book*, beginning after Page 380 of the previous book. Note that this book's pages are numbered separately, and its index begins on page 304 in the very back of the book.

A note about the DVD

The lesson files for both books are included on a single DVD-ROM.

Lesson files for the *Adobe Photoshop Elements 7 Classroom in a Book* are in a folder called "Adobe Photoshop Elements 7.0".

Some lessons in the *Adobe Photoshop Elements 7 Classroom in a Book* refer to files on an accompanying CD-ROM. Those files are all on the single Windows DVD-ROM in the back of this book.

Lesson files for *Adobe Premiere Elements 7 Classroom in a Book* are in a folder named "Adobe Premiere Elements 7.0".

ADOBE® PHOTOSHOP®
ELEMENTS 7

CLASSROOM IN A BOOK®

The official training workbook from Adobe Systems

www.adobepress.com

Adobe

WHAT'S ON THE DISC

Here is an overview of the contents of the Classroom in a Book disc

Lesson files ... and so much more

The *Adobe Photoshop Elements 7 Classroom in a Book* disc includes the lesson files that you'll need to complete the exercises in this book, as well as other content to help you learn more about Adobe Photoshop Elements 7 and use it with greater efficiency and ease. The diagram below represents the contents of the disc, which should help you locate the files you need.

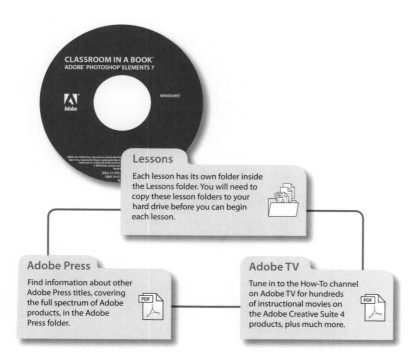

Lessons

Each lesson has its own folder inside the Lessons folder. You will need to copy these lesson folders to your hard drive before you can begin each lesson.

Adobe Press

Find information about other Adobe Press titles, covering the full spectrum of Adobe products, in the Adobe Press folder.

Adobe TV

Tune in to the How-To channel on Adobe TV for hundreds of instructional movies on the Adobe Creative Suite 4 products, plus much more.

CONTENTS

2 BASIC ORGANIZING

3   ADVANCED ORGANIZING

4   CREATING PROJECTS

5   PRINTING, SHARING, AND EXPORTING

6   ADJUSTING COLOR IN IMAGES

9 WORKING WITH TEXT

GETTING STARTED

Adobe® Photoshop® Elements 7 delivers image-editing tools that balance power and versatility with ease of use. Whether you are a home user, a professional photographer, a hobbyist, or a business user, Photoshop Elements 7 makes it easy to produce good-looking pictures and sophisticated graphics for the Web and for print.

If you've used an earlier version of Photoshop Elements, you'll find that this Classroom in a Book® will teach you advanced skills and covers the many new innovative features that Adobe Systems introduces in this version. If you're new to Adobe Photoshop Elements, you'll learn the fundamental concepts and techniques that will help you master the application.

About Classroom in a Book

Adobe Photoshop Elements 7 Classroom in a Book is part of the official training series for Adobe graphics and publishing software developed by Adobe product experts. Each lesson in this book is made up of a series of self-paced projects that will give you hands-on experience using Photoshop Elements 7.

The *Adobe Photoshop Elements 7 Classroom in a Book* includes a CD attached to the inside back cover. On the CD you'll find all the image files used for the lessons in this book, together with additional learning resources.

Prerequisites

Before you begin the lessons in this book, make sure that you and your computer are ready.

Requirements on your computer

You'll need about 380 MB of free space on your hard disk for the lesson files and the work files that you'll create as you work through the exercises.

Required skills

The lessons in this book assume that you have a working knowledge of your computer and its operating system. Make sure that you know how to use the mouse and the standard menus and commands, and also how to open, save, and close files. Do you know how to use context menus, which open when you right-click / Control-click items? Can you scroll (vertically and horizontally) within a window to see content that may not be visible in the displayed area?

If you need to review these basic and generic computer skills, see the documentation included with your Microsoft® Windows® software.

Installing Adobe Photoshop Elements 7

You must purchase the Adobe Photoshop Elements 7 software separately and install it on a computer running Windows Vista® or Windows® XP. For system requirements and complete instructions on installing the software, see the Photoshop Elements 7 Read Me file on the application CD and the accompanying documentation.

Copying the Classroom in a Book files

● **Note:** The files on the CD are practice files, provided for your personal use in these lessons. You are not authorized to use these files commercially, or to publish or distribute them in any form without written permission from Adobe Systems, Inc. and the individual photographers who took the pictures, or other copyright holders.

The CD attached to the inside back cover of this book includes a Lessons folder containing all the electronic files you'll need for the lessons. As you work through the exercises, you'll learn to organize these files using a catalog that is an essential part of many of the projects in this book. Keep the lesson files on your computer until you have completed all the exercises.

Copying the Lessons files from the CD

1   Create a new folder named **PSE7CIB** inside the *username/My Documents* folder on your computer.

2   Insert the *Adobe Photoshop Elements 7 Classroom in a Book* CD into your CD-ROM drive. If a message appears asking what you want Windows to do, choose Open Folder To View Files Using Windows Explorer, and then click OK.

If no message appears, open My Computer and double-click the CD icon to open it.

3   Locate the Lessons folder on the CD and copy it to the PSE7CIB folder you've just created on your computer.

4   When your computer has finished copying the Lessons folder, remove the CD from your CD-ROM drive and put it away.

Complete the procedures on the following pages before you begin the lessons.

Creating a work folder

Now you need to create a folder for the work files you'll create as you complete the lessons in this book.

1 In Windows Explorer, open the Lessons folder that you copied to your new PSE7CIB folder on your hard disk.

2 In the Lessons folder, choose File > New > Folder. A new folder is created in the Lessons folder. Type **My CIB Work** as the name for the new folder.

Creating a catalog file

The first time you launch Photoshop Elements, a catalog file is automatically created on your hard disk. Photoshop Elements uses this catalog file to store information about the images you import from your digital camera or your hard disk.

You will now create a new catalog to manage the image files for the lessons in this book. This will allow you to leave the default catalog untouched while working through the lessons, and to keep your lesson files together in one location where they will be easy to access.

1 Start Adobe Photoshop Elements 7. If Photoshop Elements opens without first displaying the welcome screen, click the Welcome Screen button (🏠) located at the left of the menu bar. You'll see a row of shortcut buttons across the top of the welcome screen. Click the Organize button to start Photoshop Elements in the Organizer mode.

Note: If this is the first time you have started the Organizer, an alert message may appear asking if you would like to specify the location of photos. If this alert message appears, click No.

Note: In this book, the forward arrow character (>) is used to refer to commands and submenus found in the menus at the top of the application window, for example, File, Edit, and so forth.

2 In Photoshop Elements (Organizer), choose File > Catalog.

3 In the Catalog Manager dialog box, click New. Do not change the location where the Catalog file is stored. *(See the illustration on the next page.)*

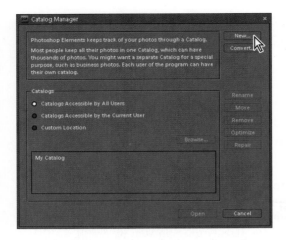

4   In the Enter A Name For The New Catalog dialog box, type **CIB Catalog** as the
    name for your new catalog, disable the Import Free Music Into This Catalog
    option, and then click OK.

5   In the Organizer, choose File > Get Photos And Videos > From Files And Folders.
    In the Get Photos From Files And Folders dialog box, click My Documents to
    open the My Documents folder. Double-click the PSE7CIB folder to open it;
    then click once to select the Lessons folder that you copied from the CD. Don't
    double-click—you do not want to open the Lessons folder.

6   In the Get Photos From Files And Folders dialog box, confirm that the Get
    Photos From Subfolders option is activated in the list of options above the
    Get Photos button. Disable the options Automatically Fix Red Eyes and
    Automatically Suggest Photo Stacks. You'll learn about these useful options
    as you work through the lessons but you won't use them just yet. *(See the
    illustration on the next page.)*

7   Click the Get Photos button. A window will open showing the photos being
    imported.

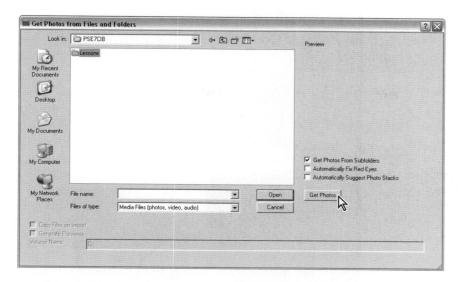

8 The Import Attached Keyword Tags dialog box opens. Click Select All below the Keyword Tags box, and then click OK.

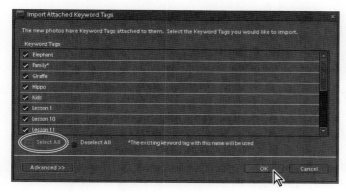

The images you are adding to the catalog contain additional information known as keyword tags, which have been applied to help you organize the images as you work through the lessons in this book. Once the image files have been imported into the catalog, the imported keyword tags are available in the Keyword Tags palette. You'll learn about using keyword tags in Lessons 2 and 3.

9   Photoshop Elements may display a dialog box informing you that the only items displayed in the Organizer are those you just imported. If this alert is displayed, click OK.

10 Click OK to close any other alert dialog box. The imported images are displayed in the Photo Browser in the main display area. Use the scrollbar at the right side to browse through the images.

11 Click the Show All button above the Photo Browser.

Reconnecting missing files to a catalog

● **Note:** To avoid missing files in your catalog, use the File > Move, File > Rename, and Edit > Delete From Catalog commands in Photoshop Elements to move, rename, or delete them, rather than doing so outside the application.

When you import a photo or video clip into Photoshop Elements, the name and location of the file is recorded in the catalog. If you move, rename, or delete a file outside Photoshop Elements after it has been added the catalog, Photoshop Elements may no longer be able to find it. If a file cannot be located, the missing file icon ( ) appears in the upper left corner of its thumbnail in the Photo Browser to alert you that the link between the file and your catalog has been broken.

If there are no files missing, you can now go on to the first lesson.

If Photoshop Elements alerts you that it cannot find an image file, you will need to carry out the following procedure to reconnect the file to your catalog.

1   Choose File > Reconnect > All Missing Files. If the message "There are no files to reconnect" appears, click OK, then skip the rest of this procedure.

2   If a message "Searching for missing files" appears, click the Browse button. The Reconnect Missing Files dialog box opens.

3 In the Browse tab on the right side of the Reconnect Missing Files dialog box, navigate to and open the moved folder.

4 Continuing to work in the Browse tab, locate and click once to select the folder that has the same name as the folder listed underneath the image thumbnail. The folder name is listed on the left side of the Reconnect Missing Files dialog box, directly under the image thumbnail.

5 After you select the appropriate folder and the correct thumbnail picture appears in the right side of the dialog box, click the Reconnect button.

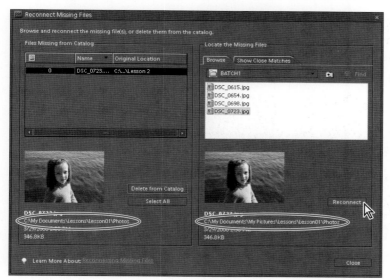

6 Repeat steps 4 and 5, continuing to select the appropriate folders and clicking the Reconnect button as you find matching files. When all the files are reconnected, click the Close button.

You can now use the Photoshop Elements Organizer to select and open files in the Photoshop Elements Editor.

Note: This procedure also eliminates error messages regarding missing files when you work with Creations, or print from the Organizer.

Additional resources

Adobe Photoshop Elements 7 Classroom in a Book is not meant to replace documentation that comes with the program, nor is it designed to be a comprehensive reference for every feature in Photoshop Elements 7. For additional information about program features, refer to any of these resources:

• Photoshop Elements Help, which is built into the Adobe Photoshop Elements 7 application. You can view it by choosing Help > Photoshop Elements Help. If you are connected to the Internet, you will be directed to the Photoshop

Elements Help and Support Center, your hub for community-based instruction, inspiration, and support that combines together the product Support pages, Design Center and Help Resource Center. If you are not connected to the Internet, you will access a subset of Help that installed with your product. For regular updates, it's best to connect to the Web for Help.

- Adobe TV, where you will find programming on Adobe products, including a How To channel. New movies are added regularly so be sure to check back if you don't find what you're looking for on your first visit to http://tv.adobe.com/.

1 A QUICK TOUR OF PHOTOSHOP ELEMENTS

Lesson Overview

This lesson will familiarize you with the Adobe Photoshop Elements 7 workspace and provide you with an overview of the tools and procedures you'll use to capture and edit your digital images.

As you work through the exercises in this lesson you'll be introduced to the following basic skills and concepts:

- Working with the Organizer and the Editor
- Attaching media
- Using the Photo Downloader
- Reviewing and comparing photos
- Sending photos in e-mail
- Using Photoshop Elements Help

 You'll probably need between one and two hours to complete this lesson.

Welcome to Adobe Photoshop Elements! Take a quick tour and get to know the Photoshop Elements workspace. You'll find all the power and versatility you'd expect from a Photoshop application in an easy-to-use, modular interface that will help you take your digital photography to a new level.

How Photoshop Elements works

Photoshop Elements has two primary workspaces: the Organizer and the Editor. You'll use the Organizer to locate, import, manage, and share your photos and media files, and the Editor for editing and adjusting your images and for creating presentations to showcase them.

About the Photoshop Elements workspaces

Once you've imported and selected a photo in the Organizer, you can open it in the Editor workspace by clicking the Editor button ( ) located near the top right corner of the Organizer window, and then choosing Quick Fix, Full Edit, or Guided Edit from the menu.

While you're working in the Editor, click the Organizer button ( ) located near the top right corner of the Editor window to open the Organizer workspace.

Use the buttons at the top of the work area to switch between the Organizer (shown in the background in the above illustration) and the Editor (shown in the foreground).

Once both the Organizer and the Editor windows are open, you can also move quickly between the two workspaces by clicking on the corresponding buttons in the Windows task bar at the bottom of your screen.

The Organizer workspace

In the Organizer workspace, the main work area is the Photo Browser pane where you can find, sort, and organize your photos and media files and preview the presentations you create to share them. At the right of the Organizer window is the Task pane, including the Organize, Fix, Create, and Share panels.

The Photo Browser pane can display a single photo or media file or show thumbnails of all the files in your catalog arranged in a variety of ways. Display your files sorted by import batch, folder location, or keywords—or if you prefer viewing your photos and media files by date, the Organizer includes a Date View workspace that lets you work with your files in a calendar format.

The Photo Browser makes it easy to browse through all the photos and assets in your catalog in one comprehensive window. It can even show previews of files that you keep stored remotely—on a CD or other removable media.

In the Organize panel of the Task pane you can sort and manage your photos by applying keyword tags and arranging them in albums. The Fix panel offers tools for the most common photographic editing tasks, such as color correction and red eye removal. (For more complex editing tasks, you'll switch to the Editor workspace by choosing Quick Fix, Full Edit, or Guided Edit from the Editor menu.) Use the Create panel to put together projects and presentations—from greeting cards to slide shows—and the Share panel to share your files with friends, family, clients or the world at large by burning a CD or DVD, sending your photos as e-mail attachments or photo mail layouts, or creating an online album.

The Editor workspace

In the Editor you'll focus on editing, adjusting, and correcting your images and creating projects and presentations to showcase them. You can choose between the Full Edit mode—with tools for color correction, special effects, and image enhancement—the Quick Fix mode with simple tools and commands to quickly fix common image problems, and the Guided Edit mode, which provides step-by-step instructions for editing tasks.

If you are new to digital imaging, the Quick Fix and Guided Edit modes make a good starting point for adjusting and correcting your photos.

If you've worked with image editing software before, you'll find that the Full Edit mode provides a more powerful and versatile image editing environment, with commands for correcting exposure and color and tools to help you make precise selections and fix image imperfections. The Full Edit tool bar also includes painting and text editing tools. You can arrange the Full Edit workspace to suit the way you prefer to work by moving, hiding, and showing palettes or arranging them in the Palette Bin. You can zoom in or out of a photo and set up multiple windows and views.

The Full Edit workspace.

Using the Palette Bin

In the Full Edit workspace, the Palette Bin of provides a convenient location to store and manage the palettes you use for image editing tasks. By default, only the Effects and Layers palettes are placed in the Palette Bin. Other palettes that you choose from the Window menu are opened in the work area. These are known as floating palettes. You can decide which palettes float and which will be stored in the Palette Bin.

To add floating palettes to the Palette Bin

1   Choose Window > [palette name] to open the palette you wish to place in the Palette Bin.

2   Drag the palette to the Palette Bin by its name tab. Dragging the palette by the bar across the top of the palette window simply repositions the palette without placing it in the Palette Bin.

Another way to add a floating palette to the Palette Bin is to choose Place In Palette Bin When Closed from the palette menu (accessed by clicking the triangle circled in the illustration below}, and then close the palette window.

To remove palettes from the Palette Bin or close palettes:

1   Remove a palette from the Palette Bin by dragging the it into the main work area by its title bar.

2   Open the palette menu and disable the option Place In Palette Bin When Closed.

3   To close a palette, choose Window > [palette name], or click the close box (▨) in the top right corner of a floating palette. When a palette is visible, a check mark is displayed adjacent to the palette's name in the Window menu; selecting a palette name that shows a check mark causes the palette window to be closed.

Adjusting the size of palettes in the Palette Bin

Adjust the size of palettes in the Palette Bin by doing either or both of the following:

•   Drag the triangle in the left border of the Palette Bin to adjust its width.

•   Drag the separator bars between palettes up or down to adjust the height of a palette.

Workflow

A typical Photoshop Elements workflow follows these basic steps:

- Bring images and media into the Organizer from a digital camera, scanner, or digital video camera.

- Sort and group images and media by a variety of methods, including applying keyword tags and creating albums, in the Organizer.

- Edit, adjust, and correct images and media or add text in the Editor.

- Share your images and media by creating projects and presentations, using e-mail or an on-line sharing service, or by burning them to CD/DVD ROM.

Importing media

Bringing your digital files into Photoshop Elements is easy.

Getting photos

To view and organize your photos in Photoshop Elements, you first need to import them into your catalog. You can bring photos into Photoshop Elements from a variety of sources and in several different ways:

- Bring images from your camera or card reader directly into the Photoshop Elements Organizer using the Adobe Photo Downloader. Getting photos directly in this way will save you time and enable you to start working with them sooner.

- Download pictures to your hard disk using the software that came with your digital camera, and then bring them into Photoshop Elements using the Get Photos And Videos > From Files And Folders command. If you prefer to work with other software to import your files to your computer, you'll first need to disable Adobe Photo Downloader. To disable the Adobe Photo Downloader, click its icon (📷) in the task bar, and then choose Disable. Do this only if you plan to use other software to import images to your computer.

- If your camera or card reader is displayed as a drive in Windows Explorer, you can drag the files to a folder on your hard disk, and then bring them into Photoshop Elements using the Get Photos And Videos > From Files And Folders command.

In most cases, you'll need to install the software drivers that came with your camera before you can download pictures to your computer. You may also need to set up the Photoshop Elements Camera or Card Reader Preferences. See "Getting photos" in Lesson 2, "Basic Organizing."

Creating a new catalog

Photoshop Elements stores information about your images in catalog files, which manage the photos on your computer but are independent of the image files themselves. As well as digital photographs, a catalog can include video and audio files, scans, PDF documents, and any presentations and layouts you might create in Photoshop Elements such as slide shows, photo collages, and CD jacket designs. When you sort and group your media in Photoshop Elements, all your work is recorded in the catalog. A single catalog can efficiently handle thousands of files, but you can also create separate catalogs for different types of work.

1 Start Photoshop Elements, either by double-clicking the shortcut on your desktop or by choosing Start > All Programs > Adobe Photoshop Elements 7.

2 Do one of the following:

- If the Welcome Screen appears, click Organize in the row of shortcut buttons across the top of the Welcome Screen, and then wait until the Organizer has finished opening.

- If the Photoshop Elements Editor window opens without first displaying the Welcome Screen, click the Welcome Screen button (🏠) located at the left in the menu bar to display the Welcome Screen, and then click Organize. Or, click the Organizer button (🔳) located at the right in the menu bar. Wait until the Organizer has finished opening.

- If the Photoshop Elements Organizer window opens without first displaying the Welcome Screen you are ready to continue with step 3.

3 In the Organizer window, choose File > Catalog.

Note: Before you start working on this lesson, make sure that you've installed the software on your computer from the application CD (see the Photoshop Elements 7 documentation) and that you have correctly copied the Lessons folder from the CD in the back of this book onto your computer's hard disk (see "Copying the Classroom in a Book files" on page 2).

4 In the Catalog Manager dialog box, click New.

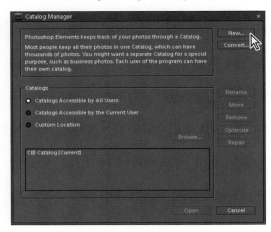

5 In the Enter A Name For The New Catalog dialog box, type Lesson1 for the catalog name, disable the option Import Free Music Into This Catalog, and then click OK.

Now you have a special catalog that you'll use just for this lesson. All you need is some pictures to put in it.

Using the Adobe Photo Downloader

The rest of this lesson is concerned with importing images into the Organizer. If you have a digital camera or memory stick reader at hand with images of your own, you can work through the steps in the next exercise; otherwise, simply follow the steps by reading through the exercise or skip to the section, "Getting photos from files and folders."

Getting photos from a digital camera or card reader

You can import image files from your camera directly into Photoshop Elements.

1 Connect your camera or card reader to your computer. For instructions on connecting your device, refer to the manufacturer's documentation that came with it.

2   Once your camera or card reader is connected to your computer, you're ready for the next step:

- If the Windows Auto Play dialog box appears, click Cancel.

- If the Photo Downloader dialog box appears automatically, continue with step 3.

- If the Photo Downloader dialog box does not appear automatically, choose File > Get Photos And Videos > From Camera Or Card Reader.

3   Under Source in the Photo Downloader dialog box, open the Get Photos From menu and choose the name of the connected camera or card reader.

4   Under Import Settings, accept the folder location listed next to Location, or click Browse to choose a new location for the files.

5   Next to Create Subfolder(s), choose one of the date formats if you want the photos to be stored in subfolders named by capture or import date. You can also choose Custom Name to create a folder using a name you type in the text box, or choose None if you don't want to create any subfolders at all. Your selection is reflected in the pathname Location pathname.

6 From the Rename Files menu, choose Do Not Rename Files and from the Delete Options menu choose After Copying, Do Not Delete Originals. If the Automatic Download option is activated, click the check box to disable it.

You will learn more about customizing import settings and the advanced features of the Adobe Photo Downloader in Lessons 2 and 3.

7 Click the Get Photos button.

The photos are copied from the camera to the specified folder location.

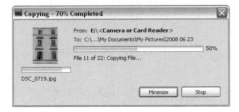

8 If the Files Successfully Copied dialog box appears, click OK.

The Getting Photos dialog box appears as the photos are imported into Photoshop Elements.

If the imported photos contain keyword metadata, the Import Attached Keyword Tags dialog box will appear. Select the keyword tags you wish to import.

The keyword tags you selected are added to the Keyword Tags palette when the photos are imported. If a keyword tag has an asterisk (*), you already have a keyword tag of the same name in your catalog and that keyword tag is attached to the photos.

9 Click OK to close any other alert dialog box.

The imported photos appear in the Photo Browser pane.

Getting photos from files and folders

Digital images stored on your computer can also be imported into Photoshop Elements.

1 Choose File > Get Photos And Videos > From Files And Folders.

2 In the Get Photos dialog box, navigate to the Lesson01 folder and click once to select the Photos folder that contains sample images.

3 Select the Get Photos From Subfolders check box. If selected, deselect the Automatically Fix Red Eyes and the Automatically Suggest Photo Stacks check boxes, and then click Get Photos. *(See the illustration on the next page.)*

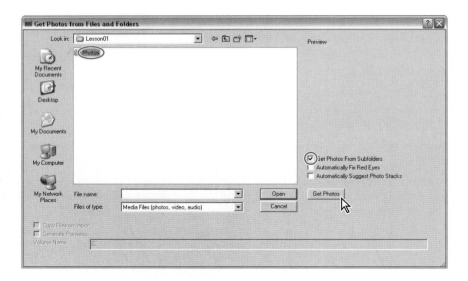

The Getting Photos dialog box appears and the photos are imported into Photoshop Elements. Since the imported photos contain keyword metadata, the Import Attached Keyword Tags dialog box appears. You will learn more about keyword tags in Lessons 2 and 3.

4   In the Import Attached Keyword Tags dialog box, click Select All, and then click OK. Click OK to close any other alert dialog box.

The imported photos appear in the Organizer.

Reviewing and comparing

Photoshop Elements provides several options to quickly and easily review and compare your images.

Viewing photos at full screen or side-by-side

The Full Screen View and Side by Side View let you review your images without the distraction of other interface items such as windows, menus and palettes.

About keyword tags

Keyword tags are personalized labels, such as "Vacation" or "Beach," that you attach to photos, video clips, audio clips and other creations in the Photo Browser to make it easier to organize and find them.

When you use keyword tags, there's no need to manually organize your photos in subject-specific folders or rename files with content-specific names.

In fact, both of the latter solutions confine a given photo to a single group. By contrast, you can assign multiple keyword tags to a photo, allowing it to be included in several different groupings. You can then easily retrieve the selection of images you want by clicking the appropriate keyword tags in the Keyword Tags palette.

For example, you could create a keyword tag called "Beach - Croatia" and attach it to every photo you took at that location. You can then instantly find all the photos with the Beach - Croatia keyword tag by clicking the Find box next to that tag in the Keyword Tags palette, even if the photos are stored in different folders on your hard disk.

You can create keyword tags to group your images any way you want. For example, you could create keyword tags for individual people, places and events in your life.

You can attach multiple keyword tags to your photos and easily run a search based on a combination of keyword tags to find a particular person at a particular place or event.

For example, you can search for all "Christine" keyword tags and all "John" keyword tags to find all pictures of Christine with her husband, John.

Or search for all "Christine" keyword tags and all "Beach - Croatia" keyword tags to find all the pictures of Christine vacationing at the beach in Croatia.

Use keyword tags to organize and find photos by their content or any other association. See Lessons 2 and 3 for more information on keyword tags.

1 Click the Display button () near the upper right corner of the Organizer window, and then choose View Photos In Full Screen from the menu.

In the Full Screen View Options dialog box, you can customize the slide show—for example, you can play an audio file as you view the images. You can also choose to display thumbnails of the selected files in a filmstrip along the right side of the screen, or add a fade between pictures.

2 Disable the Include Captions option and activate the Start Playing Automatically option; then click OK to start the slide show.

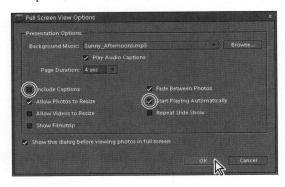

Your photos are displayed as a full-screen slide show—an enjoyable and efficient way to view a set of photos.

The control bar, which contains buttons for playing, rotating, and zooming disappears from view when you don't move the mouse for a couple of seconds.

▶ **Tip:** When you view images in full screen, you can quickly assign a rating. On the right end of the control bar, click a star to apply a rating. You can also apply the rating using the shortcut keys, 1 (for 1 star) through 5 (for 5 stars).

3 To make the control bar reappear, move the mouse.

4 Press the Esc key on your keyboard to return to the Organizer.

5 Click the Display button (⬛), and then choose Compare Photos Side By Side to display two photos simultaneously. Side by Side View is useful when you need to focus on details and differences between photos. You can select two or more photos to compare. When you click the Next Photo button (◉) in the control bar, the selected image changes to the next image in your selection. By default, image # 1 (on the left or top) is selected. To select image #2 instead, click it.

Note: The selected image has a blue border. If you have the filmstrip showing, you can click any image in the filmstrip to view it in place of the selected image.

▶ **Tip:** Choose the photos to be compared in the Organizer by holding the Ctrl key and selecting the images. Then, choose View > Compare Photos Side By Side.

Use the Side by Side View to analyze and compare composition and detail.

You can switch between views by clicking the Full Screen View button (🖥) or the Side by Side View button (🎞) in the control bar. While in either view, you can right-click an image and access further options from the context menu. For example, you can mark an image for printing, fix red eye, add a photo to an album, and delete or apply keyword tags.

6 Press the Esc key on your keyboard to return to the Organizer.

Choosing files

To select more than one photo in the Photo Browser, hold down the Ctrl key and click the photos you want to select. Ctrl-clicking enables you to select multiple non-consecutive files. To select a series of images that are in consecutive order, click the first photo, and then hold down the Shift key and click the last in the series. All the photos between the two images you Shift-clicked will be selected.

Sharing photos in e-mail

Have you ever had to wait long time for an incoming e-mail to download, and then found that the e-mail contained only a single photograph in an unnecessarily high resolution? You can avoid imposing this inconvenience on others by using the Organizer e-mail function, which exports a copy of the image that is optimized specifically for sending via e-mail.

1 In the Photo Browser, select the photo (or photos) you'd like to send by e-mail.

Note: The first time you access this feature you will be presented with the E-mail dialog box. Choose your e-mail client (such as Outlook Express or Adobe E-mail Service) from the menu, and then click Continue. You can review or change your settings later by choosing Edit > Preferences > Sharing.

2 In the Share panel of the Task pane, click the E-mail Attachments button.

3 (Optional) Drag more photos from the Photo Browser to add to your selection.

4 Select Very Small (320 x 240 px) from the Maximum Photo Size menu and adjust the image quality using the Quality slider (the higher the quality the larger the file size and the longer the download time). The resulting file size and download time for a typical 56 Kbps dial-up modem are estimated and displayed for your reference. When you're done, click Next.

5   Under Message, select and delete the "Here are the photos…" text and type a message of your own.

6   Next to Select Recipients, click the Edit Contact Book button (📇). In the Contact Book dialog box, click the New Contact button (📇). In the New Contact dialog box, type in the name (or a nickname—our example uses Mom) and e-mail address of the person to whom you want to send the picture. Click OK to close the New Contact dialog box and click OK again to close the Contact Book dialog box.

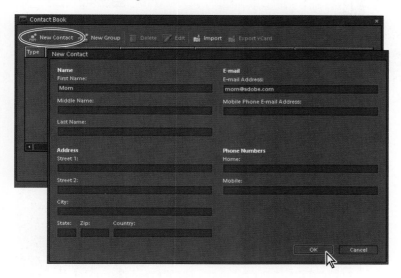

7   Under Select Recipients, click the check box next to Mom to select it, and then click Next.

Your default e-mail application immediately creates an e-mail message. You can edit the message and Subject line to say what you want. When you are finished and ready to send the e-mail, either make sure that you are connected to the Internet and click Send if you actually want to send the e-mail, or close the message without saving or sending it.

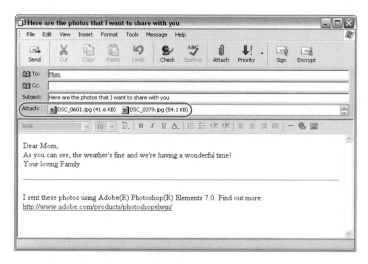

8   Switch back to Photoshop Elements (Organizer).

Creating a Photoshop.com account

Another way to share your photos and videos is by creating an online album. You'll learn how to do that in lesson 5, "Printing, Sharing and Exporting," but for now you can go ahead and create your free Photoshop.com account so that you're ready to take advantage of the exciting new Adobe-hosted Web-based services that extend the capabilities of Photoshop Elements.

With your free Photoshop.com membership you get your own personal web page, where you can not only share and showcase your images but also access your photos and videos anytime and anywhere that you can connect to the internet. You can use your Photoshop.com storage space to back up your Photoshop Elements albums and effortlessly safeguard your memories.

● **Note:** For Adobe Photoshop Elements 7, these services will be available to users in the United States only. Photoshop Elements users outside the United States will continue to share their Albums to third party sharing services via Photoshop Showcase (www. photoshopshowcase. com).

You'll also get access to the Photoshop.com Inspiration Browser, with regularly updated downloadable content such as sharing templates, page layouts, artwork, borders, frames, backgrounds, and more—as well as integrated tutorials offering tips and tricks related to whatever you're working on, providing a powerful way to advance your skill set with Photoshop Elements. (*See the illustration on the next page.*)

You can share your Photoshop.com web gallery with the world at large, or privately with friends, family, or clients to whom you chose to give the address. Check out http://bob.photoshop.com for an example of what your own sharing website could look like.

1   To sign up for your free Photoshop.com account, do one of the following:

•   In the Welcome screen, click the Join Now button.

•   In either the Organizer or Editor, click the Join Now link in the menu bar.

2   Fill out your personal details in the Photoshop.com Membership dialog box (*see the illustration on the next page*), and then click Create Account. Enjoy!

Using Help

Help is available in several ways, each one useful in different circumstances:

● **Note:** You do not need to be connected to the Internet to view Help in the application. However, with an active Internet connection, clicking the "This page on the Web" link on any page in the application's Help opens the corresponding page in LiveDocs.

Help in the application The complete user documentation for Adobe Photoshop Elements is available as Help in the application, in the form of HTML content that you can access with your default browser. Help in the application provides easy access to summarized information on common tasks and concepts. Help in the application can be especially useful if you are new to Photoshop Elements or if you aren't connected to the Internet.

LiveDocs Help on the Web This is the most comprehensive and up-to-date version of Photoshop Elements Help. It is the recommended choice if you have an active Internet connection.

Help PDF Help is also available as a PDF that is optimized for printing; just go to http://www.adobe.com/go/learn_pse_printpdf to download the PDF document. The Help PDF file is about 30 MB in size and may take a considerable time to download when using a slow Internet connection.

Links in the application Within the Photoshop Elements application there are links to additional help topics, such as the "Tell me more" link at the bottom of the panel in each guided task.

Navigating Help in the application

Choose Help > Photoshop Elements Help, or press the F1 key. Your default Web browser will open and display the starting page of the Adobe Photoshop Help in the application. Do any of the following:

- Click the Contents link in the top left corner of the window. Click a topic heading in the table of contents. Click the plus sign (+) to the left of a topic heading to see its sub-topics. Click a topic or sub-topic to display its content.

- Click the Index link in the top left corner of the window. Click on a letter to display index entries starting with that letter. Click the plus sign (+) to the left of an index header or click the index header to see its entries. Click the index entry to display its content on the right side of the window.

- Select the Search link in the top left corner of the window. Enter a search term, and then click Search. When the search has finished, click a search result in the list on the left side of the window to display its content on the right side of the window.

Search tips

Adobe Help Search works by searching the entire Help text for topics that contain all the words typed in the Search box. These tips can help you improve your search results in Help:

- If you search using a phrase, such as "shape tool," put quotation marks around the phrase. The search returns only those topics containing that specific phrase.

- Make sure that the search terms are spelled correctly.

- If a search term doesn't yield results, try using a synonym, such as "photo" instead of "picture."

Accessing LiveDocs Help on the Web

LiveDocs Help on the Web contains the most up-to-date version of Photoshop Elements Help. In addition, it enables you to search across multiple applications.

1 To access Photoshop Elements' LiveDocs Help on the Web, part of the Adobe Help Resource Center, do any of the following:

    - Click the "This page on the Web" link, located at the bottom of any topic page in Adobe Help in the application.

    - In your Web browser, open the Adobe Help Resource Center at http://www. adobe.com/support/documentation. Select Photoshop Elements from the list of products, and then click Go. On the Photoshop Elements resources page, click the LiveDocs link.

2 To switch to LiveDocs Help for a different product, select that product from the Browse menu, and then click Go.

3 To search for a topic, type the search term in the Search box, and then click Search. To search across all products, click Search All Products on the LiveDocs Search Results page, type in the search term, and then click Go.

Links to help in the application

There are some links to additional help within the Photoshop Elements application. Clicking these links will take you to the corresponding topic in either Help in the application or LiveDocs Help on the Web.

Hot-linked tips

Hot-linked tips are available throughout Adobe Photoshop Elements. These tips either display information in the form of a typical tip balloon or link you to the appropriate topic in the help file.

You've reached the end of the first lesson. Now that you know how to import photos, understand the concept of the catalog, and are familiar with the essentials of the Photoshop Elements interface, you are ready to start organizing and editing your photos in the next lessons.

Review questions

1 What are the primary workspaces in Adobe Photoshop Elements 7?

2 Define the typical Photoshop Elements workflow.

3 What is a catalog?

4 What are keyword tags?

5 How can you select multiple thumbnail images in the Photo Browser?

Review answers

1 Photoshop Elements has two primary workspaces: the Organizer and the Editor. You'll use the Organizer to locate, import, manage, and share your photos and media files, and the Editor for editing and adjusting your images and for creating presentations to showcase them. You can use the buttons on the top of the workspace windows to switch between the Organizer and the Editor.

2 A typical Photoshop Elements workflow follows these basic steps:

   • Bring images and media into the Organizer from a digital camera, scanner, or digital video camera.

   • Sort and group images and media by a variety of methods, including applying keyword tags and creating albums, in the Organizer.

   • Edit, adjust, and correct images and media or add text in the Editor.

   • Share your images and media by creating projects and presentations, using e-mail or an on-line sharing service, or by burning them to CD/DVD ROM.

3 Photoshop Elements stores information about your images in catalog files, which manage the photos on your computer but are independent of the image files themselves. As well as digital photographs, a catalog can include video and audio files, scans, PDF documents, and any presentations and layouts you might create in Photoshop Elements such as slide shows, photo collages, and CD jacket designs. When you sort and group your media in Photoshop Elements, all your work is recorded in the catalog. A single catalog can efficiently handle thousands of files, but you can also create separate catalogs for different types of work.

4   Keyword tags are personalized labels such as "House" or "Beach" that you attach to photos, creations, and video or audio clips in the Photo Browser so that you can easily organize and find them.

5   To select more than one photo in the Photo Browser, hold down the Ctrl key and click the photos you want to select. Ctrl-clicking enables you to select multiple non-consecutive files. To select a series of images that are in consecutive order, click the first photo, and then hold down the Shift key and click the last in the series. All the photos between the two images you Shift-clicked will be selected.

2 BASIC ORGANIZING

Lesson Overview

This lesson will get you started with the essential skills you'll need to import images and keep track of your growing photo library:

- Opening Adobe Photoshop Elements 7 in Organizer mode

- Creating a catalog of your images

- Importing photos from a digital camera

- Importing images from folders on your computer

- Switching between view modes in the Photo Browser

- Working with the Date view

- Creating, organizing, and applying tags to images

- Finding and tagging faces in photos

 You'll probably need between one and two hours to complete this lesson.

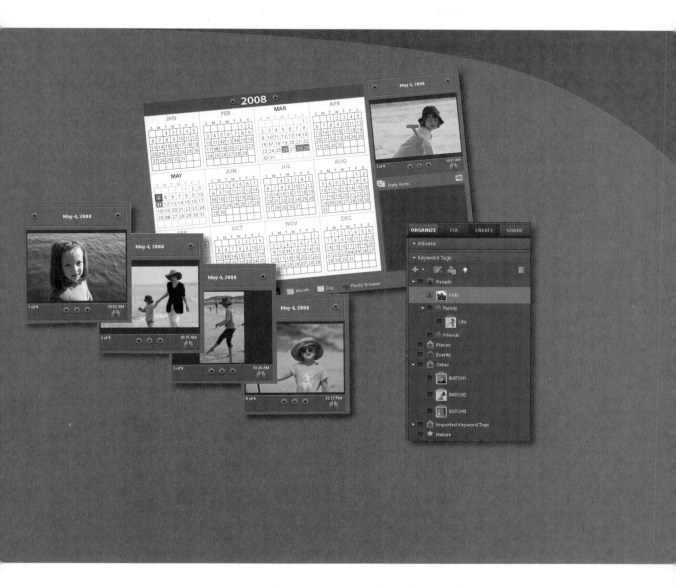

As you capture more and more images with your digital camera, it becomes increasingly important that you have ways to organize and manage your pictures on your computer so that your valuable memories are always accessible. Adobe Photoshop Elements makes it easy to import your photos from a variety of sources and provides powerful tools for sorting and searching your collection.

Getting started

● Note: Before you start working on this lesson, make sure that you've installed the software on your computer from the application CD (see the Photoshop Elements 7 documentation) and that you have correctly copied the Lessons folder from the CD in the back of this book onto your computer's hard disk (see "Copying the Classroom in a Book files" on page 2).

In this lesson, you'll be working mainly in the Photoshop Elements Organizer workspace.

1   Start Photoshop Elements, either by double-clicking the shortcut on your desktop, or by choosing Start > All Programs > Adobe Photoshop Elements 7.

2   Do one of the following:

- If the Welcome Screen appears, click Organize in the row of shortcut buttons across the top of the Welcome Screen.

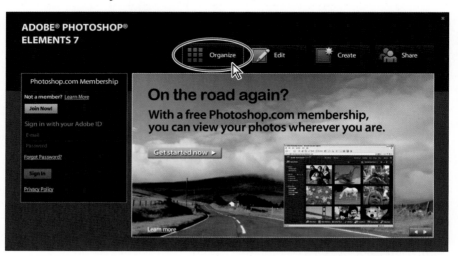

- If the Editor window opens without first displaying the Welcome Screen, click the Welcome Screen button (🏠) located to the left in the menu bar, and then click the Organize button. Alternatively, click the Organizer button (▦) located to the right in the Editor window menu bar, and then wait until the Organizer has finished opening.

- If the Organizer window opens without first displaying the Welcome Screen, you don't have to do anything more— you're all set to start with this lesson.

Getting photos

The Organizer component of Photoshop Elements provides a workspace where you can efficiently sort and organize your photos and perform some of the most common basic image editing tasks. Before you print your photographs, burn them to CD or DVD ROM, or share them by e-mail or on the Web, the first step is to assemble them in the Organizer, as you'll learn later in this lesson.

Creating a new catalog

Photoshop Elements stores information about your images in catalog files, which manage the photos on your computer but are independent of the image files themselves.

A catalog can include digital photographs, video and audio files, scans, PDF documents, and any presentations and layouts you might create in Photoshop Elements.

When you organize your files in Photoshop Elements, all your work is recorded in the catalog. A single catalog can efficiently handle thousands of files, but you can create as many catalogs as you wish to suit the way you work.

In this exercise you'll create a new catalog so that you won't confuse the practice files for this lesson with the files for the other lessons in this book.

1   In the Organizer, choose File > Catalog.

2   In the Catalog Manager dialog box, click New.

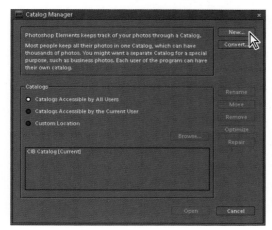

3 In the Enter A Name For The New Catalog dialog box, type Lesson2 as the catalog name, disable the option Import Free Music Into This Catalog, and then click OK.

You'll import the images for this lesson into your new catalog using a variety of different methods.

Dragging photos from Windows Explorer

Perhaps the easiest and most intuitive method of adding photographs to an Organizer catalog is by using the familiar drag-and-drop technique.

1 Minimize the Organizer by clicking the Minimize button (■) towards the right end of the Organizer window menu bar or by clicking the Organizer application button on the Windows taskbar.

2 Open the My Computer window in Windows Explorer by whatever method you usually use—double-click a shortcut icon on the desktop or use the Start menu or Windows Explorer.

3 Navigate through the folder structure to locate and open the Lesson02 folder you copied to your hard disk (see "Copying the Classroom in a Book files" on page 2).

You'll see three folders inside the Lesson02 folder: BATCH1, BATCH2, and BATCH3.

4 Drag and hold the BATCH1 folder icon over the Organizer application button on the Windows taskbar.

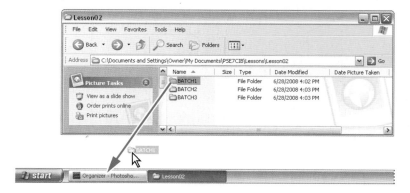

5 Wait until the Organizer becomes the foreground application, and then move the pointer with the BATCH1 over the Organizer application window and release the mouse button.

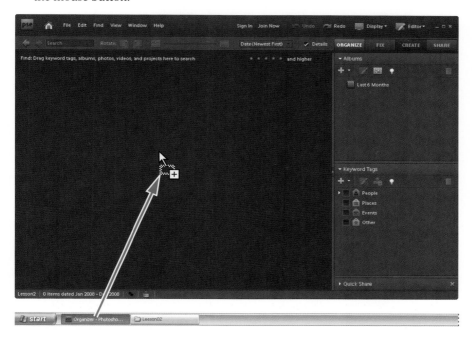

▶ **Tip:** If you can arrange the Windows Explorer window and the Organizer application window on your screen so that you can see both windows at the same time, you can also drag and drop the folder icon (or individual files) directly from the Windows Explorer window onto the Organizer application window.

The Organizer will briefly display a dialog box while searching inside the BATCH1 folder for files to import.

The files in the BATCH1 folder have keyword tags attached to them to help keep them organized, so the Import Attached Keyword Tags dialog box opens, giving you the opportunity to choose whether or not to import keywords with the images and to select which keywords to import.

6 In the Import Attached Keyword Tags dialog box, click Select All; then click OK.

The Getting Photos dialog box appears briefly as the Organizer imports the image files from the BATCH1 folder.

7   If a message appears telling you that only the newly imported items will be visible in the Photo Browser, click OK.

▶ **Tip:** If you don't want to see this message each time you import new items, select Don't Show Again before clicking OK. To have it show again, click Reset All Warning Dialogs in the General section of the Preferences dialog box.

▶ **Tip:** The timeline that you may expect to see above the Photo Browser if you're familiar with earlier versions of Photoshop Elements is now hidden by default. To toggle the visibility of the timeline, choose Window > Timeline. To toggle the visibility of the information displayed under the thumbnails in the Photo Browser, choose View > Details. If the View > Details option is active, you can show or hide File Names and Grid Lines using the View menu, where you can also choose to show or hide the borders around the thumbnails.

8   Click the Maximize button (▢) towards the right end of the menu bar in the Organizer window. This causes the window to expand and cover the entire screen.

In the Photo Browser, you can now see thumbnails of the four images you've just added to your Lesson2 catalog. Don't drag the other two batches into the Organizer—you'll use different methods to import them into your catalog.

Getting photos from specific locations

Another technique for adding items to your catalog is to use a menu command rather than re-sizing and arranging windows on the desktop.

1   Choose File > Get Photos And Videos > From Files And Folders.

2   In the Get Photos From Files And Folders dialog box, navigate to your Lesson02 folder and open the BATCH2 folder.

3   Move the pointer over each of the four image files inside the BATCH2 folder. You'll see additional information about each image displayed in a Tooltip. Click once on the file and a thumbnail image will be displayed in the Preview area.

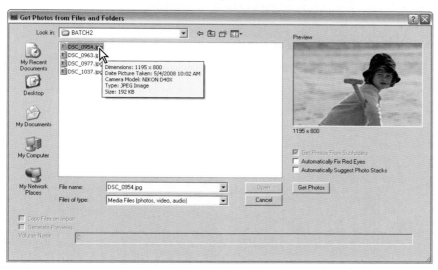

4   If the options Automatically Fix Red Eyes and Automatically Suggest Photo Stacks are activated, disable them by clicking their check boxes.

5   Press Ctrl+A or drag to marquee-select all four images in the BATCH2 folder, and then click the Get Photos button.

6   Select the keyword tag "Lesson 2" in the Import Attached Keyword Tags dialog box. You'll notice that by default the new batch of images will pick up the existing "Lesson 2" keyword tag that was already added to the catalog in the previous import.

▶ **Tip:** Select a folder icon in the Get Photos From Files And Folders dialog box, and then click Get Photos to import all items within that folder. Activate the Get Photos From Subfolders option to import items from any subfolders.

7 Click the Advanced button in the lower left corner of the dialog box. You now have the option to either assign new name to the keyword tag found in the imported items, or to use the existing tag of the same name. For now, leave the settings unchanged. Click the Reset to Basic button, and then click OK. Click OK to close any other alert dialog box.

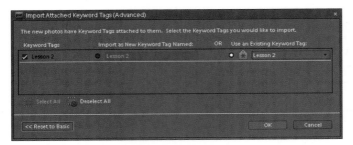

8 Click the Show All button above the Photo Browser to see all eight images.

9 Select the image of the girl with the red hat, named DSC_0977.jpg, and then click the Rotate Left button (□) above the Photo Browser.

Searching for photos to import

This method is a good choice when you're not sure exactly where on your hard disk you've stashed your photographs and other resources over the years. You might run this search on your entire hard disk or for your My Documents folder. For this demonstration, you'll limit the search to a very restricted part of the folder structure on your computer.

1 In the Organizer, choose File > Get Photos And Videos > By Searching.

Automatically fixing red eyes

The term "red eye" refers to the common phenomenon in photos taken with a flash, where the subject's pupils are red instead of black. This is caused by the flash reflecting off the retina at the back of the eye.

While none of the images for this lesson require red eye correction, for photos taken with a flash you can have Photoshop Elements remove the red eye effect automatically while importing the images. To activate this option, click the Automatically Fix Red Eyes check box in the Get Photos From Files And Folders dialog box.

More ways to fix the red eye effect will be discussed in lessons 3 and 6.

2   Under Search Options in the Get Photos By Searching For Folders dialog box, choose Browse from the Look In menu.

3   In the Browse For Folder dialog box, select the Lesson02 folder; then click OK.

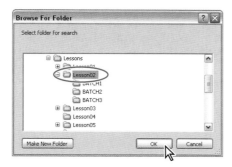

4   Under Search Options in the Get Photos By Searching For Folders dialog box, disable the Automatically Fix Red Eyes option.

5   Click the Search button located in the upper right corner of the dialog box.

6 In the Search Results box, select the BATCH3 folder and click Import Folders.

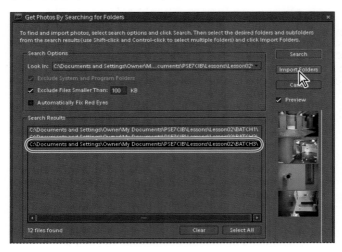

7 In the Import Attached Keyword Tags dialog box, click Select All, and then click OK. Click OK to close any other alert dialog box. Click the Show All button above the Photo Browser to see all 12 images in your Lesson2 catalog.

Importing from a digital camera

This exercise is optional and requires that you have a digital camera or memory card at hand with pictures on it. You can either step through this procedure now, or skip to the section "Viewing photo thumbnails" later in this lesson.

1 Connect your digital camera or card reader to your computer, following the manufacturer's instructions.

2 If the Windows Auto Play dialog box appears, click Cancel.

3 Do the following:

• If the Photo Downloader dialog box appears automatically, continue with step 4.

- If the Photo Downloader dialog box does not appear automatically, choose File > Get Photos And Videos > From Camera Or Card Reader.

Tip: You can also launch the Adobe Photo Downloader by double-clicking its icon (▣) in the system tray in the lower right corner of your screen.

4 Under Source in the Photo Downloader dialog box, choose the name of the connected camera or card reader from the Get Photos from menu.

5 Under Import Settings, accept the folder location listed next to Location, or click Browse to choose a new location for the files.

6 From the Create Subfolder(s) menu, choose Today's Date (yyyy mm dd) as folder name format. Your selection is reflected in the Location pathname.

7 Choose Do Not Rename Files from the Rename Files menu, and from the Delete Options menu choose After Copying, Do Not Delete Originals. If selected, deselect the Automatic Download check box.

8 Click the Advanced Dialog button.

The Advanced Photo Downloader Dialog displays thumbnail images of the photos on your camera's memory card.

9 (Optional) Click the check box below a thumbnail—removing the green check mark—to remove that photo from the selection to be imported.

10 (Optional) Select one or more photos to rotate. Click the appropriate Rotate button in the lower left corner of the dialog box.

11 Under Advanced Options, if the options Automatically Fix Red Eyes, Automatically Suggest Photo Stacks, and Make 'Group Custom Name' A Tag are activated, disable them by clicking their checkboxes, an then click Get Photos.

The selected photos are copied from the camera to the specified folder on your hard disk.

12 If the Files Successfully Copied dialog box appears, click OK.

The Getting Photos dialog box appears while the photos are being imported into Photoshop Elements.

13 Click OK to close any other alert dialog box.

The imported photos appear in the Photo Browser, already rotated where specified.

Using watched folders

You can specify any folder on your hard disk as a watched folder so that Photoshop Elements will automatically be alerted if a new photo is placed in (or saved to) that folder.

By default, the My Pictures folder is watched, but you can add additional folders to the Folders to Watch list.

You can choose to have new photos that are detected in a watched folder added to your catalog automatically or to have Photoshop Elements ask you before importing the new images. If you choose the latter option, the message "New files have been found in Watched Folders" will appear when new photos are detected. Click Yes to add the photos to your catalog or click No to skip them.

Now you'll add a folder to the watched folders list.

1   Choose File > Watch Folders.

2   Under Folders To Watch in the Watch Folders dialog box, click Add, and then browse to the Lesson02 folder.

3 Select the Lesson02 folder, and then click OK.

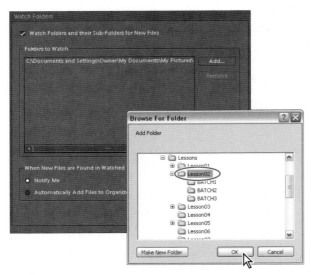

The folder name appears in the Folders to Watch list. To delete a folder name from that list, select it and then click Remove.

4 Leave the Notify Me option activated and click OK to close the Watch Folders dialog box.

This concludes this section on importing images into your catalog, but even more methods will be discussed in Lesson 3, "Advanced Organizing."

Viewing photo thumbnails in the Organizer

In the Organizer, there are several ways to view the images in your catalog. You can switch between the various viewing modes to suit different stages in your workflow or to make it easier and more efficient to perform specific organizing tasks.

Using the Photo Browser views

Up to this point, you've been working in the default Photo Browser view, the Thumbnail View, where your images are arranged by capture date and time. You can reverse the display order by choosing either Date (Oldest First) or Date (Newest First) from the menu to the right of the Thumbnail Size slider just above the Photo Browser pane.

Let's look at some of the other display options in the Organizer.

1 Use the Thumbnail Size slider to reduce the size of the thumbnails so that you can see all the images in your Lesson2 catalog.

2   Click the Display button (■) near the upper right corner of the Organizer window, and then choose Import Batch from the menu to see the thumbnails organized by their separate import sessions.

Notice the bar and film canister icons (▤) separating each row of thumbnails.

3   Try the following:

  •   Click the separator bar above any of the import batches (reading "Imported from hard disk on …") to select all the images imported in that session.

  •   Increase the thumbnail size by dragging the slider above the Photo Browser until only a few of the images in the catalog are visible in the Photo Browser.

  •   Choose Window > Timeline if the timeline is not currently visible above the Photo Browser. The timeline shows three frames representing the three import sessions that account for all the images in this catalog. Click each of the three frames in turn to jump to the first image imported in the corresponding session.

The view switches to the corresponding batch, the first image in the batch is temporarily surrounded by a green border and the capture date of that image flashes off and on.

4 Using the Display menu that you used in Step 1, select Folder Location to see the thumbnails organized according to the folders in which they are stored on your computer. Reduce the size of the thumbnails again so that you can see all the images. The divider bars between the groups now display a folder icon rather than the film canister.

● **Note:** To display the file names of the images in the Browser View, activate the menu option View > Details (or activate the Details checkbox in the bar above the Photo Browser), and then choose View > Show File Names.

5 Repeat the same steps you performed in Step 3. This time, the three frames in the timeline represent the three source folders.

6 As you click the different frames in the timeline the corresponding source folder is highlighted in the folder hierarchy displayed to the left of the Photo Browser.

Using the Date View

The Date View can be a great way to organize and access your images, particularly if you are working with a collection of photos that span a number of years.

1 Click the Display button (■) near the upper right corner of the Organizer window, and then choose Date View from the menu.

2 Select the Year option under the calendar display. Use the right and left arrows on either side of the year heading at the top of the calendar to go to 2008, if it is not already selected.

3 Select May 4, 2008 on the calendar. A thumbnail preview of the first photograph taken on May 4, 2008 appears at the right of the Organizer window.

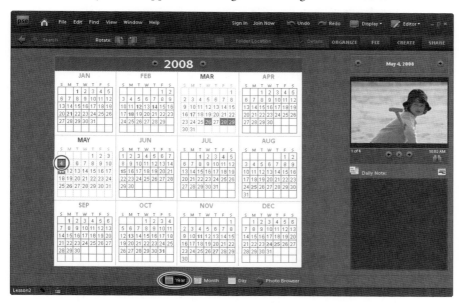

4 Use the Next Item On Selected Day button () under the thumbnail image on the right side of the Organizer window to see the other photographs taken on the same day.

You can view all the photos taken on the same day as a slide show by clicking the Start Automatic Sequencing button ( ) under the preview.

5 Under the preview thumbnail, click the Find this photo in the Photo Browser button () to switch to the Photo Browser with the current photo highlighted.

6 In the Photo Browser, click the Back To Previous View button (◀) near the upper left corner of the Organizer window to return to the Date View.

7 Select the Month option below the calendar view.

8 Click the word May at the top of the calendar, and then choose March from the months menu. If you wished to move one month at a time, you could simply click the Previous Month button twice.

9   The March page opens with the 26th already selected, as that is the first date
    for which there are photos in your Lesson2 catalog. Click in the Daily Note box
    at the bottom right of the Organizer window and type **A grand day out** to add
    a note to the selected date. An icon appears on the thumbnail for March 26th
    indicating that there is a note attached.

Now you know how to access photos via the calendar you'll be able to return and
use the Date view whenever you wish, but for the remainder of this lesson you'll
work with the Photo Browser view. Choose Photo Browser from the Display menu.

Working with star ratings and keyword tags

Most of us find it challenging to organize our files and folders efficiently. Forgetting
which pictures were stored in what folder is easy, and it can be tedious to have to
open and examine the contents of numerous folders looking for the files you want.

Photoshop Elements provides powerful and versatile organizing, tagging, and search
tools to make that kind of frustration a thing of the past. You learned earlier how
you can use the Search feature in the Organizer to find and retrieve files from multiple locations on your computer. The next set of exercises will show you how a little
time invested in applying star ratings and keyword tags can streamline the process
of sorting through your pictures, regardless of where the image files are stored.

Applying keyword tags and rating photos

Applying keyword tags to your photos and grouping keyword tag in categories make
it easy to quickly find exactly the images you're looking for. You can also apply star
ratings to your photos, providing you with yet another way to refine your searches.

In this example, you'll apply a rating and a couple of keyword tags from the default set to one of the images you imported into your catalog.

1 Click the Display button (), and then choose Thumbnail View from the menu. Make sure the Details checkbox in the bar above the Photo Browser pane is activated.

2 In the Photo Browser, move the pointer slowly from left to right over the stars beneath the thumbnail image of the mother and daughter at the seaside. When you see four yellow stars, as in the illustration below, click to apply that rating.

3 Find images based on their assigned rating using the stars and the adjacent menu located in the top right corner the Photo Browser pane. For this example set the search criteria at 2 stars and higher. Only the image with the 4-star rating is displayed in the Photo Browser.

4 Click the Show All button.

5 in the Keyword Tags palette in the Organize palette bin, click the arrow next to the People category to expand it so that you can see the Family and Friends sub-categories.

Using Star ratings and the Hidden tag

Star ratings—Use *Star ratings* to rank your photos. You can attach only one star rating value per photo. If you assign 5 stars to a photo that already has 4 stars assigned, the 5 star rating replace the previous rating.

Hidden—The *Hidden tag* hides photos in the Photo Browser, unless you select the Hidden tag as one of the search criteria. Use the Hidden tag, for example, to hide items that you want to keep, but generally don't want to see.

—From Photoshop Elements Help

6   Drag the Family sub-category tag to the thumbnail of the mother and daughter at the beach.

7   Allow the cursor to rest for a few seconds over the keyword tag icons under each thumbnail image until a Tooltip message appears identifying the keyword tags that are applied to the image.

Creating new categories and sub-categories

You can add or delete new keyword tag categories and sub-categories to group and organize your keywords tags.

1   Under Keyword Tags in the Organize pane, click the Create New button (✚) and choose New Category from the menu.

2   In the Create Category dialog box, type **architecture**, and then select the building icon from the Category Icon menu. Click OK.

3   In the Keyword Tags palette, click to select the People category, and then click the Create New button (➕) and choose New Sub-Category from the menu.

4   In the Create Sub-Category dialog box, type **Kids** in the Sub-Category Name box. Make sure that People is selected from the Parent Category or Sub-Category menu, and then click OK.

Your new keyword tag category and sub-category become part of this catalog.

Applying and editing category assignments

You can add keyword tags to several files at once, and—of course—remove keyword tag assignments.

1   In the Photo Browser, click to select any of the seven photos featuring children. Hold down the Ctrl key and click the other six photos with children to add them to the selection.

2   Drag the Kids keyword tag to any one of the selected thumbnails, as shown in the illustration on the next page. When you release the pointer, the keyword tag is applied to all seven images.

3   Keeping the same images selected, drag the architecture keyword tag to one of the un-selected images of the building interior. The keyword tag is applied to just this picture. Selecting the thumbnail or deselecting the other thumbnails is not necessary.

4   Choose Edit > Deselect, and then Ctrl-click the remaining three photos of the building interior. Drag the architecture keyword tag to any one of the selected images. The architecture keyword tag is applied to all three images at once.

5   Select the image of the mother and daughter at the beach—the one to which you applied the Family sub-category keyword tag. Then, choose Window > Properties to open the Properties palette.

6   Select the Keyword Tags tab (🔖) in the Properties panel to see which keyword tags are applied to this image.

▶ **Tip:** You can also show or hide the Properties panel by holding down the Alt key, and then pressing the Enter key.

7   Remove the Family keyword tag from the image by doing one of the following:

- Right-click the blue keyword tag image underneath the thumbnail in the Photo Browser, and then choose Remove Family Sub-Category Keyword Tag from the menu.

- Right-click the thumbnail image and choose Remove Keyword Tag > Family from the context menu.

- In the Properties palette, right-click the Family, Kids listing, and then choose Remove Family Sub-Category Keyword Tag from the menu.

8   Close the Properties palette by clicking the Close button (▣) in the upper right corner of the palette, or by choosing Window > Properties again.

Creating and applying new keyword tags

In the previous topic, you created new keyword tag categories and subcategories. In this topic, you'll create a new keyword tag and specify its location.

1   In the Keyword Tags palette in the Organize palette bin, click the Create New button (➕) and choose New Keyword Tag from the menu. The Create Keyword Tag dialog box appears.

2   In the Create Keyword Tag dialog box, choose Family (under People) for category and type Lilly for Name, and then click OK.

3 Drag the picture of the mother and child at the seaside from the previous exercise to the Lilly keyword tag under Keyword Tags.

The image becomes the icon for the new tag because it's the first image to have this keyword applied. You will adjust the tag icon in the next steps, before applying the new keyword tag to additional photos.

4 In the Keyword Tags palette in the Organize palette bin, select the Lilly keyword tag, and then click the Edit button (🖼) above the list of keyword tags. Alternatively, right-click the Lilly keyword tag, and then choose Edit Lilly Keyword Tag from the context menu.

5 In the Edit Keyword Tag dialog box, click the Edit Icon button to open the Edit Keyword Tag Icon dialog box.

6 In the Edit Keyword Tag Icon dialog box, drag the corners of the boundary in the thumbnail so that it surrounds just the little girl with the blue hat in the center of the photo.

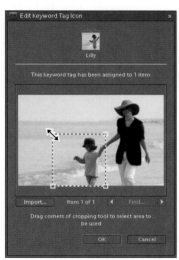

7 Click OK to close the dialog box and click OK again to close the Edit Keyword Tag dialog box.

You can update the keyword tag icon later when you find another photo that you think works better as a keyword tag icon.

8 Drag the Lilly keyword tag to the picture of Lilly digging in the sand. The Lilly keyword tag is now applied to two images.

Converting keyword tags and categories

Changing the hierarchy of categories and keyword tags is easy. Doing this will not remove the keyword tags or categories from the images to which you've assigned them.

1 Click the Find box next to the Kids sub-category. A binoculars icon (🔍) appears in the Find box to remind you that it is now activated. Only the thumbnails tagged with the Kids keyword tag are displayed in the Photo Browser.

2 Click the Show All button above the Photo Browser to see all the images in the catalog.

3 Under the People category, right-click the Kids sub-category and choose Edit Kids Sub-Category from the context menu.

4   In the Edit Sub-Category dialog box, select None (Convert to Category) from the Parent Category or Sub-Category menu, and then click OK.

Now Kids is no longer a sub-category under People but a category on its own. Its icon has been inherited from its former parent category.

5   (Optional) Select a different category icon by choosing Edit Kids category.

6   Click the empty Find box next to the Kids category. Notice that the selection of images tagged with the Kids tag did not change. Click the Show All button.

7   Under Keyword Tags, drag the Kids category to the People category.

Now the Kids category appears as a sub-category under People. Because it's no longer a category, it has the generic sub-category icon.

8   Click the empty Find box next to the Kids sub-category. Notice that the selection of images tagged with the Kids tag did not change. Click the Show All button.

9   Under the Family category, right-click the Kids sub-category and choose Change Kids Sub-Category To A Keyword Tag from the context menu.

10 Under Keyword Tags, right-click the Kids keyword tag and choose Edit Kids Keyword Tag from the context menu. In the Edit Keyword Tag dialog box, click the Edit Icon button. In the Edit Keyword Tag Icon dialog box, select a different image for this tag by clicking on the arrows under the thumbnail image.

11 Click OK to close the Edit Keyword Tag Icon dialog box and click OK again to close the Edit Keyword Tag dialog box.

Applying more keyword tags to images

There are a few simple ways to automatically tag multiple images, as well as manual methods you can use for applying custom tags.

1 Click the Display button (■) near the upper right corner of the Organizer window, and then choose Folder Location from the menu.

2 Click the Instant Keyword Tag icon on the right end of the separator bar above the thumbnails of BATCH1. That way you can quickly apply the same keyword tag to all items in that group.

3 In the Create And Apply New Keyword Tag dialog box, choose Other from the Category menu, leaving BATCH1 as the Name, and then click OK.

4 Repeat Steps 2 and 3 for the other folder groups, BATCH2 and BATCH3.

5 Switch back to Thumbnail View, using the same menu you used in Step 1.

Creating a keyword tag for your working files

You can create a keyword tag to apply to the files you create and save as you work through the lessons in this book.

1 Open the Organizer. If the Show All button is visible at the top of the Photo Browser pane, click it.

2 In the Keyword Tags palette, click the Create New button and choose New Category from the menu.

3 In the Create Category dialog box, type **Work Files** and select one of the Category icons. You can scroll to the right to see more icons. Click OK.

4 Apply this keyword tag to all the files you create and save to your My CIB Work folder as you complete the lessons in this book.

Automatically finding faces for tagging

When you use the Find Faces for Tagging feature, Photoshop Elements isolates faces in photos and displays them as individual thumbnails in the Face Tagging dialog box. This makes it quick and easy to tag faces of friends or family members. In the Face Tagging dialog box you can apply existing tags or create and apply new ones. When tag a face in the Face Tagging dialog box, Photoshop Elements removes it from view, making it simpler to work with those remaining. You can activate the Show Already Tagged Faces option if you wish the thumbnails of the faces that you've already tagged to remain visible.

1   In the Photo Browser, select the file DSC_0698.jpg, an image of four girls at the seaside.

2   Choose Find > Find Faces For Tagging, or click the Find Faces For Tagging button (🖼) at the top of the Keyword Tags palette.

Photoshop Elements searches the photo for faces. Thumbnails of the all the faces found are displayed in the Face Tagging dialog box.

As you can see, the Face Tagging dialog box is showing only three of the four girls' faces. Find Faces has missed one face. In the next exercise you'll find it.

Finding more faces

Occasionally the Find Faces feature misses a face due to unusual lighting or angle, or sometimes just because a photo is very busy or crowded with detail.

In this example, the angle of the taller girl's face combined with the strong sunlight and shadow are probably to blame, but don't worry—you can have Photoshop Elements find the missing face.

1 Click Done to dismiss the Face Tagging dialog box.

2 In the Photo Browser, make sure the file DSC_0698.jpg is still selected.

3 This time, hold down the Ctrl key on your keyboard as you choose Find > Find Faces For Tagging, or click the Find Faces For Tagging button ( ) at the top of the Keyword Tags palette.

Once more, Photoshop Elements searches the photo for faces. This time the search is slower. While Find Faces is searching, a progress bar is displayed at the bottom of the Face Tagging dialog box. The missing face has been found and there are now four faces displayed in the Face Tagging dialog box. Photoshop Elements saves the data for the found faces in the catalog file.

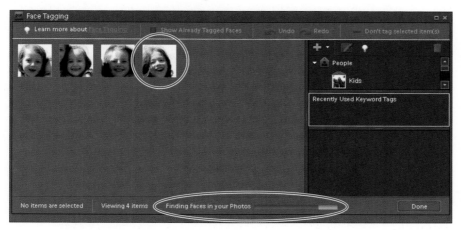

4 Click Done to dismiss the Face Tagging dialog box. In the next exercise you'll find the faces in all of the images in your Lesson 2 folder and apply some tags.

Tagging faces

Now that you know how to make sure Photoshop elements finds all the faces in your images, you can go ahead and apply the procedure to all of the photos in the Lesson 2 folder, and then you're ready to do some tagging.

1   Choose Edit > Select All to select all of the photos in the Photo Browser pane of the Organizer.

2   Just one more time, now—choose Find > Find Faces For Tagging, or click the Find Faces For Tagging button (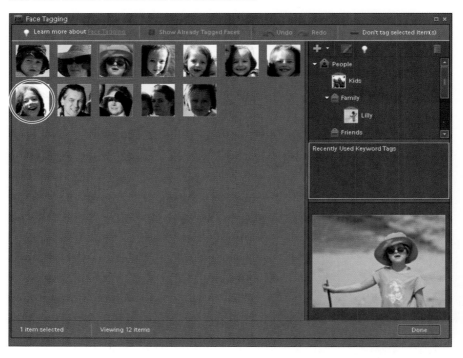) at the top of the Keyword Tags palette. You won't need to hold down the Ctrl key—the data for the extra face you found in the last exercise is already recorded in the catalog.

Photoshop Elements searches your photos for faces. Thumbnails of the all the faces found are displayed in the Face Tagging dialog box. You can see that the problematic face from the last exercise has also been found.

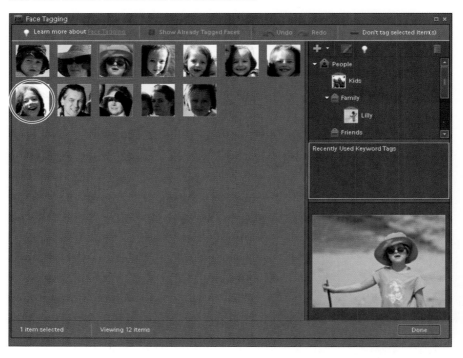

Remember: if you press Ctrl as you choose Find > Find Faces For Tagging, Photoshop Elements will produce more accurate results (for example, it will find more faces in the background of a busy photo), but it will take longer for the faces to appear. You can select your preferred searching method as default under Face Tagging in the Keyword Tags And Albums section of the Preferences dialog box (Edit > Preferences > Keyword Tags And Albums).

3   In the Face Tagging dialog box, Ctrl-click to select the three thumbnails showing Lilly's face, as shown in the illustration below. Drag the Lilly keyword tag onto any of the selected thumbnails, or drag the thumbnails onto the Lilly keyword tag. Once tagged, the thumbnails of Lilly disappear from the display.

4   Select the Show Already Tagged Faces option to show the faces already tagged.

5   Click Done to close the Face Tagging dialog box.

Using keyword tags to find pictures

Why create and apply all these keyword tags? Because they make it amazingly simple to find your pictures.

1   In the Organizer, click the empty Find box next to the Kids keyword tag. A binoculars icon appears in the Find box to remind you that it is selected. Only the thumbnails tagged with the Kids keyword tag are displayed.

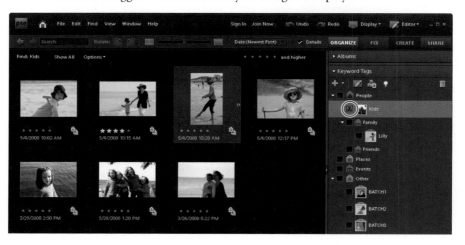

2   Leave the Kids keyword tag selected. Click the Find box for the BATCH2 keyword tag. Only four thumbnails appear: those tagged with both the Kids and the BATCH2 keyword tags.

3 From the Options menu above the Photo Browser, select Show close match results. The thumbnails display changes, also showing images that are tagged with some but not all of the selected keyword tags. These close matches are identified by a check mark in the upper left corner of the thumbnail images.

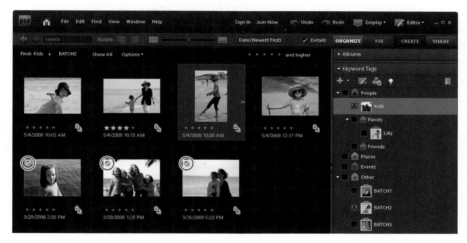

4 Click Show All to display all images.

Congratulations! You've finished the lesson and should be feeling pretty good about your accomplishment!

In this lesson, you've imported files into the Organizer using a variety of techniques and learned several different ways to view and access the images in your catalog. You've also created, edited, and applied keyword tags to individual photographs so that they'll be easy to find in future work sessions.

Review questions

1 How do you open the Organizer component of Adobe Photoshop Elements?

2 Name three methods to import photos located on your computer hard disk into your catalog.

3 What is a "watched folder"?

4 Explain the difference between the Photo Browser view and Date view in the Organizer.

Review answers

1 Click Organize in the row of shortcut buttons across the top of the Welcome Screen when you start Photoshop Elements. Alternatively, if the Editor window is already open, click the Organizer button located to the right in the menu bar.

2 This lesson demonstrated three different methods to import photos into Photoshop Elements:

   • Drag-and-drop photographs from a Windows Explorer window into the Photo Browser pane in the Organizer window.

   • In the Organizer, choose File > Get Photos And Videos > From Files And Folders, and then navigate to the folder containing your photos. You can import a whole folder, specify whether to include subfolders, or select just those images you want to add to your catalog.

   • In the Organizer, choose File > Get Photos And Videos > By Searching, and then select the folder on the hard disk that you wish Photoshop Elements to search. This method will locate all images in that folder and its subfolders and offer you the opportunity to select which images to import.

3 A watched folder is a folders on your computer that automatically alerts Photoshop Elements when a new photo is saved or added to the folder. By default, the My Pictures folder is watched, and you can add additional folders to the list. New images added to these folders can be automatically added to the Organizer.

4 The default Photo Browser view in the Organizer lets you browse thumbnail images of your photos sorted in chronological order, by folder location, or by import batch. The Date view is organized in the form of a calendar where you can quickly find photos taken on a particular day, month, or year.

3
ADVANCED ORGANIZING

Lesson Overview

In this lesson, you'll learn a few new methods of importing images and some of the more advanced techniques for organizing, sorting, and searching your growing photo collection:

- Using advanced Photo Downloader options

- Acquiring still frames from video

- Importing pictures from a PDF document

- Importing pictures from a scanner

- Using Version sets and Stacks to organize photos

- Sorting photos by location using the Map view

- Finding photos by similarity, metadata, text search, and folder location

- Grouping photos in Albums and Smart Albums

 You'll probably need between one and two hours to complete this lesson.

As your collection grows to hundreds or even thousands of images, keeping track of your photos can be a daunting task. Photoshop Elements 7 delivers advanced organizing tools that not only get the job done but in fact make the work quite enjoyable.

Getting started

● **Note:** Before you start working on this lesson, make sure that you've installed the software on your computer from the application CD (see the Photoshop Elements 7 documentation) and that you have correctly copied the Lessons folder from the CD in the back of this book onto your computer's hard disk (see "Copying the Classroom in a Book files" on page 2).

In this lesson, you'll be working mainly in the Photoshop Elements Organizer workspace, though you will switch to the Editor to capture frames from video and import images from a PDF document. You'll also create a new catalog so that you won't confuse the practice files for this lesson with the files for the other lessons in this book.

1   Start Photoshop Elements, either by double-clicking the shortcut on your desktop or by choosing Start > Programs > Adobe Photoshop Elements 7.

2   Do one of the following:

   • If the Welcome Screen appears, click Organize in the row of shortcut buttons across the top of the Welcome Screen.

   • If the Editor window opens without first displaying the Welcome Screen, click the Welcome Screen button (⌂) at the left of the menu bar, and then click the Organize button. Alternatively, click the Organizer button (⊞) located to the right in the Editor window menu bar, and then wait until the Organizer has finished opening.

   • If the Organizer window opens without first displaying the Welcome Screen, you don't have to do anything more—you're all set to continue with step 3.

3   In the Organizer, choose File > Catalog.

4   In the Catalog Manager dialog box, click New.

5 In the Enter A Name For The New Catalog dialog box, type Lesson3 as the file name, disable the Import Free Music Into This Catalog option, and then click OK.

Now you have a special catalog that you'll use just for this lesson; all you need is some pictures to put in it.

Advanced import options

In Lesson 2 you learned various methods for importing images into the Organizer and how to apply tags manually to organize your photos once they are in your catalog. In the following exercise you will find out how you can use some advanced import options to make organizing your photos even easier by having Photoshop Elements tag and group them automatically during the import process. This way, your images will already be organized by the time they arrive in your catalog. You'll also learn how to import photos from some different sources—capturing a frame from a movie, extracting images embedded in a PDF document, and acquiring an image from a scanner.

Photo Downloader options

If you have a digital camera or memory card from your camera at hand with your own photos on it, you can step through this exercise using those images. For best results, you should have several batches of pictures taken at different times on a single day. Alternatively, you can simply follow the process by studying the illustrations in the book, without actually performing the exercise yourself.

1 Connect your digital camera or card reader to your computer, following the manufacturer's instructions.

2 Do the following:

 • If the Windows Auto Play dialog box appears, click Cancel.

- If the Photo Downloader dialog box appears automatically, continue with step 3.
- If the Photo Downloader dialog box does not appear automatically, choose File > Get Photos And Videos > From Camera Or Card Reader.

3   If the Photo Downloader dialog box opens in the Advanced mode, click the Standard Dialog button located near the lower left corner of the dialog box. Under Source in the Photo Downloader dialog box, choose the name of the connected camera or card reader from the Get Photos from menu.

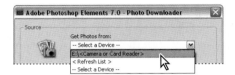

4   Under Import Settings, accept the folder location listed next to Location, or click Browse to choose a new location for the files.

5   Without making any other changes to the settings, click the Advanced Dialog button in the lower left corner of the dialog box.

The Advanced Photo Downloader Dialog displays thumbnail images of the photos on your camera's memory card. (*See the illustration on the next page.*) You have access to several options here that are not available in the Standard dialog box.

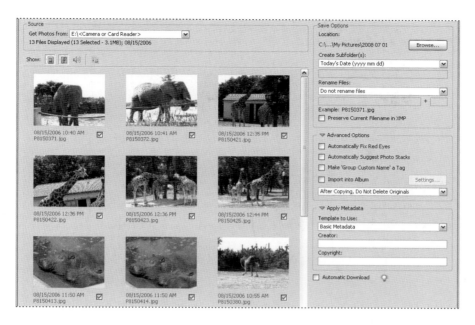

6 Under Save Options, choose Custom Groups (Advanced) from the Create Subfolder(s) menu. Your selection is reflected in the Location pathname.

The thumbnail images on the left side of the dialog box are divided into groups, based on the capture time and date.

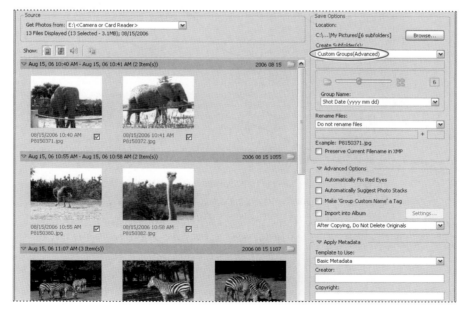

Tip: To increase or decrease the number of groups by one at a time, press Control-Shift-M or Control-Shift-L respectively on your keyboard.

7   Use the slider under the Create Subfolder(s) menu to adjust the granularity of the subdivision to suit your needs. Move the slider to the left to generate fewer groups (or subfolders) or to the right to generate more groups. Scroll down the list of thumbnail images to review the grouping of the images. The number of groups chosen is displayed in the box to the right of the slider.

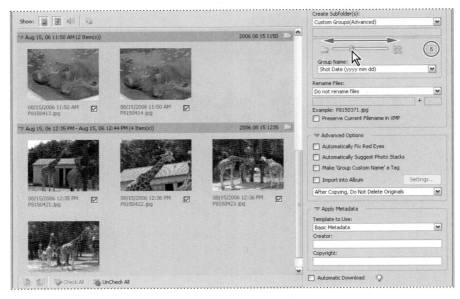

8   Choose Shot Date (yyyy mm dd) + Custom Name from the Group Name menu.

9   On the right end of the separator bar above the thumbnails of the first group, click the Custom Name field and type **Elephant** into the text box.

10 Repeat step 9 for the other groups in the thumbnail list, giving each group a distinct name (for this example, that could be **Ostrich**, **Zebra**, **Hippo**, and **Giraffe**).

11 Under Advanced Options, activate the option Make 'Group Custom Name' A Tag by clicking the check box. This will automatically create the appropriate tags and apply them to the pictures as they are imported in the Organizer. If the options Automatically Fix Red Eyes and the Automatically Suggest Photo Stacks are currently activated, disable them by clicking their checkboxes.

12 Click Get Photos.

The photos are copied from the camera to the specified folder locations.

13 If the Files Successfully Copied dialog box appears, click OK.

The Getting Photos dialog box appears and the photos are imported into your Lesson3 catalog.

The imported photos appear in the Photo Browser. You can see that Photoshop Elements has automatically created and applied tags for the groups during the import process.

The Advanced Photo Download dialog box also offers other options: you can choose to import only a specified selection of the images on your memory card, rotate images as they are imported, fix red eye effects automatically, have your photos grouped in stacks, change the file names, and add metadata such as copyright information.

The more of these import options you take advantage of when importing your photos into the Organizer, the less effort you will need to spend later on to sort and organize your files—and the easier it will be to find a specific photo months or even years after you added it to your catalog. Later in this lesson you'll learn more techniques for organizing your images, but first you'll look at some more methods of importing images into Photoshop Elements.

Acquiring still frames from a video

You can capture frames from your digital videos if they are saved in a file format that Photoshop Elements can open. Supported formats include: AVI, MPG, MPEG, WMV, ASF, and MLV. To capture frames from video, you'll need to open the Editor.

1   If you still have any image selected in the Organizer from the previous exercise, choose Edit > Deselect.

2 Click the Editor button () located near the top right corner of the Organizer window, and then choose Full Edit from the menu; then wait until the Editor has finished opening.

3 In the Editor, choose File > Import > Frame From Video.

4 In the Frame From Video dialog box, click the Browse button. In the Open dialog box, navigate to the Lesson03 folder and select the file Video.avi, and then click Open.

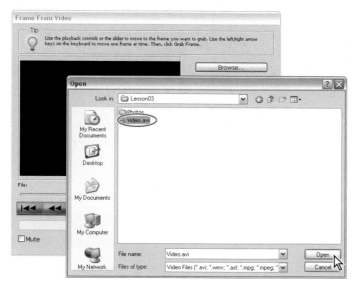

5 To start the video, click the Play button (▶). Click the Pause button (⏸) after 3 or 4 seconds, and then use the arrow keys on your keyboard to move forward or backward one frame at a time until you find a frame you want to capture.

6 To capture a frame of the video as a still image, click the Grab Frame button or press the spacebar when the frame you want is visible on the screen.

Note: Some video formats don't support rewinding or fast-forwarding. When this is the case, the Rewind (◀◀) and Fast Forward (▶▶) buttons are dimmed.

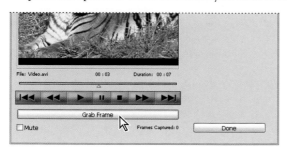

7 (Optional) You can continue to move forward and backward in the video to capture additional frames.

8 When you have all the frames you want, click Done.

Depending on your video footage and which frames you captured, you might notice artifacts in the still image resulting from the fact that a video picture consists of two interlaced half-pictures. The odd-numbered scanlines of the image, also called odd fields, constitute one half of the picture, and the even-numbered scanlines, or even fields, the other. Since the two halves of the picture were recorded at slightly different times, the captured still image might look distorted.

In Photoshop Elements you can remedy this problem by using the De-Interlace filter. With the De-Interlace filter you can remove either the odd or even fields in a video image and replace the discarded lines by duplication or interpolation from the remaining lines.

For the purposes of this exercise, it's worthwhile to deliberately choose a frame with this kind of distortion, which is most easily identified as a 'zigzag' effect that is particularly noticeable on vertical detail. *(See the illustration on the next page.)*

9 Choose the captured image with which you wish to work for this exercise. You can discard the others by clicking the Close button in the top right corner of each image window. Click No in the alert dialogs that appear to ask if you wish to save the images.

10 With your chosen image still visible in the Edit work area, switch from the Full Edit mode to the Quick Edit mode by clicking the Quick button.

11 From the View menu in the lower left corner of the image display window, choose Before & After - Vertical.

12 Click the number in the Zoom value box in the lower right corner of the image display window, type **300**, and then press Enter. Use the Hand tool to move the image in either the Before or After pane so that you can see the Tiger's eyes. (When you're working with a tiger, it's *always* a good idea to watch the eyes!)

13 Choose Filter > Video > De-Interlace. Position the De-Interlace dialog box so that you can see both the Before and After views, and then choose either Odd Fields or Even Fields under Eliminate and either Duplication or Interpolation under Create New Fields By, and then click OK. The combination of options that will produce the best results depends on the image at hand. You can Undo after each trial and repeat this step until you are satisfied with the result.

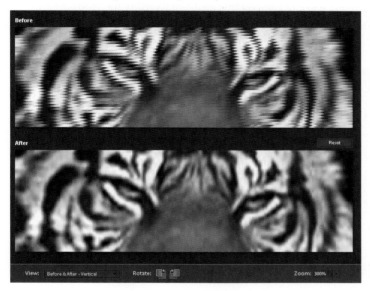

14 Return to the Full Edit mode, save the image (File > Save) in your My CIB Work folder, and then close the image window in the Editor.

Importing from a PDF document

Photoshop Elements enables you to import whole pages or just selected images from a PDF document.

1 In the Editor, choose File > Open.

2 In the Open dialog box, navigate to the Lesson03 folder and select the file ZOO. pdf, and then click Open. If you can't see the file ZOO.pdf, in the Open dialog box, choose either All Formats or Photoshop PDF (*.PDF,*.PDP) from the Files Of Type menu.

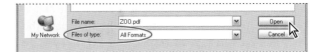

In the Import PDF dialog box, you can choose to import entire pages or just the images from the PDF file.

If you choose to import whole pages from a multiple-page PDF file, you can Ctrl-click the page thumbnails to select those pages you wish to import. Pages are rasterized according to your choice of image size, resolution, and color mode. The imported result will be an image of the page similar to that acquired by scanning a printed document.

If you choose to import just the images from the PDF file rather than full pages, you can use the same method to select the images you want.

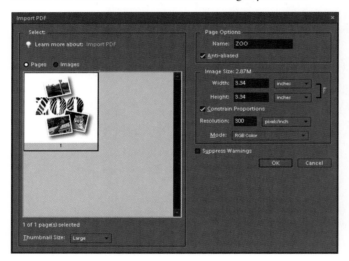

3   Under Select in the Import PDF dialog box, choose Images.

4   Select Fit Page from the Thumbnail Size menu to see the image previews at the largest possible size. Use the scrollbar at the right of the preview pane to scroll down to the last image.

5   Select Large from the Thumbnail Size menu. This enables you to see all 4 of the images in this file. Click to select an image you wish to import. Ctrl-click any additional images you would like to add to the selection to be imported, and then, click OK.

6   If any alert dialogs appear to let you know that the image files use an unsupported color mode, click Convert Mode.

Each imported image opens in its own document window in the Editor, ready for further processing.

7 For each imported image choose File > Save As, navigate to your My CIB Work folder, and save the file with a descriptive name in Photoshop (*.PSD,*.PDD) file format. Select the option Include In The Organizer before you click Save, if you wish to add the files to your catalog.

Scanning images

This exercise is optional and requires that you have a scanner available.

1 To prepare for acquiring images from a scanner, first make sure you are in the Organizer; then choose Edit > Preferences > Scanner, and then do the following:

- If you have more than one scanner or an additional video input source installed, make sure that the correct device is selected in the Scanner menu.

● **Note:** Photoshop Elements 7 also allows you to scan images using a video input source—such as a web camera—attached to your computer.

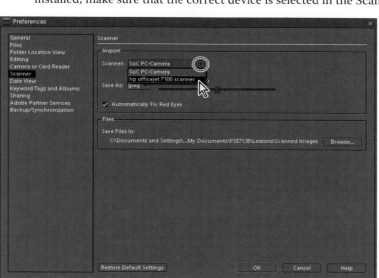

- Either accept the default settings for Save As (jpeg), and Quality (6 Medium) or, if you prefer different settings, change them now.

- Disable the Automatically Fix Red Eyes option. You will learn how to fix red eye in the Organizer in Lesson 8, "Repairing and Retouching Images."

- If you want to change the location to which the scanned files will be saved, click Browse, and then find and select the folder you want to use.

- Click OK to close the Preferences dialog box.

2 Place the picture or document you want to scan on the scanner bed and make sure your scanner is turned on.

3 If the scan dialog box does not appear automatically, go to the Organizer and choose File > Get Photos And Videos > From Scanner.

4 In the scan dialog box, click the Preview button and examine the resulting image.

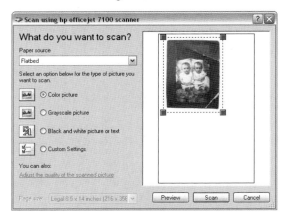

5 (Optional) If you are not satisfied with the preview, change the settings as preferred.

6 Click Scan.

When the scan is complete, the image thumbnail appears in the Organizer.

7 Click Back To All Images to see your entire catalog.

Organizing photos

Organizing your files and folders efficiently can be challenging. It's easy to forget which pictures are stored in what folder, and being forced to open and examine the content of numerous folders to find files or images can be time consuming and extremely frustrating.

The Organizer can make the whole process much simpler and more enjoyable. The next set of exercises will show you how investing a little time in organizing your pictures can streamline the process of sorting through your image files, regardless of where they are stored.

Working with Version sets

A version set groups the original imported image file with any edited versions. In the Photo Browser, you'll see all versions of the image in a single stack rather than scattered amongst the rest of the images in your catalog—making it much easier for you to find the version you want.

For this exercise you'll use Auto Smart Fix to edit an image in the organizer and create a version set containing the original and the edited version. To prepare, for the exercise, you'll clear any images you've added to your Lesson3 catalog since the beginning of this lesson.

1   In the Organizer make sure the Lesson3 catalog is open. If the Show All button is visible above the Photo Browser, click it. Choose Edit > Select All, and then choose Edit > Delete Selected Items From Catalog. If you see the options Delete All Photos In Collapsed Stacks and Delete All Items In Collapsed Version Sets in the Confirm Deletion From Catalog dialog box, activate both options by clicking their checkboxes, and then click OK.

2   Choose File > Get Photos And Videos > From Files And Folders.

3   In the Get Photos From Files And Folders dialog box, navigate to the Lesson03 folder and select the Photos folder. Select the Get Photos From Subfolders check box. If the options Automatically Fix Red Eyes and Automatically Suggest Photo Stacks are activated, disable them by clicking their check boxes, and then click Get Photos.

4   In the Import Attached Tags dialog box, click Select All, and then click OK. Click OK to close any other alert dialog box. Click the Show All button above the Photo Browser.

In the Photo Browser, you can now see thumbnails of all the images you just added to your Lesson 3 catalog.

5   In the Keyword Tags palette, click the triangle next to Imported Keyword Tags to see the newly added keyword tags.

Note: If you edit a photo in the Organizer, Photoshop Elements creates a version set for you. If you edit an image in the Editor you need to choose File > Save As, and then activate the option "Save In Version Set With Original."

6 In the Photo Browser, select the first photo of the Elephant (taken at 10:40 am) and choose Edit > Auto Smart Fix. The Auto Smart Fix command corrects the overall color balance and improves shadow and highlight detail, if necessary. The edited copy of the photo is automatically grouped with the original photo in a version set, with the edited version topmost. A version set can be identified in the Photo Browser by the version set icon in the upper right corner of the thumbnail.

Note: If you edit a photo that's already in a version set, the edited copy is placed at the top of the existing version set. To specify a different photo as the topmost, select it in the expanded view of the version set, and then choose Edit > Version Set > Set As Top Item.

7 Click the expand button on the right side of the thumbnail image, to see the original and edited images in a version set.

8 To see only the topmost photo in a version set, click the collapse button on the right side of the last thumbnail image in the expanded set, or right-click any of the thumbnail images in the set, and then choose Version Set > Collapse Items In Version Set from the context menu. Notice the other commands available from the same context menu—as well as from the Edit menu—such as Version Set > Convert Version Set To Individual Items.

About stacks

You can create stacks to group a set of related photos in the Photo Browser, making them easier to manage. Stack photos that make up a series or multiple images of the same subject to help reduce clutter in the Photo Browser.

For instance, you might create a stack for several photos of your family taken in the same pose until you have a chance to pick the best shot, or for photos taken at a sports event using your camera's burst mode or auto-bracket feature. Generally, when you take photos this way, you end up with many variations of the same photo, but you only want the best one to appear in the Photo Browser. Stacking the photos lets you easily access them all in one place instead of having them scattered across rows of thumbnails.

1 Click the empty Find box next to the Zebra tag in the Imported Tags category.

2 To marquee-select all three images, click below the first thumbnail image and drag to the top and right. When you release the pointer, all images intersected by the selection marquee are selected.

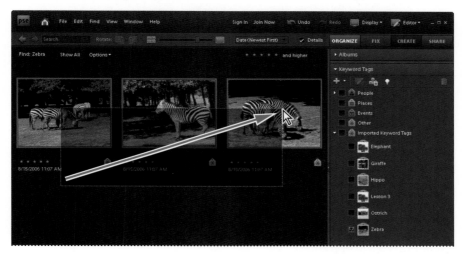

3 Choose Edit > Stack > Stack Selected Photos.

All three Zebra photos are now grouped in a stack. You can expand and collapse stacks in the Photo Browser the same way you expand and collapse version sets.

A stack can be identified in the Photo Browser by the stack icon in the upper right corner of the thumbnail.

4 Click the Show All button above the Photo Browser, and then click the empty Find boxes next to the Hippo and Ostrich tags in the Imported Tags category.

5 Choose Edit > Select All, and then choose Edit > Stack > Automatically Suggest Photo Stacks.

The Automatically Suggest Photo Stacks dialog box appears. The two photos of the hippopotamus have been successfully placed in a group already, but the ostrich photos, which have less visual similarity, will need to be grouped manually.

6 In the Automatically Suggest Photo Stacks dialog box, scroll down to the bottom of the thumbnail list. Click the image of the ostrich in the last group and drag it up to place it in the same group as the other ostrich photo.

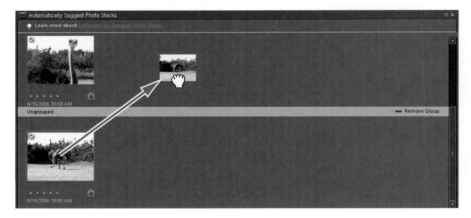

7 To split one group into two, position the cursor between two images in the group. When the cursor changes to the scissors icon, click to divide the group.

8 To exclude all photos in a group from being stacked, click the Remove Group button. Alternatively, select individual photos, and then click the Remove Selected Photo(s) button in the lower left corner of the dialog box.

9 If you change your mind about a photo excluded from being stacked, make sure the Show Removed Photos option at the bottom of the dialog box is activated, and then drag the thumbnail image from the removed photos bin to add it to a group in the main thumbnail area.

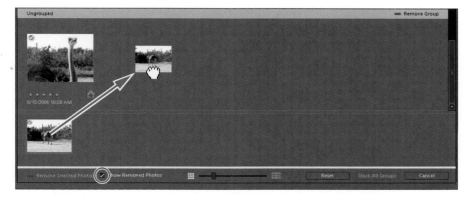

10 When you're done, click Stack All Groups to stack the photos in each group and close the Automatically Suggest Photo Stacks dialog box. Click Show All in the Photo Browser.

A stack can be identified in the Photo Browser by the stack icon in the upper right corner of the thumbnail.

Tips for working with stacks

Note: If you edit a photo that's already in a stack, the photo and its edited copy are put in a version set that is nested inside the stack.

Keep these points in mind when working with stacks:

- By default, the most recent photo is placed on top of the stack. As you create the stack, you can specify a new image as the topmost by right-clicking it and choosing from the context menu.

- Combining two or more stacks merges them to form one new stack, with the most recent photo on top of the stack. The original groupings are not preserved.

- Many actions applied to a collapsed stack, such as editing, printing, and e-mailing, are applied to the topmost item only. To apply an action to multiple images in a stack, expand the stack and select the individual images or un-stack them.

- If you apply a keyword tag to a collapsed stack, the keyword tag is applied to all items in the stack. When you run a search on the keyword tag, the top photo in the stack appears in the search results marked with the stack icon. If you want to apply a keyword tag to only one photo in a stack, expand the stack and apply the keyword tag to just that photo.

- You can access stack commands by right-clicking or by using the Edit menu.

Creating Albums

Another way of grouping photos is to organize them into albums. You can create a new album to group shots from a special occasion such as a wedding or vacation, or to assemble the images that you want to use in a project such as a presentation to a client or a slideshow. Add pictures to the album the same way you would add them to a group of pictures with the same keyword tag. The main difference between albums and keyword tags is that in an album you can rearrange the order of the photos into any order you want. Smart albums automatically search your catalog and collect the images that match any search criteria that you have specified. You'll learn about using smart albums later in this lesson in the section "Viewing and finding photos."

1 If the Albums palette is collapsed in the Organize palette bin, click the triangle in the header of the palette to expand it.

2 To create a new album, click the Create New button (➕) in the header of the Albums palette, and then choose New Album from the menu.

3 In the Create Album dialog box, type **Animals** as the name of the new album, and then click OK.

4 Ctrl-click to select two or three photos in the Photo Browser, and then drag the group onto the Animals album icon.

● **Note:** If you add a collapsed version set or a collapsed stack to an album, only the topmost picture of the version set or stack will be visible in the album. To add a different picture to the album, first expand the version set or stack.

● **Note:** You can only view the contents of one album at a time.

5 To see the contents of an album, click the album icon, or drag and drop the album icon onto the Find bar above the Photo Browser. Notice the number in the top left corner of each photo, representing its order in the album.

6 To change the order of the images in an album, select one or more photos in the Photo Browser, and then drag the selection to the desired position. The photos are reordered when you release the pointer.

7   (Optional) To remove a picture from an album, right-click the picture in the album view, and then choose Remove from Album > [album name] from the menu.

8   Click Show All above the Browser View to see all the photos in your catalog.

9   To delete an album, right-click its icon in the Albums palette, and then choose Delete [album name] album from the menu.

▶ **Tip:** You can group related albums in an album group, as you group keyword tags in a category. Change an album's properties and icon by clicking the Edit album button.

● **Note:** Deleting an album does not delete the photos in the album from your catalog. Albums store only references to the actual photos.

10 Click OK in the Confirm Album Deletion dialog box.

The Map View

In the Map view of the Organizer, you can arrange and search for photos by geographic location. Associate an image with a location by simply dragging its thumbnail from the Photo Browser directly to a location on the map.

● **Note:** You must have an active Internet connection to use this feature.

1   In the Organizer, right-click the second thumbnail image of the elephant, and then choose Place on Map from the context menu.

2   In the Photo Location On Map dialog box, type **1 Zoo Road, San Francisco, CA** in the text box, and then click Find.

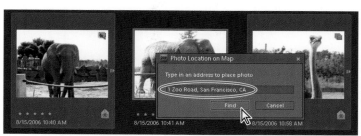

3   In the Look Up Address dialog box, click OK to confirm 1 Zoo Rd San Francisco, CA, 94132-1027 US.

4 The Map view opens to the left of the Photo Browser. You can use the Hand tool to drag the map in any direction. The red pin indicates the location for your photo.

5 Select Hybrid from the menu in the lower right corner of the Map panel, beside the Zoom, Hand, and Move tools.

6 Use the Zoom In tool and the Hand tool in combination to magnify the view on the San Francisco Zoological Gardens. Use the Move tool to reposition the red pin to exactly where you want it to appear on the map.

7 To place additional photos on the map, drag them from the Photo Browser to the Map view. If you get too close to an existing pin, the photos will be grouped under one pin location—which may or may not be what you want.

Tip: You can drag a keyword tag—for example, a keyword tag in the Places category —to the Map view to position all photos tagged with that keyword tag on the map.

8 Select the Limit Search To Map Area check box in the lower left corner of the Map View. Only photos mapped to the currently visible map area are displayed in the Browser View.

9 Click the Close button (![x]) in the upper right corner of the Map panel to close the Map view. Click the Show All button above the Photo Browser. Right-click the second thumbnail of the elephant, and then choose Show on Map from the context menu. The Map view will open, displaying the location to which the photo was mapped.

10 Close the Map view.

This concludes the section on organizing your photos. You've learned about version sets and stacks, how to group photos in albums, and how to arrange them by geographic location. In the next section, you'll learn how you can easily find photos in your catalog—even when you haven't spent a lot of time organizing them.

Viewing and finding photos

In the Organizer, Photoshop Elements offers several methods to find photos:

- **The Timeline** If necessary, choose Window > Timeline to display the timeline above the Browser View. Then, click a month or set a range to find photos and media files by date, by import batch, or by folder location.

- **The Find bar** Drag and drop a photo, keyword tag, creation, or album onto the find bar to locate similar or matching photos and media files.

- **The Find menu** Use the commands in this menu to find photos by date, caption or note, file name, history, media type, metadata, or color similarity. Commands are also available for finding photos and media files that have unknown dates, are un-tagged, or are not in an album.

Finding photos by visual similarity

You can search for photos containing similar images, color, or general appearance.

1   In the Organizer, choose Edit > Select All. Choose Edit > Stack > Unstack Photos, and then choose Edit > Version Set > Revert To Original. Click OK to close any alert dialog box that might appear.

2   Choose Edit > Deselect. Then, drag the first image with the zebras to the find bar.

The images in the Photo Browser are now displayed in decreasing order of similarity in visual appearance to the selected image. A similarity percentage appears in the bottom left corner of each image.

3   Click the Show All button.

Finding photos using details and metadata

You can search for your images by file details or metadata. Searching by metadata is useful when you want to narrow a search by using multiple criteria. For example, if you want to find all photos captured on a certain date that are also marked with a specific keyword tag, you can search using both capture date and keyword tags in the Find By Details (Metadata) dialog box.

Searchable metadata includes file name, file type, keyword tags, albums, notes, author, map location, and capture date, as well as camera model, shutter speed, and F-stop—to name just a few of the many available search criteria.

For this exercise you will search for photos taken near a specific location using the Find By Details (Metadata) dialog box.

1   Choose Find > By Details (Metadata) in the Organizer. The Find By Details (Metadata) dialog box appears.

2   Under Search Criteria, click the first menu, and then use the scrollbar to scroll down towards the end of the list. While scrolling, notice the many options available as search criteria.

Some metadata is generated automatically by your camera when you capture an image, some is added when you spend time organizing your catalog. For this exercise, choose the last entry in the list, Map Location.

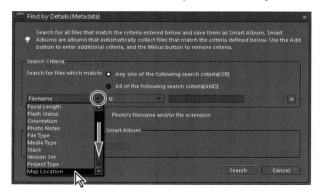

3 From the menu next to Map Location, choose Within.

4 Click the magnifying glass icon to open the Photo Location On Map dialog box. In the Photo Location On Map dialog box, type **1 Zoo Road, San Francisco, CA**, and then click Find. Click OK to close the Photo Location On Map dialog box.

5 In the Find By Details (Metadata) dialog box, type **1** as distance and choose Miles from the menu at the right.

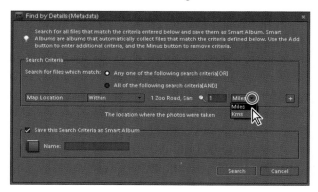

6 If it's activated, disable the option Save This Search Criteria As Smart Album by clicking its check box. You'll learn about using smart albums in the last part of this lesson. Click the Search button. Only images that match the specified criteria are displayed.

7 (Optional) To modify the search, click Options in the find bar, and then choose Modify Search Criteria from the menu. This will open the Find By Details (Metadata) dialog box with the current search criteria set. Make your changes, and then click Search to display the new search results in the Photo Browser.

8 Click the Show All button in the find bar.

Find photos using a text search

You can quickly find the photos you want using a text-based search. Type a word in the Text Search box at the left of the Find bar just above the Photo Browser, and the Organizer will display images that match the text across a wide range of criteria.

Matches can include items such as author, captions, dates, filenames, keyword tags, metadata, notes, album names, album groups, and camera information—Photoshop Elements will look for the search term in any type of text that is associated with the file.

You can use a text search as a convenient shortcut—for example, type the name of a tag, rather than navigating to the Keyword Tags palette.

Text search also supports the operators: "and," "or," and "not" if they are preceded and followed by a space. For example, you could type "vacation and kids" to find only images with both words in their metadata, not just either one.

Some words can be processed by Photoshop Elements as special instructions, not as specific search criteria. For example, you may want to search for a file tagged "Birthday," but only among your video files. You can use the Media "Type" and "Video" keywords. So, you would type "Type: Video Tag: Birthday."

For more information on using Text Search, and for a list of supported operators and special tags, please refer to Photoshop Elements Help.

Metadata support for audio and video files

Photoshop Elements 7 provides improved metadata support for audio and video files in the Organizer.

In the Properties - Metadata panel, metadata information is categorized into separate audio and video sections. For video, you'll find information such as pixel aspect ratio in the Brief view, while the audio section includes artist, album name, etc.—if that information is present in the file.

The File Properties section displays the filename, document type, creation and modification dates, and—if you activate the Complete view—the file size for your audio and video files.

1   Right-click on the audio file Temple of the Moon.wav and choose Show Properties to open the Properties - Metadata panel. Click the Info button (ⓘ) at the top of the panel, and select Complete from the view options below the Info pane to view all metadata.

2   Repeat step 1 for the video file Video.avi.

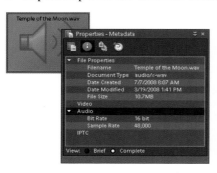 

● **Note:** You cannot edit the metadata for audio and video files in Photoshop Elements.

3   Close the Properties panel by clicking the close button in the top right corner.

Viewing and managing files by folder location

The Folder Location view in the Organizer splits the Photo Browser into three sections: a folder hierarchy pane on the left, an image thumbnail pane in the center, and the Palette Bin on the right. From this view you can manage your folders, add files to your catalog, automatically tag files using their folder name as the keyword tag, and add or remove folders from Watched Folder status.

By default, the left pane displays all the folders on your hard disk, and the center pane displays only the thumbnails of the managed files in the selected folder. Folders containing managed files have a Managed folder icon (▤). Watched folders have a Watched folder icon (▥).

1   Click the Display button () near the upper right corner of the Organizer window, and then choose Folder Location from the menu.

The folder hierarchy appears on the left side of the Photo Browser.

The contents of a selected folder are displayed in the Photo Browser when using Folder Location view.

● **Note:** You can change the default view for each panel by choosing Edit > Preferences > Folder Location View and selecting your preferred options.

2   Do one of the following to specify which files appear in the center panel:

- To view only the managed files in the selected folder, right-click in the left panel and disable the menu option Show All Files.

- To view all your managed files in the center panel grouped by folder location, right-click in the left panel and activate the menu option Show All Files.

- If you want to search all your managed files while in Folder Location view, select Show All Files.

- To find the folder location of a file, click the file's thumbnail in the center panel. The file's folder is highlighted in the left panel.

- To find files in a specific folder, click the folder in the left panel. Thumbnails for the files in that folder appear in the center panel, grouped under the folder name.

- To instantly tag files by their folder locations, click the Instant Keyword Tag icon in the Photo Browser pane. In the Create And Apply New Keyword Tag dialog box you can attach keyword tags simultaneously to all images in that folder.

3   To manage files and folders, select a folder and do any of the following:

- To move a file to a different folder, drag the file's thumbnail from the Photo Browser pane to a folder in the left panel.

- To view the folder in Windows Explorer, right-click in the left panel and choose Reveal in Explorer.

- To add or remove the folder from watched-folder status, right-click in the left panel and choose Add to Watched Folders or Remove from Watched Folders.

- To add a file in the folder to your catalog, right-click in the left panel and choose Add Unmanaged Files To Catalog.

- To rename the folder, right-click in the left panel and choose Rename Folder. Then, type a new name.

- To delete the folder, right-click in the left panel and choose Delete Folder.

4   Click the Display button (🖥), and then choose Thumbnail View from the menu. In the Photo Browser, click Show All.

Hiding files

You have already learned that you can simplify the process of working with your growing catalog by creating stacks and version sets to help reduce clutter in the Photo Browser, effectively reducing the number of images on view by stacking similar or related shots and grouping edited versions with their originals. With a stack or a version set you can choose the image in which you are most interested as the topmost in the collapsed grouping and the other images are tucked out of view until you choose to work with them.

In many cases it may be more effective to hide those images from view entirely. Once you have settled on the best shot from a stack of similar images, or the best of several edited versions in a version set, you can hide the other images from view so that they will no longer appear in search results, distract you when making selections, or need to be considered when applying commands.

Hiding photos does not delete them from their folders on your hard disk or remove them from your catalog or even from an album—you can always un-hide them if you start a new project where they might be useful or find that you could make use of a differently edited version.

1 Ctrl-click to select both of the photos of the elephant. Choose Edit > Auto Smart Fix Selected Photos. Auto Smart Fix is applied to both images and both are grouped in separate version sets with the edited versions topmost.

2 Ctrl-click to select both version sets and choose Edit > Version Set > Convert Version Set To Individual Items. There are now 4 images of the elephant in the Photo Browser: 2 originals and 2 edited copies.

3 Ctrl-click to select both of the originals of the elephant photos; then add to the multiple selection by Ctrl-clicking the first ostrich photo, the second zebra photo, the second hippo photo and the third giraffe photo. You should have six images selected. Choose Edit > Visibility > Mark As Hidden.

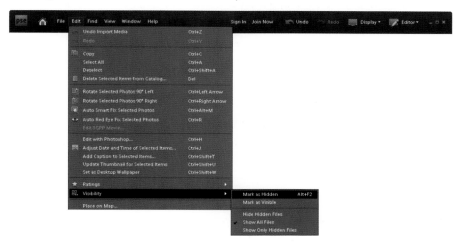

4 The Hidden File icon now appears on all six Thumbnails. Now choose Edit > Visibility > Hide Hidden Files. The six images marked as Hidden are removed from the Photo Browser view. Expand the Keyword Tags palette, if necessary, and then expand the Imported Keyword Tags category so that you can see all the imported tags.

5 Click the empty Find box beside each keyword tag in turn. The 6 hidden files do not appear in any of the search results.

6 In the Photo Browser, click Show All. Choose Edit > Visibility > Show Only Hidden Files, and then choose Edit > Visibility > Show All Files. Finally Ctrl-click to select all six thumbnails with the Hidden File icon. Choose Edit > Visibility > Mark As Visible. The Hidden File icon is removed from all 6 files.

7 Ctrl-click to select both of the edited images of the elephant and press the choose Edit > Delete Selected Items from Catalog. In the Confirm Deletion From Catalog dialog box, activate the option Also Delete Selected Items From The Hard Disk, and then click OK.

Working with smart albums

● **Note:** You cannot change the order of photos in a smart album, as you can for other albums. Nor can you add photos to a smart album by dragging them onto the album's icon; you need to modify the album's search criteria to change the content. The content of a smart album may change over time even without modifying the search criteria if photos matching the search criteria are added or removed from the catalog; for example, a smart album may be set up to contain photos captured within the last six months from the current date. Photos included in the album today may not fall within that date range tomorrow.

All albums, including smart albums, contain photos of your choosing. However, instead of manually selecting individual photos as you do for ordinary albums, you only need to specify search criteria to create a smart album. Once you set the criteria for a smart album, any photo in a catalog that matches the specified criteria will appear automatically in that smart album. As you add new photos to the catalog, those photos matching a smart album's criteria will appear automatically in that smart album. Smart Albums keep themselves up-to-date.

1   To set up search criteria for a new smart album, choose Find > Find by Details (Metadata). In the Find By Details (Metadata) dialog box, select the search criteria for the smart album. Click the plus sign (+) to add a criterion, click the minus sign (-) to remove a criterion.

2   If necessary, activate Save this Search Criteria as Smart Album. Enter **My first smart album** as the name, and then click Search.

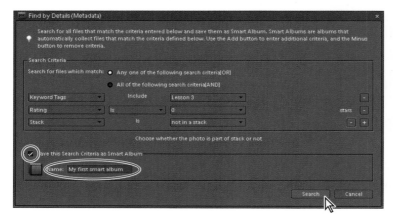

3   To display the photos in a smart album in the Photo Browser, select the smart album from the Albums palette.

4   To change the name of a smart album, do the following:

   • Select the smart album from the Albums palette.

   • Click the Edit button (▨) in the Albums palette.

   • Enter a new name in the Edit Smart Album dialog box, and then click OK.

5   To change the search criteria of a smart album, do the following:

•   Select your new smart album from the Albums palette.

•   Click Options in the find bar, and then choose Modify Search Criteria from the menu.

6   Modify the search criteria in the Find By Details (Metadata) dialog box, and select to save it as smart album. Provide a new name for the smart album, and then click Search.

7   To delete the smart album, right-click its icon in the Albums palette, and then choose Delete *[smart album name]* album from the menu. Click OK to confirm.

Note: You can save the modified search criteria using the same name, but this is not recommended. A second smart album with the same name will be created, rather than the first smart album being over- written. A dialog box will alert you about the duplicate file name. Click OK if you want to go ahead and create a second smart album with the same name anyway.

Congratulations! You've reached the end of Lesson 3. In this lesson, you've learned about advanced import options in the Photo Downloader, how to acquire still frames from a video, and how to import images from a PDF file or acquire them from a scanner. You've organized images in version sets, stacks, and albums, placed photos on a map, and learned some advanced methods for finding and managing the photos in your catalog.

Before you go on to the next lesson you can review what you've learned and test your command of the concepts and techniques presented in this lesson by working through the following questions and answers.

Review questions

1 How can you automatically create and apply tags to images while importing them from a digital camera or card reader?

2 What does the Photoshop Elements De-Interlace filter do?

3 What does the Auto Smart Fix command do?

4 What are Version Sets and Stacks?

5 What is the main difference between grouping pictures using tags and grouping them in an album?

Review answers

1 In the Advanced Photo Downloader dialog box, choose Custom Groups (Advanced) from the Create Subfolder(s) menu. Next, choose an option including Custom Name from the Group Name menu. Enter a Group Name in the Custom Name field in the separator bar above each group of thumbnails. Finally, select the Make 'Group Custom Name' A Tag check box before clicking Get Photos.

2 The Photoshop Elements De-Interlace filter can improve the appearance of still frame images acquired from a video by removing artifacts caused by the fact that a video picture consists of two interlaced half-pictures taken at slightly different times. The De-Interlace filter removes either the odd or even fields in a video image and replaces the discarded lines by duplication or interpolation from the remaining lines.

3 The Auto Smart Fix command corrects the overall color balance and improves shadow and highlight detail, if necessary. The Auto Smart Fix command groups the edited copy of the photo automatically with the original photo in a version set.

4 A version set groups an original photo and its edited versions. Stacks are used to group a set of similar photos, such as multiple shots of the same subject, or photos taken using your camera's burst mode or auto-bracket feature. A version set can be nested inside a stack: if you edit a photo that's already in a stack, the photo and its edited copy are put in a version set that is nested inside the original stack.

5 The main difference between albums and keyword tags is that in albums you can rearrange the order of the photos.

4 CREATING PROJECTS

Lesson Overview

Photoshop Elements makes it easy to create stylish, professional-looking projects to showcase your photos. Choose from preset themes and layouts—or create your own designs from scratch. Put together a range of creations from greeting cards and photo collages to animated slide shows and online albums.

This lesson will familiarize you with the Create mode by stepping you through a few basic techniques and simple projects:

- Creating a greeting card
- Animating your photos in a Slideshow
- Producing a Photo Collage
- Using the Artwork library
- Working with layers

 You'll probably need between one and two hours to complete this lesson.

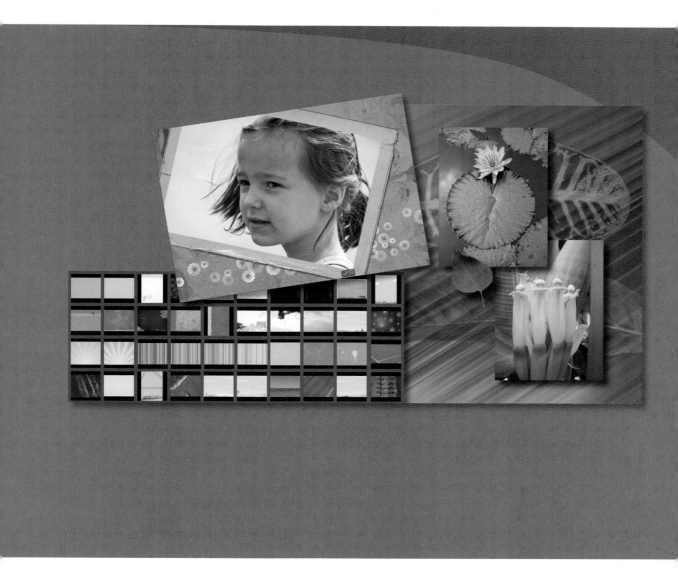

Use your own images in personalized CD or DVD jackets and labels, calendars, photo books, and digital flip-books. Combine images, text, animation, and even music and narration, to produce unique multimedia creations. Whether you're sharing your photos online, designing your own coffee table book, or making special greeting cards for your family or friends, Photoshop Elements unleashes your creativity.

Getting started

● **Note:** Before you start working on this lesson, make sure that you've installed the software on your computer from the application CD (see the Photoshop Elements 7 documentation) and that you have correctly copied the Lessons folder from the CD in the back of this book onto your computer's hard disk (see "Copying the Classroom in a Book files" on page 2).

While you're working on the projects in this lesson, you'll use the CIB Catalog you created in the "Getting Started" section at the beginning of this book. To open your CIB Catalog, follow these steps:

1 Start Photoshop Elements and click the Organize button in the Welcome Screen. Wait until the Organizer has finished opening.

2 Choose File > Catalog.

3 In the Catalog Manager dialog box, select the CIB Catalog, and then click Open.

If you don't see the CIB Catalog file, review "Copying the Lessons files from the CD" on page 2 and "Creating a catalog" on page 3 in the "Getting Started" section at the beginning of this book.

Creating a Greeting Card

Eye-catching personalized greeting cards based on your own photos are a sure way to impress family and friends—a really attractive card can spend many months on a loved one's mantelpiece, or may even get framed and displayed with pride.

As with the other photo project options, you can include one or more photos on each page of a greeting card and either print it on your home printer, order prints online, or send it via e-mail.

The Photo Projects panel in Adobe Photoshop Elements offers you a variety of templates to help you create sophisticated designs quickly and easily.

This exercise will show you how easy it is to choose a theme and format to present a photo in a creative and professional-looking manner. When you're finished, you'll have transformed your photo into a delightful greeting card.

1   In the Organizer, use the Keyword Tags palette to isolate the photos in your CIB catalog that are tagged with the keyword Lesson 4. Sselect the portrait of a little girl with the file name 4_Zoe.jpg.

▶ **Tip:** If you don't see the names of the image files displayed below the thumbnail images in the Photo Browser pane, choose View > Show File Names.

2   Click to select the purple Create tab in the Task pane to the right of the Photo Browser.

3   Choose Greeting Card from the More Options menu below the project buttons in the Create panel.

4 The Editor workspace opens. In the Photo Projects panel, scroll down to see all the options in the Choose A Theme menu. Select the "Wedding Classic" template (the third design from the end) featuring worn grey paper with pale flowers scattered across the bottom.

5 From the Choose A Layout menu, select the template "1 Tilted" (the design in the center of the second row), a horizontal layout with a single landscape format photo frame placed on an angle. Activate the option Auto-Fill With Project Bin Photos and disable the Include Captions option; then, click Done.

To move the photo, click inside its bounding box and drag it to a new position. To re-size the image, move the pointer over any one of the corner handles of the bounding box and drag the handle with the diagonal double-arrow cursor. By default, the photo will be scaled proportionally. Move the pointer close to a corner handle, outside the bounding box—when the pointer becomes a curved double-arrow cursor, drag in either direction to rotate the photo around its center point.

6 You'll see a preview of your greeting card in the Editor panel with a bounding box surrounding the photo. You can move, rotate and re-size the photo if you wish.

▶ **Tip:** To move the photo, click inside its bounding box and drag it to a new position. To re-size the image, move the pointer over any one of the corner handles of the bounding box and drag the handle with the diagonal double-arrow cursor. By default, the photo will be scaled proportionally. To rotate a photo around its center point, move the pointer close to any handle, staying outside the bounding box; when the pointer becomes a curved double-arrow cursor, drag to rotate the image in either direction.

7 When you're done re-sizing and repositioning the photo, click the green Commit button (✓) at the bottom of the bounding box to commit the changes.

▶ **Tip:** When the Move tool is active, you can use the arrow keys on your keyboard to move the elements of a selected layer in small increments instead of dragging them using your pointer. Similarly, when one of the selection tools is active you can use the arrow keys to nudge a selection.

That was quick! Composing your photo with an appropriate theme and layout can make a really distinctive card.

8 Choose File > Save. In the Save As dialog box, navigate to the My CIB Work folder and name the file 4_Greeting_Card.psd. Make sure that the option Include In The Organizer is activated. Click Save.

9 Choose File > Close. Congratulations; you've created your first photo project!

Adjusting a photo inside a frame

The theme template you used for your greeting card consists of a background and an image frame. The image frame and the photo it surrounds are on the same layer—when you scale or move the photo, the frame is scaled or moved with it.

In this case, the frame crops the edges of the photograph slightly (notably at the top and back of the girl's head) so you may want to scale, move, or even rotate the image slightly within the frame. To do this, first double-click the photo; then you can drag it to reposition it inside its frame and scale or rotate it using the handles.

Working with multiple pages

You can create multiple-page layouts with Photoshop Elements, which are perfect for projects such as photo albums where you want consistency from page to page. In the Edit menu you'll find options for adding either blank pages or pages using the same layout. The example shown below also uses the same theme that you used for the greeting card but applies a different layout template.

Animating your photos in a slide show

A Photoshop Elements slide show is a digital project that makes a dynamic, fun way to present and share your photos. You can add and edit slide transitions and zoom or pan effects, choose from an array of graphic extras and frames, add text and even music or narration.

Using the Slide Show Editor

1   In the Organizer, select the four photos with the little girls playing on a sculpture in a park. These images are tagged with the Lesson 4 keyword and are named 4_Slideshow1.jpg through 4_Slideshow4.jpg.

2 Click the purple Create tab in the Task pane, and then click the Slide Show button.

3 In the Slide Show Preferences dialog box, choose 3 sec for Static Duration, Gradient Wipe as Transition, and 2 sec for the Transition. Disable all the option checkboxes except for Landscape Photos beside Crop to Fit Slide, as in the illustration below. Click OK and your project will automatically open in the Slide Show Editor window.

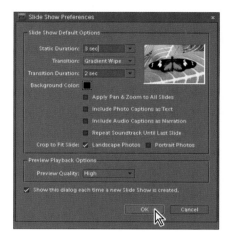

4 Click the Play button () below the preview panel or press the spacebar to start the slide show. The timing of the transitions needs adjustment, and the flow could be improved by changing the display order of the four images.

Adding Music and Narration to a slide show

Sound adds another dimension to the animation of your images and complements your presentation. You can add an ambitious full-scale sound track or record a simple voice narration.

Import music from your Photoshop Elements catalog or from any folder on your hard disk. In the Slide Show Editor window, click the Add Media button above the preview pane; then, choose Audio From Organizer or Audio From Folder and navigate to your music files.

In the Add Audio dialog box, you can listen to an audio file before adding it by selecting the clip and clicking Play.

To align the pace of the slide show with the music, select Fit Slides To Audio; the length of each slide will be updated in the film strip. You can also drag the audio file to begin playing at a specific slide.

If you have a microphone attached to your computer, you can record voice narration for a selected slide. You can also attach your narration to a photo as an audio caption. You'll find the narration button in the Extras palette of the Slide Show panel. Click the button to see the recording controls.

For more information on adding music and narration to your project, please consult Photoshop Elements Help.

Refining your Slide Show

In the next steps, you'll tweak the timing of the slideshow, change the style of the transitions, and rearrange the slides to make for smoother playback.

1   From the menu bar in the Slide Show Editor window, choose Edit > Select All Transitions.

2 In the Properties panel, choose 1 sec from the Multiple Transitions menu. To change the style of the transitions, choose Fade from the Transition menu.

3 Press the spacebar to play your slideshow, which looks more fluid with the new settings applied. However, there is still room for improvement: the first image would fit much better at the end of the show.

4 Drag the first thumbnail in the filmstrip to the right and release the mouse button when the blue line appears at the end of the series. The other three images move back one position. To work with the thumbnail images in a larger panel, which can be helpful if you are producing a slideshow with more than just a few images, click the Quick Reorder button (⬓), located above the thumbnail images at the left end of the filmstrip. When you're done in the Quick Reorder panel, click Back.

Adding Extras

Once you're happy with the image order and slide transitions, you can increase the impact of the slide show and have some fun by including a few graphic elements. First, let's add a message with a speech bubble and text.

1 In the Slide Show Editor window, select the third thumbnail image in the filmstrip—the photo of the girl in orange sitting alone on the sculpture.

2 In the Extras panel to the right of the Slide Editor pane, select the graphics category, and then scroll down to Thought & Speech Bubbles. If necessary, click the triangle next to the name to see the choice of shapes. Drag the first speech bubble close to the little girl's head. *(See the illustration on the next page.)*

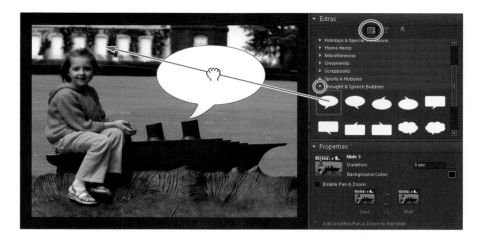

3 Position the pointer over one of the six handles around the bounding box of the graphic; when the cursor becomes a double arrow, you can drag the handle to scale the bubble or alter its shape. Try to size and shape the speech bubble as show in the illustration below. Move the pointer inside the white area and drag the graphic to move it to a new position on the image.

4 Under Extras, select the type category, and then locate the second T in the third row—a narrow black letter representing the font Myriad Pro Condensed.

5 Drag the T onto the speech bubble in the Slide Editor pane.

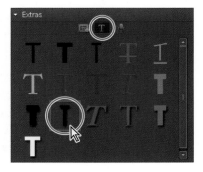

6   Choose 30 pt from the text size menu beside the font name, and then click the Edit Text button in the Properties panel. Type **BON VOYAGE!** in the Edit Text dialog box; then click OK.

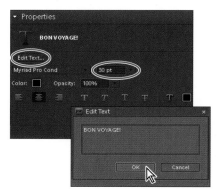

7   Drag the text box to center the message in the speech bubble.

Tip: Explore the Graphics options in the Extras panel. You can liven up your slides with costumes, frames, holiday and sports motifs, or ornamental embellishments—but remember: in design terms, less can be more!

8   Now the first slide has a prominent message, but there is so much more you could do. For example, you could add a flower behind the girl's ear and a rabbit or two to set off this slide with some fun touches. Collapse the Extras panel.

Adding a Zoom effect

Press the spacebar to preview the slide show once more.

The first three images are all framed quite closely around the group of girls playing, but the final image has a wider focus, bringing the whole of the sculpture and much more of the background into view. This creates the feeling that we are pulling back as a farewell to the scene.

As a finishing touch, we can capitalize on this impression by adding a zoom effect to the last slide.

1   Select the last slide in the filmstrip. In the Properties panel, click the checkbox beside Enable Pan & Zoom and change the Duration for this slide from 3 to 4 seconds, to allow a little extra time for the zoom effect.

2   Click the Start view (the thumbnail with the blue border) and drag the handles at the corners of the green frame to arrange the view for the beginning of the zoom as shown on the left below. Now click the End view (the thumbnail with the blue border) and drag the handles at the corners of the red frame to arrange the view for the end of the zoom as shown on the right. The green and red frames also appear on the thumbnail of the last slide in the filmstrip.

3 Click the Full Screen Preview button above the Slide Editor pane.

4 When you're done previewing your slide show, choose File > Save As. In the Adobe Photoshop Elements dialog box, type **4_Slideshow_work** as the file name, and then click Save.

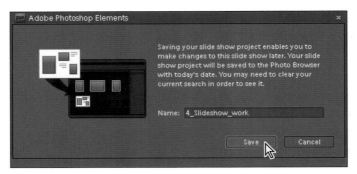

5 The Slide Show Complete dialog box appears to inform you that your project has been saved and is selected at the top of the Photo Browser. Click OK.

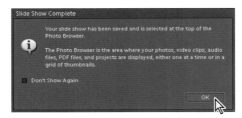

6 Note that the saved project has automatically been tagged with the Lesson 4 keyword and that it is identified as a slide show in the Photo Browser by the slide show icon in the top right corner of its thumbnail.

Done! You've completed another project and learned about some fun features along the way. There are a number of ways to share your slide show: you can publish it as a PDF or movie file, as a video CD or DVD, or in Adobe Premiere Elements for use in a video project. For more detail on sharing your presentation, please refer to Photoshop Elements Help.

Assembling a photo collage

In the next few exercises you'll create another photo project—this time, a photo collage. You can print a photo collage on your home printer, order prints on-line, or save it to your hard drive to send by e-mail or use in another digital document.

Using the Photo Projects panel

1 In the Organizer, find the items in your CIB catalog that are tagged with the Lesson 4 keyword by clicking the find box beside the Lesson 4 tag in the keyword Tags palette. Ctrl-click to select the two images of flowers, named banana_bloom.jpg and blackwater_lily.jpg.

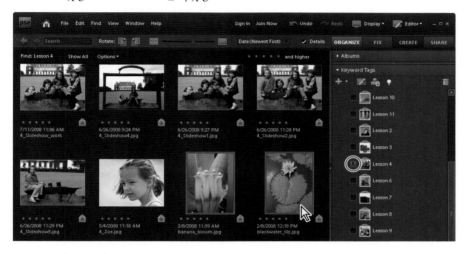

2 Click the purple Create tab at the top of the Task pane, and then click the Photo Collage button.

3 The Editor window opens in Create mode, with thumbnails of your selected photos visible in the Project Bin at the bottom of the workspace. In the Photo Projects panel at the right, choose Letter (8.5 inch x 11 inch) from the Paper Size menu. Move the pointer over the theme swatches; a Tooltip appears with the name of each theme. Locate and select the No Theme swatch in the top row.

As you saw when you created a greeting card earlier in this lesson, a theme consists of a preset combination of background artwork and photo frame style. The background and frame style can be changed later in the Editor, but for this exercise you'll start without any theme preset, and then explore the Photo Projects panel and the Artwork library to choose your own options.

4 Scroll about half-way down the Layout menu. As you move the pointer over each layout thumbnail a Tooltip appears with the name of that layout. Locate and select the 2 Portrait vertical layout. This is a layout preset to accommodate two portrait-format images, each on its own layer.

5 Activate the Auto-Fill With Project Bin Photos option to automatically place the two photos you selected from the Photo Browser into the selected layout template. Click Done.

6 Your images are placed in the selected template and your photo project opens in its own window in the work area. *(See the illustration below.)*

7 Choose View > Fit On Screen to see the layout displayed as large as possible.

Exploring the Artwork library

Photoshop Elements makes it quick and easy to create distinctive photo projects by providing an extensive collection of themes, backgrounds, frames, text styles, and clip-art shapes and graphics in the Artwork library. In this series of exercises, you'll choose a background for your collage and add graphics as you explore the options.

1 Click the Artwork button at the top of the Photo Projects panel. If necessary, expand the Content palette and collapse the Favorites palette, as shown in the illustration below, so that you can see as many of the sample swatches as possible.

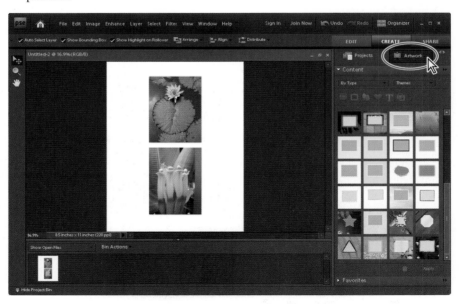

What you see displayed in the Content palette depends on the options you choose from the sorting menus above the sample swatches.

2   In the Content palette, choose By Type from the menu on the left to see the content of the artwork library sorted by functional category. In the menu on the right, the options are Backgrounds, Frames, Graphics, Shapes, Text, Themes, and Show All. Choose each option in turn and scroll the sample swatch menu to see the options available.

   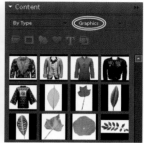

3   Set the content sorting menus to By Type and Show All, and then click the double arrow button at the top right of the Artwork panel to expand the Artwork panel to full screen view.

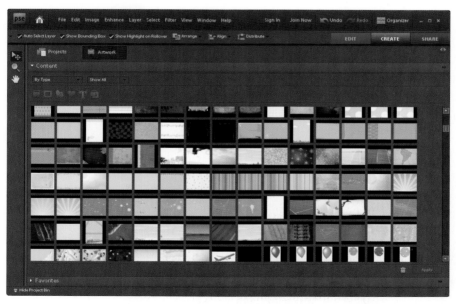

Scroll down to see the many backgrounds, frames, graphics and themes available in the library. In Show All mode, the number of choices may seem overwhelming, but

Photoshop Elements provides several options that make it easy to sort the library and locate the items you need. One of these is the Favorites palette.

4   Expand the Favorites palette at the bottom of the Artwork panel. Drag a small assortment of the items that interest you from the Content palette into the Favorites palette.

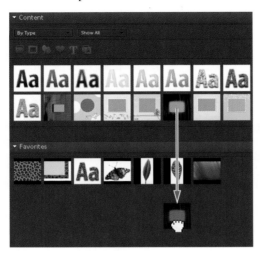

5   Click the double arrow button at the top right of the Artwork panel to collapse the Artwork panel and return to the to full Create workspace.

6   For now, collapse the Favorites palette once more so that you can see as much of the Content palette as possible.

Adding a background

In this exercise you'll choose a background from the Content palette and add it to your photo collage.

1   In the Content palette, open the sorting menu on the left. Note the options in the menu; the content in the Artwork library has been tagged with keywords that allow you to search it intuitively by activity, mood, season, and many other associations. For now, choose By Color. From the other sorting menu, choose Green.

The Content palette now displays all the items in the artwork library that are tagged with the keyword "green". This is reflected by the active state of all the Content Filter buttons above the sample

swatches. From left to right, these six buttons filter the items in the Content palette for Backgrounds, Frames, Graphics, Shapes, Text Effects, and Themes, providing another means for finding what you want in the artwork library.

2   Starting from the Filter For Themes button at the right, click to disable each of the content filters except Filter For Backgrounds. The Content palette now displays only the backgrounds in the Artwork library that are tagged with the keyword "green". Scroll down in the sample swatches menu to locate the background "Leaves 02". Click to select the Leaves 02 thumbnail, and then click Apply. Alternatively, simply double-click the Leaves 02 thumbnail to apply the background.

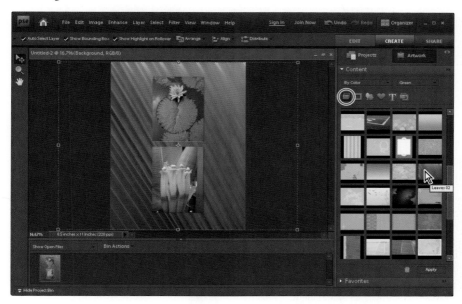

▶ **Tip:** If you had started the process of creating your photo collage by choosing a theme that included a preset background, you could use the same technique to change it.

The new background appears behind the photos in your photo collage. The background layer is selected and the background image is surrounded by a bounding box. The bounding box shows that the image is considerably wider than your photo collage page.

3   Choose View > Zoom Out. Move the pointer close to one of the handles around the bounding box for the background. When the curved double arrow cursor appears, drag to rotate the background image 90° counter-clockwise. Hold down the Shift key as you drag to constrain the rotation to 15° increments.

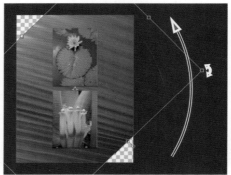

4   Drag the background image up and to the left to align the lower right corner of the bounding box with the lower right corner of the photo collage page. The bounding box snaps to the page edges to assist you in placing it precisely.

5   Click the Commit button () at the bottom of the page preview to commit the changes.

6   Choose Select > Deselect Layers. Click the Hide Project Bin button in the lower left corner of the workspace, and then choose View > Fit On Screen.

7   Click inside the photo of the water lily, and then click one of the corner handles on its bounding box. Width (W) and height (H) values appear in the bar above the work area. Ensure that the Constrain Proportions option is activated, and then double-click or swipe to select the 100% value in the width text box. Type **120**, and press the Enter key on your keyboard. The new scaling value is applied to the height box and the water lily image is scaled proportionately. Click the Commit button to accept the change.

8   Repeat step 7 for the photo of the banana flowers. Click the Commit button to accept the change, and then choose Select > Deselect Layers.

Adding graphics

1   Choose the option By Word from the sorting menu in the Content palette and type **leaf** in the text box beside it. Click to activate the Filter For Graphics button and make sure that all the other content filters that are disabled.

2 Drag Leaf 04, Leaf 08, and Leaf 11 onto your Photo collage page as shown in the illustration below: each overlapping the last, along the edge of the photograph of the water lily.

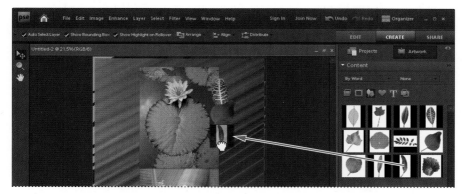

3 Choose Select > Deselect Layers.

Working with layers

Each element in your photo collage occupies its own layer. The background is at the bottom with the other images overlaid in successive layers in the order in which they were added to the project. The two photographs from the Organizer were added in the order of their capture date and time, so that the oldest is on the layer directly above the background.

1 Click the yellow Edit button above the Artwork panel. Collapse the Effects palette and expand the Layers palette if necessary so that you can see all the layers in your photo collage project.

Layers are like transparent overlays on which you can paint or place photos, artwork, vector graphics or text. The checkerboard grid areas in the layer thumbnails represent the transparent parts of the layers through which you can see the layers below.

2 Experiment by clicking the eye icons beside the layer thumbnails to hide and show each layer in turn.

3 Click to select the Move tool in the toolbox, and then click the layer names to select each layer in turn. The selected layer is highlighted in the Layers palette and its contents are surrounded by a bounding box in the editor pane to indicate their selected state.

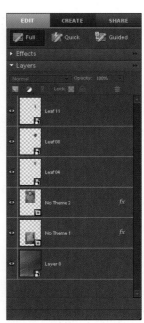

● **Note:** Backgrounds chosen from the Artwork library will always appear on the bottom layer, even when they are added to the layout after the photographs—as was the case in this project. You can use your own image as a background by converting its layer.

● **Note:** As well as photos and graphics from the artwork library layers can contain text, fills, gradients, or even saved photo projects. You can apply filters or special effects to any layer and specify the way those effects will affect other layers in the project. You can specify a layer's opacity and blending mode and create adjustment layers that allow you to tune the images on the layer or layers below.

4   Click the top layer "Leaf 11" (the last layer added) to select it. Use the corner handles of the bounding box surrounding the leaf to rotate and scale it, and then click the image and drag to position it on the page as shown in the illustration below. Click the Commit button to commit the changes.

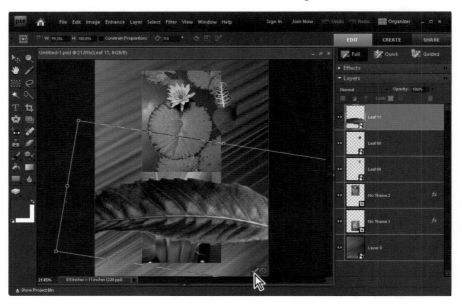

5   Click the third layer from the top "Leaf 04" and use the same techniques to achieve the result shown in the next illustration; then, click the Commit button.

6 Ctrl-click to select both of the layers you just edited, and then click the Link
   Layers button ( ) just above the top layer in the Layers palette. Both layers
   are marked with the Linked Layer icon. Drag the Leaf 04 layer down over the
   border between the background layer, Layer 0, and the layer above it, No Theme
   1, and release the mouse button when the border is highlighted. The linked
   layers move to the second and third positions and the other layers move up to
   accommodate them.

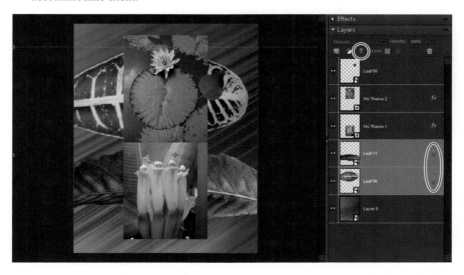

7 Select each of the two linked layers in turn and
   change their opacity to 40%, either by using the
   Opacity slider at the top of the Layers palette or
   by typing the new value directly into the Opacity
   text box and pressing Enter on your keyboard.

8 Double-click the layer name of each of the layers No Theme 1 and No Theme 2
   in turn and type **banana bloom** and **blackwater lily** respectively to rename the
   layers.

9 Select each of the top three layers in turn and drag the images to position them
   as shown in the illustration on the next page. You will also need to rotate the
   image Leaf 08 and make it slightly larger.

● **Note:** For more
detailed information
about understanding
and working with
layers, please refer to
Photoshop Elements
Help.

Applying effects

As a finishing touch you can apply a drop shadow effect to the top three layers.

Note: For more detailed information about applying effects and working with layer styles, refer to Photoshop Elements Help.

1 Select the layer "banana bloom."

2 Expand the Effects palette, click the Layer Styles button (the second button from the left at the top of the Effects palette), and choose Drop Shadows from the effects menu.

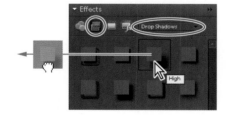

3 Locate the "High" drop shadow style. Simply drag the sample swatch from the Effects palette and drop it onto the photo of the banana flower.

4 In the Layers palette, double-click the *fx* icon at the right of the banana bloom layer. In the Style Settings dialog box, set the Lighting Angle to 135° and the Size, Distance, and Opacity values to 50, 60, and 60 respectively. Click OK.

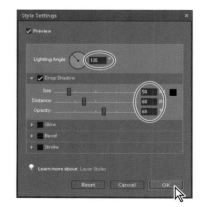

5 Choose Layer > Layer Style > Copy Layer Style; then, select the layer "blackwater lily" in the Layers palette and choose Layer > Layer Style > Paste Layer Style.

6   In the Layers palette, double-click the *fx* icon at the right of the banana bloom layer. In the Style Settings dialog box, set the Lighting Angle to 135° and the Size, Distance, and Opacity values to 70, 100, and 55 respectively. These settings will help with the illusion that the leaf is higher above the background than the two photographs. Click OK, and then choose Select > Deselect Layers.

7   Save your photo collage to your My CIB Work folder.

Congratulations! You've completed the last project in this lesson. You've learned about using the preset Theme and Layout templates, explored the Artwork library, and become familiar with a variety of methods for locating the items you need. You've also learned the basics of working with layers and applying layer styles. Before you move on to the next lesson, "Printing, Sharing, and Exporting," take a moment to refresh your new skills by reading through the review on the next page.

Review questions

1 How do you begin a new project such as a greeting card, photo collage, or slide show?

2 How do you scale and reposition a photo in a photo project?

3 How do you change the order of slides in a slide show?

4 How can you find the items you want amongst all the choices in the Artwork library?

5 What are layers, how do they work, and how do you work with them?

Review answers

1 To create a project in the Organizer, select a project option in the Create panel of the Task pane by clicking one of the project buttons or choosing from the More Options menu. The Projects panel offers prompts to guide you through choosing theme and layout presets and the Artwork panel provides access to frames, graphics and more.

2 Once you've selected and applied a theme and a layout, an edit window opens with a bounding box around the photo. You can scale or rotate the photo by dragging the bounding box handles and move it on the page by dragging the image itself. To scale, rotate, or move a photo within its own frame you need to double-click the image before using the same techniques, so that the changes affect the photo independently and are not applied to the photo and its frame together.

3 You can change the order of slides in a slideshow by dragging them to new positions in the filmstrip below the Slide Editor pane. When you are working on a slideshow with too many slides to display at a convenient size in the filmstrip, click the Quick Reorder button located above the slide thumbnails to open the Quick Reorder window, where there is plenty of room to display, select, and manipulate a large number of slides.

4 You can sort and search the items in the Artwork library by using the menus and buttons at the top of the Content palette. From the first menu you can choose options to sort the content by type, activity, mood, season, color, keywords and other attributes. Once you have set up the first menu, you use the other menu to narrow the search—to specify which type, color, or mood you want. Use the Filter buttons to limit the search results to display only backgrounds, frames, graphics, shapes, text styles, or themes with the attributes you've specified. Use the favorites palette to assemble a collection of the items you're most likely to use, rather than looking through the entire library every time you want to add an artwork item to a project.

5 Layers are like transparent overlays on which you can paint or place photos, artwork, or text. Each element in a photo project occupies its own layer—the background is at the bottom and the other elements are overlaid in the order in which they are added to the project. Photos from the Project Bin are placed in the order of their capture date, so that the oldest is on the lowest layer. You work with layers in the Layers Palette, where you can toggle their visibility and change their order. The checkerboard grid areas in the layer thumbnails represent the transparent parts of the layers through which you can see the layers below.

5 PRINTING, SHARING, AND EXPORTING

Lesson Overview

In previous lessons you imported photos, learned how to organize and search your catalog, and created projects to showcase your images. Now you'll learn how you can output your images and creations to share them with family, friends, or the world at large:

- Printing at home and ordering prints online
- Sharing photos by e-mail and Photo Mail
- Setting up a Quick Share flow
- Signing up for a Photoshop.com account
- Creating your own Online Album
- Using an online sharing service
- Burning your photos and projects to CD or DVD
- Exporting images for use on the Web

 You'll probably need between one and two hours to complete this lesson.

Now that you've learned how to find your way around the Photoshop Elements workspace, how to organize and find the photos and other media that you've brought into your catalog, and how to create photo projects and digital presentations, you're ready to share your images and creations with the world as printed output, by e-mail, or online.

Getting started

Note: Before you start working on this lesson, make sure that you've installed the software on your computer from the application CD (see the Photoshop Elements 7 documentation) and that you have correctly copied the Lessons folder from the CD in the back of this book onto your computer's hard disk (see "Copying the Classroom in a Book files" on page 2).

If you have already created a catalog for your own photos you can use that for the purposes of this exercise; otherwise, use the CIB Catalog you created at the start of the book. To open the catalog you wish to use, follow these steps:

1   Start Photoshop Elements. In the Welcome Screen, click Organize in the row of shortcut buttons across the top of the Welcome Screen.

2   The name of the currently active catalog is displayed in the lower left corner of the Organizer window. If the catalog you plan to use for this lesson is already open you can skip to the next section, "About printing." If the catalog you want is not already open, continue to step 3.

3   Choose File > Catalog.

4   In the Catalog Manager dialog box, select the catalog of your choice in the Catalogs list, and then click Open.

If you do not see the CIB Catalog file listed, review "Getting Started," the first chapter in this book. See "Copying the Lessons files from the CD" on page 2, and "Creating a catalog" on page 3.

About printing

Photoshop Elements offers several options for printing your photos or Photo Projects, such as photo albums, greeting cards, and calendars. You can order professional prints from online providers through Adobe Photoshop Services, or use your home printer. You can print your photos individually, as contact sheets (thumbnails of a selection of photos arranged in a grid layout), picture packages (one or more photos repeated at a variety of sizes on the same page), or print photo labels on commercially available label paper.

Printing individual photos

The Organizer helps you minimize wastage of expensive photographic paper by giving you the option of printing either single or multiple images on the same page, arranged on the page in the sizes you want.

1   In the Organizer, select the thumbnails of the image or images you wish to print. Ctrl-click to select more than one image.

2   Choose File > Print.

3   In the Print Photos dialog box, specify the following settings:

- Choose a printer from the Select Printer menu.

- Choose Individual Prints from the Select Type Of Print menu.

- From the Select Print Size And Options menu, choose 3.5" x 5." If you're using the lesson files in the CIB Catalog for this exercise, you may see a warning about print resolution, as some of the sample files are provided at low resolution. Click OK to dismiss this warning.

- If the One Photo Per Page option is active, click the checkbox to disable it.

4 (Optional) Do any of the following:

- Select one of the thumbnails in the menu on the left side of the dialog box, and then click the Remove button (—) below the thumbnails to remove that image from the selection to be printed.

- Click the Add button (+) under the column of thumbnails. Activate the Entire Catalog option, and then click the check box beside any image you'd like to add to the selection to be printed. Click Done.

- If you have selected more pictures than will fit on one page, you can see the other pages by clicking the arrows buttons below the Print Preview.

Note: You can only print images from Photoshop Elements if they are part of the currently active catalog. If you want to add pictures to the printing batch that are not in the currently active catalog, you must first import them using one of the methods described in chapters 1, 2 and 3.

5 Do one of the following:

- If you'd prefer to save your ink and paper for your own prints, click Cancel to close the dialog box without printing.

- If you'd like to go ahead and try printing with these sample images, click Print.

Printing a contact sheet

Contact sheets make it easy to assess a multiple selection of images by printing them at thumbnail size, arranged on the same page in a grid layout.

● **Note:** If you choose the Print command without first selecting any images, Photoshop Elements will ask if you want to print all the images currently visible in the Photo Browser.

1   In the Photo Browser, select the photos you'd like to see printed on a contact sheet. If you wish to select a consecutive series of thumbnails, click the first image in the series, and then Shift-click the last; the images in-between will be selected. If you wish to select non-consecutive images, Ctrl-click their thumbnails.

2   Choose File > Print.

3   In the Print Photos dialog box, choose a printer from the Select Printer menu.

4   Choose Contact Sheet from the Select Type Of Print menu. By default, the contact sheet layout includes all the photos in the thumbnail menu column at the left of the Print Photos dialog box. To remove a photo from the contact sheet, select its thumbnail in the menu and click the Remove button.

5   You can alter the contact sheet layout by changing the number of columns under Select A Layout. Click the arrow buttons beside the Columns number or type a number between 1 and 9 in the text box.

The thumbnail size and number of rows are adjusted according to your choice for the number of columns. If the number of photos selected for printing exceeds the capacity of a single page, more pages will be added to accommodate them.

● **Note:** Some words in the text label may be truncated, depending on the page setup and column layout.

6   To print image information labels below each image on the contact sheet, activate any or all of the Text Label options:

- Date, to print the capture date recorded in the images' metadata.

- Caption, to print any caption text embedded in the file's metadata.

- Filename, to print the filename for each photo.

- Page Numbers, to print a page number at the bottom of each page if there are more images than will fit on a single page for the specified column layout.

7   Click Print or Cancel.

Printing a Picture Package

In a Picture Package layout you can print one or more photos repeated at a variety of sizes on the same page. You can choose from a variety of layout options with an assortment of image sizes to customize your picture package print.

1   Select one or more pictures from the browser, and then choose File > Print.

2 In the Print Photos dialog box, choose a printer from the Select Printer menu.

3 Choose Picture Package from the Select Type Of Print menu. If a Printing Warning dialog box cautioning against enlarging pictures appears, click OK. For this exercise you'll print multiple images at smaller sizes.

4 Choose a layout from the Select A Layout menu, and activate the Fill Page With First Photo option. This will Result in a printed page with a single photo repeated at a variety of sizes, according to the layout you have chosen. If you selected more than one photo in the Photo Browser, a separate Print Package page will be printed for each photo selected; you can see the previews for each page by clicking the page navigation buttons below the print preview.

● **Note:** The options available in the Picture Package Layout menu depend on the paper size specified in the page setup or printer preferences. To change the paper size, click either the Page Setup button at the lower left of the Print Photos dialog box or the Show Printer Preferences button (▤) to the right of the printer menu and select your preferred paper size. Depending on your printer, you may need to look for the paper size options in the Advanced preferences settings.

5 (Optional) Choose Icicles (or another border of your preference) from the Select A Frame menu. You can select only one border style per picture package print.

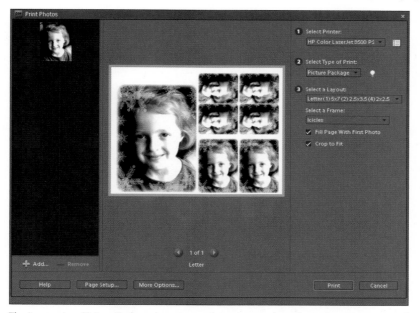

The images in a Picture Package layout are oriented to produce the optimum coverage of the printable area for the layout you have chosen. This feature is automatic and cannot be overridden. You cannot manually rotate the images in a picture package layout.

6 If your photo is of non-standard proportions, the Crop To Fit option may fit the multiple images more closely to the layout and fill the printable area better.

7 (Optional) To add more photos from your catalog to the picture package, click the Add button, select the photos you want in the Add Photos dialog box, and then click Done. The selected photos are added to the thumbnails column. To replace a photo in the layout with another, drag an image from the thumbnails menu column over an image in the print preview and release the mouse button.

8 Click Print or Cancel.

Ordering professionally printed photos online

● **Note:** You need an active Internet connection to order prints online.

If you want high quality prints of your photos—for your own enjoyment or to share with others—you can order professionally printed photos online. In this exercise you will learn how to order individual prints from the Organizer (a service available in the US, Canada, and Japan).

1 In the Organizer, select one or more pictures that you would like to have printed professionally.

2 If the Quick Share palette is not already open in the Organizer palette bin, choose Window > Quick Share to open it.

3 Drag the selected photos from the Browser view onto the *Drag photos here to create an order* target in the Quick Share palette.

The New Order Prints Recipient dialog box appears. *(See the illustration on the next page.)*

4 In the New Order Prints Recipient dialog box, enter all the required information for the person who is to receive the printed photos. For this exercise, you can enter your own name, address, and home phone number, and then click the checkbox beside This Is My Home Address. If you would prefer to import contact information from an existing contact book entry, click the Choose Existing Contact button, select a contact from the list, and then click OK.

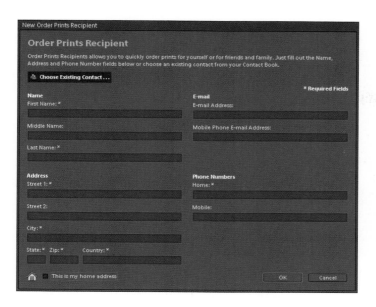

5   Click OK to close the New Order Prints Recipient dialog box.

A new target entry appears in the Quick Share palette. If you clicked the This Is My Home Address check box in the New Order Prints Recipient dialog box in step 4, you'll see a home icon next to the new target entry. The number in brackets next to the target name indicates the number of photos selected for this print order.

6   In the Quick Share palette, double-click the new target entry or click the View Photos In [Recipient's Name] button () above the list of recipients in the Quick Share panel to open the Order Prints for [Recipient's Name] dialog box. *(See the illustration on the next page.)* Do any of the following:

   • Use the slider to increase or decrease the size of the thumbnail images.

   • Select one or more photos and click Remove Selected Photo(s) to remove the selected photos from the current order.

   • Click Remove All to remove all photos from the current order.

7   When you're done, click Close to close the dialog box without confirming the order.

8   (Optional) Add additional photos to the order by dragging thumbnails from the Photo Browser onto the same target entry in the Quick Share palette.

9   In the Quick Share palette, click the Order button on the right side of the target entry. The Welcome To Adobe Photoshop Services dialog box appears.

10 In the Welcome To Adobe Photoshop Services dialog box, do one of the following:

   •   If you are already an Ofoto or EasyShare Gallery member, enter your e-mail address and password and click Next to log in.

   •   If you are not an Ofoto or EasyShare Gallery member, click Join Now.

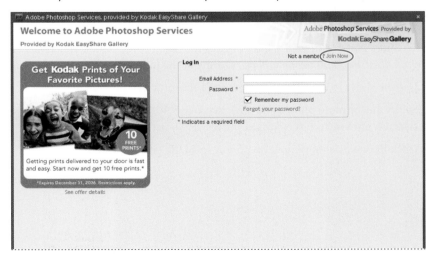

11 If you chose Joint Now in the previous step, create a new account by entering your first name, e-mail address, and a password of at least six characters. If you agree with the Terms of Service click the respective check box under Create Account, and then click Next.

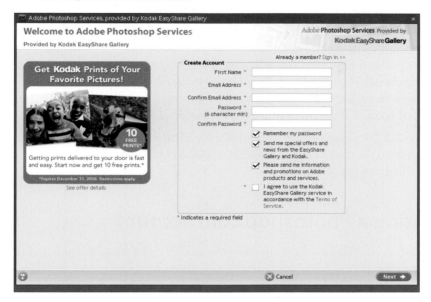

12 In the Review Order dialog box, do any of the following:

- Click Change Quantities Or Sizes for any of the photos in your order.

- Click Remove under a thumbnail image in the list on the left side of the dialog box to remove that print from your order.

- Review the Order Summary and Delivery Information.

13 When you're done reviewing your order, click Checkout.

14 If you wished to proceed with your order, you would now provide your credit card details in the Billing Information dialog box and review the information under Billing Address and Order Summary. Clicking Place Order would initiate the processing of your order and your credit card would be charged. For this exercise, click Cancel unless you want to go ahead and order prints. A dialog box appears to ask if you want to stop using this service. Click OK.

15 Right-click the target entry in the Quick Share palette and choose Cancel Order from the context menu. Click Yes in the alert dialog box to confirm the cancellation of the order.

Creating a Photoshop.com account

● **Note:** At this stage, Photoshop.com services are available only to Photoshop Elements users in the United States.

U.S.-based users of Photoshop Elements users can sign up for a free Photoshop.com membership and take advantage of exciting new Adobe-hosted Web-based services that extend the capabilities of Photoshop Elements.

Photoshop.com offers several different membership levels. The Basic membership is free and gives you your own storage space, where you can not only share and show-case your images but also access your photos and videos anytime and anywhere that you can connect to the internet. You can also use your Photoshop.com storage space to back up your Photoshop Elements albums and effortlessly safeguard your photos and creations.

Basic membership also gives you access to the Photoshop.com Inspiration Browser, with regularly updated downloadable content such as project templates, and extras such as backgrounds, frames, graphics, and more to keep your projects fresh and appealing. The Inspiration Browser also offers integrated tutorials with tips and tricks related to whatever you're currently working on, providing a powerful way to advance your skill set and helping you make the most out of your photos and creations.

You can upgrade your membership to the Premium level if you need more storage space or if you wish to access more of the special content.

Signing up from the Welcome screen

1 Start Photoshop Elements.

2 In the Welcome screen, click Join Now and follow the instructions to create your Adobe ID. An e-mail message confirms the creation of your account.

3 Follow the instructions in the e-mail to activate your account.

Signing up from the Organizer or Editor

1 In either the Organizer or Editor, click the Join Now link in the menu bar.

2 Fill out your personal details in the Photoshop.com Membership dialog box, and then click Create Account.

Signing in to your Photoshop.com account

1 Make sure, your computer is connected to the Internet, and then start Adobe Photoshop Elements.

2 In the Welcome screen, enter your Adobe ID and password, and click Sign In.

If you didn't sign in at the Welcome screen, you can always click the Sign In link at the top of either the Organizer or Editor windows.

● **Note:** You don't have to open a Photoshop.com membership account when the Welcome screen appears. You can open an account anytime you want. Links for joining and signing in are conveniently located throughout the Photoshop Elements workspace.

About sharing

In Lesson 1 you learned how to use the E-mail Attachments feature to create copies of your photos optimized as e-mail attachments (see "Sharing photos in e-mail" on page 25). Another option is to use the Photo Mail feature, which embeds your photos in the body of an e-mail within a colorful custom layout. To share items other than photos—such as slide shows, photo collages, or flipbooks—you are offered a choice of output options during the creation process.

Using Photo Mail

1 In the Organizer, select one or more photos in the Photo Browser and click the Photo Mail button in the Share panel of the Task pane.

If this is the first time you have accessed an e-mail feature in Photoshop Elements you will be presented with the E-mail dialog box. Choose your e-mail service from the menu, enter your name and e-mail address, and then click Continue. You can review or change your settings later by choosing Edit > Preferences > Sharing.

2   Activate the Include Captions option beside Items, and then click Next.

3   In the Message text box, delete the default text "Here are the photos…" and type a message of your own.

4   Select a recipient from the list in the Select Recipients pane. (If you didn't work through Lesson 1 and your recipient list is still empty, click the Edit Contact Book button ( ) and create a new entry in the Contact Book dialog box.

5   Click Next. The Stationery & Layouts Wizard dialog box appears.

6   In the Stationery & Layouts Wizard dialog box, click on each category in the list at the left of the dialog box to see the range of designs available. (*See the illustration on the next page.*) Select a stationery style appropriate to your selected photos. A preview of your photo e-mail will appear on the right side of the dialog box.

7 Click Next Step.

8 Customize the layout by choosing from the Photo Size and Layout options. Choose a font from the menu under Text. Click the color swatch beside the font menu and choose a text color from the color palette. To edit the message text, click the message in the preview to make it active, and then edit the text as you would usually do. Use the same technique to edit the caption text.

9 Click Next.

Photoshop Elements opens your default e-mail application and creates an e-mail message with your design embedded in the body of the message. You can send Photo Mail through Outlook Express, Outlook, or Adobe E-mail Service.

10 Switch back to the Photoshop Elements Organizer.

Creating a Quick Share Flow

If you find yourself sending the same kind of documents to the same group of people on a regular basis, then setting up a Quick Share Flow can help you automate the process, minimizing your effort considerably. For example, if you frequently (or even only occasionally) send your family e-mail messages with vacation or holiday season photos, you need only set up such information as the mailing list and your preferred image size for the attachments once, and then reuse these settings by simply dropping photos on the Quick Share target.

While you can create a new print order by clicking the New button in the Quick Share palette, you can only create a Quick Share Flow only from within the respective workflow. In the following steps you will set up a Quick Share Flow to send photos as e-mail attachments to a specified group of recipients.

1 Select several photos in the Photo Browser and click the Share tab in the Task pane; then, click the E-mail Attachments button.

2 From the Maximum Photo Size menu, select Very Small (320 x 240 px), which will result in a relatively small file size for an e-mail with several images attached. Use the Quality slider to adjust the image quality, remembering that a higher quality setting will equate to a longer download time.

Photoshop Elements will calculate the file size and display the estimated download time for a typical dial-up modem at 56 Kbps. When you're satisfied with the settings, click Next.

3 In the Message text box, delete the default "Here are the photos…." text and type a message of your own.

4 Choose the recipients you wish to include in this Quick Share target from the Recipients list by clicking the check boxes beside their names.

5 Under Save As Quick Share Flow?, click the radio button for Yes. Type a descriptive name for this quick share target, and then click Next.

Your default e-mail application opens and creates an e-mail message with the selected photos attached at the specified image size and quality. You can still edit the message and subject line if you wish. If you intend to send this e-mail, first make sure that you are connected to the Internet, and then click Send; otherwise, close the message without saving it.

6 Switch back to the Photoshop Elements Organizer. You'll notice the new e-mail attachments Quick Share target in the Quick Share palette. Select one or more photos in the Photo Browser; then, drag and drop your selection onto the new target.

7 (Optional). Drag and drop additional photos onto the Quick Share target. The number in brackets next to the target name indicates the number of photos selected for this Quick Share target.

8 When you're done, click the E-mail button in the Quick Share target.

With just one click your default e-mail application opens and creates an e-mail message with the selected photos attached at the specified image size and quality, ready to be sent.

9 Close your e-mail application, and then switch back to the Photoshop Elements Organizer.

Creating an Online Album

Note: At this stage, Photoshop.com membership will be available to users in the United States only. Photoshop Elements users outside the United States will continue to share their Albums to third party sharing services via Photoshop Showcase.

Another way to share and showcase your photos is by creating an Online album. You can choose from a variety of interactive layout templates that are optimized for viewing photos on the Web. Photoshop Elements guides you through the process of adding and arranging photos, applying templates, and sharing your files.

1 In the Organizer, choose View > Show File Names, if necessary, to see the file names below the thumbnails. Type **jungle** in the Text Search box at the upper left of the workspace, and then press Enter on your keyboard to find the images for this exercise. The Photo Browser shows 12 photos named "5_jungle_ruins_1.jpg" to "5_jungle_ruins_12.jpg."

2 In the Image Browser, Ctrl-click to select the top 4 photos.

3 Click the Share tab at the top of the Tasks pane, and then click the Online Album button. The 4 selected photos are added to the album and their thumbnails are displayed in the Items pane.

4 In the Album Details panel, type **Jungle Ruins** in the Album Name text box.

Adding photos to your Online Album

1 In the Photo Browser, Ctrl-click to select the next 4 photos, and then click the Add Items Selected In Photo Browser button (⊕) above the Items pane. The selected photos are added to the album and appear in the Items pane.

2 Ctrl-click to select the last 4 images in the Photo Browser and drag them into the Items pane. All 12 photos are now included in the Jungle Ruins album.

To add a photo to the album, select a thumbnail in the Photo Browser and click the Add Items Selected In Photo Browser button (⊕) above the Items pane as shown in the illustration on the left. To remove an image from the album, select a thumbnail in the Items pane and click the Remove Selected Items button (⊖) above the Items pane as shown in the illustration on the right.

Changing the order of photos in an Online Album

To change the order in which the photos will be displayed, simply drag the thumbnails to rearrange them in the Items pane. If you wish, you can arrange them in the order in which they were intended to be displayed by referring to the numbering in their file names.

1   When you're satisfied with the order of the images, click Share. The 12 photos are displayed in an animated Online Album preview, using the default template.

2   Click any of the image thumbnails across the bottom of the preview to see an enlarged view of that image. Click the navigation buttons above the enlarged photo to cycle through the images in the album.

3   Click the Change Template button to see the options available. You can experiment with the templates later, but for now leave the template as it is. Click Cancel.

Choosing a sharing option for your Online Album

1   Click the radio button beside one of the options under Share To:

   • Choose Photoshop.com if you are a US resident and have already signed up for Photoshop.com membership.

   • Choose Export To CD/DVD if you wish to make a backup of your album, if you don't have access to an online sharing service, or if you wish to share your album with someone who does not have an internet connection.

   • Choose Export To FTP if you plan to upload your album to a web server.

2   Click Next.

3   Type **Angkor** as the on-screen title for your online album, type **Cambodia** for the subtitle, and then click Next.

4   Depending on your choice of sharing option, do one of the following:

- If you chose Export To CD/DVD, choose a destination drive from the menu, type a name for the disc, and then click Export. When the process is complete, skip the rest of the steps in this exercise and move on to the next section, "Sharing an existing album."

- If you chose Export To FTP, type the server name for your web server, your user name and password for that server, and a folder name for the folder into which you want to upload your files, and then click Export. When the process is complete, skip the rest of the steps in this exercise and move on to the next section, "Sharing an existing album."

- If you chose Export To Photoshop.com, you can move on to step 5.

5 Click a radio button to specify whether you wish to share your album publicly for everyone to see or privately with only those friends to whom you choose to send an invitation.

6 Type a message to be e-mailed with your invitation in the Message text box.

7 Under Send E-mail To, select those contacts to whom you wish to e-mail an invitation by clicking the checkboxes beside their names in the list.

8 Specify whether you wish to allow viewers to download photos or order prints, and then click Share.

Photoshop Elements informs you that the album is now being shared and will be available online as soon as the upload is complete.

9 Return to the Organizer. In in the Albums palette, the Jungle Ruins album is marked with an Online Album icon (). Click the entry for the new online album. The Stop Sharing button () to the right of its name indicates that the Jungle Ruins album is currently being shared.

Sharing an existing album online

If you have a Photoshop.com account it's easy to convert any Photoshop Elements album into an Online Album.

1 In the Organizer, click Show All above the Photo Browser pane.

● **Note:** This feature is currently only available to Photoshop Elements users in the US who have signed up for Photoshop.com membership.

2 In the Keyword Tags panel, click the Find box beside the Lesson 1 tag.

3 Select the four images of New York buildings.

4 Click the Create New Album Or Album Group button (✚) at the top of the Albums palette and choose New Album from the menu.

5 In the Album Details dialog box, type **New York** as the name for the new album, click the checkbox to disable the Backup/Synchronize option, and then click Done.

The entry for the new album in the Albums palette is marked with the standard Album icon (▣). In the Image Browser, the thumbnails if the images included the new album are also marked.

6 In the Albums palette, click the entry for the New York album, and then click the Share button (▣) to the right of the album name.

7 The Album Details dialog box appears. You can change the template if you wish, and follow steps 5, 6, and 7 from the previous exercise to specify sharing options and invite your friends to view your album by e-mail.

8 Specify whether you wish to allow viewers to download photos or order prints, and then click Share.

9 Return to the Organizer. In in the Albums palette, the New York album is now marked with an Online Album icon (▣). Click the entry for the new online album. The Stop Sharing button (◉) to the right of its name indicates that the New York album is currently being shared.

Backing up and synchronizing albums

● **Note:** This feature is currently only available to Photoshop Elements users in the US who have signed up for Photoshop.com membership.

If you have signed up for Photoshop.com membership, you can choose to synchronize the files in your Photoshop Elements catalog and your Photoshop.com account, making your photos and videos available to you from any web browser through Photoshop.com and Photoshop Express.

You can manage your media from any web browser: add, delete, edit, or re-organize items at home or on the road. Any changes you make online will be synchronized back to Photoshop Elements on your desktop. Don't worry; the Synchronization feature will not overwrite anything on your base computer—Photoshop Elements creates a Version Set on your computer, so you will still have the original. If you delete something online, a copy is kept on your computer unless you confirm that you really do want it deleted from your Photoshop Elements Catalog.

Only Albums can be backed up and synchronized in this way. If you wish to protect photos from your catalog you must first place them in an album.

1 In the Organizer, click Show All above the Photo Browser pane.

2 In the Keyword Tags panel, click the Find box beside the Lesson 1 tag.

3 Select the six images of flowers.

4 Click the Create New Album Or Album Group button (➕) at the top of the Albums palette and choose New Album from the menu.

5 In the Album Details dialog box, type **Flowers** as the name for the new album, make sure that the Backup/Synchronize option is activated, and then click Done.

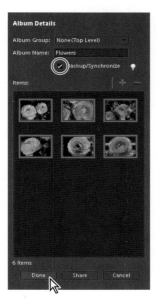

The entry for the new album in the Albums palette is marked with the Synchronized Album icon (⬛). The Share button (⬛) to the right of the album name indicates that the album is not being shared.

▶ **Tip:** You can also access the Backup/ Synchronization Preferences by choosing Edit > Preferences > Backup/ Synchronization.

6 Click the entry for the Flowers album, and then click the Backup/ Synchronization Preferences button (⬛) at the top of the Albums palette.

The Backup/Synchronization Preferences dialog box opens.

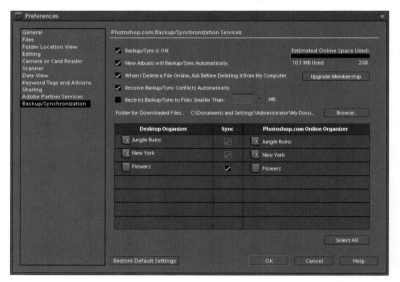

7 Notice the settings in the Backup/Synchronization Preferences:

• Backup/Synchronization is active and new albums are set to backup and synchronize by default.

• By default, when you delete a file online Photoshop Elements will ask before deleting it from your computer.

• You can choose whether conflicts between the data in your catalog and your backed-up data online will be resolved automatically, or whether you wish to control which data is changed, and you can restrict backup to exclude large (time and CPU intensive) files.

There is also a status bar showing how much online space you've used, a button for upgrading your Photoshop.com membership, and a setting to specify a folder for downloads.

8   Now look at the table below the preferences settings. Synchronization is enabled for all three albums. The Sync checkboxes for the Jungle Ruins and New York albums are greyed out—the settings cannot be changed because both are Online Albums that are currently shared and therefore enabled for synchronization by default. To disable synchronization for an Online Album, you first need to stop sharing that album.

9   Click OK to close the Backup/Synchronization Preferences dialog box.

You can also set Backup/Synchronization preferences from the Welcome Screen (once you log in to your Photoshop Express account) and even from within Photoshop.com's Photoshop Express. For more detailed information on backup and synchronization options, please refer to Photoshop Elements Help.

Using an online sharing service

From within Photoshop Elements you can use Adobe Photoshop Services to upload your images and creations to online sharing service providers. You can also use these services to download photos.

1   In the Organizer, select the photos you wish to share from the Photo Browser.

2   In the Share panel of the Task pane, click the More Options button, and then choose Share With Kodak Easyshare Gallery from the menu to access the Kodak® EasyShare Gallery service.

3   If the Welcome to Adobe Photoshop Services dialog box appears, do one of the following:

   • If you are already an Ofoto or EasyShare Gallery member, click Sign in, and then use the e-mail address and password associated with your existing online account to sign in.

   • Create a new account by entering your first name, e-mail address, and a password of at least six characters. If you agree with the Terms of Service, select the respective check box under Create Account, and then click Next.

● **Note:** If you are still signed in to Adobe Photoshop Services from the previous exercise, you don't need to sign in again. Just click Next to continue.

4　In the Share Online dialog box, click Add New Address.

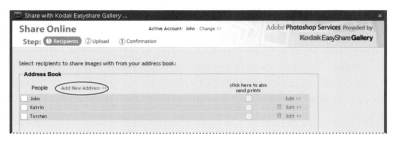

5　In the Add Address dialog box, complete the address information for the person with whom you wish to share your photos, and then click Next.

6　In the Share Online dialog box, select the newly added address book check box. Under Message, type **Photos** in the subject field and **Enjoy!** in the message field; then, click Next and your photos will be uploaded.

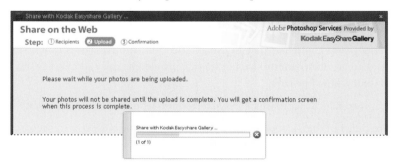

7　In the Share Online Confirmation dialog box, click Done. Alternatively, if you wish to purchase prints of your photos click Order Prints, and then follow the on-screen directions.

An e-mail will be sent to the recipient you specified in step 6, containing a Web link to the photos which can be viewed as an online slide show.

About exporting

Even though Photoshop Elements offers a variety of ways to share your photos and creations, there may be situations where you wish to export copies of your files for use in another application. In the Organizer, you can move or copy your files to CD or DVD. In the Editor, you can export you photos optimized for use in a web page design application.

Burning photos to CD or DVD

Choose File > Make A CD/DVD in the Organizer to copy a set of photos to a CD or DVD. You might do this in order to share a large number of photos at full size with a friend, or when you want to backup only selected images. Alternatively, use the Copy/Move to Removable Disk command to copy or move photos to any removable storage device—an external hard disk, USB memory stick, network drive, or CD/DVD writer—connected to your computer.

1   In the Photo Browser, select the items you want to burn to CD or DVD. Make sure you have a blank writable disc in the CD or DVD drive connected to your computer, and then choose File > Make A CD/DVD.

If you haven't selected any files, you'll see a dialog box giving you the option of copying all the files currently visible in the Photo Browser.

2   In the Make A CD/DVD dialog box, select a destination drive, and then click OK. If you'd prefer to stop now, without copying any files, click Cancel.

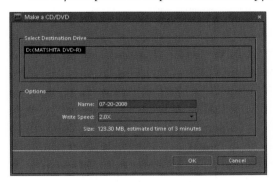

3   In the Photo Browser, select the items you want to copy or move, and then choose File > Copy/Move To Removable Disk. The Copy/Move To Removable Disk wizard appears.

Note: The Move Files option deletes the original files from your hard disk after they are copied to the new location, storing only a smaller low-resolution proxy file and a reference to the new location of the original file in your catalog. This is useful if you only need to access the original files occasionally and wish to save hard disk space on your computer.

4   If the Move Files option is activated under Offline Media, click the checkbox to disable it.

5   Under Stacks and Version Sets, you have the option to copy/move only the topmost file or all the files in a stack or version set. If there are no stacks or version sets in your selection, these options are dimmed.

6   Click Next.

7   Select a destination drive in the Destination Settings dialog box. If you want to specify a target folder, click Browse and select the folder in the Browse For Folder dialog box.

8   Click Done to copy your files to the target location or Cancel to exit the Copy/Move To Removable Disk wizard without copying or moving any files.

The File > Export > As New File(s) command gives you the additional option to export your photos in file formats other than the original. You can choose between JPEG, PNG, TIFF, or PSD file formats and specify image sizes, location, and custom file names.

Saving copies of your images for use on the Web

As a final exercise in this lesson you'll convert a file to JPEG format and optimize it for use on the Web. The JPEG file format reduces the file size and can be displayed by web browsers such as Internet Explorer. If your file contains multiple layers, the conversion to the JPEG file format will flatten them into one layer.

For this operation you'll use the Save for Web feature, which enables you to tweak the export settings while comparing the original image file with the proposed web-ready version of the image.

1   In the Photo Browser, select a photo you want to export for use on the Web.

2   Click the Editor button (🖊) located near the top right corner of the Organizer window, and then choose either Quick Fix, Full Edit, or Guided Edit from the menu. Alternatively, click either the Quick Fix, Full Edit, or Guided Edit button in the lower part of the Fix panel in the Organizer Task pane.

3   Wait until the Editor workspace has loaded, and then choose File > Save For Web.

4   In the Save For Web dialog box, choose Fit On Screen from the Zoom menu in the lower left corner of the dialog box. *(See the illustration on the next page.)*

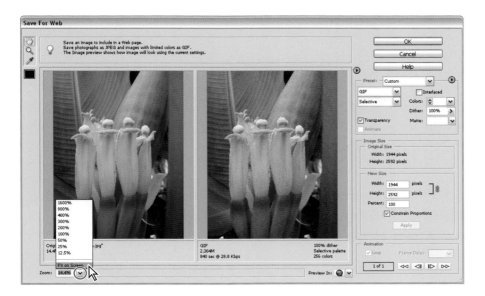

Note: When you're previewing photos in the Save For Web dialog box, you can magnify an image by clicking with the Zoom tool (Q) from the toolbox in the upper left corner of the dialog box. Alt-click with the zoom tool to zoom out. While you're zoomed in, you can drag either image with the Hand tool (✋) to move both images at once so that you see the same details in both views.

5 Notice the file-size information under each view of the image. The image on the left displays the file size of the original document.

6 On the right side of the dialog box, select JPEG Medium from the Preset menu. Notice the change in file size for the JPEG image on the right.

7 Under New Size, select Constrain Proportions and type **300** in the Width field. The Height is adjusted automatically to retain the image's original proportions.

8 In the New Size section of the Save For Web dialog box, click the Apply button. Again, notice the change in the file size displayed beneath the JPEG view of the image. If necessary, choose Fit On Screen from the Zoom menu.

9 Click OK. Navigate to the My CIB Work folder in the Save Optimized As dialog box, add _**Work** to the end of the file name, and then click Save.

The JPEG format reduces the file size by using JPEG compression which discards some of the data. The amount of data lost, and therefore the resulting image quality will vary depending on the image you're working with and the settings you choose.

Note: If you need to further reduce the file size, choose the JPEG Low setting, which reduces the file size by discarding more image data and further compressing the image. You can specify intermediate levels between these options by tweaking the Quality setting, either by typing a new value or by clicking the arrow and dragging the slider.

10 In the Editor, choose File > Close, without saving changes.

Congratulations! You've completed this lesson and should now have a working understanding of the basics of printing, sharing, and exporting. You've learned how to set up single or multiple images for printing at home and how to order professional prints online. You've learned how to share photos in Photo Mail or to an online sharing service and you've seen how a Quick Share Flow can automate frequently performed sharing tasks. You've created on Online Album and exported photos for use on the Web. Before you move on to the next lesson, take a few moments to work through the following review.

Review questions

1 How do you print multiple images on a single sheet of paper?

2 What is Photo Mail?

3 What is a Quick Share Flow?

4 What command can you use to backup all photos in your catalog to a CD or DVD?

5 How do you convert an existing album to an Online Album?

6 Is synchronization only possible for shared Online Albums?

7 Is the Save For Web command also available in Quick Fix mode?

Review answers

1 In the Organizer, select the photos you want to print and choose File > Print. Choose Individual Prints as the Type Of Print, select a print size that's small enough for multiple images, and then deselect the One Photo Per Page check box. Alternatively, choose Picture Package or Contact Sheet from the Select Type Of Print menu and experiment with different layout options.

2 The Photo Mail feature embeds selected photos in the body of an e-mail within a colorful custom layout. You can tweak the layout and image size, choose backgrounds, frames, and effects, and add text messages and captions. You can send Photo Mail through Outlook Express, Outlook, or Adobe E-mail Service.

3 A quick share flow can help you automate sharing tasks you perform frequently. Save your settings within a sharing workflow—such as attaching photos to an e-mail to be sent to all the members of your family—as a Quick Share Flow, and then perform the same task by simply dropping photos onto your new target in the Quick Share palette.

4 In the Organizer, choose File > Backup Catalog. After the first full backup, you can choose to perform only an incremental backup. To copy or move only selected files in your catalog, use the File > Copy/Move Offline command.

5 You need a Photoshop.com account to be able to convert any album into an Online Album. In the Albums palette, click the entry for the album, and then click the Share button to the right of the album name. You can select a template if you wish, and specify sharing options.

6   No. Synchronization is enabled for shared Online Albums by default, but you can choose whether or not you wish to enable backup and synchronization to Photoshop.com for any album in your catalog. You can either specify that an album is synchronized when you create it, or change it's status later in the Backup/ Synchronization Preferences dialog box.

7   Yes, the Save For Web command is available in all three modes of the Editor, Quick Fix, Full Edit, and Guided Edit.

6 ADJUSTING COLOR IN IMAGES

Lesson Overview

This lesson introduces you to a variety of tools and techniques for fixing color problems in your photos:

- Correcting color in Guided Edit mode
- Auto-correcting in Quick Fix and Full Edit mode
- Using automatic options to improve images
- Adjusting skin tones
- Correcting an image using Smart Fix
- Using Color Variations to correct color balance
- Whitening teeth and removing red eyes effects
- Selecting and saving selections
- Adjusting color in selected areas
- Troubleshooting color printing
- Working with color management

 You'll probably need about two hours to complete this lesson.

Explore the many powerful and versatile tools and options available in Photoshop Elements for correcting color problems in your photos—starting with a few of the easy-to-use, one-step image correction features, and then experimenting with some of the more advanced features and adjustment techniques that can be mastered easily.

Getting started

Note: Before you start working on this lesson, make sure that you've installed the software on your computer from the application CD (see the Photoshop Elements 7 documentation) and that you have correctly copied the Lessons folder from the CD in the back of this book onto your computer's hard disk (see "Copying the Classroom in a Book files" on page 2).

For the exercises in this lesson you'll be working in the Editor in Full Edit mode, Quick Fix mode, and Guided Edit mode. You'll be using the CIB Catalog you created in the "Getting Started" section at the beginning of this book.

1   Start Photoshop Elements and click the Organize button in the Welcome Screen. The name of the currently active catalog is displayed in the lower left corner of the Organizer window.

2   If your CIB Catalog is not already open choose File > Catalog and select the CIB Catalog in the Catalog Manager dialog box. If you don't see the CIB Catalog file listed, see "Creating a catalog" on page 3.

3   Once you have loaded your CIB Catalog, click the Editor button (🖊) near the top right corner of the Organizer window and choose Full Edit from the menu.

Before you begin the exercises, you can set up the Editor workspace so that what you see on screen corresponds to the illustrations in this section.

Note: You cannot add or remove palettes in Quick Fix mode. For detailed instructions on adding palettes to (and removing them from) the Palette Bin in Full Edit mode, see "Using the Palette Bin" in Lesson 1, "A Quick Tour of Photoshop Elements."

4   In Full Edit mode, choose from the Window menu to show the Tools palette, the Palette Bin, and the Project Bin. In both Full Edit and Quick Fix modes, you can expand or collapse palettes in the Palette Bin by clicking the arrow beside the palette name on the palette title bar.

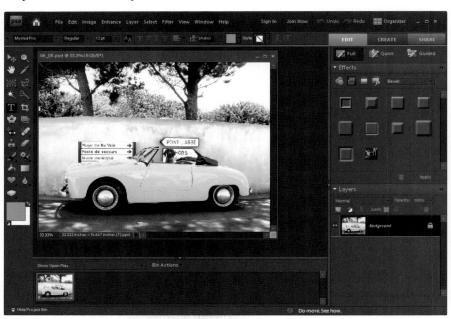

The Editor workspace in Full Edit mode.

Each of the three Edit modes offers a different set of tools, controls and views.
In the Guided Edit mode, the Palette Bin is replaced by a list of guided tasks.

The Editor workspace in Quick Fix mode.

The Editor workspace in Guided Edit mode.

Correcting color problems

You may have noticed that not all the photographs used for the lessons in this book are of professional quality. Many of the pictures were selected to illustrate common image faults—the kind of challenges that people typically face when attempting to make the most of their photographs.

Artificial light sources, unusual shooting conditions, and incorrect camera exposure settings can all cause tonal imbalances and unwelcome color casts in an image. In the following exercises we'll look at some of the ways Photoshop Elements can help you correct such problems.

In the Editor, you can make adjustments using the simple controls in the Quick Fix mode or be stepped through a wide range of editing tasks in Guided Edit mode. You can have Photoshop Elements apply corrections automatically, processing your photos in batches, or work in Full Edit mode to perform sophisticated edits selectively.

Fixing files in batches

Photoshop Elements allows you fix multiple photographs with one command by processing them as a batch. In this exercise, you'll apply automatic fixes to all the image files to be used in this lesson.

You'll save the auto-adjusted files as copies so that at the end of each project you can compare these automatic results to the edits you have made to the original files using various other techniques.

1   In the Editor, choose File > Process Multiple Files. The Process Multiple Files dialog box opens.

2   In the Process Multiple Files dialog box, set the source and destination folders as follows:

 • Choose Folder from the Process Files From menu.

 • Under Source, click the Browse button. Find and select the Lesson06 folder in the Lessons folder. Click OK to close the Browse For Folder dialog box.

 • Under Destination, click Browse. Then, find and select the My CIB Work folder that you created at the start of the book. Click OK to close the Browse For Folder dialog box.

3   Under File Naming, select Rename Files. Select Document Name from the menu on the left and type **_Autofix** in the second field. This adds the appendix "_Autofix" to the existing document name as the files are saved.

4   Under Quick Fix on the right side of the dialog box, select all four options: Auto Levels, Auto Contrast, Auto Color, and Sharpen.

5   Review all the settings in the dialog box, comparing them to the illustration below. Make sure that the Resize Images and Convert Files options are disabled.

6   When you are sure that the settings are correct, click OK.

Photoshop Elements goes to work, automatically opening and closing image windows. All you need to do is sit back and wait for the process to finish, then move on to the next exercise.

To see the how the images look after the Quick Fix operations, you can either use Windows Explorer, or import them into your catalog (as you will do in the next exercise) where you can view them in the Photo Browser. For more information on the Photo Browser, see Photoshop Elements Help.

An error message warning that files are missing indicates that the Lessons folder has been moved or was not expanded correctly. See "Copying the Classroom in a Book files" on page 2 and redo that procedure, following the instructions exactly.

Note: If an error message appears warning that some files couldn't be processed, you can ignore it. This error is often caused by a hidden file that is not an image, so it has no effect on the success of your project.

Adding the corrected files to the Organizer

For most files modified in the Editor, the Include In Organizer option is activated in the Save, Save As, and Save Optimized As dialog boxes by default.

However, when you batch-edit files with the Process Multiple Files feature, this option isn't part of the process—you must add the edited files to the Organizer manually.

1 In the Editor, click the Organizer button (⊞) to open the Organizer workspace.

2 In the Organizer, choose File > Get Photos And Videos > From Files And Folders.

3 In the Get Photos From Files And Folders dialog box, locate and open your My CIB Work folder.

4 Ctrl-click or marquee-select all six files with the _Autofix suffix.

5 Activate the Automatically Fix Red Eyes option, disable the Automatically Suggest Photo Stacks option, and then click Get Photos.

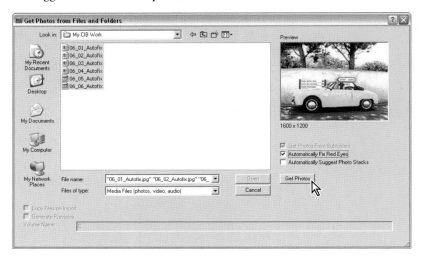

6 The Import Attached Keyword Tags dialog box opens. Click OK without selecting any keyword tags—you'll be adding keyword tags manually in the next few steps.

7 If the Auto Red Eye Fix Complete dialog box appears, click OK.

8 If a message appears reminding you that only the new photos will appear in the Photo Browser, click OK.

The files are imported to your CIB Catalog and the Organizer displays thumbnails of the newly added images in the Photo Browser.

9 Choose Edit > Select All, or press Ctrl+A.

10 If necessary, click the triangle beside the Imported Keyword Tags category in the Keyword Tags palette to expand the category entry so that you can see the imported keyword tags. Drag the Lesson 6 keyword tag to any of the selected image thumbnails to apply it to all selected images. *(See the illustration on the next page.)*

11 Click the Show All button above the Photo Browser.

In this lesson you saw how easy it is to have Photoshop Elements apply Quick Fix corrections to a batch of image files automatically. In the next exercises you'll explore some other methods for correcting color.

Using Guided Edit

If you are new to digital photography, the Guided Edit mode in Photoshop Elements is a great place to start when it comes to learning how to fix many common image problems. Even more experienced users can enjoy the ease and simplicity of performing editing tasks using the Guided Edit mode, and may just pick up some new tricks!

Removing a color cast using Guided Edit

One of the photos in the Lesson 6 folder, an image of three glass vases, has a very obvious color cast—a result of inadequate artificial lighting. In this exercise, you'll correct that color problem using the Guided Edit mode in the Editor.

1 If you are not still in the Organizer from the last exercise, switch to it now.

2 In the Keyword Tags palette, click the Find box for the Lesson 6 keyword tag.

The Image Browser is updated to show twelve images tagged with the Lesson 6 keyword: each of the six original photos from the Lesson06 folder is displayed beside the edited copy of the same image from your My CIB Work folder.

● **Note:** As you gain advanced skills in Photoshop Elements 7, you might require additional information to solve any problems you may encounter. For help with common problems you might have while working through the lessons in this book, see "Why won't Photoshop Elements do what I tell it to do?" later in this lesson.

3   Select the original photo of the three vases, 06_01.jpg, to make it active. Make sure not to confuse the original file with the copied file 06_01_Autofix.jpg, to which color correction—among other Quick Fix adjustments—has already been applied.

▶ **Tip:** To see the file name below each thumbnail image in the Photo Browser, choose View > Show File Names.

4   Click the Editor button () near the top right corner of the Organizer window, and then choose Guided Edit from the menu.

5   Wait until the Editor workspace has loaded and the image of the three vases has opened in Guided Edit mode.

6   If necessary, click the triangle beside the Color Correction entry in the guided tasks menu so that you can see the nested options. Choose Remove A Color Cast from the Color Correction submenu.

7 Click the display mode button near the bottom of the Guided Edit task panel to change the display to the Before & After - Horizontal view.

8 Read the instructions under Correct Color Cast. Then, using the Color Cast Eyedropper tool, click near the top left corner of the Before image to remove the color cast. Notice the change in the After image.

9 (Optional) If you are not satisfied with the result, click the Undo button (⟲) in the menu bar at the top of the organizer window, and then click a different area in the Before image with the Color Cast Eyedropper tool. To clear the Undo/Redo history and start all over with the original version of the image, click the Reset button in the Guided Edit panel.

10 When you are satisfied with the result of the color correction in the After image, click the Done button near the bottom of the Guided Edit task panel.

Adjusting lighting using Guided Edit

As is often the case with poorly exposed photos, this image has more than just one problem. After the color cast has been removed, the image looks as if it could benefit from some lighting adjustments.

1 If necessary, click the triangle beside the Lighting And Exposure entry in the guided tasks menu so that you can see the nested options, and then choose Lighten Or Darken from the submenu of Lighting And Exposure tasks.

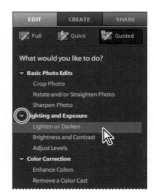

2   In the Lighten Or Darken A Photo task panel, click the Auto button. Notice the substantial improvement in the appearance of the image.

3   Use the Lighten Shadows, Darken Highlights, and Midtone Contrast sliders to fine-tune the lighting for this image. We set a value of 30 for Lighten Shadows, left the Darken Highlights slider at 0, and set a value of 32 for Midtone Contrast. Your choices may vary, depending on the results of your color correction and your preferences for the look of the final image.

4   When you are satisfied with the results of the lighting adjustment as they are shown in the After image, click the Done button near the bottom of the Guided Edit task panel.

5   (Optional) In the guided tasks menu, choose Sharpen Photo from the Basic Photo Edits submenu. Click the Auto button near the top of the Sharpen Photo task panel. Use the slider to manually fine-tune the sharpening to your liking, and then click Done.

6   Choose File > Save As. In the Save As dialog box, navigate to and open your My CIB Work folder. Leaving the JPEG file format selected, name the file **06_01_Guided**, activate Include In The Organizer, disable Save in Version Set with Original, and then click Save.

7   In the JPEG Options dialog box, click OK without making any changes.

8   In the Editor, choose File > Close, and then switch back to the Organizer.

Note: To avoid the image artifacts that can result from over-sharpening, sharpening is best applied at a magnification of 100%. Use the display mode button near the bottom of the Guided Edit task panel to change the display to the After Only view, and then choose View > Actual Pixels.

9 In the Organizer, type the word **guided** in the Text Search text box above the Photo Browser. The Photo Browser is updated to display only the newly added image 06_01_Guided.jpg. Drag the Lesson 6 keyword tag from the Keyword Tags palette onto the image thumbnail in the Photo Browser.

10 Click the Show All button above the Photo Browser.

With just a few clicks you have improved the appearance of the photo dramatically. You don't need to have prior experience using an image editor to get good results in Guided Edit mode. Try the Guided Activities ("Touch Up Scratches, Blemishes Or Tear Marks", "Guide For Editing A Photo", and "Fix Keystone Distortion") that each step you through several image editing tasks in the recommended order to get professional results. In the exercise to follow, you'll move on to the next level in editing—working in the Quick Fix mode.

Using Quick Fix for editing

The Quick Fix workspace conveniently assembles many of the basic photo fixing tools in Photoshop Elements. If one control doesn't work for your image, click the Reset button and try another one. Whether you've used the Quick Fix mode before or not, the intuitive slider controls make adjusting your image easy.

Applying automatic adjustments separately

When you apply a combination of automatic fixes to a set of images using the Process Multiple Files feature, the process happens too fast for you to see the changes made to each image at each stage of processing.

In this exercise, you'll apply some of the same automatic fix options separately, one at a time. This enables you to see how each editing step affects an image, and provides the opportunity to fine-tune the correction process by adjusting the default settings to optimize the results.

Opening image files for Quick Fix editing

Once again, you can use the Keyword Tags palette to find the sample image you want, and then open it in Quick Fix mode from the Organizer.

1 If the Organizer is not currently active, switch to it now.

2 In the Keyword Tags palette, click the Find box next to the Lesson 6 keyword tag.

3 Select the original version of the image with three glass vases, 06_01.jpg.

4 Click the Editor button (🖊) near the top right corner of the Organizer window and choose Quick Fix from the menu.

Note: To see the file names for images in the Photo Browser, choose View > Show File Names.

5 Choose Before & After - Horizontal from the View menu in the lower left corner of the image window. If you prefer the before and after images one above the other rather than side-by-side, choose the Before & After - Vertical view.

Using Smart Fix

In the Quick Fix workspace the Palette Bin at the right contains five palettes—General Fixes, Lighting, Color, Sharpen, and Touch Up. In the General Fixes palette, the first option available is the Smart Fix feature, which corrects overall color balance and improves shadow and highlight detail in your image. As with the other editing features in Quick Fix mode, you can click the Auto button to apply corrections automatically or you can use the slider controls to fine-tune the adjustments. You can even combine these methods, as you will in this exercise.

1 In the General Fixes palette, click the Smart Fix Auto button. Notice the immediate effect on the image.

2 Now, move the Amount slider to change the color balance and highlight and shadow detail settings for your image. Experiment to find the setting you prefer. In our example the slider has been moved to the middle position.

3 Click the Commit button (✔) in the title bar of the General Fixes palette to commit the changes.

Applying other automatic fixes

More automatic fixes are available in the Lighting, Color, and Sharpen palettes.

1   In the Lighting palette, click the Auto button for the Levels feature. Depending on the adjustment you made to the Smart Fix edit, you may or may not see a big shift in the lighting of this image.

2   Click the Auto buttons for Contrast, Color, and Sharpen in turn, noticing the affects of each of these adjustments on the After image.

3   Experiment with the slider controls in each palette. When you're satisfied with an adjustment, click the Commit button (✔) in title bar of the respective palette to commit the changes.

4   If you wish to undo your modifications and start again using the original version of the image, click the Reset button above the After view.

5   When you have achieved the results you want, choose File > Save As. In the Save As dialog box, navigate to and open your My CIB Work folder, rename the file **06_01_Quick** and select the JPEG format. Select Include In The Organizer. If Save In Version Set With Original is selected, deselect it. Click Save.

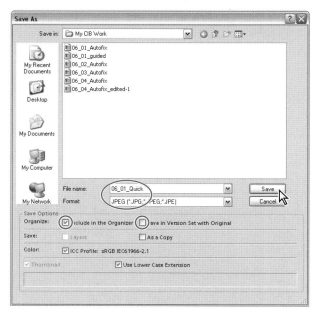

6   When the JPEG Options dialog box appears, select High from the Quality menu, and then click OK.

7   In the Editor, choose File > Close, and then switch back to the Organizer.

8   In the Organizer, type the word **quick** in the Text Search text box above the Photo Browser. The Photo Browser is updated to display only the newly added image 06_01_Quick.jpg. Drag the Lesson 6 keyword tag from the Keyword Tags palette onto the image thumbnail in the Photo Browser.

9   Click the Show All button above the Photo Browser.

Using the Touch Up tools

The last palette in the Quick Fix Palette Bin is the Touch Up palette. The four tools in the Touch Up palette all enable you to apply corrections and adjustments selectively to specific parts of an image:

- The Red Eye Removal tool removes red eye effects in flash photos of people and red, green, or white eye effects in flash photos of pets.
- The Whiten Teeth tool brightens smiles.
- The Blue Sky tool can bring new life to an image.
- The Black And White - High Contrast tool simulates the high-contrast image effects that black and white film photographers produce by placing a red filter over the camera lens.

Except for Red Eye Removal, all Touch Up adjustments are applied on a separate adjustment layer; they do not discard or permanently edit any information on the image layer. You can always change adjustment settings without degrading the original image.

Brightening a smile

We'll be looking closer at the Red Eye Removal feature in a later exercise. For now, let's try the Whiten Teeth tool.

1 If the Organizer is not currently active, switch to it now.

2 In the Keyword Tags palette, click the Find box next to the Lesson 6 keyword tag.

3 Select the original version of the image 06_02.jpg, showing a couple photographed in bright sunlight. Take care not to select the "_Autofix" file.

4 Click the Editor button (⬚) near the top right corner of the Organizer window and choose Quick Fix from the menu.

● **Note:** The Whiten Teeth, Blue Sky, and Black And White - High Contrast tools in Quick Fix mode are all variants on the Smart Brush tool in Full Edit mode. For more information on the Smart Brush, see "Using the Smart Brush" later in this lesson or refer to Photoshop Elements Help.

● **Note:** To see the file names for images in the Photo Browser, choose View > Show File Names.

Setting up the Quick Fix workspace

1 Collapse all the palettes in the Palette Bin except for the Touch Up palette.

2 To maximize the space available for editing, hide the Project Bin by clicking the triangle in the lower left corner of the Editor window.

3 From the View menu at the left below the Quick Fix editing preview, choose Before & After - Vertical.

4 Set the Zoom level to 200%. Either use the slider or type **200** in the text box.

5 Use the hand tool to drag either the Before or After image within the preview window. The images will move together. Position them so that you can see the man's teeth.

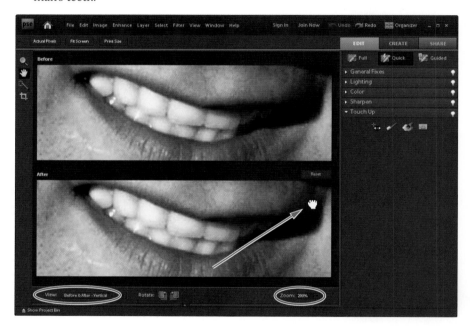

Using the Whiten Teeth tool

Now it's time for a little dental magic. With the Whiten Teeth tool, as with the other Touch Up tools, you'll work directly into the After image—the tools have no effect on the Before image.

1 Click to select the Whiten Teeth tool (■) in the Touch Up palette.

2 Notice that settings and controls for the Whiten Teeth tool are now available at the top left of the Editor window, just above the Tools palette.

3   In the Whiten Teeth tool settings, click the triangle to open the Brush picker. As the image you're using for this exercise is of a fairly low resolution, you'll need a small brush—set the Diameter to 5 px. Set the Hardness value to 50%, and then click the triangle again to close the Brush picker.

4   Move the pointer over the After image. A small cross-hair cursor indicates the brush size set for the Whiten Teeth tool: Notice that in the tool settings at the top left of the Editor window, the brush icon on the left is highlighted to indicate that the tool is in New Selection mode. Drag the cross-hair across two of the brightest teeth as shown below, and then release the mouse button.

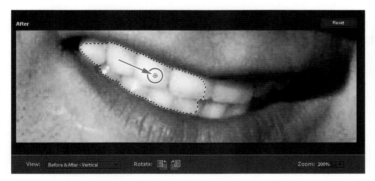

Adding to and subtracting from an adjustment selection

The Whiten Teeth tool, like the Blue Sky and Black And White Touch Up tools, is both a selection tool and an image adjustment tool. You have just used the tool to create a selection through which the tooth whitening adjustment is applied once. While this selection is active, you can add to or subtract from it, without re-applying the adjustment.

The Whiten Teeth selection and edit is being made on an adjustment layer separate from the original image. The edit remains active on its adjustment layer—so you can always alter the selection area or the way the adjustment is being applied without degrading the original image.

1   Notice that in the tool settings at the top left of the Editor window, the brush icon in the center is now highlighted. Now that there is already an active selection, the brush has automatically switched to Add To Selection mode.

2   To add the shadowed teeth on the right to the selection, drag with the Add To Selection brush as shown below, and then release the mouse button. Don't worry if parts of the lips are also selected—you'll deal with that in the next step.

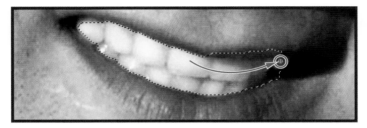

3   Hold down the Alt key. The cursor changes to that of the Subtract From Selection brush. Notice that in the tool settings at the top left of the Editor window, the brush icon on the right is now highlighted. Sill holding down the Alt key, carefully drag with the Subtract From Selection brush to remove the lip areas from the adjustment selection as shown below.

4   Release the Alt key. The brush returns to Add To Selection mode. Drag carefully as shown below to include the shadowed tooth on the left corner.

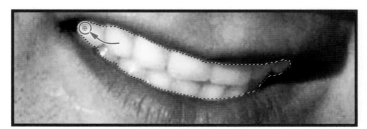

The selection is complete. The Whiten Teeth adjustment has been applied to the selected area on an adjustment layer separate from the original image. Although the adjustment has had a noticeable effect, you can improve the image by using the Whiten Teeth feature again.

5 With the Whiten Teeth tool still active, choose Select > Deselect to deselect the current adjustment. Using the Whiten Teeth tool on the After image now will create a new adjustment selection on a new layer—applying a second instance of the adjustment.

6 Use the brush picker to change the Hardness of the brush to 10%. Drag using very short strokes as shown in the illustration on the left below, to create an irregular selection area including only the brighter areas of the smile. Avoid shadowed teeth—the whitening will look unnatural if applied too evenly. Alternate between the Add To Selection and Subtract From Selection brushes.

7 With the Whiten Teeth tool still active, choose Select > Deselect to deselect the current adjustment. Create a third adjustment layer by dragging in the After image, using short strokes to make a small selection as shown in the illustration on the right below. choose Select > Deselect to deselect the current adjustment.

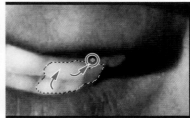

The Whiten Teeth adjustment is applied a second and third time through the new selections. The irregular selections and the softer brush setting help to create a more natural effect than re-applying the adjustment to the entire smile.

Modifying the Touch Up adjustment

Each time you applied The Whiten Teeth tool a separate adjustment layer was created in the image. Each edit remains active on its own adjustment layer—you can still alter the selection area or the way the adjustment is applied for each layer.

1 Click the Full Edit button at the top of the Task Panel to open the current photo in Full Edit mode.

2   In Full Edit mode, Expand the Layers panel if it is currently collapsed. If you don't see the layers panel, choose Window > Layers. Notice that there are three adjustment layers stacked above the original image in the Background layer. Click the eye icons to toggle each layer's visibility in turn, noticing the effect in the preview window.

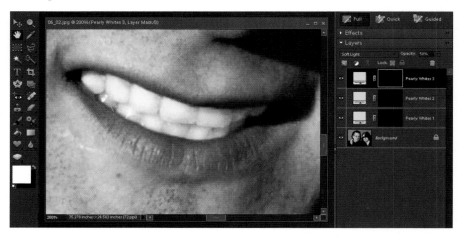

3   For the Whiten Teeth tool, Soft Light is the preset blending mode and the opacity for each layer is set to 50%. Use the controls at the top of the Layers palette to experiment with the Blending Mode and the Opacity value for each layer in turn. When you're done experimenting, choose File > Save As. Name the edited file **06_02_Dental**, select the Photoshop (*PSD, *PDD) format, and then save the file to your My CIB Work folder. Choose File > Close.

Using the Smart Brush tool

The Whiten Teeth, Blue Sky, and Black And White - High Contrast tools in the Quick Fix mode Touch Up palette are all variants on the Smart Brush tool in Full Edit mode. The Smart Brush is both a selection tool and an image adjustment tool. It creates a selection based on similarity of color and texture through which a preset edit called a Smart Paint adjustment is applied. While the selection is active, you can add to or subtract from it, without re-applying the adjustment. Each Smart Brush edit is made on a separate adjustment layer and does not affect the original image. The Smart Brush edit remains active on its adjustment layer—so you can always alter the selection area, change the way the adjustment is being applied, or even delete the adjustment layer without degrading the original image.

Applying a Smart Paint adjustment

For this exercise you'll work with a photo from the Lesson01 folder.

1 In the Organizer, use the Lesson 1 keyword tag to find the image DSC_0363.jpg.

2 Click the Editor button (![icon]) near the top right corner of the Organizer window and choose Full Edit from the menu.

3 Wait until the image DSC_0363.jpg opens in the Editor; then Collapse the Effects palette, expand the Layers palette and choose View > Fit On Screen.

4 Select the Smart Brush (![icon]) from the Tools palette; then resize the Smart Paint presets menu and drag it to a convenient position, leaving the image clear.

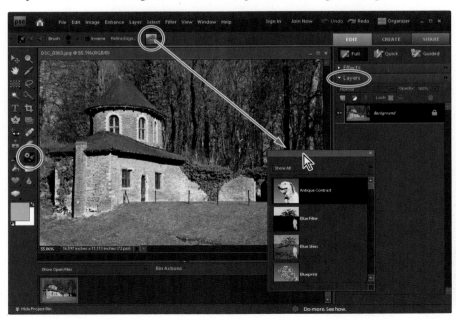

5   Click the categories menu in the moveable Smart Brush presets menu. For this exercise choose the category Nature. Scroll down through the options in the Nature category and select Greenery.

6   In the Brush Picker in the bar above the preview window, set the brush diameter to 35 pixels. Drag across about half of the lawn in front of the old building, and then release the mouse button.

Tweaking a Smart Paint adjustment

The Greenery brush has not made a very dramatic difference to the lawn. Let's try some methods for modifying the adjustment to boost the effect.

1   The Smart Paint adjustment you just applied shows a pin—a marker identifying a Smart Paint edit when the Smart Brush tool is active—at the point in the image where you began applying the Smart Brush.
Right-click the pin and choose Change Adjustment Settings from the menu.

2 Experiment with using the sliders and options to in the Hue/Saturation dialog box to modify the Smart Paint adjustment. When you're done, click Cancel—you'll be looking at another way to modify the effects of the Greenery brush yet.

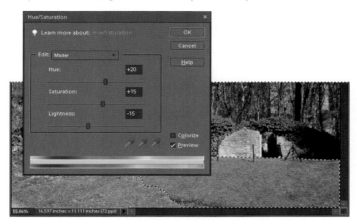

3 In the layers palette, you'll notice that the active layer is your new Greenery edit. Change the layer's Opacity to 75%, and the Blending Mode to Multiply.

4 This modification is much more effective. If you wish, you can go ahead and paint over the rest of the lawn with the new adjustment layer settings.

5   When you're done, choose File > Close without saving the changes.

Applying multiple Smart Paint adjustments

You can use the Smart Brush on the same area as many times as you wish. You can re-apply the same Smart Paint preset more and the effects are usually cumulative, though the results will vary depending on the layer blending mode for that preset. You can also apply different Smart Paint presets to the same image area.

1   Open the image DSC_0639.jpg in the Full Edit mode. Hint: this photo has the Lesson 1 keyword tag. When the image opens, choose View > Fit On Screen.

2   Select the Smart Brush tool. If the Smart Brush preset palette is not visible, select another tool for a moment, and then click the Smart Brush to select it again.

3   Move the Smart Brush preset palette to a convenient position. Choose the Nature category once more, and then select the Blue Skies brush. Drag horizontally across the sky starting from the far left, just above the horizon.

4   Choose Select > Deselect Layers to make the last edit inactive, and then use the Cloud Contrast brush, starting at the far right and dragging left. There are now two Smart Brush pins showing on the image.

5   Choose Select > Deselect Layers to make the last edit inactive, and then use the Dark Sky brush, starting at the upper left. Choose Select > Deselect Layers. You can see three pins, and there are three new layers in the Layers palette.

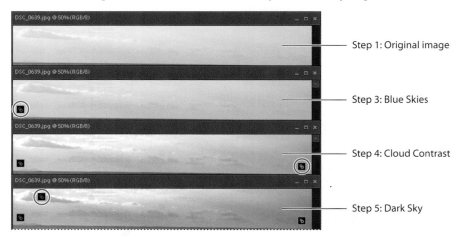

Step 1: Original image

Step 3: Blue Skies

Step 4: Cloud Contrast

Step 5: Dark Sky

6   Close the file without saving.

Before you return to the Organizer for the next lesson, open a few more files and explore more of the many options in the Smart Paint menu. Right-click the pins to try the options and experiment with the adjustment layers. For more detail on using the Smart Brush, refer to Photoshop Elements Help.

Comparing methods of fixing color

The automatic correction features in Photoshop Elements do an excellent job of bringing out the best in most photographs, but each image—and each image problem—is unique. Some photographs don't respond well to automatic fixes and require a more hands-on approach to color correction.

Photoshop Elements offers many ways to deal with color correction. The more techniques you master, the more likely you'll be able meet the challenge of fixing a difficult photograph. In this section, you'll study three different methods for correcting a color problem, and then compare the results.

Creating extra working copies of an image

In the following exercises you'll compare three different approaches to correcting the same color problem, so you'll need three copies of the same photograph.

1   In the Organizer, use the Lesson 6 keyword tag to find the file 06_03.jpg. Take care not to confuse the original file with the file 06_03_Autofix.jpg.

2   Select the file 06_03.jpg in the Photo Browser. Click the Editor button (⬛) near the top right corner of the Organizer window and choose Quick Fix from the menu. In the Quick Fix workspace, click the triangle in the lower left corner of the Editor window to show the Project bin.

3   Choose File > Duplicate. In the Duplicate Image dialog box, click OK to accept the default name 06_03 copy.jpg.

4   Repeat Step 3 to create another duplicate, 06_03 copy 2.jpg.

Leave all three copies of the image file open for the next procedures. You can tell that the files are open because their thumbnails appear in the Project Bin below the Editor preview. The image file names will appear in Tooltips when you hold the pointer over each thumbnail in the Project Bin.

Correcting color automatically

At the beginning of this lesson, you applied all four Quick Fix options to each of the six images in the Lesson06 folder and saved the results to a separate location. In this exercise, you'll apply just one Quick Fix adjustment.

1   In the Project Bin, double-click the original image—06_03.jpg—to make it the active file.

● **Note:** By now, you should have mastered the techniques of using keyword tags and text search to locate the files you need in the Organizer. From now on, the instructions for opening files will be summarized rather than stepped through in detail.

2   In the Color palette, click Auto to correct only the color.

Compare the Before and After views of the file. Although there is a small change noticeable in the skin tones and the lighter part of the background behind the girl's head, it appears that this image is not a good candidate for an automatic color fix.

3   Choose File > Save. Save the file in your My CIB Work folder in JPEG format, changing the name to **06_03_Work**. Make sure that the Save In Version Set With Original option is disabled. Click Save, leaving all the other options unchanged in the Save dialog box and the JPEG Options dialog box.

Adjusting the results of an automatic fix

1   In the Photo Bin, double-click the image 06_03 copy to make it the active file.

2   In the Color palette, click Auto. For this image, the results are minimal.

3   Drag the Temperature slider a small amount to the left.

This makes the colors in the image cooler, reducing the predominant red and orange tones while enhancing blues and greens.

4   Examine the results, paying particular attention to the skin tones.

5 Adjust the Temperature slider until you are satisfied with the realistic balance. While removing the overly orange cast from the image, watch the right side of the girl's face, taking care to preserve a warm, natural skin tone. When you are happy with the results, click the Commit button (✔) at the top of the Color palette.

6 Choose File > Save. Save the file in your My CIB Work folder in JPEG format, changing the name to **06_03 copy_Work**. Notice that the Save In Version Set With Original option is not available, since the file 06_03 copy.jpg has not been added to the catalog. Click Save, leaving all the other options unchanged in the Save dialog box and the JPEG Options dialog box.

Tweaking results from an automatic fix

The top six commands in the Enhance menu apply the same image adjustments as the various Auto buttons in the Quick Fix palettes. These commands are available in both the Quick Fix and Full Edit modes, but not in Guided Edit.

Both the Quick Fix and Full Edit modes also offer other methods of enhancing color in images. These are found in the lower half of the Enhance menu. In this exercise, you'll use a one of these options to tweak the results produced by an automatic fix button.

1 In the Photo Bin, double-click the image 06_03 copy 2 to make it the active file.

2 In the Color palette, click Auto to apply the automatic color correction.

3 Choose Enhance > Adjust Color > Color Variations. The Color Variations dialog box appears.

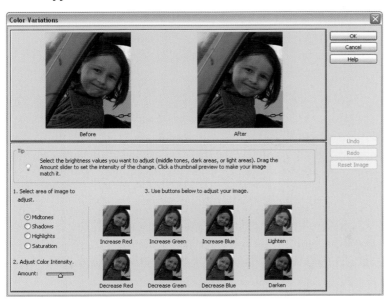

● **Note:** If you aren't happy with the results you're getting with the slider and wish to start over, click the Cancel button in the header of the Color palette. If click the Commit button, and then decide that you want to undo the color fix, click the Reset button above the image in the editing preview. This will revert the image to its original condition.

4 In the lower left area of the Color Variations dialog box, make sure that Midtones is selected, and then move the Amount slider down to about the one-third position. Click the Decrease Red thumbnail twice.

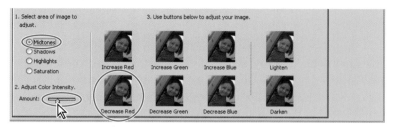

5 In the lower left area of the Color Variations dialog box. Make sure that Highlights is selected. Click the Increase Blue thumbnail twice and the Lighten thumbnail twice. Click OK.

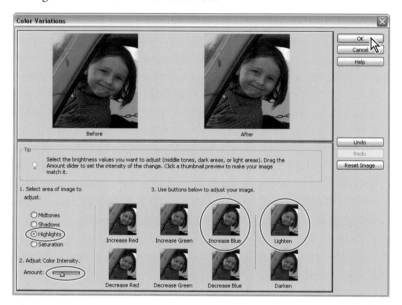

This reduces the amount of blue in the images, probably even too much. To try again, using a smaller value or a different combination of adjustments, you can undo the changes and start again. (Choose Edit > Undo Color Variations, and then try again, starting with Step 3.)

6 Choose File > Save As, and navigate to the My CIB Work folder. Rename the file **06_03 copy 2_Work**, and select the JPEG format. Click Save, leaving all other options in the Save and JPEG Options dialog boxes unchanged.

About viewing modes and image window arrangements

When you work in Quick Fix mode, only one image—the active file—appears in the work area, regardless of how many files are open. The inactive open files appear only as thumbnails in the Photo Bin.

When you work in Full Edit mode, other arrangements are possible. You can usually adjust the size and placement of image windows in the work area. If you can't arrange individual windows freely, your view is probably set to Maximize Mode. If opening or closing a file sometimes causes unexpected rearrangements of image windows, your view is probably set to Tile.

Maximize Mode (below, left) fills the work area with the active image window.

Tile (below, center) re-sizes and arranges all open images so that the image windows cover the work area. If Tile mode is active when you close an image file or open a new one, Photoshop Elements will rearrange the image windows in tile formation.

Cascade (below, right) enables you to resize, arrange, or minimize files.

There are two ways to switch from one mode to another:

- Use the Window > Images menu and choose Maximize Mode, Tile, or Cascade. If there is a check mark on the Maximize Mode command, choose Maximize Mode again disable it and switch to the mode you were using previously.

- Use the buttons on the far right end of the window title bar. The available buttons vary, depending on which viewing mode is active, and on the size of the work area on your monitor. If the work area is reduced, these buttons may not appear.

For more information, see "Working in the Editor: Viewing images in the Editor" in Adobe Photoshop Elements Help.

Comparing results

As you can tell by checking the Photo Bin, all three of your saved work files are still open in the Editor. Let's compare them to the autofix file from the batch process at the beginning of this lesson.

1   Choose File > Open. Locate and open your My CIB Work folder. Select the file 06_03_Autofix, and then click Open.

2   At the top of the Tasks pane, click the Full tab (📝) to switch to Full Edit mode.

3   Choose Window > Images > Tile.

4   Use the Zoom tool and the Hand tool to see an area of interest in one of the images, and then choose Window > Images > Match Zoom and Windows > Images > Match Location.

5   In the toolbox, select the Zoom tool (🔍).

6   In the tool options bar above the Tools palette, activate the Zoom Out mode for the Zoom tool.

7 Click in the active image window until you can see the entire photo. Then, choose Window > Images > Match Zoom. Choose Window > Images > Match Zoom again to disable the feature.

8 In the tool options bar above the Tools palette, activate the Zoom In mode for the Zoom tool, and then click the checkbox to activate the Zoom All Windows option. Click in the active image window until you can see a detail of interest.

● **Note:** At any given time there is only one active window. Look at the text in the title bars of the open image windows; the text is dimmed in the title bars of all but the active image window.

9 In the toolbox, select the Hand tool ( ).

10 In the tool options bar, activate the Scroll All Windows option.

11 Click and drag within the active window to examine different areas of the image. Compare the four images and decide which looks best. Drag any corner edge of the image window to resize it so it fills the available space, and then turn off Tile mode in the Widow > Images menu.

12 Choose View > Fit On Screen to enlarge the image so it fits in the window. You can cycle through all open windows by pressing Ctrl-Tab or Ctrl-Shift-Tab.

Adjusting skin tones

Sometimes the combination of ambient light and reflection from colored objects around your subject can cause the skin tones in your image to be tinted with unwanted color. Photoshop Elements offers a unique solution that is available in both the Full Edit and Quick Fix modes.

To adjust color for skin tones do the following:

1 Choose Enhance > Adjust Color > Adjust Color For Skin Tone. The Adjust Color For Skin Tone dialog box appears.

2 In the Adjust Color For Skin Tone dialog box, make sure the Preview option is activated. As you move the pointer over the image, the cursor changes to an eyedropper tool.

Before you click, it's worth considering the peculiarities of the image at hand. Quite apart from the general orange color cast, the little girl has yellow light on one side of her face caused by light shining through colored glass. If you sample an area of the girl's skin on which this yellow light is falling, the image will be corrected too far into the blue range. Look for a relatively neutral area of skin towards the other side of the girl's face and click with the eyedropper tool.

▶ **Tip:** Even while the Adjust Color For Skin Tone dialog box is open, you can still select the Zoom or Hand tools in the Editor Tools palette to help you focus on a different area of the image. When you're ready to sample a skin tone in the image, pick up the eyedropper tool from the Tools palette.

Photoshop Elements automatically adjusts color balance for the entire photo using the color of the child's skin as reference.

3   If you're unsatisfied with the correction, click Reset and sample a different point in the image or move the Tan, Blush, and Temperature sliders to achieve the desired result.

4   When you're happy with the skin tone, click OK to close the Adjust Color For Skin Tone dialog box, and then choose File > Close All. Don't save the changes.

Working with red eye

The red eye effect occurs when a camera flash is reflected off the retina at the back of the eye so that the dark pupil looks bright red. Photoshop Elements can automatically correct red eye effects during the process of importing images into the Organizer. Simply activate the Automatically Fix Red Eyes option in the Get Photos dialog box when you're importing your photos (see the *Automatically Fixing Red Eyes* sidebar in Lesson 2). Alternatively, you can apply the red eye fix feature to images already in your catalog. In Lesson 8 you will learn how red eyes can be fixed without leaving in the Organizer, but for this exercise you'll use the tools available to you in the Editor.

Using automatic Red Eye Fix in the Editor

In Quick Fix mode, you can apply an automatic red eye correction with a single click—just as you did earlier in this lesson with the Smart Fix feature. This technique may not be suitable for some images, but for those Photoshop Elements provides other options.

In this exercise you'll be working in the Editor in Quick Fix mode, but first you'll use the Organizer to find the image for this lesson in your catalog.

1   In the Editor, click the Organizer button to load the Organizer workspace. If necessary, click the Show All button above the Photo Browser.

2   Use the Keywords Tags palette to find all images with the Lesson 6 keyword tag.

For our red eye removal exercise, you need the image 06_04.jpg—the uncorrected photo of three little girls dressed for Halloween. Take care not to confuse this file with the version that had auto red eye fix applied as part of the batch edit. If necessary, choose View > Show File Names.

3   In the Photo Browser, click the image 06_04.jpg to select it. Then, click the Editor button located near the top right corner of the Organizer window and choose Quick Fix from the menu. Wait until the Editor has finished opening the file.

4   Select Before & After - Vertical from the View menu below the preview pane. Use the Zoom and Hand tools to focus on the eyes of the girl in the centre of the photo.

5   In the Palette Bin, under General Fixes, click the Auto button next to Red Eye Fix. There is no slider available for this correction.

● **Note:** The Auto Red Eye Fix feature is also available as a command available from the Enhance menu in both the Quick Fix and Full Edit modes, together with other automatic features such as Auto Smart Fix.

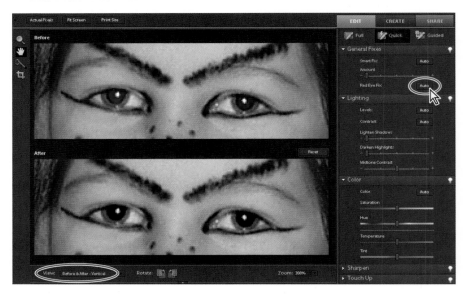

As you can see, automatic red eye correction does a great job for this little girl. Unfortunately, it hasn't worked for her sisters.

6   Use the Zoom and Hand tools to check the eyes of the other two girls.

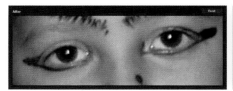

The automatic adjustment had no discernible effect for the girls at either side of the photo. Admittedly, the red eye effect is less pronounced in both cases, but it is also more complex and difficult to remove. The pupils of the girl in the center are crisply defined against her blue irises while there is less contrast in the hazel irises of the other girls.

7   Click the Reset button above the After image to revert the photo to its state before the Auto Red Eye Fix was applied.

The Auto Red Eye Fix feature works well for most images, but when you want more control you need to use the Red Eye Removal tool.

Using the Red Eye Removal tool

For stubborn red eye problems, the Red Eye Removal tool () is a simple and efficient solution. In this exercise you'll now learn how to customize the Red Eye Removal tool to fix difficult cases.

1   If the image 06_04.jpg is not already open in Quick Fix mode—and reverted to its unedited state—from the last exercise, open it in the Editor now, in either Quick Fix or Full Edit mode.

2   Zoom and position the image so that you can focus on the eyes of the girl on the left of the photo. In Quick fix, use the Before And After - Vertical view.

3   In Full Edit mode, select the Red Eye Removal tool () from the tool palette. In Quick Fix mode, you'll find the Red Eye Removal tool in the Touch Up palette.

4   In the Red Eye Removal tool options in the bar above the Tools palette, change the Pupil Size value to 10% and the Darken Amount to 50%. You can either use the slider controls, type the new values in the text fields, or simply drag left or right over the Pupil Size and Darken Amount text.

5   With the Red Eye Removal tool selected, click once (in the After image, if you are in Quick Fix) in the reddest part of each pupil. If there is little result, Undo and click a slightly different spot.

The red is removed from both eyes. The adjustment has also darkened the less defined parts of the irises, but we'll accept that for now.

6   Use the Zoom and Hand tools to position the image so that you can focus on the eyes of the girl on the right of the photo.

7   In the Red Eye Removal tool options in the bar above the Tools palette, change the Pupil Size value to 100% and the Darken Amount to 75%.

8 With the Red Eye Removal tool still selected, drag a marquee rectangle around each eye in turn.

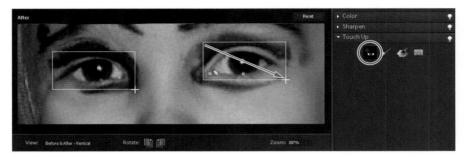

You may need to experiment with the size and positioning of the rectangle you drag around an eye to get the best results. Just Undo and try again.

9 Finally, you can re-instate the Auto Red Eye Fix for the little girl in the Middle. Zoom out to see all three faces. If you are in Quick Fix mode, click the Auto Red Eye Fix button in the General Fixes palette. If you're in Full Edit mode, choose Enhance > Auto Red Eye Fix.

10 Choose File > Save As and navigate to the My CIB Work folder. Rename the file **06_04_Work** and select the JPEG format. Disable the Save In Version Set With Original option and click Save, leaving all other options in the Save and JPEG Options dialog boxes unchanged.

11 Choose File > Close and return to the Organizer.

Making selections

By default, the entire area of an image or image layer is active: any adjustments you make are applied across the whole photo. If you want to make changes to a specific area or object within an image, you first need to make a selection. Once you have made a selection it becomes the only active area of the image—the rest of the image layer is protected or masked from the effects of your edits.

Typically, the boundaries of a selection are indicated by a selection marquee—a flashing border of dashed black and white lines. You can save a selection and re-use it at a later time. This can be a terrific time-saver when you need to use the same selection several times.

You can use several different tools to create selections; you'll get experience with most of them in the course of the lessons in this book. Selections can be geometric in shape or free form, and they can have crisp or soft edges. Selections can be created manually the mouse pointer, or calculated by Photoshop Elements based on similarities of color within the image.

Perhaps the simplest, most effective way to create a selection is to paint it on an image. This exercise focuses on the use of two selection tools in Photoshop Elements, the Selection Brush tool and the Quick Selection tool.

1   Using the Organizer, select the original image of the water lily, 06_05.psd. Click the Editor button located near the top right corner of the Organizer window and choose Full Edit from the menu or use the keyboard shortcut Ctrl+I. Wait until the Editor has finished opening the file.

Notice that this file has been saved as a Photoshop file and not as a JPEG file. The Photoshop file format can store additional information along with the image data. In this case, a portion of the flower has previously been selected and the selection has been saved in the file.

2   With the image 06_05.psd file open in the Editor, choose Select > Load Selection. In the Load Selection dialog box, choose "petals" as the Source Selection. In the Operation options, activate New Selection, and then click OK.

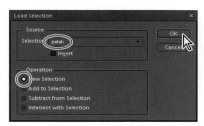

The saved selection "petals" is loaded. The flower is surrounded by a flashing selection marquee to indicate that it has become the active portion of the image.

One petal needs to be added to make the selection of the flower complete. In the following exercise, you'll add the missing petal and modify the saved selection.

3   Choose Select > Deselect to clear the current selection.

4   In the toolbox, select the Selection Brush tool, which is grouped with the Quick Selection tool.

Using the Selection Brush tool

The Selection Brush tool makes selections in either of two ways. In Selection mode, you simply paint over the area you want to select. In Mask mode you paint a semi-opaque overlay over areas you don't want selected.

1   In the tool options bar, set the Selection Brush controls to match the illustration below. Click the Add To Selection button at the far left, set the brush Size to 25 pixels wide, choose Selection from the Mode menu, and set the brush Hardness value to 100%.

2   Drag with the Selection Brush to paint over the interior of the petal at the front. Don't try to paint the edges; you'll do that in the next step.

Notice that you're actually painting a live selection onto the image, surrounded with a flashing dashed selection marquee. Release the mouse every second or two.

Now you need to reduce your brush size to paint around the edges of the petal, adding to your selection.

You could move the Size slider to change your brush size, but it's probably more convenient to press the open bracket key ([) to reduce the brush size in increments and the close bracket key (]) to enlarge it.

3   Press the left bracket key ([), to reduce the Selection Brush size to 10 pixels.

4   Drag with the Selection Brush to paint the selection to the edges of the petal. Use the bracket keys to change the brush size as needed, until the selection outline completely surrounds the petal.

▶ **Tip:** Use the Zoom tool to magnify the area of interest in the photo when you need to make a detailed selection.

▶ **Tip:** If you have accidentally selected an area you didn't want to select, use the buttons at the left of the tool options bar to switch the brush mode from Add To Selection to Subtract From Selection and paint back over the unwanted area.

If you found using the Selection Brush tool tedious, you'll appreciate learning about the Quick Selection tool later in this lesson. But first, you'll make use of your hard work and save the results.

Editing a saved selection

In this exercise you'll add your current selection to the "petals" selection that was saved with the file. You can modify saved selections by either replacing them, adding to them, or subtracting from them.

1   With your selection still active, choose Select > Load Selection.

Note: The New Selection option replaces the saved selection with the current selection. The Subtract from Selection option subtracts the current selection from the saved selection. Intersect with Selection replaces the saved selection with the intersection between the current selection and the saved selection.

2   In the Load Selection dialog box, choose the saved selection "petals" as the Source Selection. In the Operation options, activate the Add To Selection option, and then click OK. This setting will combine your current selection of the front-most petal with the saved selection of the rest of the flower.

You should now see the entire water lily outlined by the flashing selection boundary.

Note: Once you have loaded a saved selection you can also add to it or subtract from it by Shift-dragging or Alt-dragging with any of the selection tools.

If you've missed a spot, simply paint it in with the Selection Brush tool. If you've selected too much, switch to Subtract From Selection mode in the options bar, set an appropriate brush size, and then paint out your mistakes.

3   Choose Select > Save Selection. In the Save Selection dialog box, choose petals as the Selection name, activate Replace Selection in the Operation options, and then click OK.

4   Choose Select > Deselect.

Using the Quick Selection tool

The Quick Selection tool enables you to select an area in the image by simply drawing, scribbling, or clicking on the area you want to select. You don't need to be precise, because while you are drawing, Photoshop Elements expands the selection border based on color and texture similarity.

In this exercise, you'll use the Quick Selection tool to select everything but the water lily, and then swap the selected and un-selected areas in the photo to establish the selection you want. This technique can be a real time-saver in situations where it proves difficult to select a comples object directly.

1   In the Tools palette, select the Quick Selection tool ( ). Remember; the Quick Selection tool is grouped in the Tools palette with the Selection Brush you used earlier.

2   In the tool options bar just above the Tools palette, make sure the New Selection mode button on the far left is activated. Set a brush diameter in the Brush picker. For the purposes of this exercise, you can use the default brush diameter of 30 pixels.

3   Scribble over the area around the water lily, making sure to touch some of the yellow, green, and black areas as shown in the illustration on the left below. Release the pointer to see the result. As you draw, Photoshop elements automatically expands the selection based on similarity of color and texture.

4   With an active selection already in place, the Quick Selection tool defaults to Add To Selection mode (below, right). Scribble over, or click into, un-selected areas around the water lily until everything is selected but the flower itself.

▶ **Tip:** If you want to simply scribble-select an area in the image, you can use a larger brush. If you need more control to draw a more precise outline, choose a smaller brush size.

5   Finally, turn the selection inside out by choosing Select > Inverse, thereby masking the background and selecting the flower—ready for the next exercise.

Working with selections

Now that you have an active selection outline around the water lily, you can apply any adjustment you like and only the flower will be affected.

1   With the water lily still selected, click the Quick tab at the top of the Task pane to switch to Quick Fix mode.

2   To make comparison more convenient, choose Before & After - Horizontal from the View menu at the left below the editing preview pane.

3   In the Color palette on the right, click and drag the Hue slider to the left or right to change the color of the water lily.

Notice that the water lily changes color, but the background does not. Only the pixels inside a live selection are effected by edits or adjustments.

4   Click the Cancel button in the Color palette to undo your changes.

You could also invert the selection to apply changes to the background instead of the water lily.

5   Click the Full button at the top of the Edit panel to switch to Full Edit mode.

6   With the water lily still selected, choose Select > Inverse.

7   With the background around the water lily selected, choose Enhance > Convert To Black And White.

8   In the Convert To Black And White dialog box, choose Urban/Snapshots under Select A Style.

9 (Optional) Select a different style to see the effect on the image. Use the Adjustment Intensity sliders to vary the amount of change for red, green, blue, and contrast. Click Undo if you made adjustments you don't like.

10 Click OK to close the Convert To Black And White dialog box.

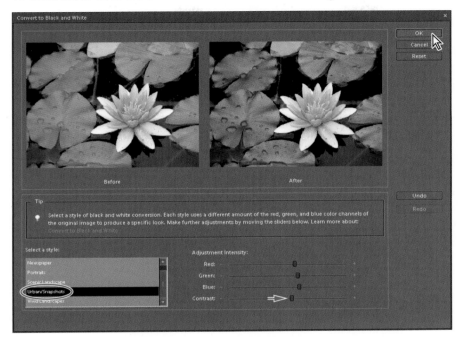

11 Choose Select > Deselect.

12 Choose File > Save As and save the file in the My CIB Work folder. In the File Name text box, type **06_05_Work**. Make sure that the Format setting is Photoshop (PSD). If the option Save Tn Version Set With Original is activated, disable it before you click Save.

13 Choose File > Close, and then switch back to the Organizer.

Congratulations, you've completed another exercise. You've learned how to use the Selection Brush tool and the Quick Selection tool to isolate areas of an image. You've also learned to mask out areas to which you don't want changes applied. You've also learned how to add a new selection to existing, saved selection. These techniques will be invaluable as you learn to use other selection tools.

Why won't Photoshop Elements do what I tell it to do?

In some situations, the changes you try to apply to an image may not seem to work. You may hear a beep, indicating that you're trying to do something that's not allowed. The following list offers explanations and solutions for common issues that might be blocking your progress.

Commit is required

Several tools, including the Type tool require you to click the Commit button before you can move on to another task. The same is true when you crop with the Crop tool or resize a layer or selection with the Move tool.

Cancel is required

The Undo command isn't available while you have uncommitted changes made with some tools—for example, the Type tool, Move tool, and Crop tool. If you want to undo these edits, click the Cancel button instead of using the Undo command or shortcut.

Edits are restricted by an active selection

When you create a selection (using a marquee tool, the Quick Selection tool, or the Selection Brush tool, for example), you limit the active area of the image. Any edits you make will apply only within the selected area. If you try to make changes to an area outside the selection, nothing happens. Edits are restricted by an active selection. If you want to deactivate a selection, choose Select > Deselect, and then you can work on any area of the image.

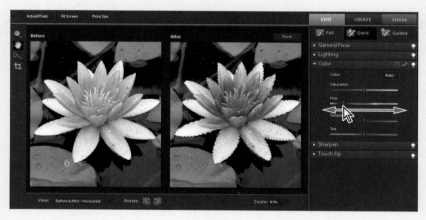

Move tool is required

If you drag a selection, the selection marquee moves, not the image within the selection marquee. If you want to move a selected part of the image or an entire layer, use the Move tool .

(continued on next page)

Why won't Photoshop Elements
do what I tell it to do? *(continued)*

Background layer is selected

Many changes cannot be applied to the Background layer. For example, you can't erase, delete, change the opacity, or drag the Background layer to a higher level in the layer stack. If you need to apply changes to the Background layer, double-click it and rename it (or accept the default name, Layer 0).

Active layer is hidden

In most cases, the edits you make apply to only the currently selected layer—the one highlighted in the Layers palette. If an eye icon does not appear beside that layer in the Layers palette, then the layer is hidden and you cannot edit it. Or, if the image on the selected layer is not visible because it is blocked by an opaque upper layer, you will actually be changing that layer, but you won't see the changes in the image window.

The active layer is hidden, the view is blocked by an opaque upper layer, or the active layer is locked.

Active layer is locked

If you lock a layer by selecting the layer and then selecting the Lock in the Layers palette, the lock prevents the layer from changing. To unlock a layer, select the layer, and then select the Lock at the top of the Layers palette to remove the Lock.

Active layer is locked.

Wrong layer is selected (for editing text)

If you want to make changes to a text layer, be sure that layer is selected in the Layers palette before you start. If a non-text layer is selected when you click the Type tool in the image window, Photoshop Elements creates a new text layer instead of placing the cursor in the existing text layer.

Replacing the color of a pictured object

Photoshop Elements offers two methods of swapping a color in a photo: the Color Replacement tool and the Replace Color dialog box. The Color Replacement tool is grouped in the toolbox with the Brush tool, the Impressionist Brush tool, and the Pencil tool and enables you to replace specific colors in your image by painting over a targeted color with another. You can also use the Color Replacement tool for color correction.

Using the Replace Color dialog box is faster and more automatic than using the Color Replacement tool, but it doesn't work well for all types of images. This method is most effective when the color of the object you want to change is not found in other areas of the image. The photograph of a yellow car used for the following exercises is a good candidate for this approach as there is very little yellow elsewhere in the image.

Replacing a color throughout the image

In this exercise, you'll change the color of a yellow car. You'll do your work on a duplicate of the Background layer, which makes it easy to compare the finished project to the original picture.

What's great about the Replace Color feature is that you don't have to be too careful or meticulous when you apply it, yet you can still produce spectacular results. You'll do this exercise twice. First, you'll work on the entire image area, which will show you how much the color changes will affect the areas other than the car, such as the trees in the background. For the second part of the exercise you'll use an area selection to restrict the changes.

1   Using the Organizer, find the file 06_06.psd, a picture of a yellow car, and then open it in the Editor in Full Edit mode.

2   In the Editor, choose Layer > Duplicate Layer and accept the default name. Alternatively, drag the Background layer up to the New Layer button () in the Layers palette. By duplicating the layer, you have an original to return to should you need it.

3 With the Background copy layer still selected in the Layers palette, choose Enhance > Adjust Color > Replace Color.

4 In the Replace Color dialog box, make sure the Eyedropper tool—the left-most of the three eyedropper buttons—is activated, and then click Image in the Selection options so that you can see the color thumbnail of the car. Click with the Eyedropper tool to sample the yellow paint of the car.

5 Below the thumbnail image in the Replace Color dialog box, change the Selection option from Image to Selection, so you see the extent of the color selection indicated as white on a black background.

6 Drag the Hue slider (and optionally the Saturation and Lightness sliders) to change the color of the selected area. For example, set the Hue value to −88 to change the yellow to pink.

7 To adjust the area of selected color—or color-application area—start by clicking the second of the three eyedropper buttons to activate the Add to Sample mode for the Eyedropper tool, and then click in the edit window in the areas where the paint on the car still appears yellow.

8 Drag the Fuzziness slider left or right until you find an acceptable compromise between full coverage on the car and the effect on other areas in the image. Try to avoid picking up any color in the wall.

9   When you're satisfied with the results, click OK to close the Replace Color dialog box.

Depending on what color and color characteristics you used to replace the yellow, you probably can see a shift in the color of the trees in the background. If this is a compromise you can live with, that's great—if not, you may need to try another technique. In the next exercise you'll do just that.

Replacing a color in a limited area of the image

In this exercise you'll repeat the previous procedure, but this time you'll limit the color change to a selected area of the photograph.

1   Choose Edit > Undo Replace Color, or select the step before Replace Color in the Undo History palette (Window > Undo History).

2   In the toolbox, select the Lasso tool and draw a rough selection marquee around the car. It's OK if some of the road and the wall in the background are included in the selection.

Note: In the Tools palette, the Lasso tool is grouped with the Magnetic Lasso tool and the Polygonal Lasso tool. To switch from one lasso tool to another, click the tool in the toolbox and hold the mouse button down until a menu appears. Choose the desired tool from the menu.

3 In the tool options bar, click the Subtract From Selection button to set that mode for the Lasso tool.

4 Using the Lasso tool in Subtract From Selection mode, draw a shape around the yellow sticker on the windshield to remove it from the selection.

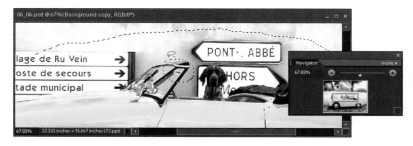

● Note: It may be helpful to zoom in for this part of the process. To avoid switching from the Lasso to the Zoom tool, choose Window > Navigator and zoom in using the slider in the Navigator palette. You can also zoom in using the keyboard shortcut Ctrl+ = (equal sign).

5 Choose Enhance > Adjust Color > Replace Color.

6 Using the same techniques and settings you used in the previous procedure, make adjustments in the Replace Color dialog box to change the color of the car. (See "Replacing a color throughout the image," steps 4-8.)

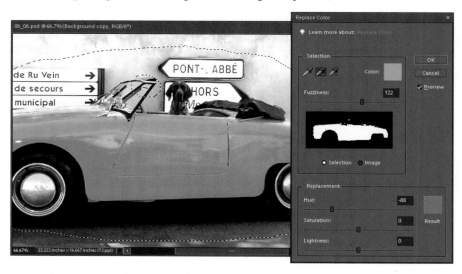

7 When you are satisfied with the results, click OK to close the Replace Color dialog box.

8 Choose Select > Deselect, or press Ctrl+D.

9   Choose File > Save As and save the file in the My CIB Work folder. Type
    06_06_Work for the new file name. Make sure that the Format option is set to
    Photoshop (PSD). If the Save In Version Set With Original option is activated,
    disable it before you click Save.

10 Choose File > Close, to close the file and return to the Organizer.

Take a bow—you've finished all the exercises in this lesson. In the last exercise, you
learned how to make a selection with the Lasso tool and also how to edit that selection. You replaced one color with another using the Replace Color dialog box and in
the process you were introduced to the Undo History palette and the Navigator.

About printing color pictures

Color problems in your photos can result from a variety of causes, such as incorrect exposure, the quality of the camera, or the conditions under which a photograph was taken. If an image is flawed, you can usually improve it by editing it with
Photoshop Elements, as you did with the images in this lesson.

Sometimes, pictures that look great on your computer don't turn out so well when
you print them. There are things you can do to make sure that what you get from the
printer is closer to what you see on screen.

It's important that you calibrate your monitor regularly so that it's set to display the
range of color in your photographs as accurately as possible.

Your prints may also look bad if your color printer interprets color information differently from your computer. You can correct that by activating the appropriate type
of color management.

Working with color management

Moving a photo from your camera to your monitor and from there to a printer
makes shifts the colors in the image. This shift occurs because every device has a
different color gamut or color space—the range of colors that the device is capable
of interpreting and producing. To achieve consistent color between digital cameras,
scanners, computer monitors, and printers, you need to use color management.

Color management software acts as a color interpreter, translating the image colors
so that each device can reproduce them in the same way. This software knows how
each device and program understands color, and adjusts colors so that those you see
on your monitor are similar to the colors in your printed image. It should be noted,
however, that not all colors may match exactly.

Note: When you save a file, select ICC Profile in the Save As dialog box.

Color management is achieved through the use of profiles, or mathematical descriptions of each device's color space. If these profiles are compliant with the standards of the ICC (International Color Consortium), they help you maintain consistent color.

Photoshop Elements' color management controls are located under the Edit menu.

Setting up color management

1 In the Editor, choose Edit > Color Settings.

2 Select one of these color management options:

- **No Color Management** uses your monitor profile as the working space. It removes any embedded profiles when opening images, and does not apply a profile when saving.

- **Always Optimize Colors For Computer Screens** uses sRGB as the working space, preserves embedded profiles, and assigns sRGB when opening untagged files.

- **Always Optimize For Printing** uses Adobe RGB as the working space, preserves embedded profiles, and assigns Adobe RGB when opening untagged files.

- **Allow Me To Choose** lets you choose to assign sRGB (the default) or Adobe RGB when opening untagged files.

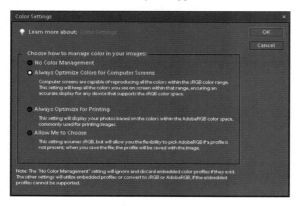

3 Click OK to close the Color Settings dialog box.

Further information on color management, including monitor calibration, can be found in a series of topics in Help. To access this information, choose Help > Photoshop Elements Help and search for these subjects.

Review questions

1 What are the key differences between adjusting images in Full Edit mode, Quick Fix mode, or Guided Edit mode?

2 Can you apply automatic fixes when you are in Full Edit mode?

3 What tools can you use to fix the red-eye phenomenon created by some flash cameras?

4 What makes selections so important for adjusting color?

5 Name at least two selection tools and describe how they work.

Review answers

1 Full Edit provides a more flexible and powerful image correction environment. Full Edit offers lighting and color correction commands, tools for fixing image defects, making selections, adding text, and painting on your images. Quick Fix provides easy access to a range of basic image editing controls for making quick adjustments and corrections. If you are new to digital photography, Guided Edit is the best place to start. Guided Edit steps you through each procedure to help you get professional results.

2 Yes. The Enhance menu contains commands that are equivalent to the Auto buttons in the Quick Fix palettes: Auto Smart Fix, Auto Levels, Auto Contrast, Auto Color Correction, and Auto Red Eye Fix. The Enhance menu also provides an Adjust Smart Fix command, which opens a dialog box in which you can specify settings for automatic adjustments.

3 You can fix red eye automatically during the process of importing photos into the catalog. To fix red eye after the photos have been imported, choose Edit > Auto Red Eye Fix in the Organizer. In either the Full Edit or Quick Fix mode of the Editor, choose Enhance > Auto Red Eye Fix. Finally, the Red Eye Removal tool located in the toolbox enables you to specify the tool settings to fix difficult cases.

4 You use a selection to define an area as the only part of a layer that can be altered. The areas outside the selection are protected from change for as long as the selection is active. This aids greatly in image correction, as it enables you make adjustments selectively, targeting specific areas or objects in an image.

5 The first tool you used in this lesson to make selections is the Selection Brush tool, which works like a paintbrush. The Quick Selection tool is similar to the Selection Brush tool, but is in most cases a faster, more flexible option. The Lasso tool creates free-form selections. There are more selection tools than are discussed in this lesson. The Magic Wand tool selects all the areas with the same color as the color on which you click. The Rectangular Marquee tool and the Elliptical Marquee tool make selections of fixed geometric shape. The Magnetic Lasso tool helps to draw selections along even quite irregular object edges, while the Polygonal Lasso tool restricts drawing to straight lines, making it the tool of choice to select straight-sided objects.

7 FIXING EXPOSURE PROBLEMS

Lesson Overview

You can use Photoshop Elements to fix images that are too dark or too light and to rescue photos that are dull, flat, or simply fading away. Start with Quick Fix and Guided Edit and work up to Full Edit mode.

In this lesson you'll be introduced to a variety of techniques for dealing with exposure problems:

- Brightening underexposed photographs
- Correcting parts of an image selectively
- Saving selection shapes to reuse in later sessions
- Working with adjustment layers
- Choosing layer blending modes
- Using layer opacity settings
- Enhancing overexposed and faded photographs

 You'll probably need between one and two hours to complete this lesson.

Learn how to make the most of images that were exposed incorrectly due to unusual lighting conditions such as strong backlighting. Retrieve detail from photos that are too dark and liven up images that look dull and washed-out. Find out how you can save those fading memories. Photoshop elements provides powerful, easy-to-use tools for correcting exposure problems in all three of its Edit modes.

This lesson assumes that you are already familiar with the main features of the Photoshop Elements workspace and that you recognize the two Photoshop Elements modules: the Organizer and the Editor. If you need to learn more about these subjects, see Lesson 1, "A Quick Tour of Photoshop Elements" and Photoshop Elements Help. This lesson builds on the skills and concepts covered in the earlier lessons.

Getting started

● **Note:** Before you start working on this lesson, make sure that you've installed the software on your computer from the application CD (see the Photoshop Elements 7 documentation) and that you have correctly copied the Lessons folder from the CD in the back of this book onto your computer's hard disk (see "Copying the Classroom in a Book files" on page 2).

For the exercises in this lesson you'll use the CIB Catalog you created in the "Getting Started" section at the beginning of this book. To use the CIB Catalog, follow these steps:

1   Start Photoshop Elements and click the Organize button in the Welcome Screen. The name of the currently active catalog is displayed in the lower left corner of the Organizer window. If the CIB Catalog is open, begin the first exercise, "Correcting images automatically as batch process." If the CIB Catalog is not open, complete the following steps.

2   Choose File > Catalog.

3   In the Catalog Manager dialog box, select the CIB Catalog and click Open.

If you don't see the CIB Catalog file listed, you should review the procedures in "Getting Started" at he beginning of this book. See "Copying the Lessons files from the CD" on page 2, and "Creating a catalog" on page 3.

Correcting images automatically in batches

You'll start this lesson in the same way that you began your work in Lesson 6—by batch-processing the photos in the lesson folder to apply the Photoshop Elements automatic fix adjustments. Later you can compare the automatic results with the results of the techniques you'll learn in the exercises.

▶ **Tip:** From the Welcome Screen you can go directly to the Full Edit mode by clicking the Edit button.

1   In the Organizer, click the Editor button () near the top right corner of the workspace window and choose Full Edit from the menu.

If you already have the Editor open, switch to Full Edit mode by clicking the Full tab in the Task pane.

2   In the Editor, choose File > Process Multiple Files. The Process Multiple Files dialog box opens.

3 In the Process Multiple Files dialog box, set the source and destination folders as follows:

- Choose Folder from the Process Files From menu.

- Under Source, click the Browse button. Find and select the Lesson06 folder in the Lessons folder. Click OK to close the Browse For Folder dialog box.

- Under Destination, click Browse, and then find and select the My CIB Work folder that you created at the start of the book. Click OK to close the Browse For Folder dialog box.

4 Under File Naming, select Rename Files. Select Document Name from the menu on the left and type **_Autofix** in the second field. This adds the appendix "_Autofix" to the existing document name as the files are saved.

5 Under Quick Fix on the right side of the dialog box, activate all four options: Auto Levels, Auto Contrast, Auto Color, and Sharpen.

6 Review all the settings in the dialog box, comparing them to the illustration below. Make sure that the Resize Images and Convert Files options are disabled, and then, click OK.

Photoshop Elements takes a few seconds to process the files. Image windows will open and close automatically as the adjustments are applied. There's nothing else you need to do. If any alerts or warnings appear, click OK.

At the end of this lesson, you can compare the results of these basic, automatic fixes with the results you achieve by applying the manual techniques as you work through the exercises. In some cases, the automatic method of fixing images may be sufficient to meet your needs.

Brightening an underexposed image

Slightly underexposed photographs tend to look dull and flat, or too dark. While the auto-fix lighting feature does a terrific job of brightening up many of these photos, in this exercise you'll learn some different methods for adjusting exposure.

Applying the Quick Fix

1 If you are still in the Editor, switch to the Organizer now.

2 In the Keyword Tags palette, click the Find box next to the Lesson 7 keyword tag.

Note: To see the file names for images in the Photo Browser, choose View > Show File Names.

3 Click to select the file kat_and_kind.jpg, an underexposed image of a mother and child at the seaside.

4 Click the Editor button (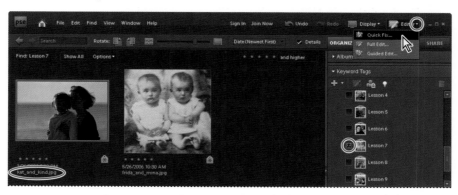) near the top right corner of the Organizer window and choose Quick Fix from the menu.

Photoshop Elements will load the Editor workspace and open the image in Quick Fix mode.

5   In the General Fixes palette, click the Smart Fix Auto button. The photo becomes a little brighter but the skin tomes are still quite dark.

6   In the Lighting palette, drag the Lighten Shadows slider to the right—just a little past the first divider bar. Drag the Midtone Contrast slider about half-way to the next divider to the right, as shown in the illustration below.

The image is substantially improved, though the skin tones are still a little cool.

7   In the Color palette, drag the Temperature and Hue sliders just fractionally to the right. Take care not to make the sky too pink or yellow.

8   When you are satisfied with the result, click the Commit button (✔) in the Color palette title bar to commit the changes.

Original image   Auto Smart Fix - Lighting sliders   Temperature & Hue tweaked

9   Choose File > Save As. In the Save As dialog box, navigate to and open the My CIB Work folder, rename the file kat_and_kind_Quick and choose the JPEG format. If the option Save In Version Set With Original is activated, disable it. Click Save. In the JPEG Options dialog box, choose High from the Quality menu, and then click OK.

10 Choose File > Close and return to the Organizer.

Without much effort the image has improved significantly. Let's try some other methods to adjust the lighting in the image and you can compare the results later.

Exploring Guided Edit

1   With the image kat_and_kind.jpg still selected in the Photo Browser, click the Editor button, and then choose Guided Edit from the menu.

The Editor workspace will load and open the original underexposed photo you used for the previous exercise—but this time in Guided Edit mode.

2   In the guided tasks menu, click the triangle beside Lighting and Exposure if necessary to see the options, and then choose Lighten Or Darken.

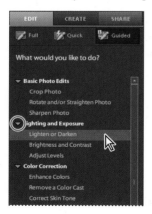

3   The Lighten Or Darken A Photo task panel opens. Click the Auto button near the top right corner of the Lighten Or Darken A Photo panel. You'll notice that in this case the result is not quite as good as you would expect. Click the Reset button at the bottom of the task panel, or choose Edit > Undo Auto Levels to revert the image to its original state.

4   Use the sliders to adjust the lighting in the image manually. Drag the Lighten Shadows slider to a value of 50 and the Midtone Contrasts to a value of 20; then, click Done.

5   Choose File > Save As. In the Save As dialog box, navigate to and open the My CIB Work folder, rename the file kat_and_kind_Guided and select the JPEG format. If the option Save In Version Set With Original is activated, disable it. Click Save. In the JPEG Options dialog box, choose High from the Quality menu, and then click OK.

6   Choose File > Close and return to the Organizer.

Again, the image now looks considerably better than its original; however, it would be ideal if the mother and child could be treated separately from the background of sea and sky.

Fixing an image in Full Edit mode

Underexposure problems are very often caused when your camera cuts down exposure to compensate for backlighting. In the case of our example image, the large area of relatively light sea and sky may contribute to the problem in this way, compounded by the fact that the lighting on our subjects is fairly low and indirect. Perhaps the camera's exposure settings were also incorrect. If your photo is a particularly difficult case, more elaborate methods than those you've used in the Quick Fix and Guided Edit modes might be necessary to achieve the best results.

In the Full Edit mode you can work with layers and blending modes and make selections to isolate different parts of an image for special treatment.

Using Blending modes

When an image file has multiple layers, each layer has its own blending mode that defines the way it will effect the layer or layers below it in the stacking order. By default, a new layer has a Normal blending mode: it will not blend with the layer below except where it contains transparency or when the opacity for the layer is set to less than 100%. The Darken and Lighten blending modes will blend a layer with the layer below it only where the result will darken or lighten the lower layer. Other blending modes produce more complex results.

If a photo is too dark, duplicating the base layer and applying the Screen blending mode to the new layer may correct the problem. If this technique produces too strong an affect, us the layer opacity setting to tone it down. Inversely, if your photo is overexposed—too light—duplicating the base layer and applying the Multiply blending mode to the new layer might be a solution.

1 With the image kat_and_kind.jpg still selected in the Photo Browser, click the Editor button, and then choose Full Edit from the menu. The Editor workspace will load and open the image in Full Edit mode.

2 In the Palette Bin, make sure that the Layers palette is open. The image has only one layer: the Background.

3 Do any one of the following to duplicate the Background layer:

- With the Background layer selected in the Layers palette, choose Layer > Duplicate Layer, and then click OK in the Duplicate Layer dialog box, accepting the default name.

- Right-click the Background layer in the Layers palette and choose Duplicate Layer from the context menu. Click OK in the Duplicate Layer dialog box, accepting the default name.

- Drag and drop the Background layer onto the New Layer button () in the Layers palette.

The new Background copy layer is highlighted in the Layers palette, indicating that it is the selected (active) layer.

4 With the Background copy layer selected in the Layers palette, choose Screen from the layer blending mode menu. Notice how the image becomes brighter.

● **Note:** If the layer blending mode menu is disabled, make sure that the copy layer, not the original Background layer, is selected in the Layers palette.

5 Choose File > Save As.

6 In the Save As dialog box, name the file **kat_and_kind_Screen**, choose Photoshop (PSD) from the Format menu, and make sure the Layers option is activated. Save the file to your My CIB Work folder. If the Save In Version Set With Original is activated, disable it before you click Save. If the Photoshop Elements Format Options dialog box appears, keep Maximize Compatibility selected and click OK.

7 In the Layers palette, click the eye icon to the left of the Background Copy layer to toggle its visibility so that you can compare the original with the adjusted image. When you've finished comparing, close the file without saving and return to the Organizer.

In this exercise you've seen how using a blending mode can brighten up a dull image. However, you should be careful about applying a blending mode over an entire image, as it can sometimes adversely affect parts of the photos that were OK to begin with. In this example, the sky is now overexposed and some subtle color detail has been lost. In the following exercises, you'll use other blending modes that are useful for correcting a wide range of image problems.

Adjusting color curves

Using the Adjust Color Curves command is a great way to fix common exposure problems, from photos that are too dark as a result of backlighting to images that appear washed-out due to overly harsh lighting. You can choose one of the preset adjustment styles as a solution or as a useful starting point—or improve color tones by adjusting the highlights, mid-tones, and shadows separately.

In the Adjust Color Curves dialog box, you can quickly see the results of each preset in the before and after preview. To fine-tune the adjustment, simply use the sliders. To preserve your original image, experiment with color curve adjustments on a duplicate layer.

To open the Adjust Color Curves dialog box, choose Enhance > Adjust Color > Adjust Color Curves. To adjust only a specific area of the image, select it with one of the selection tools before you open the Color Curves dialog box.

For of our sample image, the Lighten Shadows style preset made a good starting-point for some manual fine-tuning, mainly to the shadows and mid-tones.

Adding adjustment layers

Sometimes you need to go back and tweak an adjustment after you have had time to assess your first efforts. You may even want to alter your settings during a much later work session—perhaps to fit the image to a particular purpose for a project or presentation. This is when you will appreciate the power and versatility of adjustment layers and fill layers.

An adjustment layer is like a overlay or lens over the underlying layers, perhaps darkening the image, perhaps making it appear pale and faded, or intensifying its hues—but remaining separate. Any effects applied on an adjustment layer can be easily revised, because the pixels of the image are not permanently modified. This is an appreciable advantage, especially when you wish to apply the same changes to several images. You can either copy the adjustment layer and place it on top of the layers in another photo, or use the Process Multiple files command (for more information please refer to Photoshop Elements Help).

Creating adjustment layers for lighting

In this next exercise, we'll continue to use the same underexposed photograph to explore the possibility of improving the image by using an adjustment layer.

1 With the image kat_and_kind.jpg still selected in the Photo Browser, click the Editor button, and then choose Full Edit from the menu.

2 With the Background layer selected in the Layers palette, click the Create Adjustment Layer button (◑) and choose Brightness/Contrast from the menu.

3 In the Brightness/Contrast dialog box, make sure that the Preview box is checked. Drag the dialog box aside, if necessary, so that you can see most of the image in the preview window. Drag the Brightness and Contrast sliders to set values of +80 and +25 respectively, and then click OK.

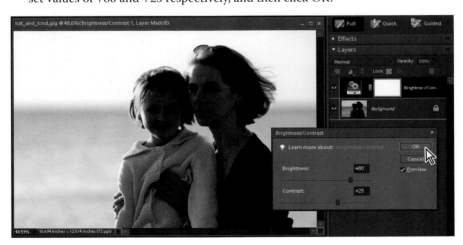

4 Click the Create Adjustment Layer button again, but this time choose Levels (instead of Brightness/Contrast) from the menu. Levels is an effective tonal and color adjustment tool. Notice the additional layer created in the Layers palette.

5 In the Levels dialog box, drag the black, gray, and white arrows (assigned to shadows, mid-tones and highlights respectively) under the graph to the left or right until the balance of dark and light areas looks right to you. We used values of 11, 1.2, and 250.

6 Click OK to close the Levels dialog box.

7 Choose File > Save As. In the Save As dialog box, name the file **kat_and_kind_ Adjustment**, choose the Photoshop (PSD) format, make sure the Layers option is activated. If the option Save In Version Set With Original is activated, disable it before saving the file to your My CIB Work folder. If the Photoshop Elements Format Options dialog box appears, keep Maximize Compatibility selected and click OK.

8 Close the file and return to the Organizer.

The beauty of adjustment layers is that you can always return to adjust your settings, even in future work sessions—as long as you have saved the file in the Photoshop (PSD) format, preserving the layers (the default). If you reopen the file you just closed and double-click the adjustment controls icon in the Brightness/Contrast layer, your original settings (+80 and +25) will still appear in the Brightness/Contrast dialog box—the adjustment is still live and can be refined. If necessary, you could even revert to the original, uncorrected image by either hiding or deleting the adjustment layers.

Correcting parts of an image

Although the adjustment layers do a lot to help bring out the color and image detail from our dark original image, the background is now overexposed. So far in this lesson, all the corrections you've made to the image have been applied to the entire photo. In the next exercise you'll apply adjustments selectively to just part of the image.

Creating a selection

In this exercise you'll divide the image into two parts: our subjects in the foreground, and the sea and sky in the background. You'll start by selecting the silhouette of the mother and child and saving the selection.

There are different ways of making a selection—you've already explored some of them in Lesson 6. The choice of selection tool depends largely on the picture. For this exercise, we'll start with the Quick Selection tool, which makes a selection based on similarity in color and texture. All you need to do is scribble inside a pictured object and the Quick Selection tool automatically determines the selection borders for you.

1   With the image kat_and_kind.jpg still selected in the Photo Browser, click the Editor button, and then choose Full Edit from the menu.

2   In the toolbox, select the Quick Selection tool (✎), which is grouped with the Selection Brush tool.

3   Make sure the New Selection mode is selected for the Quick Selection tool in the tool options bar.

4   Place the cursor at the lower right corner of the woman and slowly drag a line to the top of her head and then down across the child's face and body. Notice that the active selection automatically expands to create a border around the silhouette of our subjects. Not bad at all for a quick first pass.

Next you need to refine the border a little to capture the silhouette as closely as possible. You'll need to deselect the small area of background between the child's shoulder and her mother's chin and pay attention to hair and highlight areas. To refine your selection, you'll alternate between the Quick Selection tool's Add To Selection () and Subtract From Selection () modes. Buttons for these modes are located next to the New Selection mode button in the tool options bar.

5　Choose the Subtract From Selection (✎) mode for the Quick Selection tool from the tool options bar.

6　With the Subtract From Selection tool, click in the space between the girl's shoulder and her mother's chin. The selection contracts to exclude this background area.

7　Keeping the Quick Selection tool active, press Ctrl+= (equal sign) to zoom in to the image, and hold the spacebar for the Hand Tool to move the image as required. Press the left bracket key '[' on your keyboard repeatedly to reduce the brush size for the Quick Selection tool. Alternate between the Add To Selection (✎) and Subtract From Selection (✎) modes and use a combination of clicks and very short strokes to modify the selection border around the area you deselected in step 6, paying attention to the hair and the small spaces in-between.

8　Without being overly fussy, continue to refine the selection around the subjects' heads using the same technique. Your work will be much simpler if you use the keyboard shortcuts to navigate in the image and for the tool settings. Press Ctrl+= (equal) and Ctrl+- (minus) to zoom in and out. Hold the spacebar for the hand tool to move the image in the preview window. Increase and decrease the brush size by pressing the right and left bracket keys: ']' and '['. With the Quick Selection tool in New Selection mode, you can switch temporarily to Add To Selection mode by holding the Shift key, and to Subtract From Selection mode by holding the Alt key.

9   Finally, pay attention to the brightly highlighted area that runs from the little girl's right cheek down her arm and includes a portion of her mother's fingers. You should end up with a tight flashing selection outline around the silhouettes of both of the subjects.

10 To soften the hard edges of the selection, you can smooth and feather the outline. Click Refine Edge in the tool options bar.

11 In the Refine Edge dialog box, enter a value of 2 for Smooth and 1 pixel for Feather. These settings are quite low, but should be appropriate for our lesson image, which has a relatively low resolution. Notice that the Refine Edge dialog box has its own Zoom and Hand tools to help you get a better view of the details of your selection. Click OK.

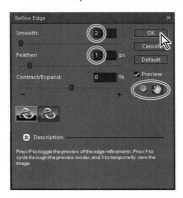

12 Choose Select > Save Selection. In the Save Selection dialog box, choose New from the Selection menu, type **Mother and Child** to name the selection, and then click OK. Saving a selection is always a good idea, because you may find you wish to re-use it later—after assessing your adjustments you can always reload the selection and modify them.

Using layers to isolate parts of an image

Now that you've created a selection that includes only the figures in the foreground of the photo, you can adjust the exposure and color for the subjects and the background independently. You can bring out the shaded detail in the faces without overexposing the sky, and bring out the blue in the background without making the skin tones too cold.

The approach is to divide and conquer—to apply different solutions to different areas of the image. The next step in this process is to use your selection to isolate the foreground and background areas on separate layers. To make the job easier, let's make sure that the layer thumbnails are of a satisfactory size.

1   Choose Palette Options from the Layers palette Options menu.

2   In the Layers Palette Options dialog box, select either the large or medium thumbnail option. Any thumbnail size will work, just as long as you don't choose None—seeing the layer thumbnails can help you visualize the layers you're working with. Click OK.

3   Choose View > Fit On Screen or, if the Zoom tool is active, click the Fit Screen button in the tool options bar so that you can see the entire image.

4   Do one of the following:

    •   If the selection you made in the previous exercise is still active, choose Select > Inverse, and then go on to Step 5.

    •   If the selection you made in the previous exercise is not still active, choose Select > Load Selection. Under Source, select Mother and Child from the

Selection menu and click the check box to activate the Invert option. Make sure New Selection is selected under Operation, and then click OK.

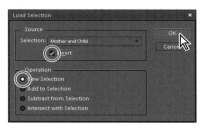

5   Choose Edit > Copy to copy the selected area.

6   Choose Edit > Paste. The copied area is pasted onto a new layer, named *Layer 1* by default.

You can see the new layer in the Layers palette, already selected. In the image window the selection is no longer active.

7   In the Layers palette, select the Background layer. Choose Select > Load Selection. Under Source, choose Mother And Child from the Selection menu, but this time do not activate the Invert option. Click OK.

8   Choose Edit > Copy.

9   With the Background layer still selected in the Layers palette, choose Edit > Paste.

Now you have three layers: Layer 1 with the sea and sky, Layer 2 with the figures in the foreground, and the Background layer with the entire image.

A new layer, whether it's created by pasting into the image or by clicking the new layer button or using the menu command—always appears immediately above the selected layer. The checker-board pattern in layers 1 and 2 indicates transparent areas.

10 You'll find it easier to work with the Layers palette if you name your layers descriptively—especially when you're working with images with a lot of layers. Double-click the name of Layer 2. The pointer changes to the text cursor and the name text is selected. Type **Figures** as the new name for the layer. Change the name of Layer 1 to **Sea & Sky**.

Now you're ready to work on each layer independently to improve the photo as a whole.

Correcting underexposed areas

We can now apply the most effective technique from the earlier exercises to the subjects of our photo selectively, and then fine-tune the result.

1 In the Layers palette, select the Figures layer and choose Screen from the blending menu. The figures are brighter and clearer, while the Sea & Sky layer remains unchanged.

2 Choose Enhance > Adjust Color > Adjust Color For Skin Tone. The pointer becomes an eyedropper. Sample a neutral skin area such as the center of the child's forehead, and then click OK.

Adding more intensity

Now that the figures in the foreground looks so much better, the sea and sky in the background need to be adjusted to appear less dull and murky.

1 In the Layers palette, select the Sea & Sky layer.

2 Choose Enhance > Auto Levels. Not only do the sea and sky look blue again —and far more vibrant—but we have also recovered a lot of textural detail in the background. However, the effect is too strong to sit well with the subdued late-afternoon light in the foreground.

3 Change the opacity of the Sea & Sky layer to 60% by dragging the Opacity slider or typing the new value into the text box.

With these few adjustments to the separate layers, the photograph now looks much more lively. There are still a lot of possibilities to continue playing around with for improving different areas of the image; for example you could separate the sky onto a new layer and intensify the cloud contrast. There is also more you could do with blending modes and layer opacity—you'll learn more about those techniques later in this lesson and as you work further through this book.

4 Choose File > Save As.

5 In the Save As dialog box, name the file kat_and_kind_Layers and save it to your My CIB Work folder, in Photoshop (PSD) format with the Layers option activated. The option Save In Version Set With Original should be disabled.

If the Photoshop Elements Format Options dialog box appears, keep Maximize Compatibility selected and click OK.

6 Close the file and return to the Organizer.

In Lesson 6 you learned how you can tile image windows to best compare the results of your different methods for adjusting an image. It's a good idea to use that technique now to compare the six adjusted and saved versions of this photo before moving on to the next exercise.

Improving faded or overexposed images

In this exercise, you'll work with the scan of an old photograph that has faded badly and is in danger of being lost forever—a photo of a beloved grandmother and her twin sister when they were babies. Like our example, such a photo may not be an award-winning shot, but it could represent a valuable and treasured aspect of personal history, which you might want to preserve for future generations.

The automatic fixes you applied to a copy of this image at the beginning of this lesson (see "Correcting images automatically in batches") improved the photograph markedly. In this project, you'll try to do even better using other techniques.

Creating a set of duplicate files

You'll compare a variety of techniques during the course of this project. You can begin by creating a separate file to test each method. You'll name each file for the technique it demonstrates.

1   If the Organizer is not currently active, switch to it now. In the Keyword Tags palette, click the Find box next to the Lesson 7 keyword tag.

2   In the Photo Browser, click to select the image frida_and_mina.jpg, a faded photo of twin babies.

3   Click the Editor button ( ) near the top right corner of the Organizer window and choose Full Edit from the menu. In the Full Edit workspace, open the Project Bin by clicking the triangle in the lower left corner of the window.

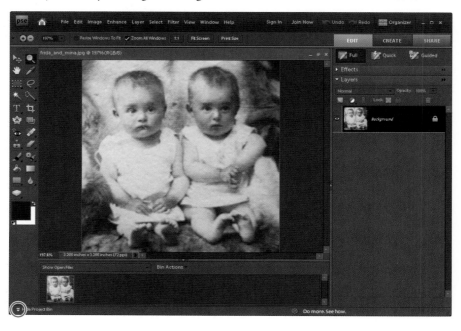

4   In the Editor, choose File > Duplicate. In the Duplicate Image dialog box, type
    frida_and_mina_Shad_High, and then click OK.

5   Repeat Step 5 twice more, naming the duplicate files frida_and_mina_Bright_
    Con and frida_and_mina_Levels.

6   In the Project Bin, double-click the frida_and_mina.jpg thumbnail to make that
    image active. You can see the name of a file in the Project Bin displayed in a
    Tooltip window when you hold the pointer over the thumbnail image.

7   Choose File > Save As. In the Save As dialog box, type **frida_and_mina_Blend_
    Mode** as the new file name and select Photoshop (PSD) from the Format menu.
    Select your My CIB Work folder as the Save In location. If Save In Version Set
    With Original is activated, disable it before you click Save.

8   Click OK to accept the default settings in any dialog boxes or messages that
    appear. Leave all four images open for the rest of the project.

While you're working in the Editor, you can always tell which images you have
open—even when a single active photo fills the edit window—by looking in the project bin. When you can see more than one photo in the edit window, you can identify
the active image by the un-dimmed text in its title bar.

9   Choose Window > Images > Tile.

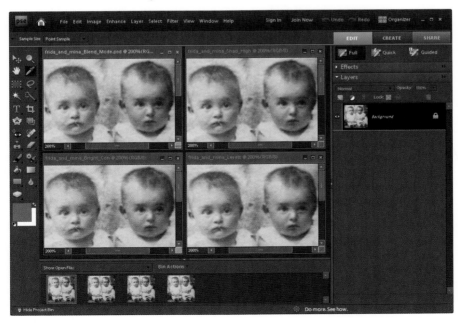

Using blending modes to fix a faded image

Blending modes make layers interact with the layers beneath them in a variety of ways. The Multiply mode intensifies or darkens pixels in an image. The Overlay mode tends to brighten an image while preserving its tonal range. For this project, you'll use the Overlay mode to add clarity and brilliance without canceling out the effect of the Multiply blending mode you'll use on the underlying layers.

1   Make sure that the image frida_and_mina_Blend_Mode.psd is the active window. If necessary, double-click its thumbnail in the Project Bin to make it active.

2   Duplicate the Background layer by choosing Layer > Duplicate Layer. Click OK in the Duplicate Layer dialog box, accepting the default name, Background copy.

Leave the Background copy layer selected in the Layers palette for the next step.

3   In the Layers palette, choose Multiply from the layer blending mode menu.

4   Drag the Background copy layer with its Multiply blend mode onto the New Layer button ( ) in the Layers palette to create a copy of the Background copy layer. Accept the default name, Background copy 2.

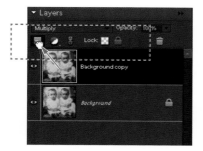

5   In the Layers palette, change the blending mode for the Background copy 2 layer from Multiply to Overlay. Set the layer's Opacity value to 50%, either by dragging the Opacity slider or by typing the new value in the text field.

The stacking order of the layers makes a difference to how blending modes affect an image In our example, if you drag the layer with the Multiply blending mode to a position above the layer with the Overlay mode, you'll see slightly different results.

6   (Optional) Fine-tune the results by adjusting the Opacity settings for the two background copy layers until you achieve a pleasing balance.

The Multiply blending mode made the image bolder and the Overlay blending mode brightens it considerably, but the contrast is still unimpressive.

7   Choose File > Save to save the file in the My CIB Work folder. Leave the file open.

8   If a message appears about maximizing compatibility, click OK to close it, or follow the instructions in the message to prevent it from appearing again.

Adjusting shadows and highlights manually

Although both Auto-fix and the technique using blending modes do a good job of correcting fading images, some of your own photos may be more challenging. You'll try three new techniques in the next exercises.

The first method involves making manual adjustments to the Shadows, Highlights, and Midtone Contrast of the image.

1   In the Project Bin, double-click the thumbnail for the image frida_and_mina_Shad_High to make it the active window.

2   Choose Enhance > Adjust Lighting > Shadows/Highlights.

3   Activate the Preview option in the Shadows/Highlights dialog box if it is not already active. If necessary, move the dialog box so that you can also see most of the frida_and_mina_Shad_High image window.

By default, the Lighten Shadows setting is 25%. You can see difference in the image by toggling the Preview option on and off in the Shadows/Highlights dialog box.

4   In the Shadows/Highlights dialog box, set the Lighten Shadows value to 30%, the Darken Highlights value to 15%, and the Midtone Contrast slider to +20%.

▶ **Tip:** The controls you are using to make the adjustments for this technique are also available in the Lighting palette in Quick Fix mode.

5   Adjust the three settings as needed until you think the image is as good as it can be. When you're done, click OK to close the Shadows/Highlights dialog box.

6   Choose File > Save As and save the file as frida_and_mina_Shad_High to your My CIB Work folder, in JPEG format. Click OK to accept the default settings in the JPEG Options dialog box and leave the file open in the Editor.

Adjusting brightness and contrast manually

The next approach you'll take to fixing an exposure problem uses another command that is available from the Enhance > Adjust Lighting menu.

1   In the Project Bin, double-click the image frida_and_mina_Bright_Con to make it active.

2   Choose Enhance > Adjust Lighting > Brightness/Contrast.

If necessary, drag the Brightness/Contrast dialog box aside so that you can see most of the frida_and_mina_Bright_Con image window.

3   In the Brightness/Contrast dialog box, click the checkbox to activate Preview, if it is not already active.

4   Drag the Brightness slider to -20, or type -20 in the text field, being careful to include the minus sign when you type. Set the Contrast to +40.

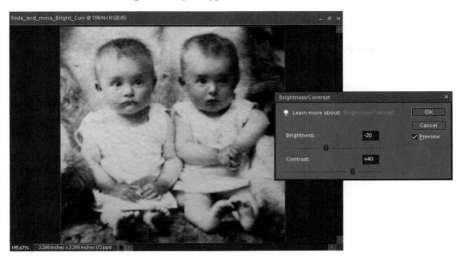

5   Adjust the Brightness and Contrast settings until you are happy with the quality of the image. Click OK to close the Brightness/Contrast dialog box.

6   Choose File > Save As and save the file as frida_and_mina_Bright_Con to your My CIB Work folder, in JPEG format. Click OK to accept the default settings in the JPEG Options dialog box and leave the file open in the Editor.

Adjusting levels

The Levels controls (again, available from the Enhance > Adjust Lighting menu) affect the range of tonal values in an image—the degree of darkness or lightness, regardless of color. In this exercise, you'll enhance the photograph by shifting the reference points that define the spread of those tonal values.

1   In the Project Bin, double-click the image frida_and_mina_Levels to make it active.

2   Choose Enhance > Adjust Lighting > Levels.

3   Activate the Preview option in the Levels dialog box, if it is not already active.

The Levels graph represents the distribution of pixel values in the image. As you can see, in this image there are no truly white pixels or truly black pixels. By dragging the end sliders inward to where the pixels start to appear in the graph, you redefine which levels are calculated as black or white. This will enhance the contrast between the lightest pixels in the image and the darkest ones.

If necessary, drag the Levels dialog box aside so that you can also see most of the image window.

4   In the Levels dialog box, drag the black triangle below the left end of the graph to the right and position it under the point where the graphed curve begins to climb. The value in the first Input Levels box should be approximately 42.

5   Drag the white triangle from the right side of the graph until it reaches the end of the steepest part of the graphed curve. The value in the third Input Levels box should be approximately 225.

6   Drag the gray triangle below the center of the graph toward the right to set the mid-tone value to approximately 0.90. Click OK to close the Levels dialog box.

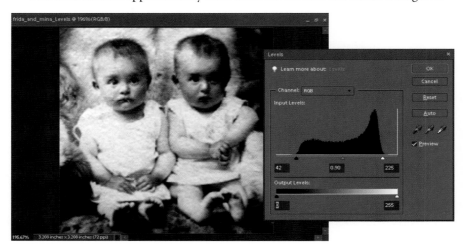

7   Choose File > Save As and save the file to your My CIB Work folder as frida_and_mina_Levels, in the JPEG format. Click OK to accept the default settings in the JPEG Options dialog box and leave the file open in the Editor.

Comparing results

You can now compare the six versions of the image: the original file, the four files you saved showing the results of the preceding exercises, and image that was fixed automatically as part of a batch process at the beginning of this lesson.

1   In the Editor, choose File > Open. Locate and open the file frida_and_mina_Autofix.jpg in the My CIB Work folder. If you don't see the file in the Open dialog box, make sure All Formats is selected in the Files Of Type menu.

2   Repeat the same process to open the file frida_and_mina.jpg in the Lesson 7 folder. Again, if you don't see the file in the Open dialog box, make sure All Formats is selected in the Files Of Type menu.

3   Check the Project Bin to make sure that only the six files for this project are open: the original image, frida_and_mina.jpg, and five others with the appendixes _Blend_Mode.psd, _Shad_High.jpg, _Bright_Con.jpg, _Levels.jpg,

and _Autofix.jpg. To see the file names displayed under the thumbnails in the Project Bin, right-click an empty area in the Project Bin and choose Show Filenames from the context menu.

4   Choose Window > Images > Tile.

5   Now you'll set the zoom level for all active windows. Select the Zoom tool. In the tool options bar, click the Zoom Out button and activate Zoom All Windows. Click in any of the image windows so that you can see a large enough area of the photo to be able to compare the different results. Zoom in to focus on details. Select an area of interest in one window, and then choose Window > Images > Match Zoom and Windows > Images > Match Location.

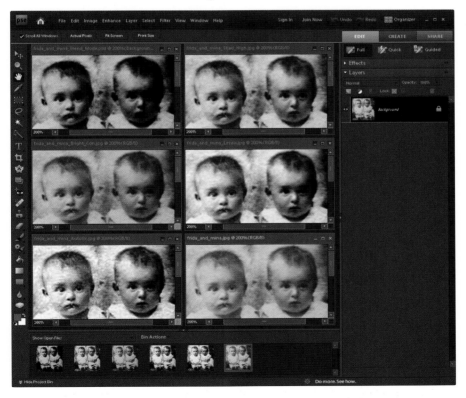

6   Compare the results and pick your favorite. The best method for fixing a file depends on the type of problem being addressed, the areas of the image that are affected, and how you intend to use the adjusted image.

7   Choose Window > Images > Cascade or Window > Images > Maximize to disable image tiling.

8   Choose File > Close All. Save your changes to your CIB Work folder if you're prompted to do so and return to the Organizer.

Congratulations! You've finished another lesson. In the exercises in this lesson you used a variety of both automatic and manual techniques for correcting exposure problems. You've tried auto-fixes, layer blending modes, and lighting adjustment controls. You've learned how to apply these different methods either to layers, in selections, separately, and in combination to get the most from a problem image.

Review questions

1. Describe two ways to create an exact copy of an existing layer.

2. Where can you find the controls for adjusting the lighting in a photograph?

3. How do you change the arrangement of image windows in the work area?

4. What is an adjustment layer and what are its unique benefits?

Review answers

1. Photoshop Elements must be in Full Edit mode to copy a layer. You can select the layer you want to duplicate in the Layers palette, and then choose Layer > Duplicate Layer. Alternatively, drag the layer to the New Layer button in the Layers palette. In either case, you get two layers, identical in all but their names, stacked one above the other.

2. You can adjust the lighting for a photo in either Full Edit, Guided Edit, or Quick Fix mode. In Full Edit, you can use the Enhance > Adjust Lighting menu to open various dialog boxes that contain the controls. Or, you can choose Enhance > Auto Levels, Enhance > Auto Contrast, or Enhance > Adjust Color > Adjust Color Curves. In the Guided Edit mode, choose Lighting and Exposure. In Quick Fix mode, you can use the Lighting palette in the Palette Bin.

3. You cannot rearrange image windows in Quick Fix and Guided Edit modes, which display only one photograph at a time. In the Full Edit workspace, there are several ways you can arrange them. One is to choose Window > Images, and select one of the choices listed there. Another method is to use the maximize or tile windows buttons in the upper right corner of each edit window. A third way is to drag the image window title bar to move an image window, and drag a corner to resize it (provided Maximize mode is not currently active).

4. An adjustment layer does not contain an image. Instead, it modifies some quality of all the layers below it in the Layer palette. For example, a Brightness/Contrast layer can alter the brightness and contrast of any underlying layers. One advantage of using an adjustment layer instead of adjusting an existing layer directly is that adjustment layers are easily reversible. You can click the eye icon for the adjustment layer to remove the effects instantly, and then restore the eye icon to apply the adjustments again. You can change a setting in an adjustment layer at any time—even in a later editing session when the file has already been saved.

8 REPAIRING AND RETOUCHING IMAGES

Lesson Overview

Sometimes you may need to deal with image flaws other than color or exposure problems. You may have an antique photograph that is damaged or a scanned image with dust and scratches. Your photo may be tilted or spoilt by red eye effect or spots and blemishes on a person's skin.

In this lesson, you'll learn some techniques for repairing and retouching flawed images:

- Using the Straighten tool
- Removing red eyes in the Organizer
- Retouching skin with the Healing Brush tool
- Repairing creases with the Clone Stamp tool
- Using the Selection Brush tool
- Masking parts of an image

 You'll probably need between one and two hours to complete this lesson.

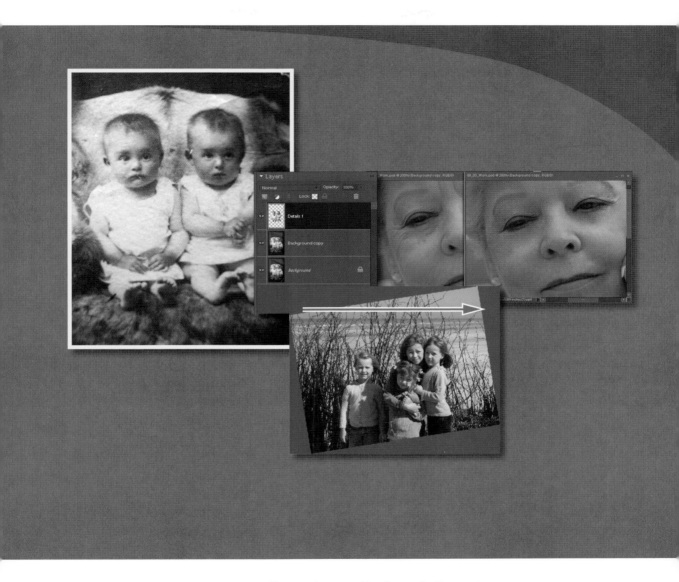

Not every image problem is a result of incorrect exposure or color imbalance. Learn how to improve an image by straightening it or by retouching blemishes on your subject's skin. The same techniques and tools used to remove spots or repair creases and tears when restoring a treasured keepsake can be used creatively to remove an object that's spoiling an image, or even to add one that would enhance it.

259

Getting started

● **Note:** Before you start working on this lesson, make sure that you've installed the software on your computer from the application CD (see the Photoshop Elements 7 documentation) and that you have correctly copied the Lessons folder from the CD in the back of this book onto your computer's hard disk (see "Copying the Classroom in a Book files" on page 2).

The lesson includes four independent exercises—you can do them all at once or in separate work sessions. The first three projects vary only slightly in length and complexity, while the fourth is a little more involved. For the exercises in this lesson you'll use photos from the CIB Catalog you created in the "Getting Started" section at the beginning of this book.

1   Start Photoshop Elements and click the Organize button in the Welcome Screen.

The name of the currently active catalog is displayed in the lower left corner of the Organizer window.

If the CIB Catalog is already open, you can skip ahead to step 3. If the CIB Catalog is not already open, complete step 2 first.

2   Choose File > Catalog. In the Catalog Manager dialog box, select the CIB Catalog and click Open.

If you don't see the CIB Catalog file listed, you should review the procedures in "Getting Started" at he beginning of this book. See "Copying the Lessons files from the CD" on page 2, and "Creating a catalog" on page 3.

3 In the Keyword Tags palette, click the Find box next to the Lesson 8 keyword tag. Click to select the file 08_01.jpg in the Photo Browser. If you don't see the filenames below the thumbnails in the Photo Browser, choose View > Show File Names.

4 In the Organizer, click the Editor button (🖉) near the top right corner of the workspace window and choose Full Edit from the menu. The photo 08_01.jpg opens in the Editor.

As you can see, the picture is not exactly horizontal. When you're taking a photo it's easy to be distracted or rushed by awkward shooting conditions or the need to focus your attention on live subjects and the result is often an image that would be just fine—if only it were straight!

Using the Straighten tool

With the Straighten tool you can manually specify a line in a tilted image that should be horizontal or vertical and Photoshop will straighten the image accordingly.

1 In the toolbox, select the Straighten tool (🔳).

2 For this image, the horizon is visible and can be used as a natural reference. With the Straighten tool, drag a line along the horizon from the top left to the right border.

▶ **Tip:** If you wish to straighten a photo relative to an element in the image that should be vertical—such as an architectural detail or perhaps a signpost—hold down the Ctrl key on your keyboard as you drag with the Straighten tool. The image will be rotated so that your line is vertical.

3 When you release the mouse button, Photoshop Elements straightens the image relative to the line you've just drawn.

4   In the toolbox, select the Crop tool (✄). Drag a cropping rectangle inside the image, which is now displayed at an angle, being careful not to include any of the gray area around the photo. When you're satisfied with the crop, click the green Commit button in the lower right corner of the cropping rectangle.

▶ **Tip:** For some images, you may want to consider using the commands Image > Rotate > Straighten Image or Image > Rotate > Straighten and Crop Image, which perform straightening functions automatically.

5   The straightened and cropped image is much more comfortable to look at than the tilted original. Choose File > Save As. In the Save As dialog box, navigate to your My CIB Work folder. Disable the Save in Version Set with Original option, choose JPEG from the Format menu, name the file **08_01_Straight.jpg**, and then click Save.

6   Click OK in the JPEG Options dialog box to accept the default settings.

7   Choose File > Close to close the file.

Removing red eye in the Organizer

The red eye effect is caused by the reflection of the camera's flash from the subject's retinas. You'll see it more often when taking pictures in a darkened room, because the subject's pupils are then wide open.

You can have Photoshop Elements automatically fix red eyes as part of the import process (see the sidebar "Automatically Fixing Red Eyes" in Lesson 2). Lesson 6 discusses the tools available in the Editor for fixing red eye effects (see "Using automatic Red Eye Fix in the Editor" and "Using the Red Eye Removal tool" in Lesson 6).

For this exercise you'll fix the problem without even leaving the Organizer. You can use a menu command to remove the red eye effect from one or more selected photos while viewing them in the Photo Browser.

1   In the Organizer, click the Find box next to the Lesson 8 keyword tag.

2   In the Photo Browser, click to select the file 08_02.jpg, a picture of a startled child staring straight into the camera. If you don't see the filenames below the thumbnails in the Photo Browser, choose View > Show File Names.

3   In the Fix panel of the Task pane, click the Auto Red Eye Fix button. If you prefer to use a menu command, choose Edit > Auto Red Eye Fix. Both commands trigger the same process.

A progress window will appear displaying the progress of the red eye fix.

When the fix is complete, the Auto Fix Red Eye dialog box may appear informing you that a version set was created. Version sets are identified by the version set icon in the upper right corner of the thumbnail. *(See the illustration on the next page.)*

4   Click OK, to close the Auto Red Eye Fix Complete dialog box.

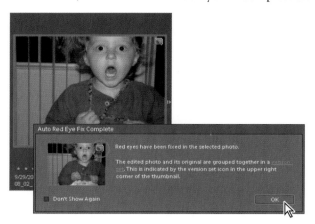

5   If it's not still selected, click to select the image 08_02.jpg in the Photo Browser. To view the results in the Editor, click the Editor button located near the top right corner of the Organizer window and choose Full Edit from the menu. Alternatively, click the Full Edit button in the Fix panel of the Task pane.

6   In the Editor, click the Zoom tool (🔍) in the toolbox. Select the Zoom In mode for the tool in the tool options bar, and then click the photo to view the results of the Auto Fix Red Eye fix. The red has been removed from the child's eyes.

7   Choose File > Close to close the file and return to the Organizer.

Removing wrinkles and spots

In this exercise, you'll explore several techniques for retouching skin flaws and blemishes to improve a portrait photograph. Retouching skin can be a real art, but luckily Photoshop Elements provides several tools that make it easy to smooth out lines and wrinkles, remove blemishes, and blend skin tones.

1   In the Organizer, find and select the file 08_03.jpg, which is tagged with the Lesson 8 keyword tag. If you don't see the filenames below the thumbnails in the Photo Browser, choose View > Show File Names.

2   Click the Editor button located near the upper right corner of the Organizer workspace window and choose Full Edit from the menu.

3   The Editor opens in Full Edit mode. If the Palette Bin and Project Bin are not already open, you can open them now by choosing Window > Palette Bin and Window > Project Bin. You should see a check mark beside both menu options.

4   If the Layers palette is not visible in the Palette Bin, choose Windows > Layers to open it now.

Note: For help working with palettes and the Palette Bin, see "Using the Palette Bin" in Lesson 1, "A Quick Tour of Photoshop Elements."

Preparing the file for editing

Before you actually start retouching, you'll set up the layers that you'll need and save the file with a new name to make it easy to identify as your work file.

1   In the Layers palette of the Editor, drag the Background layer to the New Layer button () in the Layers palette to create another layer, which will be called Background copy. Drag the Background copy layer to the New Layer button to create a third layer, which will be called Background copy 2.

2   Choose File > Save As and save the file in Photoshop (PSD) format as **08_03_Work** in your My CIB Work folder. If the option Save In Version Set With Original is activated, disable it before you click Save. Make sure the Layers checkbox is selected.

Using the Healing Brush tool

Now you're ready to retouch the subject's skin using the Healing Brush tool.

1   Make sure the layer Background copy 2 is still active. Zoom in on the upper half of the photo, as you'll be retouching the skin around the woman's eyes first.

2   Select the Healing Brush tool ( ), which is grouped with the Spot Healing Brush tool in the toolbox.

3 In the tool options bar, click the small arrow to open the Brush Picker and set the Diameter to 15 px. Set the brush Mode to Normal and the Source to Sampled. Disable the Aligned and All Layers options, if they are active.

4 With the Healing Brush tool, Alt-click a smooth area of skin on the woman's right cheek to sample that area as the reference texture. The Healing Brush tool won't work until you establish the sample area. If you switch to another tool and then back to the Healing Brush, you'll need to repeat this step.

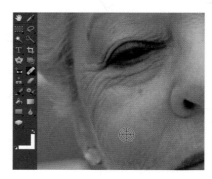

5 Draw a short horizontal stroke under the left eye. As you drag, it looks as if you're creating a strange effect, but when you release the mouse button, the color is blended and natural skin tones fill in the area.

▶**Tip** Be very careful to keep your brush strokes short. You can also try just clicking rather than dragging. Longer strokes may produce unacceptable results. If that happens, choose Edit > Undo Healing Brush, or use the Undo History palette to backtrack. Also, make sure that Aligned is not selected in the tool options bar.

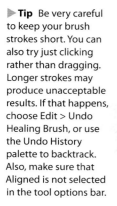

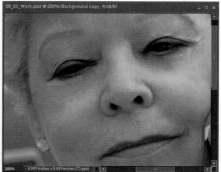

6 Continue to smooth the skin on the face, hands, and neck with the Healing Brush. Avoid the areas very close to the eyes or near the edges of the face. As you work, reestablish the reference texture occasionally by Alt+clicking in other parts of the face to sample different skin tones.

7 Use the Undo History palette (Window > Undo History) to quickly undo a series of steps. Every action you perform is recorded in chronological order from top to bottom of the palette. To restore the file to an earlier state, simply select an earlier action in the Undo History palette. If you change your mind before making any further changes to the file, you can still restore the image to a later state by selecting a step lower in the list.

The Healing Brush tool copies texture from the source area, not color. It samples the colors in the target area—the area it brushes—and arranges those colors according to the texture of the reference area. Consequently, the Healing Brush tool appears to be smoothing the skin. So far, the results are not convincingly realistic, but you'll work on that in the next exercise.

▶ **Tip:** To remove spots and small imperfections in your photo, try the Spot Healing Brush as an alternative to the Healing Brush. You can either click or drag with the brush to smooth away imperfections.

Refining the healing brush results

In this next exercise, you'll use layer opacity and another texture tool to finish your work on this image.

1 Use the Navigator palette (Window > Navigator) to zoom in to the area of the woman's face around the eyes and mouth.

Extensive retouching can leave skin looking artificially smooth, like molded plastic. Reducing the opacity of the retouched layer gives the skin a more realistic look by allowing some of the wrinkles on the original Background layer to show through.

2 In the Layers palette, change the Opacity of the layer Background copy 2 to about 60%, using your own judgment to set the exact percentage.

3 Select the layer Background copy to make it the active layer.

4   In the toolbox, select the Blur tool (💧). In the tool options bar, set the brush diameter to approximately 13 px and set the Blur tool's Strength to 50%.

5   With the layer Background copy selected and active, drag the Blur tool over some of the deeper lines around the eyes, mouth, and brow. Use the Navigator palette to change the zoom level and shift the focus as needed. Reduce the Blur tool brush diameter to 7 px, and then smooth the lips a little, avoiding the edges.

Compare your results to the original, the version retouched with the Healing Brush, and final refined version below. Toggle the visibility of the retouched layers to compare the original image with your edited results.

Original

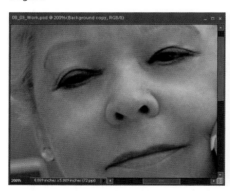

Healing Brush 100% Opacity

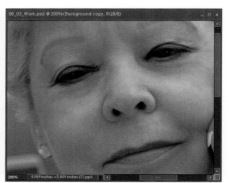

Healing Brush 60% Opacity with Blur tool

6   Choose File > Save to save your changes, and then close the file and return to the Organizer.

In this exercise, you've learned how to set an appropriate source for the Healing Brush tool, and then sample the texture of the source area to repair flaws in another part of the photograph. You also used the Blur tool to smooth textures, and an opacity change to create a more realistic look.

Restoring a damaged photograph

All sorts of nasty things can happen to precious old photographs—or precious new photographs, for that matter—and it is often impossible to locate the negative. For this exercise you'll work with an uncropped version of one of the photos you adjusted in the previous chapter.

The scanned image of an antique photograph that you'll use in this project is a challenging restoration job, because of large creases in the original print, among other flaws.

Unfortunately, there's no way to fix such significant damage in just one or two keystrokes but to rescue an important heirloom photograph like this one, a little effort is worthwhile and the results can be dramatic.

Photoshop Elements provides the tools you'll need to restore this picture to a convincing simulation of its original condition. You'll repair creases and replace parts of the image that are actually missing, fix frayed edges, and remove dust and scratches. You may be surprised to discover how easy it is to achieve impressive results.

Preparing a working copy of the image file

The first thing you need to do is to set up a work file with a duplicate layer.

1   In the Organizer, find and select the file 08_04.psd, a scanned antique photo of twin babies, tagged with the Lesson 8 keyword tag. Click the Editor button in the upper right of the Organizer window and choose Full Edit from the menu.

2   In the Editor, choose File > Save As. In the Save As dialog box, name the file **08_04_Work** and choose Photoshop (PSD) from the Format menu. If the option Save In Version Set With Original is active, be sure to disable it before you save the file to your My CIB Work folder.

3   Choose Layer > Duplicate Layer and in the Duplicate Layer dialog box, click OK to accept the default name: Background copy.

Using the Clone Stamp tool to fill in missing areas

The first thing you'll do is to eliminate the creases using the Clone Stamp tool. The Clone Stamp tool paints with information sampled from an image, which is perfect for both covering unwanted objects and replacing detail that is missing, as is the case for the worn areas along the creases.

1   With the help of the Navigator palette or the Zoom tool, zoom in on the crease in the lower right corner.

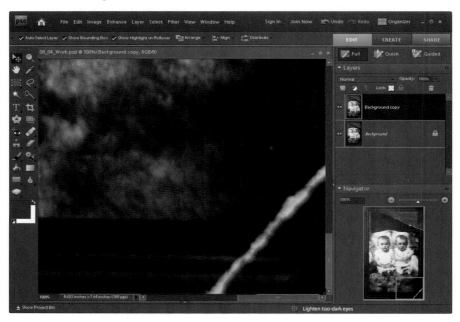

2   In the toolbox, select the Clone Stamp tool ( ), which is grouped with the Pattern Stamp tool.

3   On the left end of the tool options bar, click the triangle and choose Reset Tool from the menu.

The Reset Tool command reinstates the default values for the Clone Stamp tool: Size: 21 px, Mode: Normal, Opacity: 100%, and the Aligned option is activated.

4 In the tool options bar, open the Brush Picker. Choose Basic Brushes from the Brushes menu, and then select a hard mechanical brush with the size of 48 pixels. Set the Mode to Normal, the Opacity to 100%, and select Aligned.

5 Move the Clone Stamp tool to the left of the crease at the bottom of the picture. Hold down the Alt key and click to set the source position—the area to be sampled. Centering the source on a horizontal line makes it easier to align the brush for cloning. The tool duplicates the pixels at this point in your image as you paint.

6 Position the brush over the damaged area so that it is aligned horizontally with the source reference point. Click and drag to the right over the crease to copy the source image onto the damaged area. As you drag, cross-hairs appear, indicating the source—that is, the area that the Clone Stamp tool is sampling.

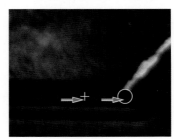

Note: If necessary, you can reset the source by at any time by Alt-clicking in a different location.

7 To repair the upper part of the crease, set the source position in the area above the crease and drag downwards. This will help you blend the repair with the vertical edges of the photograph's mount.

8 Continue to drag the brush over the creased, damaged area, resetting the source position as necessary, until the repair is complete.

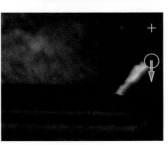

The cross-hairs follow the movement of the brush. With the Aligned option activated in the tool options bar, the cross-hairs maintain the same position relative to the brush that was set when you made the first brush stroke. When the Aligned option is disabled, the cross-hairs return to their original position at the beginning of each new stroke, regardless of where it is made.

9   Now, smooth out the crease across the upper right corner. For this operation the Healing Brush tool () is the best choice, because the crease is quite severe and has caused significant variations in the background color. The Healing brush set to a small brush size is also the right tool to restore large white speck on the ear of the baby on the right.

10 Choose File > Save to save your changes.

Using the Selection Brush tool

The next step in restoring this photo is to use the Dust & Scratches filter to remove the stray spots and frayed edges from the scanned image. This filter smooths out the pixels by blurring the image just slightly. This is fine for the background, but the subjects—the children—should be kept as detailed and sharp as possible. To do that, you'll need to create a selection that includes only the areas you want to blur.

▶ **Tip:** In the same way that the Spot Healing Brush tool can provide a quicker alternative to the Healing Brush, the Quick Selection tool is a faster alternative to the Selection Brush. However, the Quick Selection Brush tool automatically makes a selection based on similarities in color and texture, so it's more effective in some situations than others.

1   In the toolbox, select the Selection Brush tool (), which is grouped with the Quick Selection tool. Be careful to not select a painting brush tool by mistake.

2   In the tool options bar, select a round brush shape and set the brush size to about 60 pixels. Leave the other options at the default values: Mode should be set to Selection and Hardness should be set to 100%.

3   Drag the brush around the edges of the photograph and move inwards. Increase or decrease the brush size as needed as you paint the selection to include everything but the children. There's no need to be too precise around the outlines of the babies. It's no problem if some of your strokes overlap on the children; you'll be refining the selection in the next exercise.

4   Choose Select > Save Selection.

5   Name the new selection **Backdrop** and click OK to close the Save Selection dialog box.

Painting a selection with the Selection Brush tool is an intuitive way to create a complex selection. In images like this one, where there are no distinct color blocks, few sharp boundaries between pictured items, and few crisp geometric shapes, the Selection Brush tool is especially useful.

Another advantage of the Selection Brush tool is that it is very forgiving. You can hold down the Alt key while dragging to remove an area from a selection. Alternatively, you can use the Selection Brush in Mask mode, which is another intuitive way of refining the selection, which you'll be doing in the next exercise.

What is a mask?

A mask is simply the opposite of a selection. A selection is an area that you can modify; everything outside the selection is unaffected by the changes you make. A mask protects an area from changes, just like the solid areas of a stencil or the masking tape you'd put on window glass at home before you paint the frame.

Another difference between a mask and a selection is the way Photoshop Elements presents them visually. You're familiar with the flashing black and white dashed outline that indicates a selection marquee. A mask appears as a colored, semi-transparent overlay on the image. You can change the color and opacity of the mask overlay using the overlay color and opacity settings that become available in the tool options bar when the Selection Brush tool is set to operate in Mask mode.

Refining a saved selection

As you progress through this book, you're gathering lots of experience with saving selections. In this procedure, you'll amend a saved selection and replace it with your improved version.

1 In the work area, make sure that your Backdrop selection is still active in the image window. If it's not still active, choose Selection > Load Selection, choose the saved selection, and then click OK.

2 Make sure the Selection Brush tool () is still selected in the toolbox.

3 In the tool options bar, select Mask from the brush Mode menu. You can see the mask as a semi-transparent colored overlay on the unselected—or protected—areas of the image. In this mode, the Selection Brush tool paints a mask rather than a selection.

4 Examine the image, looking for unmasked areas with details that should be protected (places where the Selection Brush strokes overlapped onto the children) and parts of the backdrop that are masked and should not be.

   Use the Navigator palette slider or the Zoom tool (🔍) to adjust your view of the image, as necessary.

5   Reduce the brush size for the Selection Brush to about 30 pixels, and then paint in any areas you want to mask. Press the Alt key while painting to remove an area from the mask.

6   Switch back and forth between Selection and Mask modes, making corrections until you are satisfied with the selection (or the mask, if you like). Your goal is to make sure that fine details you want to preserve are masked.

7   Choose Select > Save Selection. In the Save Selection dialog box, choose Backdrop from the Selection menu. Under Operation, activate the Replace Selection option and click OK.

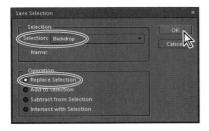

8   While the Selection Brush tool is still active, make sure that the Selection mode—not the Mask mode—is selected in the Mode menu in the tool options bar. Keep the selection active for the next procedure.

Filtering flaws out of the backdrop area

Now that you've made your selection, you're ready to apply the filter that will soften the selected areas, reducing the tiny scratches and dust specks in the background of the image.

1   If the Backdrop selection is no longer active, choose Select > Load Selection and choose Backdrop before you click OK to close the dialog box.

2   Choose Filter > Noise > Dust & Scratches.

3 In the Dust & Scratches dialog box, make sure that Preview is selected, and then drag the Radius slider to 6 pixels and the Threshold slider to 10 levels. Move the dialog box so that you can see most of the image window, but don't close it yet.

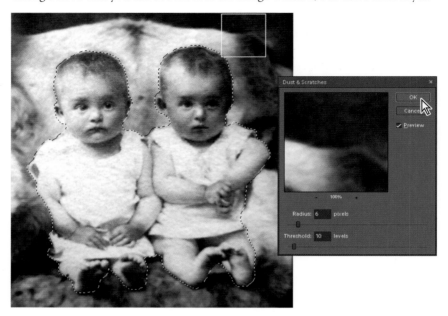

4 Examine the results in the image window. The frayed edges of the image should be softened and the stray dust and tiny scratches eliminated. Move the cursor inside the magnified preview in the Dust & Scratches dialog box and drag with the hand tool to change the area of the image that is displayed.

5 Make adjustments to the Radius and Threshold values until you are satisfied with the results, and then click OK to close the Dust & Scratches dialog box.

6 Choose Select > Deselect, and then choose File > Save to save your work.

The Dust & Scratches filter does a good job of clearing away spots created by flaws on the negative, without affecting the unselected—or masked—areas.

Adding definition with the Smart Brush

The Smart Brush provides a quick and easy way to apply an adjustment to just part of a photo. Unfortunately, like the Quick Selection tool, the Smart Brush makes its selection based on similarities of color and texture in an image, which makes it a little difficult to use on an image such as our example. However, you have already spent time with the Selection Brush to create a selection that will isolate the subjects of the photo from the background; for this exercise you can use that saved selection to quickly tidy up any effect from the Smart brush that extends outside the area you intend to adjust.

1   In the Layers palette, select the layer Background copy and choose Layer > Duplicate Layer. In the Duplicate Layer dialog box, click OK to accept the default name for the new layer: Background copy 2.

2   Select the Smart Brush tool (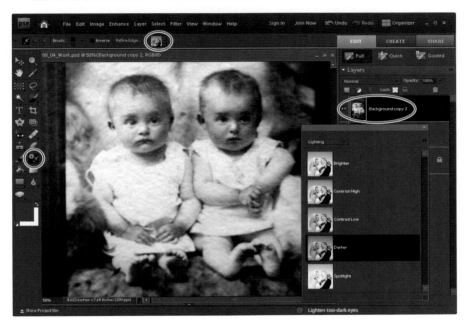) in the toolbox. The floating Smart Paint palette appears. If the palette does not appear, you can open it by clicking the colored thumbnail in the tool options bar. Drag the Smart Paint palette aside so that you can see the two babies in the Edit window.

3   From the categories menu at the top of the Smart Paint palette, choose Lighting, and then select Darker from the list of Smart Paint adjustments.

4   In the tool options bar, open the Brush Picker and set the brush Diameter to 30 px and the Hardness to 75%.

5   Make sure the layer Background copy 2 is selected. With the Smart Brush, paint over the face of the baby on the left and over the arms and legs of both babies. You can hold down the Alt key as you paint to remove areas from the selection. Don't worry about the selection spilling over onto the background, but try to exclude the babies' clothes.

6   Choose Select > Deselect Layers to make the adjustment inactive.

7   From the categories menu at the top of the Smart Paint palette, choose Portrait, and then select Details from the list of Smart Paint adjustments.

8   With the Smart Brush, paint completely over both babies and their clothes. This time you can be even more casual with your brushwork; don't worry at all if the effect spills over onto the background—you'll tidy it up in a moment.

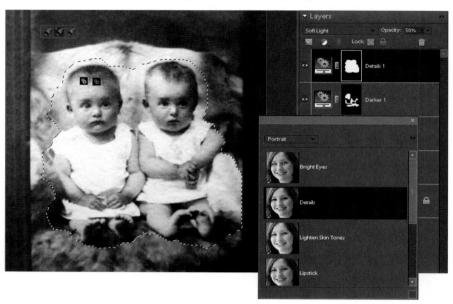

9   Choose Select > Deselect Layers to make the adjustment inactive and close the floating Smart Paint adjustments palette.

Merging layers

You'll now merge the two Smart Brush adjustment layers with the Background copy 2 layer beneath them.

1   In the Layers palette, Ctrl-click to select the top three layers: Background copy 2, Darker 1, and Details 1.

2   Choose Layer > Merge Layers. The three selected layers are merged into one. The new merged layer takes its name from the layer that was on top in the stacking order: Details 1. The Smart Brush adjustments are no longer active or able to be edited.

3   Make sure the new merged layer is still active in the Layers palette and choose Select > Load Selection.

4   In the Load Selection dialog box, choose the saved selection Backdrop from the Selection menu, and then click OK.

5   Choose Edit > Delete, and then Select > Deselect. The background is removed from around the two babies in the merged layer Details 1.

6   To see the effects of your Smart Brush adjustments, toggle the visibility of the layer Details 1 by clicking the eye icon beside its name in the Layers palette.

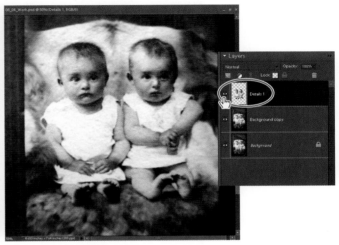

7   In the Layers palette, Ctrl-click to select the top two layers: Background copy and Details 1.

8   Choose Layer > Merge Layers. The two selected layers are merged into one. The new merged layer takes its name from the layer that was on top in the stacking order: Details 1.

Finishing up the project

Compared to the original condition of the photograph, the image is already vastly improved, but if you're in a perfectionist mood you can fix just a few more areas before saving your work.

1   Use the Zoom and Hand tools—or the Navigator palette—to examine the entire image, looking for dark or light flecks created by dust on the negative or the ravages of time, especially in the dark areas of the photograph.

2   In the toolbox, select the Blur tool ( ) and type **40 px** as the brush Size in the tool options bar.

3 Click or drag the tool over any dust spots you find, to blend them into the surrounding area.

4 Use the Clone Stamp tool to remove the pink smudge from the dress of the baby on the right and the Healing Brush to remove the black mark on the calf of the child on the left.

5 Choose File > Save, and then close the file.

Original

Retouched

Congratulations, you've finished this lesson on repairing and retouching images. You've explored a variety of techniques for fixing visual flaws in your photos, from straightening an image to smoothing wrinkles from skin. You sampled one area of an image to repair another with both the Clone Stamp and the Healing Brush and worked with selections and masks. You learned how to reset a tool to its default settings and worked more with layers and the Smart Brush. Take a moment to review the lesson by reading through the review on the next page before you move on to chapter 9, "Working with Text."

Review questions

1 What tools can you use to fix the red eye effect sometimes caused by a flash?

2 How can you quickly undo a whole series of edit steps at once?

3 What are the similarities and differences between the Healing Brush tool and the Spot Healing Brush tool for retouching photos?

4 Why was it necessary to make a selection before applying the Dust & Scratches filter to restore our damaged photograph?

5 What is the difference between a selection and a mask?

Review answers

1 You can choose to have red eye effects corrected automatically during the import process—simply activate the Automatically Fix Red Eye option in the Import dialog box. To fix red eye after the photos have been imported, choose Edit > Auto Red Eye Fix in the Organizer. In either the Full Edit or Quick Fix mode of the Editor, choose Enhance > Auto Red Eye Fix. Alternatively, you can fine-tune the Red Eye Removal tool from the toolbox if you need more control.

2 Use the Undo History palette to quickly undo a series of steps at once. Every action performed on the file is recorded in chronological order in the Undo History palette. To restore the file to an earlier state, simply select an earlier action—higher in the list—in the Undo History palette. If you change your mind before making any further changes to the file, you can still restore the image to a later state by selecting a step lower in the list.

3 Both the Healing Brush tool and the Spot Healing Brush tool blend pixels from one part of an image into another. The Spot Healing Brush tool, especially with the Proximity Match option selected, enables you to remove blemishes more quickly than does the Healing Brush, because it only involves clicking and/or dragging on an imperfection to smooth it. The Healing Brush can be customized, and requires that you Alt-click to establish a source reference area.

4 The Dust & Scratches filter smooths out pixels in an image by blurring them slightly, effectively putting detail slightly out of focus. It was necessary to create a selection so that only the background was blurred, preserving sharpness and detail in the subjects.

5   A mask is simply the opposite of a selection. A selection is an active area to which adjustments can be applied; everything outside the selection is unaffected by any changes that are made. A mask protects an area from changes. Another difference between a mask and a selection is the way Photoshop Elements presents them visually. A selection marquee is indicated by a flashing border of black and white dashes, whereas a mask appears as a colored, semi-transparent overlay on the image. You can change the color and opacity of the mask overlay using the Overlay Color options that appear in the tool options bar when the Selection Brush tool is set to operate in Mask mode.

9 WORKING WITH TEXT

Lesson Overview

Adding text messages to your photos is another way to make your images and compositions even more memorable and personal.

In this lesson you'll learn the skills and techniques you need to work with text in Photoshop Elements:

- Adding a border to an image
- Formatting and editing text
- Overlaying text on an image
- Copying a text layer from one image to another
- Applying effects and Layer Styles
- Warping text
- Hiding, revealing, and deleting layers
- Creating a type mask

 You'll probably need between one and two hours to complete this lesson.

Photoshop Elements provides you with the tools you'll need to add crisp, flexible, and editable type to your pictures. Whether you want classic typography or wild effects and wacky colors, it's all possible in Photoshop Elements. Apply effects and layer styles to make your text really stand out or blend it into your image using transparency. Create a type mask and fill your text with any image you can imagine.

For the exercises in this lesson, you'll use images from the CIB Catalog you created earlier in the book. If necessary, open this catalog in the Organizer by choosing File > Catalog and selecting the CIB Catalog in the Catalog Manager dialog box.

Getting started

This lesson assumes that you are already familiar with the Photoshop Elements interface, and that you recognize the Organizer and Editor workspaces. If you find that you need more background information as you go along, review "Getting Started" and "A Quick Tour of Photoshop Elements" at the start of this book, or refer to Photoshop Elements Help.

This lesson includes several projects, each of which builds on the skills learned in the previous exercises.

Placing text on an image

The first project involves creating a text layer, and then formatting and arranging text on a photograph. You'll add a border and a greeting to a photo so it can be printed as a card or even mounted in a picture frame.

The original photograph and the completed project file.

Using Text Search in the Organizer to find a file

If you've worked through previous chapters you're already very familiar with locating the files for a lesson by their keyword tags. Although the image files for this lesson are tagged "Lesson 9," all of them also have descriptive names, which will make it easy to find just the file or files required for each exercise, rather than all the files in the Lesson09 folder.

1 Open Adobe Photoshop Elements, and click the Organize button in the Welcome screen.

2 Once the Organizer has opened, type the word **happy** in the Text Search box, at the left of the bar above the Photo Browser pane.

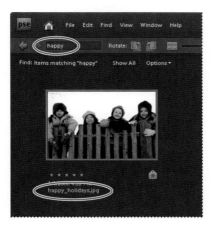

3 The Photo Browser displays a single photo—happy_holidays.jpg—an image of four young girls in the snow. Select the image in the Photo Browser, click the Editor button (⬜) at the top right of the Organizer window, and choose Full Edit from the menu. The photo happy_holidays.jpg opens in the Editor.

Adding an asymmetrical border

In this exercise you'll enlarge the canvas without increasing the size of the image. By default, the canvas—which is the equivalent of the paper on which a photo is printed—is the same size as the image.

By increasing the size of the canvas without enlarging the image you can effectively add a border. By default, the extended canvas, and therefore the border, takes on the Background color as set in the color swatches at the bottom of the Toolbox.

You'll create the border in two stages in order to make it asymmetrical.

1 Choose Image > Resize > Canvas Size.

2 Set up the Canvas Size dialog box as shown in the illustration:

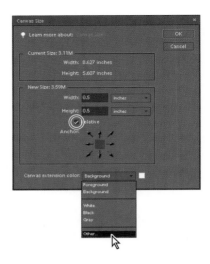

- Activate the Relative option.

- Choose Inches from the units menus and type **0.5** for both the Width and Height of the border.

- Leave the default centered setting for the Anchor control.

- From the Canvas Extension Color menu, choose Other. The Select Canvas Extension Color dialog box appears, with a color picker.

3 The pointer becomes an eye-dropper cursor when you move it over the image. Sample a purple-blue from the glove of the girl on the left.

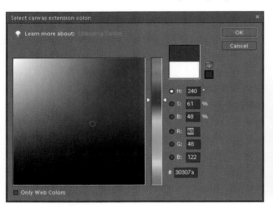

4 This color could make a good choice for the new border, as it's reflected at several points throughout the image; however, it is a little dark. Lighten the color by dragging the circular indicator upwards and to the left in the color field, or type new values of 45% for Saturation (S) and 70% for Brightness (B), and then Click OK.

5 Click OK to close the Canvas Size dialog box. The new colored border appears around the photo in the edit window.

6 Now let's extend the border above the image to create a space for the text greeting. Choose Image > Resize > Canvas Size. In the Canvas Size dialog box, confirm that the Relative check box is still activated.

7 Set the Width value to **0** and the Height to **1**. In the Anchor control diagram, click the center square in the bottom row. Leave the Canvas Extension Color setting unchanged and click OK.

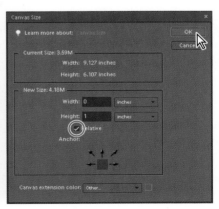

Now the border around the image is deeper at the top, providing a perfect stage for the text you'll add in the next exercise.

Adding a quick border

When precision isn't important, you can quickly add a border to an image by using the Crop tool, rather than increasing the size of the canvas.

1 Zoom out far enough so that you can see some of the gray art-board surrounding the image in the edit window.

2 Use the crop tool to drag a cropping rectangle right around the image.

3 Drag the corner handles of the crop marquee outside the image area onto the art-board to define the size and shape of border that you wish to create.

4 When you're satisfied, click the Commit button in the lower right corner of the image. The canvas expands to fill the cropping rectangle, taking on the background color set in the color swatch at the bottom of the toolbox.

Adding a text layer

With the Horizontal Type and Vertical Type tools you can place type anywhere on your image. When you use the Type tool, Photoshop Elements automatically creates a new text layer in your image. The type you enter remains active on the text layer—you can edit it, resize it, reposition it, or change the text color at any time.

● **Note:** Photoshop Elements includes several variants of the Type tool. Throughout the remainder of this lesson, the term Type tool will always refer to the Horizontal Type tool, which is the default variant.

1 In the toolbox, select the Horizontal Type tool (**T**).

2 Set up the tool options bar as shown in the illustration below. Choose Myriad Pro from the Font Family menu, Bold from the Font Style menu, and type **44** pt in the Font Size box. Choose Center Text (▤) from the paragraph alignment options and set the Leading value to 30 pt. Click the triangle beside the color swatch—not the swatch itself—and select white as the text color.

3 Click in the colored border area above the photo to set the cursor, and then type **HAPPY HOLIDAYS!** in uppercase.

4 Click the Commit button (✔) in the tool options bar to accept the text. Don't worry about the positioning of the text or any typing errors—you'll get a chance to correct those later.

● **Note:** Don't press the Enter or Return keys on the main part of your keyboard to accept text changes. When the Type tool is active, these keys add a line break in the text. Click the Commit button in the tool options bar to accept the text or press the Enter key in the numeric keypad potion of your keyboard.

Notice that in the Layers palette—in the Palette Bin at the right of the workspace—the image now has two layers: a locked Background layer containing the image and a text layer containing your holiday greeting. Most of the text layer is transparent, so only the text itself blocks your view of the Background layer.

5 Make sure the text layer is still selected in the Layers palette, and then select the Move tool (▶⊕) in the toolbox.

6 Place the cursor inside the text and drag so that the message is centered horizontally in the border above the image.

Editing a text layer

Adding vector-based text is a nondestructive process; your original image is not overwritten by the text. If you save your file in native Photoshop (PSD) format, you can reopen it and move, edit, or delete the text layer without affecting the image.

Using the Type tool is much like typing in a word processing application. If you want to edit the message, select the text and type over it. To change the font style or text color, select the characters you want to change, and then adjust the settings.

1   If necessary, choose View > Zoom In to enlarge the image until you can comfortably read the text you added in the previous exercise.

2   Confirm that the text layer HAPPY HOLIDAYS! is still selected in the Layers palette and the Type tool is still active.

3   Click to the right of "HOLIDAYS!," and then press Enter to add a line break in the text. Type **Season's Greetings from The Evans Family,** (this time in upper and lowercase) so that the text reads:
"HAPPY HOLIDAYS!
Season's Greetings from The Evans Family".

Now we want to change the font style, size, and color for the second line of text.

4   Zoom out far enough so that you can select all of the text in the second line. Don't worry that the text seems to disappear outside the image—you can still drag to select it. In the tool options bar, leave MyriadPro selected as the Font Family, choose Regular from the Font Style menu, and set the Font Size to 30 pt.

5   This time, click the color swatch to open the Color Picker. When you move the pointer over the image it becomes an eye-dropper cursor. Use the eye-dropper to sample the purple color from the border you created.

6 In the Color Picker, set the Saturation (S) value to 10% and the Brightness value to 90% so that the text will stand out against the background color.

You should keep this in mind when you're choosing color for text—always choose light colors against a dark or bold background and vice versa. Click OK.

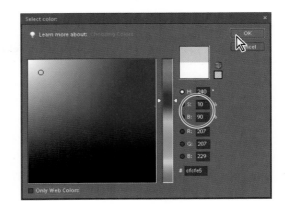

▶ **Tip:** If you need to correct any typing errors you may have made, remember that using the Type tool is like working in a word processing application. Click once to place the insertion point within the text. Use the arrow keys to move the text cursor forward or back. Drag to select multiple characters. Type to add text or to overwrite selected characters. Press Backspace or Delete to erase characters. Click the Commit button in the tool options bar to accept your editing changes.

7 If you need to adjust the position of the text, make sure the text layer is selected, and then select the Move tool in the toolbox. The text is surrounded by a bounding box. You can now either drag the text with the Move tool or use the arrow keys on your keyboard to nudge it in small increments.

Saving a work file with layers

You can save your work file complete with layers so you can return to it later. As long as you save in the right format, text and adjustment layers remain editable.

1 Choose File > Save. The Save As dialog box opens. Navigate to your My CIB Work folder, name the file **happy_holidays_Work,** and choose Photoshop (PSD) from the Format menu.

2 Under Save Options, confirm that the options Include In The Organizer and Layers are activated, and that the option Save In Version Set With Original is disabled.

3 Review your settings and click the Save button. If the Photoshop Elements Format Options dialog box appears, keep Maximize Compatibility selected and click OK.

4 Choose File > Close.

Bravo, you've finished your first text project. In this section, you've formatted and edited text, and worked with a text layer. You've also created a photo border by increasing the canvas size without enlarging the image itself.

Distinguishing between Pixel-based and Vector Graphics

Computer graphics can be divided into two types: pixel-based images (otherwise called bit-mapped, or raster images), which are primarily created by cameras and scanners, and vector images—graphics constructed with drawing programs.

Pixel-based images such as photos are made up of pixels that you can detect when you zoom in. To produce a medium quality print of a photo, you need to make sure that the file is at least 250 ppi (pixels per inch). For viewing on screen, 72 ppi is fine.

Vector images consist of artwork formed from paths, like a technical line drawing. Vectors may form the outlines of an illustration, a logo, or type. The big advantage of vector images over pixel-based images is that they can be enlarged or reduced by any factor without losing detail. Live type on a text layer has this advantage.

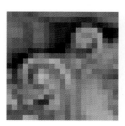
Pixel-based image

Vector type

Rasterized type

About Type

A font is a collection of characters—letters, numerals, punctuation marks, and symbols—in a particular typeface, which share design characteristics such as size, weight, and style. A typeface family is a collection of similar fonts designed to be used together. One example is the Myriad typeface family, which is a collection of fonts in a number of styles including Regular, Bold, Italic, Condensed and other variations. Other typeface families might consist of different font style variations.

Font family
Myriad Pro
Font style
Regular, **Bold**, *Italic*, Condensed

Times New Roman
Regular, **Bold**, *Italic*

Traditionally, font sizes are measured in points, but can also be specified in millimeters or inches, as with large lettering on signs, for example. The most common formats for computer fonts are Type 1 PostScript, TrueType, and OpenType.

Each font conveys a feeling or mood. Some are playful or amusing, some are serious and businesslike, while others might convey an impression of elegance and sophistication. To get a feel for which typeface best suits your project, it's a good idea to try out several fonts. One way to find out more about type is to go to www.adobe.com/type. Adobe Type offers more than 2,200 fonts from the world's leading type designers, which you can browse by categories such as style, use, theme, classification, and designer. This will make it easy to find the perfect font for any assignment. You can even type in your sample copy and compare different fonts.

Fixing Blemishes

There are three main tools in Photoshop Elements for fixing flaws in your photos:

The Spot Healing Brush tool

The Spot Healing Brush is the easiest way to remove wrinkles in skin and other small imperfections in your photos. Either click once on a blemish or click and drag to smooth it away. By blending the information of the surrounding area into the problem spot, imperfections are made indistinguishable.

The Healing Brush tool

The Healing Brush can fix larger imperfections with ease. You can define one part of your photo as a source to be sampled and blended into another area. The Healing Brush is so flexible you can even remove large objects from a uniform background—such as a person in a wheat field.

The Clone Stamp tool

Rather than blending the source and target areas, the Clone Stamp tool paints directly with a sample of an image. You can use the Clone Stamp tool to remove or duplicate objects in your photo. This tool is great for getting rid of garbage, power lines, or a signpost that may be spoiling a view.

Overlaying text on an image

In the last exercise, you preserved the layering of your work file by saving in a file format that supports layers. This gives you the flexibility to make changes to the images, text, and effects even after the file has been saved, without needing to rebuild the image from the beginning or modify the original. Your layers have kept the text and effects separate from the image itself.

In this project, you'll do what professional photographic studios sometimes do to protect proprietary images—stamp a copyright notice over the photo. You'll apply a style to a text layer so that it appears as if the type is set in clear glass overlaid on the images.

Creating a new document for the text

You'll start by preparing the text in its own file. In this procedure, you'll see a gray-and-white checkerboard pattern. This pattern indicates 100% transparency, where an area or complete layer acts like a pane of clear glass onto which you can place text or graphics.

1   If you're not already in the Editor, switch to it now. Make sure the Editor is in Full Edit mode. In the Editor, choose File > New > Blank File.

2   In the New dialog box, name the file **Overlay**. Type **600** for both the Width and Height values and choose Pixels from both units menus.

3   Set the file Resolution to **72** pixels/inch, the Color Mode to RGB Color, and the Background Contents to Transparent. Click OK.

The edit window should show only a checkerboard pattern. If it does not, choose Edit > Undo and repeat the first three steps, being careful to select Transparent from the Background Contents menu. If you still don't see a checkerboard pattern, check your preferences:. Choose Edit > Preferences > Transparency. The checkerboard pattern represents the transparent background that you specified when you created the file.

4   Select the Type tool (**T**), and then set up the tool options bar as shown in the illustration below. Choose Arial from the Font Family menu, choose Bold from the Font Style menu, and type **120** pt in the Font Size box. Choose Centered for the paragraph alignment. Click the triangle beside the color swatch—not the swatch itself—and choose black as the text color.

5   Click near the left side of the image window and type **copyright 2009**. Click the green Commit button (✔) in the tool options bar to accept the text you've typed.

6   Select the Move tool (▶⊕) in the toolbox and drag the text to center it in the image window. Position the Move tool outside a corner of the text bounding box so that the pointer changes to a rotate cursor—a curved, double-ended arrow. Drag the text counter-clockwise around its center so it appears at an angle.

7   Click the Commit button near the lower left corner of the bounding box.

● **Note:** You can scale or reshape the text by dragging the corners of the bounding box with the Move tool. Because Photoshop Elements treats text as vector shapes, the letter shapes remain smooth even if you enlarge the text. If you tried this with bit-mapped text, you'd see jagged, stair-step edges in the enlarged text.

Applying a Layer Style to a text layer

Next, you'll apply an effect to your text by adding a Layer Style. Layer Styles are combinations of adjustments that can be applied to your text layer in one easy action. Photoshop Elements gives you a wide variety of choices, from bevels and drop shadows to imaginative chrome and neon effects.

● **Note:** For help working with palettes and the Palette Bin, see "Using the Palette Bin" in Lesson 1, "A Quick Tour of Photoshop Elements."

1 In the Palette Bin, click the triangle in the upper left corner of the Effects palette to expand it. If you don't see the Effects palette in the Palette Bin, choose Window > Effects.

2 At the top of the Effects palette, Click the Layer Styles button (▤), and then choose the second last category in the effects categories menu, Wow Plastic.

3 In the top row of the Effects palette, select the Wow Plastic Clear effect and click Apply. You could also apply the effect to the selected text layer by double-clicking the swatch, or even by dragging the effect swatch directly onto your text.

When you apply a Layer Style to a Text layer, both the text and the effect remain editable. You could go back and change the year of the copyright in the text layer without affecting the layer style, or double-click the *fx* icon on the text layer and edit, replace, or remove the effect without affecting your ability to edit the text.

4   Choose File > Save and save the file to your My CIB Work folder in Photoshop (PSD) format. Make sure you activate the Layers option. You don't want to create a version set. Click Save. If the Photoshop Elements Format Options dialog box appears, keep Maximize Compatibility selected, and then click OK.

Adding text to multiple images

Now that you've prepared the copyright text, you'll place it onto a series of images.

1   Click the Organizer button at the top right of the Editor window to switch to the Organizer.

2   In the Organizer, type **x file** in the Text Search box at the left of the bar above the Photo Browser pane to find the images you'll use for this exercise.

3   Control-click to select the four images of paintings named **x_file_01.jpg** to **x_file_04.jpg**. Click the Editor button ( ) and choose Full Edit from the menu.

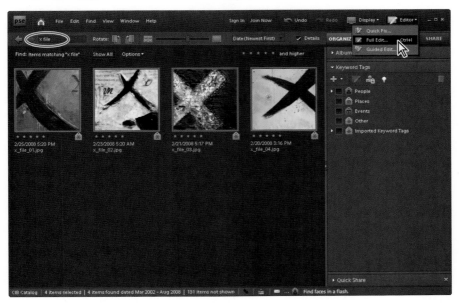

4   To see all the images that are open in the Editor, choose Window > Images > Tile.

To view the same corner of all the open images, choose Window > Images > Match Location. The view in all of the windows will shift to match the active image. To see each image at the same magnification as the active image, choose Window > Images > Match Zoom.

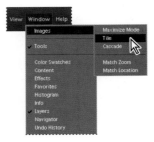

5   Now choose Window > Images > Cascade. Press Ctrl+= (equal sign) or Ctrl+-
    (minus sign) to zoom in or out for the foremost image until the image window is
    small enough to see the entire image and arrange it in the edit window with the
    others at the same size as in the illustration below. Make sure you have the Photo
    Bin open at the bottom of the edit window.

6   In the Photo Bin (the row of thumbnails across the bottom of the workspace),
    click the file Overlay.psd to make it the active file. The title bars of all the other
    files are dimmed. The Layers palette shows the text layer copyright 2009.

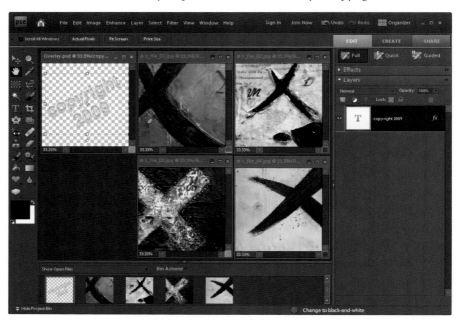

7   Hold down the Shift key and drag the text layer copyright 2009 from the Layers
    palette onto the image of the red painting, x_file_01.jpg.

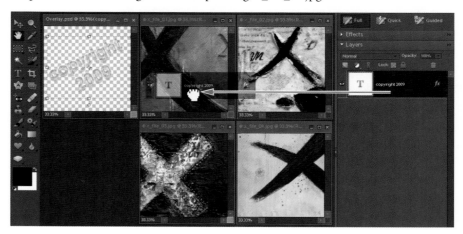

8 To make the overlay more transparent, reduce the opacity to 50% either by typing **50** into the box, or by dragging the Opacity slider to the left.

9 Make sure that the image of the red painting, x_file_01.jpg, is still the active file. In the Layers palette, double-click the *fx* icon on the copyright 2009 layer. The Style Settings dialog box appears.

10 In the Style Settings dialog box, you need to change only one setting. In the Glow options, change the size of the Outer Glow from 22 pixels to 10 pixels. Click OK to close the Style Settings dialog box.

11 Hold down the Shift key and drag the copyright 2009 text layer with its refined layer style from the image x_file_01.jpg onto the other three images. Zoom in to each image and use the Move tool to position the copyright message as you wish for each image independently. The copyright message looks less visible against some of the images than it does against the red painting. Tweak the Opacity value for the text layer on each of the other three images accordingly.

12 Choose File > Close All. If you wish, you can save your efforts to your My CIB Work folder. If you do save the files, be sure to activate the Layers option for the Photoshop (PSD) format so that the layers in the files are preserved.

Done! In this project, you've created a new Photoshop (PSD) format document without an image and added text to that document. You've used the Effects palette to apply a Layer Style to the text layer, copied the text layer to other image files, and edited the layer style and opacity.

Using Layer Styles and distortions

In this next exercise you'll have more fun with text. You'll distort text and apply effects, all the while keeping the text layer live and editable.

Adding a layer style

You can start by finding the image file that you'll use for this project.

1   If you're still in the Editor, click the Organizer button located at the top right of the Editor workspace to switch to the Organizer.

2   In the Organizer, type the word **sky** in the Text Search box at the left of the bar above the Photo Browser pane. The Photo Browser displays only one image named **big_sky.jpg**.

3   Select the image in the Photo Browser, click the Editor button, and then choose Full Edit from the menu.

4   Select the Type tool (**T**) from the toolbox, and then set up the tool options bar as shown in the illustration below. From the Font Family menu, choose a bold sans-serif style such as Impact (as an alternative, you could choose Arial Black). Type **200** pt in the Font Size box, and choose Centered from the paragraph alignment options. Click the triangle beside the color swatch (not the swatch itself) to open the color palette. For the text color, choose Pastel Cyan Blue.

5   Using the Type tool, click near the center of the image and type **MAYBE**—all in upper case.

6   Click the Commit button (✓) in the tool options bar to accept the text.

7   Choose the Move tool (▶⊕) in the toolbox and drag the text to center it as shown in the illustration below.

8   Expand the Effects palette and click the Layer Styles button (▤). Choose the category Bevels from the effects categories menu and double-click the last effect in the second row: Simple Sharp Outer.

9   In the Layers palette, change the opacity of the text layer to 75%, either by typing the new value directly into the text box or by dragging the Opacity slider.

10 Save the file in your My CIB Work folder. Name the file big_sky_Work, choose the Photoshop (PSD) format and make sure the Layers option is activated.

Warping text

It's easy to stretch and skew text into unusual shapes using the Photoshop Elements Warp Text effects; the difficulty is in avoiding overusing the effects!

Note: It's not necessary to highlight the text because warp effects are automatically applied to the entire text layer.

1 Make sure the Type tool is active, and then click anywhere on the text "MAYBE" in the image window.

2 In the tool options bar, click the Create Warped Text button ( ) to open the Warp Text dialog box. Choose the Fisheye effect from the Style menu.

3 The Horizontal and Vertical orientation options are unavailable because the fisheye effect is applied on both axes by default. Set the Bend value to **+75**% and click OK to close the Warp Text dialog box.

4 The text layer is still editable. You can check this out by dragging to select the word MAYBE with the Type tool, and then typing over it.

5 Choose Edit > Undo Edit Type Layer, and then File Save.

Creating an un-stylized copy of the text layer

In the next exercise, you'll experiment with an effect that requires your type layer to be simplified, meaning that the vector text will be converted to a bitmap image and will therefore no longer be editable. For this purpose you'll create a separate copy of the text layer.

1 In the Layers palette, select the text layer. Click the double triangle in the upper right corner of the palette to open the Layers palette Options menu. From the palette Options menu, choose Duplicate Layer. Click OK to accept the default layer name: MAYBE copy.

▶ **Tip:** You can also duplicate a layer by dragging it onto the New Layer button at the top left of the Layers palette, or by selecting the layer and choosing Layer > Duplicate Layer.

2 Click the eye icon to the left of the original text layer: MAYBE. The layer becomes invisible in the image window.

3 In the Layers palette, change the opacity of the layer MAYBE copy to 100%. The warped text once more appears as solid blue.

4 Right-click / Ctrl-click on the text layer Maybe copy and choose Clear Layer Style from the context menu.

    The warped text now appears without the bevel effect, as it did before you applied the Layer Style.

Simplifying text and applying a pattern

You can now add a different look to the copy of the text layer. In preparation, you'll lock the transparent pixels on the text layer, which will enable you to paint on the shapes in the layer without needing to be careful about the edges.

1 In the toolbox, select the Pattern Stamp tool, which is grouped with the Clone Stamp tool. Set up the tool options bar as shown in the illustration below: set the brush Size to **50** px, the brush Mode to Normal, and the Opacity to 100%. Click on the triangle next to the Pattern swatch to open the Pattern menu. Choose the Pink Fur pattern.

2   Make sure that the text layer MAYBE copy is selected in the Layers palette, and then click once on the text in the image window with the Pattern Stamp tool. A message appears, asking if you want to simplify the layer. Click OK.

3   In the Layers palette, click the Lock Transparent Pixels button to prevent changes being made to the transparent areas of the simplified MAYBE copy layer. Notice that there is now a lock icon displayed on the MAYBE copy layer.

4   Make sure the Pattern Stamp tool is still selected in the toolbox and paint over the text in the image window, applying the pattern as solidly or as unevenly as you like. The pattern is applied only to the simplified text; the locked transparent pixels remain unaffected.

Of course, the pattern is painted only onto the selected layer (the simplified text) and does not affect the Background layer or the text layer that is currently hidden.

Remember that once you simplify a text layer, the text is no longer live—it can no longer be edited with the Type tool. However, you can still change the appearance of the simplified text by painting it as you've done in this exercise, by changing the layer's blending mode and opacity, or by adding a Layer Style such as a Bevel or Drop Shadow using the Effects palette.

Hiding and revealing layers

Toggling the visibility of layers by clicking the eye icons in the Layers palette makes a great way to assess different design solutions within one file.

1   In the Layers palette, click the eye icon beside the top text layer, MAYBE copy, to hide it. The eye icon is hidden also, leaving an empty box to indicate that the layer is not visible.

Note that although the layer is selected, the Blending Mode and Opacity options are dimmed and unavailable. You cannot edit a hidden layer.

2 In the Layers palette, click the empty box to the left of the text layer MAYBE. The eye icon reappears and the warped blue text with the bevelled effect is once more visible in the document window.

Deleting layers and layer styles

You can now delete the layer with the pink fur pattern, leaving just the Background layer with the original image, and the text layer MAYBE just above it. Deleting layers that you no longer need reduces the size of your image file.

1 To delete the layer MAYBE copy, first make sure the layer is visible—you should be able to see the eye icon to the left of the layer's name in the Palette menu. Right-click / Ctrl-click the layer and choose Delete Layer from the context menu.

You can use this method to delete more than one layer at the same time—just make sure all the layers are visible and selected, and then right-click / Ctrl-click any of them. You can also delete selected layers by choosing Layer > Delete Layer from the main menu bar, or by clicking the double triangles at the right of the Layers palette's title bar and choosing Delete Layer from the Layers palette Options menu.

2 In the Layers palette, select the remaining text layer, MAYBE. Right-click / Ctrl-click the layer and choose Clear Layer Style from the context menu. Alternatively, choose Layer > Layer Style > Clear Layer Style or choose Clear Layer Style from the Layers palette Options menu.

The type in text layer MAYBE no longer has a bevelled effect, but it is still warped.

3 In the toolbox select the Type tool, and then click the Create Warped Text button in the tool option bar to open the Warp Text dialog box. Choose None from the Style menu, and then click OK to close the Warp Text dialog box.

4 Now you're back to where you began, before applying the bevelled Layer Style and before you added the fisheye text warp effect. Choose File > Save. Save the file to your My CIB Work folder as big_sky_Work, in Photoshop (*.PSD, *.PDD) file format with the Layer option activated. If the option Save In Version Set With Original is activated, disable it before you click Save. If the Photoshop Elements Format Options dialog box appears, keep Maximize Compatibility selected and click OK.

5 Choose File > Close.

In this section, you've applied a Layer Style to live text, warped it, and painted it with pink fur. You should be ashamed of yourself! You learned about locking transparent pixels on a layer and how to edit or clear layer styles and text effects. You also learned how to hide, reveal or delete a layer.

Working with Paragraph type

With point type, or headline type, each line of type is independent—the line expands or shrinks as you edit it, but it doesn't wrap to the next line. Point type (the name derives from the fact that it is preceded by a single anchor point) is perfect for small blocks of text like headlines, logos, and headings for Web pages. Probably most of the text you add to your images will be of this type.

If you work with larger blocks of type and you want your text to reflow and wrap automatically, it's best to use the paragraph type mode. By clicking and dragging with the type tool you'll create a text bounding box on your image. The bounding box can be easily resized to fit your paragraph text perfectly.

Creating a type mask

You can have a lot of fun with the Type Mask tool. The Type Mask tool has two variants—one for horizontal type and the other for vertical type. The Type Mask tool turns text outlines into a mask through which an underlying image is visible.

1   If you are still in the Editor, switch to the Organizer now.

2   In the Organizer, type the word **stripes** in the Text Search box at the left of the bar above the Photo Browser pane. The Photo Browser displays only one image named **stripes.jpg**.

3   Click the Editor button at the top right of the Organizer window and choose Full Edit from the menu.

Working with the Type Mask tool

The Type Mask tool ( ) enables you to fill letter shapes with parts of an image. This can create a much more interesting effect than using plain text filled with a solid color.

1   In the tool box, select the Horizontal Type Mask tool (🅣).

2   Set up the tool options bar as shown in the illustration below: choose Stencil from the Font Family menu, Bold from the Font Style menu, and set the font Size to 100 pt. Choose Left Align Text from the text alignment options. You don't need to worry about the color attributes as the type will be filled with detail from an image.

3   Click near the point where the front zebra's hind leg meets its belly and type the word **ZOO**.

4   The background pattern of zebra stripes shows through the shapes of the letters you just typed, while the rest of the picture is masked, as indicated by the red, semi-transparent overlay. Click the green Commit button in the tool options bar. The outline of the text becomes an active selection. If you are not satisfied with the placement of the text, you can use the arrow keys on your keyboard to nudge it into place.

5 Select Edit > Copy, and then Edit > Paste. you'll notice that the new type image has been placed onto a new layer.

6 In the Layers palette, hide the layer Background by clicking the eye icon to the left of the layer's name.

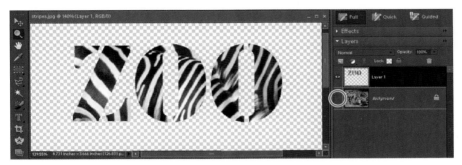

The text is no longer live—it was converted to a selection outline and can no longer be edited; however, you can still apply a layer style or an effect to enhance it or make it more prominent.

7 Select Layer 1 in the Layers palette to make it the active layer.

8 Expand the Effects palette and click the Layer Styles button (▦). Select the effects category Drop Shadows from the menu.

9 In the Drop Shadows palette, double-click the shadow effect called Noisy: the second drop-shadow effect in the second row.

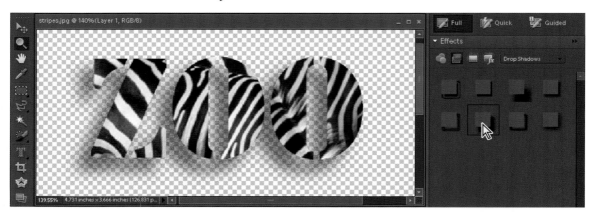

You can tweak the drop shadow effect by double-clicking the *fx* icon on Layer 1 in the Layers palette. The Style Settings dialog box appears, where you can change the angle, distance, color, and opacity of the drop shadow as you wish.

10 Since you no longer need the background layer with the photo of the zebras, delete it by choosing Flatten Image from the Layers palette Options menu. Click OK in the dialog box that appears to ask whether you want to discard the hidden layer.

11 Choose File > Save As. In the Save As dialog box, name the file **stripes_Work**, choose Photoshop (PSD) as the file format, and save the file to your My CIB Work folder.

Congratulations! You've completed another lesson. You've learned how to format and edit text, and how to work with a text layer. You've created a photo border by working with the document canvas, used the Effects palette to apply Layer Styles, warped and painted your text, and created a text mask. You learned about locking transparent pixels on a layer and how to edit or clear layer styles and text effects. You also learned how to hide, reveal and delete a layer. Take a moment to work through the lesson review on the next page before you move on.

Review questions

1   What is the advantage of having text on a separate layer?

2   How do you hide a layer without removing it?

3   In the Layers palette, what do the lock buttons do and how do they work?

4   What's the difference between point type and paragraph type?

Review answers

1   Because the text remains separate from the image, Photoshop Elements text layers remain "live"—text can be edited in later work sessions, just as it can be in a word processing application.

2   You can hide a layer by clicking the eye icon to the left of the layer's name in the Layers palette. To make the layer visible again, click the empty box where the eye icon should be to restore it.

3   Lock buttons prevent changes to a layer. The Lock All button, which looks like a padlock, locks all the pixels on the selected layer so that the layer is protected from changes. Blending and Opacity options become unavailable. The Lock Transparent Pixels button, which looks like a checkerboard, locks only the transparent pixels on a layer. To remove a lock, select the locked layer and click the active lock icon to toggle it off. (This does not work for the Background layer, which can be unlocked only by renaming and converting it into an ordinary layer.)

4   Point type is ideal for headlines, logos and other small blocks of text where each line is independent and does not wrap to the next line. Paragraph text is used where you want larger amounts of text to wrap automatically to the next line. The size of the paragraph text bounding box can be easily changed to fit the text perfectly to your design.

10 COMBINING MULTIPLE IMAGES

Lesson Overview

You can do a lot to improve a photo with tonal adjustments and color corrections, but at times the best way to produce the perfect image is to fake it!

In this lesson you'll learn some of the tricks you'll need for combining multiple photos to create that great shot that you didn't actually get:

- Merging multiple photos into a panorama

- Assembling the perfect group shot

- Removing unwanted elements

- Combining images using layers

- Resizing and repositioning selections

- Creating a gradient clipping mask

- Defringing a selection

 You'll probably need between one and two hours to complete this lesson.

If you're ready to go beyond fixing pictures in conventional ways, this lesson is for you. Why settle for that scenic photo that just doesn't capture the way it looked when you were there? Or that group portrait where someone's eyes are closed? Combine images to produce the perfect shot. Merge photos to make a stunning panorama, remove obstructions from the view, and even get little Jimmy to stop making faces.

317

Getting started

Note: Before you start working on this lesson, make sure that you've installed the software on your computer from the application CD (see the Photoshop Elements 7 documentation) and that you have correctly copied the Lessons folder from the CD in the back of this book onto your computer's hard disk (see "Copying the Classroom in a Book files" on page 2).

For this lesson you'll be using images from the CIB Catalog you created at the start of the book. To open your CIB Catalog, follow these steps:

1   Start Photoshop Elements. In the Welcome Screen, click the Organize button. The name of the currently active catalog is displayed in the lower left corner of the Organizer window. If the CIB Catalog is open, skip to the first exercise: "Merging photos into a panorama." If the CIB Catalog is not open, complete the following steps.

2   Choose File > Catalog.

3   In the Catalog Manager dialog box, select the CIB Catalog from the list, and then click Open.

If you don't see the CIB Catalog listed, you should review the procedures in "Getting Started" at he beginning of this book. See "Copying the Lessons files from the CD" on page 2, and "Creating a catalog" on page 3.

Merging photos into a panorama

The images you'll use for this first exercise are two slightly overlapping photos taken at Mont Saint Michel in France. The camera lens used for these shots did not have a wide enough angle to capture the entire scene. These pictures provide an ideal opportunity for learning how to create a panorama, having Photoshop Elements do most of the work for you.

1   If you're not already in the Organizer, switch to it now.

2   In the Keyword Tags palette, click the Find box next to the Lesson 10 keyword tag.

3   Ctrl-click to select the two pictures of Mont Saint Michel, named 10_01_a.jpg and 10_01_b.jpg in the Photo Browser.

Note: If you don't see the file names displayed below the thumbnails in the Photo Browser, choose View > Show File Names.

4 Choose File > New > Photomerge Panorama.

Photoshop Elements will load the Editor workspace in Full Edit mode and open the Photomerge dialog box.

5 Under Source Files in the Photomerge dialog box, select Files from the Use menu, and then click the Add Open Files button.

6 Under Layout, select Auto, and then click OK.

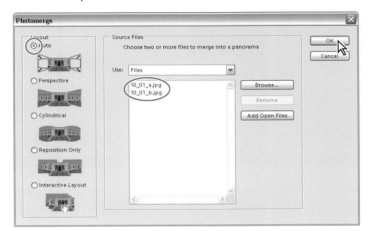

● **Note:** You can use more than two files to create a Photomerge Panorama composition.

▶ **Tip:** Select Folder from the Use menu, and then click Browse to add all the photos from a specific folder on your hard disk. To remove photos from the selection, select them in the source file list, and then click Remove.

Choosing a Photomerge layout option

Auto Photoshop analyzes the source images and applies either a Perspective or Cylindrical layout, depending on which produces a better photomerge.

Perspective Creates a consistent composition by designating one of the source images (by default, the middle image) as the reference image. The other images are then transformed (repositioned, stretched or skewed as necessary) so that overlapping content across layers is matched.

Cylindrical Reduces the "bow-tie" distortion that can occur with the Perspective layout by displaying individual images as on an unfolded cylinder. Overlapping content across layers is still matched. The reference image is placed at the center. Best suited for creating wide panoramas.

Reposition Only Aligns the layers and matches overlapping content, but does not transform (stretch or skew) any of the source layers.

Interactive Layout Choose this option to open the source images in a dialog and position them manually for the best result (see "Creating a Photomerge Panorama interactively").

—From Photoshop Elements Help

7 Wait while Photoshop Elements creates the panorama and opens it in a new image window.

That's really all there is to it! All that remains to crop the image and save your work. But first, let's have a closer look at how good a job Photoshop Elements did of merging the two images. Depending on your source files, you might sometimes spot little problem areas, in which case you'd then need to try a different layout option to merge your photos.

8 In the Layers panel, click the eye icon (👁) beside the top layer to hide it.

In the edit window, you can now see which part of the image in the lower layer was used to create the panorama. The unused portion is hidden by a layer mask. You can see a black and white thumbnail of the layer mask in the Layers palette; black represents the masked area of the image and white represents the part of the image that has contributed to the panorama.

9   Choose View > Actual Pixels, or zoom in even closer if you wish, and then use the Hand tool to move the image in the edit window so that you can inspect the edge of the layer mask. Click the eye icon (👁) for the top layer repeatedly to hide and reveal that layer while you look for irregularities along the edge between the two images. Look for pixels along the masked edge of one image that appear misaligned with pixels in the other. Use the Hand tool to inspect the entire edge of the mask.

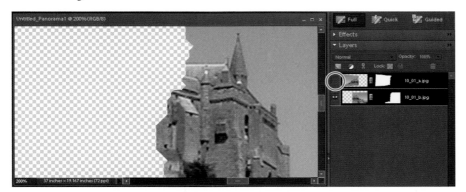

Hide the top layer to reveal the edge of the image mask.

Show the top layer and check for irregularities along the edge between the two source images.

10 If your inspection does not reveal any problem areas, make the top layer visible and you're ready to crop the picture and save it. If you do find problems in a merged panorama, close the file without saving it and repeat the procedure trying a different Photomerge layout option when you get to step 6. Later in this lesson, the section "Creating a Photomerge Panorama interactively" explains the interactive layout option, which gives you the most control over the way the panorama is put together.

Cropping the merged image

As the merged image has an irregular outline, you'll use the Crop tool to create a uniform edge. The Crop tool removes those parts of an image that fall outside an adjustable cropping rectangle. Cropping can also be very useful for changing the visual focus of a photo. When you crop an image, the resolution remains unchanged.

1 Choose View > Fit On Screen.

2 Choose Image > Crop. A cropping rectangle appears on the image. Drag the handles of the cropping rectangle to make it as large as possible, being careful not to include any of the checkerboard areas where the image is transparent. When you're happy with the result, click the Commit button in the lower right corner of the cropping rectangle.

▶ **Tip:** You could also select the Crop tool directly from the toolbox. In Quick Fix mode you can choose between the Image > Crop command or the Crop tool in the toolbox. In Guided Edit mode you'll find a Crop Photo procedure in the Basic Photo Edits palette. In the Organizer, you can use the Crop button in the Fix pane.

3 Choose File > Save and save the merged image to your My CIB Work folder as **10_01_Work**, in Photoshop (*.PSD,*PDD) format, making sure that the Layers option is activated. Saving your file in Photoshop format preserves the layers, so that you can always return to adjust them if necessary. If you save in JPEG format the layer information will be lost.

Cropping ratio options

Though you won't need to do so for this exercise, you can set options for the Crop tool in the tool options bar.

In the Aspect Ratio menu you can choose between several options. The option No Restriction lets you crop the image to any proportions. The option Use Photo Ratio retains the aspect ratio of the original photo. The menu also offers a range of preset sizes for your cropped photo, should you want your final output to fit a particular layout or a favorite picture frame.

The Width and Height fields enable you to specify custom dimensions that are not available from the Aspect Ratio menu.

4 Choose File > Close to close the file 10_01_Work.psd, but keep the two source files, 10_01_a.jpg and 10_02_b.jpg, open in the Editor.

Creating a Photomerge Panorama interactively

The automatic layout options in the Photomerge dialog box usually do a good job, but if you need manual control over the way source images are combined to create a panorama, choose the Interactive Layout option in the Photomerge dialog box.

1 With the files 10_01_a.jpg and 10_02_b.jpg still open in the Editor, choose File > New > Photomerge Panorama.

2 Under Source Files in the Photomerge dialog box, select Files from the Use menu, and then click the Add Open Files button. Under Layout, select Interactive Layout, and then click OK.

3 Wait while Photoshop Elements opens the interactive Photomerge dialog box.

● **Note:** If the composition can't be assembled automatically, a message will appear on screen. You can assemble the panorama manually in the Photomerge dialog box by dragging photos from the photo bin into the work area, and arranging them as you wish.

4 Explore the tools and controls in the Photomerge dialog box:

- Use the Zoom tool ( ) or the Navigator controls to zoom in or out of the image. Drag the red rectangle in the Navigator to shift the view in the zoomed image.

- Use the Select Image tool ( ) to select any of the photos in the work area. Drag with the pointer or use the arrow keys on the keyboard to reposition a selected image. To remove a photo from the composition, drag it from the work area into the light box strip above. To add an image to the composition, drag it from the light box into the work area.

- Use the Rotate Image tool ( ) to rotate a selected photo.

- Choose between the Reposition Only and Perspective settings.

- With the Perspective option activated, you can click in the selected image with the Set Vanishing Point tool ( ) to set a new vanishing point—the reference around which the other images will be composed.

5   When you're satisfied with the result, click OK. The Photomerge dialog box closes, and Photoshop Elements goes to work. You'll see windows open and close as you wait for Photoshop Elements to create the panorama.

6   If you like your new composition better than the one you created in the previous exercise, crop the image and save your work in the My CIB Work folder.

7   Choose File > Close All to close all open windows. When asked whether you want to save your changes, click No.

8   Switch back to the Organizer.

Vanishing Point

A vanishing point is the point at which receding parallel lines seem to meet when seen in perspective. For example, as a road stretches out ahead of you, it appears to grow narrower with distance, until it has almost no width at the horizon. This is the vanishing point.

You can change the perspective of the Photomerge Panorama composition by specifying the location of the vanishing point. Select Perspective under Settings in the Photomerge dialog box, and then click in the image with the Vanishing Point tool to reset the location of the vanishing point in reference to which the Photomerge Panorama will be composed.

Creating a composite group shot

Shooting the perfect group photo is a difficult task, especially if you have a large family of squirmy kids. Fortunately, Photoshop Elements offers a solution: a powerful photo blending tool called Photomerge Group Shot. The next exercise will show you how multiple photos can be blended together into one with amazing precision. Gone are those family photos where someone has their eyes closed, someone else has looked away at the wrong moment, and you-know-who has just made an even odder facial expression than usual. Photomerge Group Shot lets you merge the best parts of several images into the perfect group photo.

1   If the Organizer is not currently active, switch to it now.

2   In the Keyword Tags palette, click the Find box for the Lesson 10 keyword tag.

3 In the Photo Browser, Ctrl-click to select the three pictures of a girl sitting on a wall: 10_02_a.psd, 10_02_b.psd, and 10_02_c.psd.

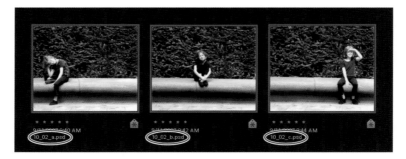

For the purposes of this exercise, we'll use these three distinctly different source images to make it easier for you to learn the technique but you would usually use the Photomerge Group Shot feature to create a merged image from a series of very similar source images such as you might capture with your camera's burst mode.

▶ **Tip:** The Photomerge Faces tool works similarly to the Photomerge Group Shot tool, except that it's specialized for working with faces. You can have a lot of fun merging different faces into one. Try merging parts of a picture of your own face with one of your spouse to predict the possible appearance of future offspring. Choose File > New > Photomerge Faces, or click the Faces button in the Photomerge palette In Guided Edit mode to create your own Frankenface.

4 Choose File > New > Photomerge Group Shot.

Photoshop Elements will load the Editor workspace and start the Photomerge Group Shot process.

5 (Optional) If you want to work with photos not currently in the Organizer (or you want to avoid switching to the Organizer first), you can also open the photos directly in the Editor. Select the image thumbnails in the Project Bin, switch to Guided Edit mode, and select Group Shot under Photomerge.

6 Photoshop Elements has automatically placed the first image (10_02_a.psd) as the source image. Drag the yellow framed image (10_02_b.psd) from the Project Bin and drop it into the Final image area on the right.

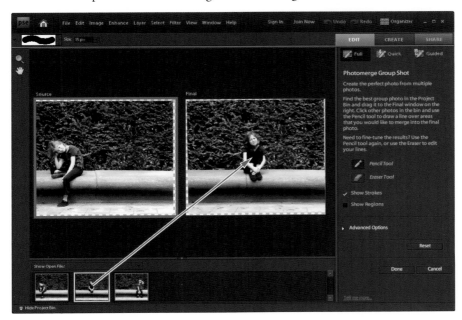

7 Use the Zoom tool to zoom in on the image so you can see all of the girl in the Source image and at least part of the girl in the Final image. Use the Hand tool to reposition the view if necessary.

8 In the Photomerge Group Shot panel, select the Pencil Tool.

9 With the Pencil tool( ), draw one stroke from head to toe of the girl in the source image, as shown in the illustration below. When you release the pointer, Photoshop Elements will merge the girl from the Source image into the Final image—including her shadow on the stone! Seeing the magic of this tool in action will probably cause you some healthy mistrust whenever you come across an unlikely photo in the future. If necessary, use the Pencil tool to add additional image areas from the source. You can use the Eraser tool ( ) to delete a stroke—or parts of a stroke—drawn with the Pencil tool. The image copied to the Final image will be adjusted accordingly.

● **Note:** Sometimes it can be a little tricky to make the perfect selection—especially when you're working with a more complex source image than our example. You may find you are copying more of the source image than you want. If you've switched several times between the Pencil and Eraser tools but you still can't get the selection right, it's better to undo the operation and start again. Try modifying the shape that you're drawing with the Pencil tool and making shorter strokes.

10 Double-click the green framed image (10_02_c.psd) in the Project Bin to make it the Source image. Use the Hand tool to move the Source image in its frame so you can see the girl, and then use the Pencil tool to add her to the Final image.

11 To see which part of each of the three source images was used for the merged composition, first click the Fit Screen button above the edit pane so that you can see the entire image, and then activate the Show Regions option in the Photomerge Group Shot panel. The regions in the Final image are color coded.

12 Click the Actual Pixels button above the edit pane, or zoom in even closer, and then use the Hand tool to position the image at a region boundary in the Final image. Toggle Show Regions off and on while you look for imperfections along the region boundaries in the merged image. If necessary, you can use the Pencil and Eraser tools to add to or subtract from the portions of the source images that are being merged to the Final image. When you are satisfied with the result, click Done in the Photomerge Group Shot panel.

13 The merged image needs to be cropped slightly. In Full Edit mode, choose Image > Crop to place a cropping rectangle on the image. In Guided Edit mode, click Crop Photo in the Basic Photo Edits palette. In Full Edit mode, hold the Shift key as you drag the handles of the cropping rectangle to constrain the aspect ratio to that of the original photo. In Guided Edit mode, choose Use Photo Ratio from the Crop Box Size menu to maintain the original proportions. Click the Commit button at the bottom right of the cropping rectangle.

● **Note:** The menu command File > Close All is available only in the Full Edit mode. In the Quick Fix and Guided Edit modes you can close only one file at a time using the File > Close command.

14 Choose File > Save and save the merged image to your My CIB Work folder as **10_02_Work**, in Photoshop (*.PSD,*PDD) format, making sure that the Layers option is activated. If you are not in Full Edit mode, switch to it now, and then choose File > Close All and return to the Organizer.

Removing unwanted intruders

The Photomerge Scene Cleaner helps you improve a photo by removing passing cars, tourists, and other unwanted elements. This feature works best when you have several shots of the same scene, and when the objects that you wish to remove were moving. In fact, when you're sightseeing you should deliberately take a few extra shots of any busy scene so that later you can use the Photomerge Scene Cleaner to put together an unobstructed view.

Using the Scene Cleaner tool

In this first exercise, you'll politely remove a tourist who walked into shot at just the wrong moment.

1   In the Organizer, click the Find box next to the Lesson 10 keyword tag in the Keyword Tags palette. In the Photo Browser, Ctrl-click to select the images 10_03_a.jpg and 10_03_b.jpg. Click the Editor button at the top right corner of the Organizer window and choose Full Edit from the menu.

2   In the Editor, Ctrl-click to select both photos in the Photo Bin, and then choose File > New > Photomerge Scene Cleaner. Wait while Photoshop Elements auto-aligns the photos.

3   The first image in the Photo Bin, 10_03_b.jpg (framed in blue), has been loaded as the Source image. Drag the image framed in yellow, 10_03_a.jpg, into the Final pane. This is the image we will clean: the base image for your composite.

Note: You can use up to ten images in a single Scene Cleaner operation; the more images you use, the more chance that you'll produce a perfect result.

4   Zoom in and use the Hand tool to position the images so that you can see the lower right corner. Scroll down in the Photomerge Scene Cleaner Guided Edit panel so that you can see the tools at the bottom.

5   Select the Pencil tool (✐) in the Photomerge Scene Cleaner panel and drag a line through the man's head in the foreground of the Final image.

6   Move the pointer away from the image window and wait a moment while information is copied from the source photo to cover the unwanted area in the Final image.

►**Tip:** You can hold down the Shift key as you drag with the Pencil tool to constrain the movement to a straight line.

7   Click the Fit Screen button above the edit window. You can see that the Source image has some information across the top and down the right hand side of the photo that is missing from the Final image. Make sure the Pencil tool is selected, and then drag a line through those areas in either image. *(See the illustration on the next page.)*

8 Working with only two images, there's not a lot more we can do. Click Done in the Photomerge Scene Cleaner panel, and then click the Fit Screen button above the edit window.

9 You can see that there are small empty patches in both the top left corner and the bottom right corner of the photo. You can crop the image to remedy that. Choose Image > Crop and drag the corner handles of the cropping rectangle to maximize the image while avoiding the empty areas. When you're satisfied, click the Commit button in the corner of the bounding box.

10 Choose File > Save. Name the file **10_03_Work** and save it to your My CIB Work folder, in Photoshop (PSD) format with the Layers option activated. Choose File > Close All and return to the Organizer.

Combining multiple photographs in one file

In this project, you'll combine three photos into one. You'll apply a clipping mask to one image to blend it into the background photo. Then, you'll add a selection from another image and learn how to remove the fringe that is often visible surrounding such a selection. Your final work file will contain all the original pixel information from all three source images, so that you can go back and make adjustments to your composition at any time.

Arranging the image layers

In this first exercise, you'll combine two images to act as a background to which you'll add foreground figures later. You'll blend an image of an airplane into the sky in a photograph of King Ludwig's castle in Bavaria—the masterpiece that inspired the design of Disney's Sleeping Beauty castle.

1   In the Organizer, click the Find box next to the Lesson 10 keyword tag in the Keyword Tags palette.

2   In the Photo Browser, Ctrl-click to select the images 10_04_a.jpg and 10_04_b.jpg: photos of a castle and an airplane. Click the Editor button at the top right corner of the Organizer window and choose Full Edit from the menu.

3   In the Editor, choose Window > Images > Tile to see both image windows.

4   Click the title bar of the image 10_04_b.jpg—the image of the airplane—to make it the active window. Select the Move tool (▶⊕). Hold down the Shift key and drag the airplane onto the image of the castle (10_04_a.jpg). Release the mouse button when you see a selection outline around the castle photo, and then release the Shift key.

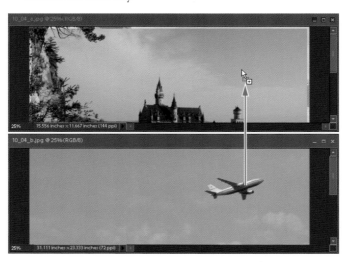

5 Close the image 10_04_b.jpg (the one you just copied from).

6 In the Layers palette, select Layer 1 (the airplane). Choose Image > Resize > Scale. In the tool options bar, make sure Constrain Proportions is selected, and then type **50%** in the W (width) field. The image is scaled proportionally. Click the Commit button in the lower right corner of the bounding box.

7 With the Move tool, drag the airplane on Layer 1 right into the upper right corner of the image. Drag the lower left handle of the bounding box to reduce the size of the airplane image further, as shown in the illustration below.

8   Release the mouse button, and then click the Commit button in the corner of the bounding box to accept the changes.

Creating a gradient clipping mask

A clipping mask allows part of an image to show while hiding the rest by making it transparent.

In the next steps you'll create a gradient that fades from fully opaque to fully transparent, and then use this gradient as a clipping mask to blend the castle and aircraft layers together.

1   In the Layers palette, click the New Layer button (⬛) to create a new blank layer, named Layer 2.

2   In the toolbox, select the Gradient tool (⬛) and click the Default Foreground And Background Colors button beside the foreground and background color swatches, or press the D key on your keyboard.

3   In the tool options bar, click the arrow to open the gradient selection menu. Locate the Foreground to Transparent thumbnail (the name of the swatch appears in a tooltip when you roll the cursor over it). Double-click the Foreground To Transparent gradient swatch.

4   Make sure that the other settings in the tool options bar are as set up as you see in the illustration. Click the Radial Gradient (⬛) button. Set the Mode to Normal, the Opacity to 100%, disable Reverse, and activate Transparency.

5 Make sure that Layer 2 is still selected in the Layers palette. Drag a short line downwards from the center of the airplane with the Gradient tool, and then release the mouse button.

The circular gradient appears on layer 2, fading from opaque black in the center and gradually becoming transparent towards the edges. You'll use this gradient as a clipping mask for the image of the airplane in Layer 1, making the airplane visible while the sky that surrounds it blends smoothly into the sky of the background image.

Applying the clipping mask to a layer

Now that you have your gradient layer, it's time to put it to work.

1 In the Layers palette, drag Layer 2—the layer with the new gradient—into the position below Layer 1.

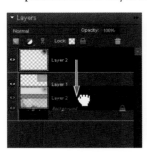 

2 Select Layer 1, now the top layer, and then choose Layer > Group With Previous.

This action defines Layer 2 as the clipping mask for Layer 1. In the Layers palette, Layer 1 is now indented and shows a tiny arrow beside its thumbnail, pointing down to Layer 2. In the image window, the image of the airplane image now blends nicely with the castle photo.

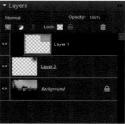

3   Choose File > Save As. In the Save As dialog box, name the file **10_04_Work** and save it to your My CIB Work folder, in Photoshop (PSD) format with the Layers option activated. If Save in Version Set with Original is selected, disable it before you click Save. If the Photoshop Elements Format Options dialog box appears, keep Maximize Compatibility selected and click OK.

Creating a clean edge with defringing

Defringing removes the annoying halo of color that often surrounds a selection pasted into another image. In this exercise you'll composite an image of a family so that they appear to be standing in front of the fence in the castle picture by selecting and deleting the background and using the Defringe feature to blend the selection halo into the background.

1   Switch to the Organizer, select the file 10_04_c.jpg, the picture of the family, and open it in Full Edit mode.

2 With the image 10_04_c.jpg selected as the active window in the edit pane, choose Select > All. Choose Edit > Copy, and then File > Close. Select the Background layer of the image 10_04_Work. psd, and then choose Edit > Paste. The image of the family is placed on a new layer, named Layer 3, just above the background layer.

3 With Layer 3 still selected in the Layers palette, choose Image > Resize > Scale.

4 In the tool options bar, make sure Constrain Proportions is selected, and then type **80%** in the W (width) field. Click the Commit button near the lower right corner of the bounding box to accept the changes.

5 If necessary, scroll to see the lower left corner of the image in the document window. Select the Move tool and drag the image in Layer 3 to position it flush with the lower left corner of the castle image.

6 Select the Magic Wand tool ($\small\diagdown$). In the tool options bar, set the Tolerance to **25**, activate Anti-alias, and disable Contiguous and All Layers. Click on the pink-colored background of the family image with the Magic Wand tool. If necessary, hold down the Shift key and click to select any unselected pink areas in the background.

7   Press the Delete key to delete the pink background. Press Ctrl+D, or choose Select > Deselect to clear the selection.

8   Zoom in to the area between the man's right hand and his sweater in the lower left corner of the image. A pinkish fringe or halo is clearly visible here.

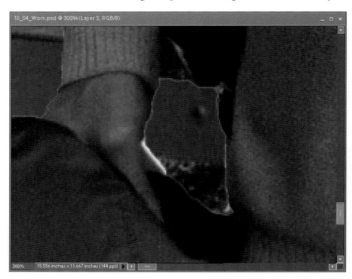

9   Choose Enhance > Adjust Color > Defringe Layer. In the Defringe dialog box, enter **1** pixel for the width and click OK. The fringe is eliminated.

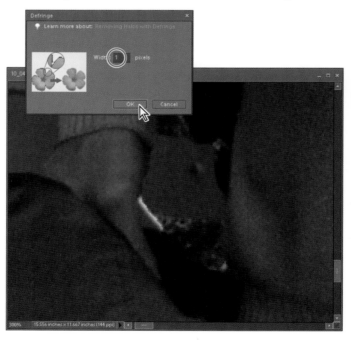

10 Double-click the Hand tool in the toolbox, or click the Fit Screen button in the tool options bar, to fit the whole image in the edit window.

11 Make sure that Layer 3 is still selected in the Layers palette. Select the Move tool in the toolbox and drag the top right handle of the selection rectangle to enlarge the image of the family so that they become more the focus of the composition. Click the Commit button near the lower right corner of the selection rectangle to accept the changes.

12 Choose File > Save, and then close the document and return to the Organizer.

Congratulations, you've completed the last exercise in this lesson. You've learned how to create a stunning composite panorama, how to merge multiple photos into the perfect group shot, how to remove obstructions from a view, and how to compose several photos into a single image by arranging layers and using a gradient layer as a clipping mask. Take a moment to work through the lesson review on the next page before you move on to the next chapter, "Advanced Editing Techniques."

Review questions

1 In the Photomerge dialog box, which tools can be used to fine-tune a panorama created from multiple images, and how do they work?

2 What does the Photomerge Group Shot tool do?

3 Why is it that sometimes when you think you're finished with a transformation in Photoshop Elements you cannot select another tool or perform other actions?

4 What is a fringe and how can you remove it?

Review answers

1 The Select Image tool is used to select a specific image from within the merged panorama. This tool can also be used to drag an image so that it lines up more closely with the other images in the panorama. The Rotate Image tool is used to rotate merged images so that their content aligns seamlessly. The Set Vanishing Point tool is used to specify the vanishing point for the perspective in the panorama. Setting the vanishing point in a different photo changes the point around which the other photos will be stretched and skewed to match the perspective.

2 With the Photomerge Group Shot tool you can pick and choose the best parts of several pictures taken successively, and merge them together to form one perfect picture.

3 Photoshop Elements is waiting for you to confirm the transformation by clicking the Commit button, or by double-clicking inside the transformation boundary.

4 A fringe is the annoying halo of color that often surrounds a selection pasted into another image. When the copied area is pasted onto another background color, or the selected background is deleted, you can see pixels of the original background color around the edges of your selection. The Defringe Layer command (Enhance > Adjust Color > Defringe Layer) blends the halo away so you won't see an artificial-looking line.

11 ADVANCED EDITING TECHNIQUES

Lesson Overview

In this final chapter you'll learn some advanced editing techniques and try some of the innovative tools that Adobe Photoshop Elements provides to help you improve the quality and clarity of your images.

This lesson will introduce some essential concepts and skills for making the most of your photos:

- Working with raw images
- Save conversions in the DNG format
- Using a histograms to assess a photo
- Improving the quality of highlights and shadows
- Resizing and sharpening an image
- Creating custom effects in the filter gallery
- Using the Cookie Cutter tool

 You'll probably need between one and two hours to complete this lesson.

Discover the advantages of working with raw images in the Camera Raw window, where the easy-to-use controls make it simple to correct and adjust your photos like a professional. Learn how to use the Histogram palette to help you understand what a less-than-perfect picture needs and to give you visual feedback on the solutions you apply. Finally, have some fun putting together your own filter effects.

Getting started

● Note: Before you start working on this lesson, make sure that you've installed the software on your computer from the application CD (see the Photoshop Elements 7 documentation) and that you have correctly copied the Lessons folder from the CD in the back of this book onto your computer's hard disk (see "Copying the Classroom in a Book files" on page 2).

The exercises in this chapter build on the skills and concepts covered in earlier lessons. This lesson assumes that you are already familiar with the Photoshop Elements interface, and that you recognize the Organizer and Editor workspaces. If you find that you need more background information as you go along, review "Getting Started" and "A Quick Tour of Photoshop Elements" at the start of this book, or refer to Photoshop Elements Help.

1 Start Adobe Photoshop Elements, and choose Organize in the Welcome screen.

2 For the exercises in this lesson, you'll use images from the CIB Catalog you created earlier in the book. The name of the currently active catalog is displayed in the lower-left corner of the Organizer window. If necessary, choose File > Catalog and select the CIB Catalog in the Catalog Manager dialog box.

If you don't see the CIB Catalog, you should review the procedures in "Copying the Lessons files from the CD" on page 2, and "Creating a catalog" on page 3.

3 In the Organizer, type the word **coast** into the Text Search box at the left of the bar above the Photo Browser. The Photo Browser shows only the file 11_01_coastline.ORF, a raw image from an Olympus digital camera. Select the file in the Photo Browser, click the Editor button at the upper right of the Organizer window and choose Full Edit from the menu.

4 The Camera Raw dialog box appears. Make sure that Preview is activated.

What is a raw image?

Raw files are referred to as such because, unlike many of the more common image file formats that you may recognize, such as JPEG or GIF, they are unprocessed by the digital camera or image scanner. In other words, a raw file contains all the image data captured for every pixel by the camera's sensors, without any software instructions about how that data is to be interpreted and displayed as an image on any particular device.

A limited but basically effective analogy or model for understanding the distinction is the difference between sending a film off for automatic processing by a commercial machine and using your own darkroom where you can control everything from the development of the negative to the way the image is exposed and printed onto paper.

The benefits of a raw image

Raw images are high-quality image files that contain the maximum amount of original image data in a relatively small file size. Though larger than a compressed image such as a JPEG file, a raw image contains more data than a TIFF image and uses less space.

Many types of image processing result in loss of data, effectively degrading the quality of the image. If a camera produces compressed files for instance, some data deemed superfluous is discarded. If a camera maps the whole range of captured image data to a defined color space, the spread of the image data can be narrowed. Processes such as sharpening and white balance correction will also alter the original captured data.

Whether you are an amateur photographer or a professional, it can be difficult to understand all the process settings on your digital camera and just what they mean in terms of data loss and image degradation. One solution is to use the camera's raw setting. Raw images are derived directly from the camera's sensors, prior to any camera processing. Not all digital cameras have the capability to capture raw images, but many of the newer and more advanced cameras do offer this option.

Capturing your photos in a raw format means you have more flexibility when it comes to producing the image you want. Many of the camera settings such as sharpening, white balance, levels, and color adjustments can be undone when you're working with your image in Photoshop Elements. For instance, automatic adjustments to exposure can be undone and recalculated based on the raw data.

Another advantage is that, because a raw image has 12 bits of data per pixel, you are able to extract shadow and highlight detail that would have been lost in the 8 bits/channel JPEG or TIFF formats.

Raw files provide an archival image format, much like a digital negative. In much the same way that you could produce a range of vastly different prints from the same film negative in a darkroom, you can reprocess a raw file repeatedly to achieve whatever results you want. Photoshop Elements doesn't save your changes to the original raw file; rather, it saves the settings you used to process it.

Note: Raw filenames have different extensions, depending on the camera used to capture the image. Examples are Canon's .CRW and .CR2, Epson's .ERF, Fuji's .RAF, Kodak's .KDE and .DER, Minolta's .MRW, Olympus'.ORF, Pentax's .PTX and .PEF, Panasonic's .RAW, and the various flavors of Nikon's .NEF.

Improving a camera raw image

Note: Any adjustment you make to an image results in a loss of data. Because you are working with much more information in a RAW file, any changes you make to settings such as exposure and white balance will have less impact in this way than if you made the same changes in a .PSD, TIFF, or JPEG file.

On the right side of the Camera Raw window is a control panel with three tabs: Basic, Detail and Camera Calibration. The Basic tab contains controls for image correction that allow you to make adjustments that are not possible with the standard editing tools in Photoshop Elements. The Detail tab contains controls for applying sharpening and reducing noise. For this exercise you'll use the controls in the Basic tab.

When you open a camera raw file, Photoshop Elements reads information in the file to ascertain which model of camera created it and applies the appropriate camera settings to the image data. In the control panel Options menu you can save the current settings as the default for the camera that created the image by choosing Save New Camera Raw Defaults, or have Photoshop Elements use the default settings for your camera by choosing Reset Camera Raw Defaults.

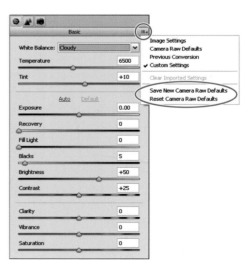

Adjusting the white balance

White balance presets can be helpful when you need to compensate for color casts in a photo caused by poor lighting conditions when the image was captured or incorrect camera settings. For example, if your camera was not set up correctly to deal with sunny conditions, you could correct the image by choosing the Daylight preset from the White Balance menu.

1   Experiment with some of the presets available in the White Balance menu. Compare the As Shot, Auto, Daylight, and Cloudy settings. Notice the effects on the preview image as you change the white balance preset. In the following pages you'll discover why setting the correct white balance is so important to the overall look of the image.

2   For now, choose As Shot from the White Balance presets menu.

3   Zoom into the image by choosing 100% from the Zoom Level menu in the lower left corner of the preview window.

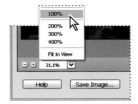

4   Select the Hand tool () from the toolbar above the preview window, and drag the image in the preview window so that you can see parts of the blue sky as well as some of the green grass on top of the cliffs.

5   Select the White Balance tool (🖋), right beside the Hand tool in the toolbar.

6   Sample a neutral color in the image—a good choice is a medium-light gray that is neither too warm or too cool—by clicking it with the White balance tool.

The White Balance is now set to Custom and the image has lost its blue cast.

Camera Raw white balance settings

A digital camera records the white balance at the time of exposure as metadata, which you can see when you open the file in the Camera Raw dialog box. This setting usually yields the correct color temperature. You can adjust it if the white balance is not quite right. The Basic tab in the Photoshop Camera Raw dialog box includes three controls for correcting a color cast in your image:

White Balance Sets the color balance of the image to reflect the lighting conditions under which the photo was taken. A white balance preset may produce satisfactory results or you may want to customize the Temperature and Tint settings.

Temperature Fine-tunes the white balance to a custom color temperature. Move the slider to the left to correct a photo taken in light of a lower color temperature; the plug-in makes the image colors bluer to compensate for the lower color temperature of yellowish ambient light. Move the slider to the right to correct a photo taken in light of higher color temperature; the plug-in makes the image colors warmer to compensate for the higher color temperature of bluish ambient light.

Tint Fine-tunes the white balance to compensate for a green or magenta tint. Move the slider to the left to add green to the photo; move it to the right to add magenta.

To adjust the white balance quickly, click an area in the preview image that should be a neutral gray or white with the White Balance tool. The Temperature and Tint sliders automatically adjust to make the selected color as close to neutral as possible. If you're using a white area to set the white balance, choose a highlight area that contains significant white detail rather than a specular highlight.

—From Photoshop Elements Help

Working with the Temperature and Tint settings

The White Balance tool accurately removes any color cast or tint from an image but you may still want to tweak the Temperature and Tint settings. Depending upon the subject matter and the effect you wish to achieve, you might actually want a slight, controlled color tint. In this instance, the color temperature seems fine, but you can fine-tune the green/magenta balance of the image using the Tint control.

1   Zoom out to view the entire picture either by double-clicking the Hand tool or by choosing Fit In View from the Zoom Level menu in the lower left corner of the preview window.

2   Test the Temperature slider in the Basic tab by dragging it from one end of its range to the other. You'll see that the colors of the image become cooler or warmer as you move the slider. In this case, the corrected temperature of the image seemed fine but this slider could help you on other occasions—for toning down the overly warm tones resulting from tungsten lighting, for example.

3   Reset the Temperature control to the corrected value of 6050 either by dragging the slider or typing the value 6050 into the Temperature text box.

4   Experiment with the extremes of the Tint slider. The corrected value was +6. Change the setting to +10 with the slider or type **+10** into the Tint text box.

Using the tone controls on a raw image

The settings for tonal adjustments are located below the White Balance controls in the Basic tab. In this exercise, you'll use these controls to correct exposure, check highlights and shadows, and adjust brightness, contrast, and saturation. Before you adjust any of the settings, you should understand what each of the controls does:

Exposure adjusts the lightness or darkness of an image. Underexposed images are too dark and look dull and murky; overexposed images are too light and look washed out. Use the Exposure control to lighten an underexposed image or correct the faded look of an overexposed image.

Recovery attempts to recover details from burned-out highlights. The Recovery control can reconstruct some details in areas where one or two color channels are clipped to white. Clipping occurs when a pixel's color values are higher or lower than the range of values that can be represented in the image; over-bright values are clipped to output white, and over-dark values are clipped to output black.

Fill Light recovers details from shadows, without brightening blacks. The Fill Light control does something close to the inverse of the Recovery control, reconstructing detail in areas where one or two color channels are clipped to black.

Blacks specifies which input levels are mapped to black in the final image. Raising the Blacks value expands the areas that are mapped to black.

Brightness adjusts the brightness of the image, much as the Exposure slider does. However, instead of clipping the image in the highlights (areas that are completely white, with no detail) or shadows (areas that are completely black, with no detail), Brightness compresses the highlights and expands the shadows when you move the slider to the right. In general, use the Brightness slider to adjust the overall brightness after you have set the white and black clipping points with the Exposure and Blacks sliders.

Contrast is the amount of difference in brightness between light and dark areas of an image. The Contrast control determines the number of shades in the image, and has the most effect in the midtones. An image without enough contrast can appear flat or washed out. Use the Contrast slider to adjust the midtone contrast after setting the Exposure, Blacks, and Brightness values.

Clarity sharpens the definition of edges in the image. This process helps restore detail and sharpness that tonal adjustments may reduce.

Vibrance adjusts the saturation so that clipping is minimized as colors approach full saturation, acting on all lower saturated colors but having less impact on higher saturated colors. Vibrance also prevents skin tones from becoming oversaturated.

Saturation is the purity, or strength, of a color. A fully saturated color contains no gray. The Saturation control makes colors more vivid (less black or white added) or more muted (more black or white added).

First you'll adjust the Exposure setting, checking for clipping in the brighter areas.

1 Hold down the Alt key as you drag the Exposure slider to see where clipping occurs in the highlights—which parts of the image will be forced towards white. Set the Exposure to +0.25. You can also see the clipping in the histogram.

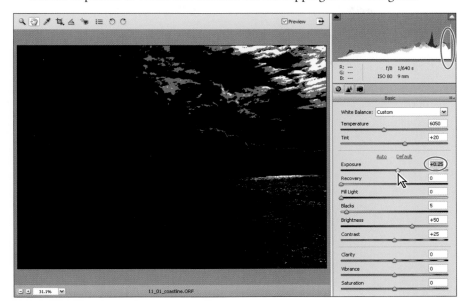

2 Hold down the Alt key as you drag the Recovery slider to 60. Most of the clipping is corrected, as you can see in both the preview and the histogram.

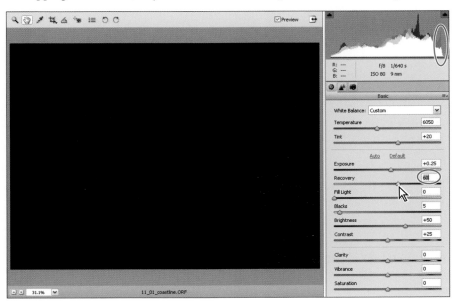

3 Hold down the Alt key and drag the Black slider. Any areas that appear in the clipping preview will be forced to a solid black. Release the mouse button when only the deepest areas of shadow in the image register as black. We moved the slider to 10.

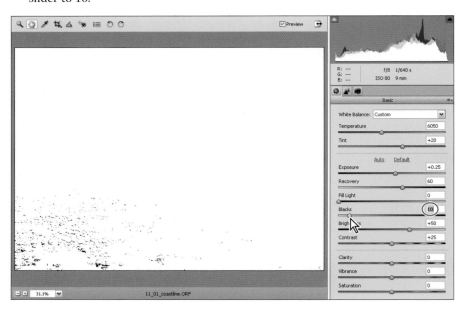

▶ **Tip:** For an interesting effect, drag the Saturation slider all the way to the left, essentially creating a three-color gray-scale.

4 Click the Brightness slider and press the up arrow on the keyboard to increase the value to 64. Click the Contrast slider and press the up arrow key on the keyboard to increase the value to +50. Drag the Clarity slider to 28.

The image, which was shot on a cloudy day and looked a little dull, now shows a larger range of detail and is more vivid and warmer in color.

Saving the image

You can reprocess this raw file repeatedly to achieve the results you want by saving it in the DNG format. Photoshop Elements doesn't save your changes to the original raw file—it saves only the settings you used to process it.

About the DNG format

Raw file formats are becoming common in digital photography. However, each camera manufacturer has its own proprietary raw format. This means that not every raw file can be read by software other than that provided with the camera. This may make it difficult to use these images in the future, as the camera manufacturers might not support these file formats indefinitely. Proprietary formats are also a problem if you want to use software other than that supplied by the camera manufacturers.

To help alleviate these problems, you can save raw images from Photoshop Elements in the DNG format, a publicly available archival format for raw files generated by digital cameras. The DNG format provides an open standard for files created by different camera models, and helps to ensure that you will be able to access your files in the future.

1 To convert and save the image, click the Save Image button at the lower left of the Camera Raw dialog box. The Save Options dialog box appears.

2 Under Destination, click the Select Folder button. In the Select Destination Folder dialog box, click your My CIB Work folder, and then click Select.

3 Under File Naming, leave Document Name selected in the menu on the left. Click the menu on the right and select 1 Digit Serial Number. This adds the number 1 following the name.

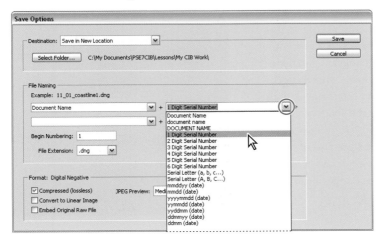

4 Click Save. The file, along with the present settings, will be saved in DNG format, which you can reprocess repeatedly.

5 Click the Open Image button in the right lower corner of the Camera Raw dialog box. Your image will open in the Editor window of Photoshop Elements.

6 In the Editor, choose File > Save. Navigate to your My CIB Work folder, name the file 11_01_coastline_Work.psd, choose the Photoshop format, and then click Save.

7 Choose File > Close.

You've now experienced some of the advantages of using a camera raw format. Even though this format gives you more control and allows you to edit your image in a non-destructive way, a lot of professionals choose not to use raw format. Raw files are usually considerably bigger than high-quality JPEGs and take much longer to be saved in your camera—quite a disadvantage for action shots or when you're taking a lot of pictures.

About histograms

For your images in JPEG, TIFF, and PSD formats, you'll do most of your serious editing in Full Edit mode. In this part of the lesson, you will learn how to use the histogram to understand what changes can be made to your images to improve their quality.

In the next exercises, you'll work on an image that was shot in poor lighting and also has a slight magenta cast. This is quite a common problem—many digital cameras introduce a slight color cast into images.

Using the histogram

A histogram is a graph representing the spread of tonal ranges present in an image. The Histogram palette in the Editor (Window > Histogram), indicates whether the image contains enough detail in the shadows (at the left end of the curve), midtones, and highlights (at the right end of the curve). The histogram can help you recognize where changes need to be made in the image.

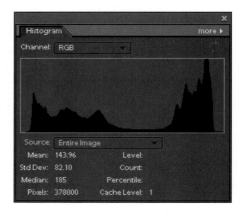

In the histogram below it's very apparent that there is not a good spread of tonal information in this image. You can see clearly that the image is deficient in the mid-tones, which is why it has a flat appearance, lacking in midtone contrast.

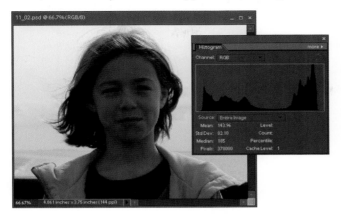

Tonal corrections such as lightening an image remove information. Excessive correction causes posterization, or color-banding in the image. The histogram in the illustration below reveals that this image is already lacking detail. You can see gaps, bands, and anomalous spikes in the curve. Any further modifications made to the image will degrade it even more.

Understanding highlights and shadows

In the next part of this lesson, you'll adjust the highlights and shadows and make additional tonal corrections to a photo while keeping an eye on the Histogram.

1 In the Editor, make sure you are in Full Edit mode. Choose File > Open, navigate to your Lesson11 folder, select the file 11_02.psd, and click Open.

2 Choose File > Save As. Name the image **11_02_Work** and save it to your My CIB Work folder in Photoshop (PSD) format.

3   If the Histogram palette is not already visible, choose Window > Histogram.

4   In order to see the effects of your adjustments more directly, you can drag the Histogram palette and position it beside the face of the girl. You'll notice that the face is a little dark.

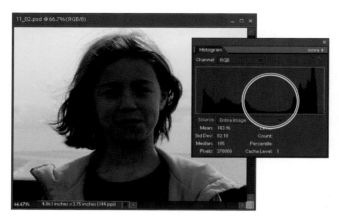

According to the histogram, there is a lack of data in the midtone range for this image—it needs more information in the midtones and less in the shadows and highlights. You'll adjust the tonal range of this image using the Levels controls.

Adjusting levels

1   Choose Enhance > Adjust Lighting > Levels. The Levels dialog box appears. Make sure that Preview is activated.

In this exercise you'll use the shadows (left), midtone (middle), and highlights (right) sliders below the histogram graph in the Levels palette as well as the Set Black Point (left), Set Gray Point (middle), and Set White Point (right) eyedroppers.

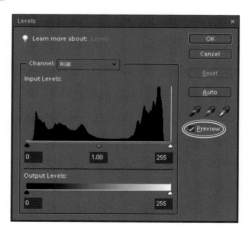

Although the midtones range is the most problematic area of this image, it is important to first adjust the highlights and shadows correctly.

We'll look at two slightly different methods for setting the white and black points in the image using the Levels controls.

2   In the Levels dialog box, hold down the Alt key as you drag the highlights slider to the left to a value of 242—just inside the right-hand end of the tonal curve. The clipping preview shows you where the brightest parts of the image are: a few highlights in the girl's hair and a portion of the sky near the upper right corner of the image.

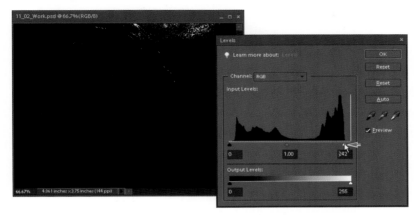

3   Watch the histogram as you release first the Alt key and the mouse button. The curve in the histogram shifts—possibly a bit far—to the right. You can see that the right-hand end of the curve is truncated. Move the highlights slider in the Levels controls to a value of 245. The histogram is adjusted accordingly.

4   In the Levels dialog box, click Reset and we'll try another method for adjusting the highlights. Select the Set White Point Eyedropper tool and watch the histogram as you click in the brightest part of the sky.

▶ **Tip:** If your image has an easily identified neutral tone, you can remove a color cast quickly using the Set White Point Eyedropper tool. Neutrals are areas in the image that contain only a gray tone mixed with as little color as possible.

The result is very similar to the previous method, but it won't be as easy to fine-tune the clipping at the right end of the curve. Now you'll correct the shadows.

5   Hold down the Alt key and drag the shadow slider to the right to a value of 16, where the area below the girl's right ear shows as a dark spot in the clipping preview. Watch the histogram as you release the mouse button and the Alt key.

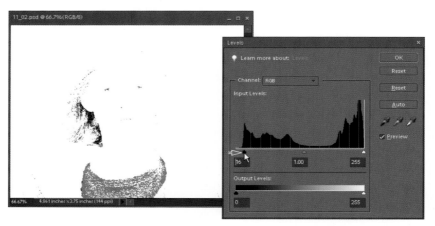

6   In the Levels controls, drag the midtone slider (the gray triangle below the center of the graph) to the left to set the midtone value to 1.50.

7   Notice the change in the Histogram. Compare the original data (displayed in gray) to the data for the corrections that you have made (displayed in black). Some gaps have been created. You want to avoid creating large gaps—even if the image still looks fine on screen, large gaps may cause a loss of data that will be visible as color banding when printed.

8   Click OK to close the Levels dialog box. If an Adobe Photoshop Elements alert dialog box appears, click Yes.

9   Select Edit > Undo Levels, or press Ctrl+Z to see how the image looked prior to redistributing the tonal values. Choose Edit > Redo Levels, or Press Ctrl+Y to reinstate your corrections. Leave this image open for the next part of this lesson.

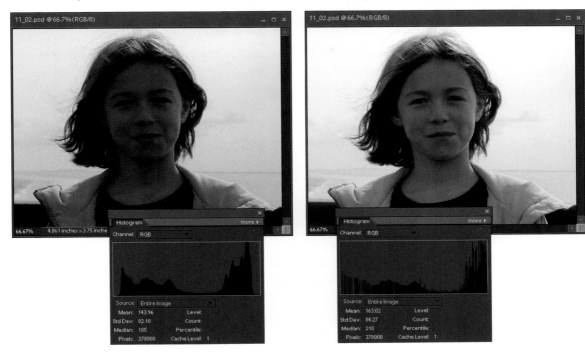

About Unsharp Mask

Now you can add some crispness to the image, which will make it look much better when printed. Using the sharpening tools correctly can improve an image significantly.

In this exercise you'll use the Unsharp Mask feature in Photoshop Elements. How can something be *un*sharp and yet sharpen an image? The term unsharp mask has it roots in the print production industry: the technique was implemented by making an out-of-focus negative film—the unsharp mask—and then printing the original in a sandwich with this unsharp mask. This produced a halo around the edges of objects—optically giving them more definition.

If you are planning to resize an image, do it before you apply the Unsharp mask filter. The halo effect mentioned above can appear as an obvious artefact if it is scaled with the image.

1   With the file 11_02_Work.psd still open in the Editor, choose Image > Resize > Image Size.

This image needs to be made smaller, but with a higher resolution (pixels per inch).

2   If necessary, disable the Resample Image check box at the bottom of the dialog box, and then type **300** in the Resolution text field. Notice that the width and height values adjust. This method increases the resolution in the image without losing information.

Resolution refers to the fineness of detail you can see in an image, measured in pixels per inch (ppi): the more pixels per inch, the greater the resolution. Generally, the higher the resolution of your image, the better the printed result.

3   Now select Resample Image, to reduce the height and width of the image without affecting the resolution. Click OK.

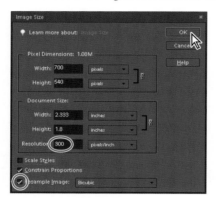

4   Choose File > Save. Keep the file open for the next part of this lesson.

Applying the Unsharp Mask filter

Before you apply any filter in Adobe Photoshop Elements, it is best to set the zoom level to 100%.

1   With the file 11_02_Work.psd still open in the Editor, choose View > Actual Pixels.

2   Choose Enhance > Unsharp Mask. The Unsharp Mask dialog box appears.

The amount of unsharp masking that you apply is determined by the subject matter. A portrait, such as this image, should be softer than an image of an object such as an automobile. The adjustments range from 1 to 500, with 500 being the sharpest.

3   Drag the Amount slider or type **125** in the Amount text field. Leave the Radius at 1 pixel.

4   Increase the Threshold only slightly to 2 pixels. Threshold is a key control in this dialog box, as it tells the filter what not to sharpen. In this case the value 2 means that a pixel will not be sharpened if it is within 2 shades of the pixel beside it (on a scale of 255).

▶ **Tip:** Disable the preview in the Unsharp Mask window by clicking on the preview pane and holding down the mouse button. When you release the mouse button, the preview is enabled again. To see another part of the image, drag the image in the preview pane.

5   Click OK to close the Unsharp Mask dialog box.

6   Choose File > Save, and then File > Close.

Without sharpening.

Unsharp mask applied.

As you've seen, the Unsharp Mask filter can't mysteriously correct the focus of your image. It only gives the impression of crispness by increasing the contrast between adjacent pixels. As a rule of thumb, the Unsharp Mask filter should be applied to an image only once, as a final step in your processing. If you use Unsharp Mask too much, you'll run the risk of over sharpening your image producing artefacts that will give it a flaky, grainy look.

● **Note:** There are other ways to adjust the sharpness of your photos: Choose Enhance > Auto Sharpen or, if you want more control over the sharpening process, choose Enhance > Adjust Sharpness.

Creating effects using the filter gallery

You can have a lot of fun experimenting with filter effects using the Filter Gallery, where you can apply multiple filters to your image and tweak the way they work together, effectively creating new custom effects. Each filter has its own slider controls, giving you a great deal of control over the effect on your photo. The possibilities are endless—it's up to you to make the most of these filters and to apply them with discretion. Have a look at "About Filters" in Photoshop Elements Help to find out more about the different filters.

1   In the Organizer, use the Lesson 11 keyword tag to find the file 11_03.jpg in your Lesson 11 folder, Select the image in the Photo Browser, click the Editor button, and choose Full Edit from the menu.

2   Choose File > Save As. Navigate to your My CIB Work folder, name the file 11_03_Work, choose the Photoshop (*.PSD,*.PDD) format, and then click Save.

Many filters use the foreground and background colors currently active in the toolbar to create effects, so you should take a moment to set them now.

3   Click the Default Foreground And Background Color button beside the color swatches at the bottom of the toolbar. This resets the default colors: black in the foreground and white for the background.

4   Choose Filter > Filter Gallery. The Filter Gallery dialog box appears.

5   If necessary, use the menu in the lower left corner of the dialog box to set the magnification level at 100%. This view brings the image much closer so that the effects of the filters you apply are more obvious.

6 When you move the pointer over the image in the preview pane, the pointer changes into the hand tool (✋). Drag the image in the preview pane so that you can see the two kids on the right of the photo.

The center pane in the Filter Gallery window lists the available filters by category.

7 Expand the Brush Strokes category by clicking the arrow to the left of the category name, and then choose the Crosshatch filter.

8 Experiment with the control sliders. You can see the effect of the filter in the preview pane. Set the sliders as shown in the illustration below.

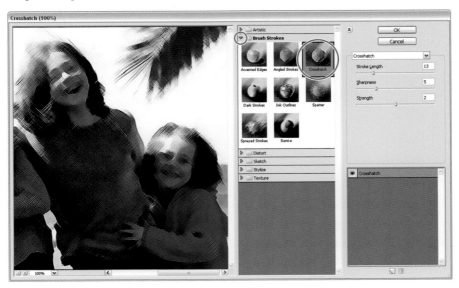

9   Click the New Effect layer button () at the lower right of the Filter Gallery dialog box, expand the Artistic filters category, and choose the Sponge filter. The Crosshatch and Sponge filters are applied simultaneously.

10 Set the Brush Size to 0, Definition to 2, and Smoothness to 8.

11 Click the New Effect Layer button again. If necessary, scroll down in the list of filters to see the Texture category. Expand the Texture category and select the Patchwork filter. Set both sliders to 0. Once again, the image has changed totally.

Experimenting with filters in the gallery

The possibilities are endless for the effects that you might create in your image by combining different filters at varied settings.

▶ **Tip:** It's a good idea to apply filters to a duplicate layer in your image, as it is not possible to undo filters after you've saved your file. Press Ctrl+J to duplicate a layer.

1 Click the button at the top right of the filters pane to hide the filters menu. Choose Fit In View from the zoom menu at the bottom left of the Preview pane.

2 Experiment with the three filters that you've applied, turning them off or on by clicking the eye icon to the left of each filter name.

3 Re-arrange the order of the filters by dragging them to new positions in the list. This will alter the way the filters interact.

4 There is no need to apply the changes to the image. Click Cancel to close the Filter Gallery dialog box, keeping the file open for the next exercise.

Using the Cookie Cutter tool

The Cookie Cutter tool enables you to crop an image with one of a library of Cookie Cutter shapes. In this exercise, you'll crop the image with a heart-shaped cutter.

1 Select the Cookie Cutter tool from the toolbox.

Tip: There are many more cutout shapes available. Click the double arrow in the upper right corner of the shapes palette to see a menu of 22 different categories.

2 Click the Shapes menu in the tool options bar to view the default selection of shapes.

3 Double-click to select the shape named Heart Card (the shape of a heart). The name of each shape appears as a tool tip when you move the pointer over its swatch.

4 From the Set Shape Options menu in the tool options bar, choose From Center.

Set Shape Options

Unconstrained Draws the shape to any size or dimension you'd like.

Defined Proportions Keeps the height and width of the cropped shape in proportion.

Defined Size Crops the photo to the exact size of the shape you choose.

Fixed Size Specifies exact measurements for the finished shape.

From Center Draws the shape from the center.

Enter a value for **Feather** to soften the edges of the finished shape.

Note: Feathering softens the edges of the cropped image so that the edges fade out and blend in with the background.

—From Adobe Photoshop Elements Help

5   Drag in the image to create the cutter shape. Press the Shift key as you drag to maintain the original aspect ratio of the shape, or press the Space key to reposition the shape. After releasing the pointer, you can use the handles on the bounding box to scale the shape. Click inside the bounding box and drag the shape to reposition it.

6   Click the Commit button at the lower right corner of the bounding box, or press Enter to crop the image. To cancel the cropping operation, click the Cancel button or press the Esc key.

7   Choose File > Save, and then File > Close.

Congratulations, you have finished the lesson on advanced editing techniques in Adobe Photoshop Elements. You discovered how to take advantage of the Camera Raw plug-in and learned how to correct images using the Histogram palette as both a diagnostic tool and a feedback reference. You also found out how to create custom effects using the Filter Gallery had a little fun with the Cookie Cutter tool.

Learning more

We hope you've gained confidence in using Photoshop Elements to bring out the best in your photographs. You've picked up some great tricks and techniques, but this book is just the start. You can learn even more by using the Photoshop Elements Help system, which is built into the application. Also, don't forget to look for tutorials, tips, and expert advice on the Adobe website, www.adobe.com.

Review questions

1 What is a camera raw image, and what are some of its advantages?

2 What are the different methods for adjusting the white balance in the Camera Raw window?

3 How do you use the Levels controls to correct highlights and shadows?

4 What is the Cookie Cutter tool used for?

Review answers

1 A raw file is one that is unprocessed by a digital camera. Not all cameras create raw files. One of the advantages of raw images is the flexibility of having detailed control over settings that are usually pre-applied by the camera. Image quality is another plus—because raw formats have 12 bits of available data, it's possible to extract shadow and highlight detail that would have been lost in an 8 bits/channel JPEG or TIFF file. Finally, raw files provide an archival image format, much like a digital negative: you can reprocess the file repeatedly to achieve the results you want, while your raw data remains unchanged.

2 In the Camera Raw window you can set the white balance in an image automatically by using the White Balance eyedropper. Clicking on a neutral color with the White Balance eyedropper automatically adjusts the Temperature and Tint sliders. Alternatively, you can choose a preset from the White Balance menu. The options include corrections based on a range of common lighting conditions. It's also possible to correct the white balance manually with the Temperature and Tint sliders.

3 In the Levels dialog box, you can adjust the shadows and highlights in your image by using either the slider controls below the Levels histogram, or the Set Black Point and Set White Point eyedroppers. You can hold down the Alt key as you drag a slider to see a clipping preview, which gives you visual feedback on the location of the darkest and lightest areas of your image. With the Set Black Point and Set White Point eyedroppers you can click directly in the image to define the white and black points, or double-click the eyedroppers to call up the color picker where you can define the values precisely.

4 The Cookie Cutter tool is used to crop an image into a variety of shapes. Use the default shapes set, or select a shape from an extensive library.

INDEX

Production Notes

The *Adobe Photoshop Elements 7 Classroom in a Book* was created electronically using Adobe InDesign CS3. Art was produced using Adobe InDesign, Adobe Illustrator, and Adobe Photoshop. The Myriad Pro and Warnock Pro OpenType families of typefaces were used throughout this book.

References to company names in the lessons are for demonstration purposes only and are not intended to refer to any actual organization or person.

Team credits

The following individuals contributed to the development of this edition of the *Adobe Photoshop Elements Classroom in a Book*:

Project coordinators, technical writers: Torsten Buck & Katrin Straub

Production: Manneken Pis Productions (www.manneken.be)

Copyediting & Proofreading: John Evans

Designer: Katrin Straub

Special thanks to Christine Yarrow.

Typefaces used

Adobe Myriad Pro and Adobe Warnock Pro are used throughout the lessons. For more information about OpenType and Adobe fonts, visit www.adobe.com/type/opentype/.

Photo Credits

Photographic images and illustrations supplied by Katrin Straub, Torsten Buck, John Evans, Han Buck, and Adobe Systems Incorporated. Photos are for use only with the lessons in the book.

Contributors

Torsten Buck has been involved in the development of software for the design and desktop publishing industries in Japan, China and the United States for almost 20 years. A Masters in Computer Science combined with a passion for typography have shaped a career that took Torsten from the development of ground-breaking Asian font technology in Hong Kong to a position as Head of Type Development at Adobe Systems in the USA. Currently he is the Director of Manneken Pis Productions and has authored a wide range of design software training books including several versions of *Adobe Photoshop Elements Classroom in a Book* and *Adobe Premiere Elements Classroom in a Book, Creating a Newsletter in InDesign: Visual QuickProject Guide*, and more recently *Adobe Photoshop Lightroom 2 Classroom in a Book* and *Adobe Creative Suite 4 Classroom in a Book*.

Katrin Straub is an artist, an MA in media studies, a graphic designer, and author. Her award-winning print, painting, and multimedia work has been exhibited worldwide. With more than 15 years experience in design, Katrin has worked as Design Director for companies such as Landor Associates and Fontworks in the United States, Hong Kong, and Japan. Her work includes packaging, promotional campaigns, multimedia, website design, and internationally recognized corporate and retail identities. She holds degrees from the FH Augsburg, ISIA Urbino, and The New School University in New York and has authored many books in the past 5 years, from *Adobe Creative Suite Idea Kit* to Classroom in a Book titles for Adobe Photoshop Lightroom 2, Adobe Creative Suite 4, Adobe Soundbooth, and several versions of *Adobe Photoshop Elements Classroom in a Book* and *Adobe Premiere Elements Classroom in a Book*.

John Evans has worked in computer graphics and design for more than 20 years—initially as a graphic designer, and then since 1993 as a multimedia author, software interface designer, and technical writer. His multimedia and digital illustration work associated with Japanese type attracted an award from Apple Computer Australia and was featured in Japan's leading digital design magazine. His other projects range from music education software for children to interface design for innovative Japanese font design software. As a technical writer his work includes software design specifications, user manuals, and more recently copyediting for *Adobe Lightroom 2 Classroom in a Book* and *Adobe Creative Suite 4 Classroom in a Book*.

Tao Buck and her sisters have been volunteering as photo models for the last three editions of *Photoshop Elements Classroom in a Book*. When she is grown up, Tao wants to work for WWF and make the world a better place, especially for all the cute animals.

Zoë Buck loves to juggle with numbers, play chess, do gymnastics, and at this very moment is considering becoming a vet.

Han Buck would like to become a painter (actually, she is one already) or else "work from home and do nothing like her parents."

Mia Buck strives to become a great pianist (although she does not believe in practicing).

ADOBE® PREMIERE® ELEMENTS 7

CLASSROOM IN A BOOK®

The official training workbook from Adobe Systems

www.adobepress.com

Adobe

CONTENTS

GETTING STARTED

Adobe® Premiere® Elements 7 delivers video-editing tools that balance power and versatility with ease of use. Adobe Premiere Elements 7 is ideal for home users, hobbyists, business users, and professional videographers—anyone who wants to produce high-quality movies and DVDs.

If you've used earlier versions of Adobe Premiere Elements, you'll find that this Classroom in a Book® covers the many new advanced skills and innovative features that Adobe Systems introduces in this version. If you're new to Adobe Premiere Elements, you'll learn the fundamental concepts and techniques that help you master this application.

About Classroom in a Book

Adobe Premiere Elements 7 Classroom in a Book is part of the official training series for Adobe graphics and publishing software developed by Adobe product experts. Most lessons in this book include self-paced projects that give you hands-on experience using Adobe Premiere Elements 7.

The *Adobe Premiere Elements 7 Classroom in a Book* includes a DVD attached to the inside back cover of this book. On the DVD you'll find all the files used for the lessons in this book. As an overview, in the first two lessons, you'll learn your way around Adobe Premiere Elements' interface, how to set up a project, and how to customize critical preferences.

In Lesson 3, you'll learn how to capture and otherwise import video into Adobe Premiere Elements. Starting with Lesson 4, and continuing through Lesson 13, you'll open projects on the DVD and learn how to convert your raw, captured clips into a polished movie.

Prerequisites

Before you begin working on the lessons in this book, make sure that you and your computer are ready.

Requirements for your computer

You'll need about 4.3 gigabytes (GB) of free space on your hard disk for the lesson files and the work files you'll create. Note that the lessons assume that you installed all templates and associated content available with the DVD version of Adobe Premiere Elements 7. If you see a template that's not installed on your computer, you should be able to simply choose another template and continue with the lesson.

Required skills

The lessons in this *Adobe Premiere Elements 7 Classroom in a Book* assume that you have a working knowledge of your computer and its operating system. This book does not teach the most basic and generic computer skills. If you can answer *yes* to the following questions, then you're probably well qualified to start working on the projects in these lessons. You will probably get most benefit from working on the lessons in the order in which they occur in the book.

- Do you know how to use the Microsoft Windows Start button and the Windows task bar? Can you open menus and submenus, and choose items from those menus?

- Do you know how to use My Computer, Windows Explorer, or Internet Explorer to find items stored in folders on your computer, or to browse the Internet?

- Are you comfortable using the mouse to move the pointer, select items, drag, and deselect? Have you used context menus, which open when you right-click items?

- When you have two or more open applications, do you know how to switch from one to another? Do you know how to switch to the Windows Desktop?

- Do you know how to open, close, and minimize individual windows? Can you move them to different locations on your screen? Can you resize a window by dragging?

- Can you scroll (vertically and horizontally) within a window to see contents that may not be visible in the displayed area?

- Are you familiar with the menus across the top of an application and how to use those menus?

- Have you used dialogs (special windows in the interface that display information), such as the Print dialog? Do you know how to click arrow icons to open a menu within a dialog?

- Can you open, save, and close a file? Are you familiar with word processing tasks, such as typing, selecting words, backspacing, deleting, copying, pasting, and changing text?
- Do you know how to open and find information in Microsoft Windows Help?

If there are gaps in your mastery of these skills, see the Microsoft documentation for your version of Windows. Or, ask a computer-savvy friend or instructor for help.

Installing Adobe Premiere Elements 7

Adobe Premiere Elements 7 software (sold separately) is intended for installation on a computer running Windows Vista® or Windows® XP. For system requirements and complete instructions on installing the software, see the Adobe Premiere Elements 7 application CD and documentation. To get the most from the projects in this book, you should install all the templates included with the software. Otherwise, you may notice missing-file error messages.

Copying the Classroom in a Book files

The DVD attached to the inside back cover of this book includes a Lessons folder containing all the electronic files for the lessons in this book. Follow the instructions to copy the files from the DVD, and then keep all the lesson files on your computer until after you have finished all the lessons.

● **Note:** The videos on the DVD are practice files provided for your personal use in these lessons. You are not authorized to use these videos commercially, or to publish or distribute them in any form without written permission from Adobe Systems, Inc., or other copyright holders.

Copying the Lessons files from the DVD

1   Insert the *Adobe Premiere Elements 7 Classroom in a Book* DVD into your DVD-ROM drive. If a message appears asking what you want Windows to do, select Open folder to view files using Windows Explorer, and click OK.

    If no message appears, open My Computer and double-click the DVD icon to open it.

2   Locate the Lessons folder inside the Adobe Premiere Elements 7 folder on the DVD and copy it to any convenient folder on your computer. Just remember where you copied it, because you'll be opening the lesson files frequently throughout the book. Inside the Lessons folder you will find individual folders containing project files needed for the completion of each lesson.

3   When your computer finishes copying the Lessons folder (which could take several minutes), remove the DVD from your DVD-ROM drive, and store it in a safe place for future use.

Additional resources

Adobe Premiere Elements 7 Classroom in a Book is not meant to replace documentation that comes with the program, nor is it designed to be a comprehensive reference for every feature in Adobe Premiere Elements 7. For additional information about program features, refer to any of these resources:

- Premiere Elements Help, which is built into the Adobe Premiere Elements 7 application. You can view it by choosing Help > Premiere Elements Help.

- The Premiere Elements 7 Quick Reference Card, which is included either in the box with your copy of Adobe Premiere Elements 7 or in PDF format on the installation DVD for the application software. If you don't already have Adobe Reader (or if you don't have the latest version of Adobe Reader, formerly called Acrobat Reader) installed on your computer, you can download a free copy from the Adobe website (www.adobe.com).

- Visit Adobe Premiere Elements Help and Support web page (www.adobe.com/designcenter/premiereelements/), which you can view by choosing Help > Adobe Premiere Elements Help. You can also choose Help > Online Support for access to the Premiere Elements Support Center on the Adobe website. Both of these options require that you have Internet access.

- The Adobe Premiere Elements 7 User Guide, which is included either in the box with your copy of Adobe Premiere Elements 7 or in PDF format on the installation DVD for the application software (E:\English\User Documentation|Adobe Premiere Elements Help.pdf). If you don't already have Adobe or Acrobat Reader installed on your computer, you can download a free copy from the Adobe website (www.adobe.com).

Photoshop.com

Various chapters in this book will refer to features of and services provided by Photoshop.com. Please note that currently, Photoshop.com services are available only for Adobe Premiere Elements users in the United States.

Adobe certification

The Adobe Training and Certification Programs are designed to help Adobe customers improve and promote their product-proficiency skills. The Adobe Certified Expert (ACE) program is designed to recognize the high-level skills of expert users. Adobe Certified Training Providers (ACTP) use only Adobe Certified Experts to teach Adobe software classes. Available in either ACTP classrooms or on-site, the ACE program is the best way to master Adobe products. For Adobe Certified Training Programs information, visit the Partnering with Adobe website at http://partners.adobe.com.

1 THE WORLD OF DIGITAL VIDEO

This lesson describes how you'll use Adobe™ Premiere™ Elements 7 to produce movies and introduces you to the key panels, workspaces, and views within Adobe Premiere Elements. You'll also learn the benefits of subscribing to Adobe Photoshop.com.

This lesson will introduce the following concepts:

- Navigating the Adobe Premiere Elements workspaces
- Importing and tagging media
- Uploading and sharing content with Photoshop.com

 This lesson will take approximately 45 minutes.

The Adobe Premiere Elements workspace.

How Adobe Premiere Elements
fits into video production

All video producers are different, and each will use Adobe Premiere Elements differently. At a high level, however, all producers will use Adobe Premiere Elements to import and organize footage (video, stills, and audio)—whether from a camcorder, digital camera, or other source—and then edit the clips into a cohesive movie.

From a video perspective, such editing will include both trimming away unwanted sections of your source clips, correcting exposure and adjusting color as needed, and then applying transitions and special effects and adding titles. On the audio front, perhaps you'll add a narration to your productions, or a background music track. Once your movie is complete, you may create menus for recording to DVD and/or Blu-ray Discs, and then output the movie for sharing with others via disc (such as DVD or Blu-ray) and/or file-based output.

Adobe Premiere Elements facilitates this workflow with a simple three-panel interface with custom workspaces for each of the four production steps: clip acquisition and organization, editing, creating disc menus, and sharing. This chapter will introduce you to the Adobe Premiere Elements interface and these four workspaces.

You undoubtedly purchased Adobe Premiere Elements to start producing movies as soon as possible. Taking a few moments now for this overview will not only get you up and running in Adobe Premiere Elements more quickly, it will also help you understand how this book is organized, and where to find the content that details the operations you'll be pursuing in future projects.

The Adobe Premiere Elements workspace

When you start Adobe Premiere Elements, a Welcome screen appears. From here, you can choose to create an InstantMovie, open a project, or create a new project. On the left, the Welcome screen will display the status of your Photoshop.com Membership, and provide access to your Account Details, your Shared Gallery, and Adobe Premiere ElementsTutorials. The large center screen will also contain information about tutorials available to Plus Members on Photoshop.com.

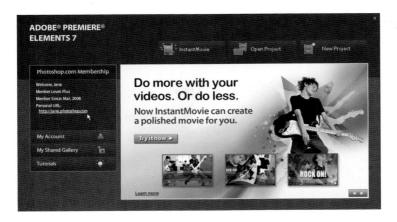

1. Start Adobe Premiere Elements and click the Open Project button in the Welcome screen, then select the Open folder. If Adobe Premiere Elements is already open, choose File > Open Project.

2. Let's open the final project in the book, to show you what you'll be working towards. Navigate to your Lesson12 folder and select the project file Lesson12_ Start.prel. Click the Open button to open your project. If a dialog appears asking for the location of rendered files, click the Skip Previews button. The Adobe Premiere Elements work area appears, with the Organize workspace selected in the Tasks panel. Note that your Organize workspace will probably look different than that shown in the figure, especially if you've edited with Adobe Premiere Elements on this computer before.

A. Monitor panel.
B. Tasks panel (Organize workspace selected. Note that your Organize workspace may contain different items). **C.** My Project panel (Sceneline selected).

The Adobe Premiere Elements workspace is arranged in three main panels: the Monitor panel, the Tasks panel, and the My Project panel. The following gives you an overview of these panels and the role they play when you are working on a movie project.

Monitor panel

The Monitor panel serves multiple purposes. It enables you to edit as well as to view your movie in one convenient place. You can navigate to any position in the movie and preview a section or the entire movie. In this role, the Monitor panel previews the movie that you are building in the My Project panel, using the VCR-like controls beneath the playback window. Other chapters will detail the Monitor panel's controls and operation; here you can experiment with the playback controls to get a feel for their operation.

In other roles, the Monitor panel also offers tools to trim unwanted footage and split clips. You can drag one scene onto another to create picture-in-picture effects, and add titles and other text directly in the Monitor panel. The Monitor panel adjusts its appearance for some edit tasks. When creating menus, the Monitor panel switches to become the Disk Layout panel; in title-editing mode the Monitor panel displays additional tools to create and edit text.

My Project panel

This panel lets you assemble your media into the desired order and edit clips. The My Project panel has two different views:

- **Sceneline:** In the Sceneline of the My Project panel, the initial frame represents each clip. This display makes it easy to arrange clips into coherent series without regard to clip length. This technique is referred to as *storyboard-style editing*. The Sceneline is useful when you first start editing a movie because it allows you to quickly arrange your media into the desired order; trim unwanted frames from the beginning and ends of each clip; and add titles, transitions and effects.

- **Timeline:** The Timeline of the My Project panel presents all movie components in separate horizontal tracks beneath a timescale. Clips earlier in time appear to the left, and clips later in time appear to the right, with clip length on the Timeline representing a clip's duration. The Timeline is useful later in the project, and for more advanced editing, because it lets you better visualize content on different tracks, such as picture-in-picture effects and titles, or narration and background music.

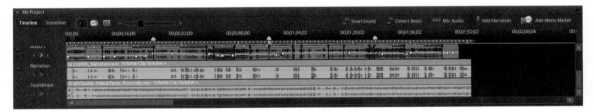

Tasks panel

The Tasks panel is the central location for adding and organizing media; finding, applying, and adjusting effects and transitions; creating DVD and Blu-ray Disc menus; and sharing your finished projects. It is organized into four main task workspaces: Organize, Edit, Disc Menus, and Share. Within each workspace are all the tools you need to accomplish your tasks.

Organize workspace

The Organize workspace (frequently referred to as the Organizer) is divided into four views to input media, create an InstantMovie, tag your content, and apply Smart Tagging. This is the workspace you'll use to start most projects.

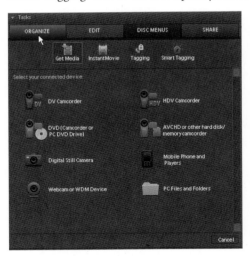

The Organize workspace (Get Media view selected).

- **Get Media:** This view shows buttons to access all the different methods for acquiring media for your movie: DV Camcorder, HDV Camcorder, DVD (Camcorder or PC DVD Drive), AVCHD or other hard disk/memory camcorder, Digital Still Camera, Mobile Phone and Players, Webcam or WDM Device, and PC Files and Folders, which you'll use to retrieve files already existing on your hard disk.

- **InstantMovie:** This view automatically and quickly steps you through the selection and editing portion of movie creation, adding theme-based effects, title, transitions, and audio.

- **Tagging:** Clicking this icon opens the Tagging panel, where you can create and apply keyword tags and albums to manage and organize your media (video, still image, and audio files). Tags, Smart Tags, Albums, Smart Albums, and any combination of these let you limit what appears in the Organizer so that you can easily and quickly find the files you want. You can add keywords for anything, such as people's names, places, or events.

- **Smart Tagging:** Clicking here opens the Smart Tagging panel and automatically analyzes selected video clips. When you analyze your videos, Adobe Premiere Elements automatically adds quality tags, such as shaky or bright; or interest tags, such as faces or motion. You can use these tags to quickly find your highest quality video. The InstantMovie feature uses Smart Tags when arranging clips for movies.

Edit workspace

If you were working on a real project, after importing and tagging your media, you'd be ready to edit. After importing and tagging your media, you're ready to edit. Click Edit to enter the Edit workspace, which is divided into five views to access media, select movie themes, apply effects, and apply transitions, and create movie titles from templates.

The Edit workspace
(Project view selected).

- **Project:** In this view you can view, sort, and select media you have captured or imported into your project. Media can be presented in List view or Icon view, selected by buttons at the lower-left corner of Project view.

- **Themes:** This view displays movie themes that you can use to instantly and dramatically enhance your movies. Using Themes enables you to create professional-looking movies quickly and easily. Themes come pre-configured with effects, transitions, overlays, title and closing credit sequences, intros, sound effects, and more. You can choose to simply apply all the available options in a theme, or select just the options you want.

- **Effects:** This view shows video and audio effects and presets you can use in your movie. You can search for effects by typing all or part of the name into the search box, browse through all available effects, or filter the view by type and category. The menu in the upper-right corner of the panel lets you choose between List view and Thumbnail view. You can apply video effects to adjust exposure or color problems, apply perspective or pixelate, or add other special effects. Audio effects help you improve the sound quality, add special effects like delay and reverb, and alter volume or balance.

- **Transitions:** This view shows video and audio transitions you can use in your movie. You can search for transitions by typing all or part of the name into the search box, browse through all available transitions, or filter the view by type and category. The menu in the upper-right corner of the panel lets you choose between List view and Thumbnail view. Transitions between clips can be as subtle as a cross-dissolve, or quite emphatic, such as a page turn or spinning pinwheel.

- **Titles:** This view shows groups of pre-formatted title templates you can use in your movie. You can browse all available templates, or filter the view by categories such as Entertainment, Travel, and Wedding. Title templates include graphic images and placeholder text that you can modify freely, delete from, or add to, without affecting the templates themselves.

Disc Menus workspace

Use the Disc Menus workspace to add menus to your movies before burning them onto DVDs or Blu-ray discs. The Disc Menus workspace lets you preview and choose pre-formatted menu templates you can use for your movie. You can browse the available templates by categories such as Entertainment, Happy Birthday, Kid's Corner, and New Baby.

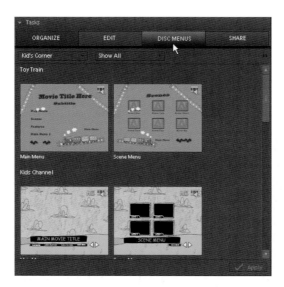

These are templates in the Kids Corner category.

Share workspace

After you've completed editing your movie, and you're ready to burn a disc or save your movie for viewing online or on a mobile phone, PC, videotape, or other device, click Share. The Share workspace shows buttons to access all the different methods for exporting and sharing your movie: Disc, Online, Personal Computer, Mobile Phones and Players, and Tape. Quick share lets you create and reuse sharing options.

Properties view

Often during editing or when producing disc menus, you'll need to customize effect parameters or menu components after applying or selecting them. Properties view (Window > Properties) lets you view and adjust parameters of items—such as video or audio clips, transitions, effects, or menus—when selected in the Monitor or My Project panel.

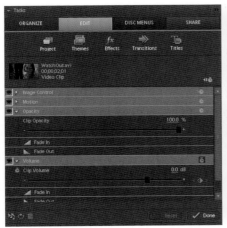
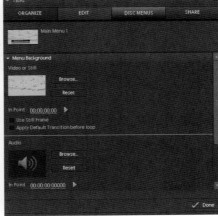

Info and History panels

The Info panel displays information about a selected clip in the Timeline. This panel can be helpful in identifying the duration of a clip, among other things.

● **Note:** The Info panel is dynamic, and the fields can vary slightly depending on what is selected. For clips selected in the Timeline, the Info panel lists a start and end point; for clips selected in Project view, it lists In and Out points.

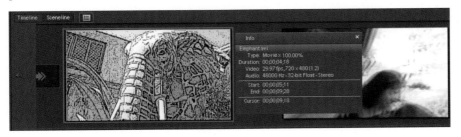

1 To open the Info panel, choose Window > Info. Once opened, you can drag the Info panel by its title bar to reposition it on the screen, if necessary.

2 Click to select a clip in Project view or the My Project panel. The Info panel displays the clip's name, type, duration, video and audio attributes, its location in the Timeline/Sceneline, and the position of the pointer.

▶ Tip: In addition to the History panel, Adobe Premiere Elements supports multiple undos by choosing Edit > Undo, or by pressing Ctrl+Z. Each time you press Ctrl+Z, you are undoing another step. You can also redo a step by choosing Edit > Redo, or pressing Ctrl+Shift+Z.

The History panel (Window > History) keeps a running list of every step you take during a project, and adds each action to the bottom of its list. To undo an editing step, click it in the History panel. To undo multiple steps, click the earliest step that you'd like to undo, and Adobe Premiere Elements will also undo all editing steps after that point. For example, in the History panel shown, the Set Out Point will be reversed, as will all subsequent edits.

These are the most prominent panels and workspaces within Adobe Premiere Elements. Now let's take a brief look at Photoshop.com, which is where you'll back up and share your photos and movies.

Working with Photoshop.com

Photoshop.com is an online photo and video hosting, editing, and sharing site. If you're using Adobe Premiere Elements in the United States, you can register for a free Basic Membership, or opt for the Plus Membership (check www.photoshop.com for pricing). All members can back up images and movies on the site, with the Basic members allocated 2 gigabytes (GB) of storage space, and Plus members having access to 20 GB of storage, or about 4 hours of DVD-quality video.

If you're already a member of Photoshop.com, you can login from Adobe Premiere Elements by clicking Sign In on the upper right toolbar. If not, you can click Join Now to register for the service.

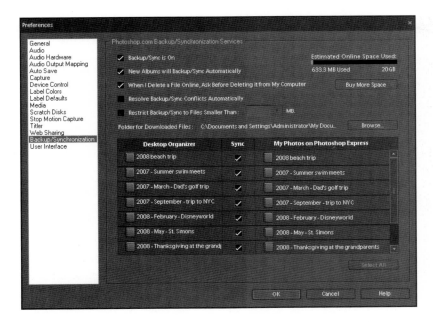

All members control the content that gets uploaded to Photoshop.com with this Preferences panel, which you access by choosing Edit > Preferences > Backup/Synchronization.

Photoshop.com Plus members also receive free access to online moviemaking ideas and tutorials. If you have a Plus Membership, Adobe Premiere Elements will display these tutorials in the Welcome screen that opens when you first run the program and, from time to time, on the lower right of the My Project panel.

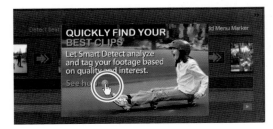

Click the tutorial title to display a short description of the tutorial, and then click See How to view the tutorial in the Adobe Photoshop.com Inspiration Browser.

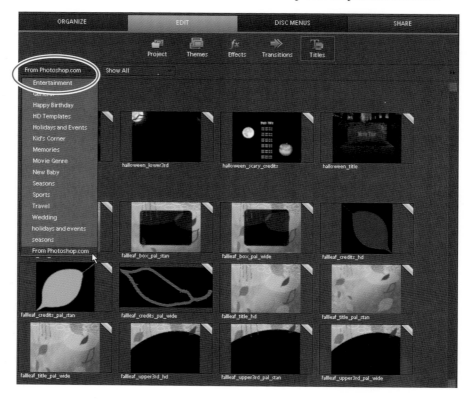

Plus members all receive free content from Photoshop.com, such as the titles shown above. Note that Adobe Premiere Elements will download these files automatically once they're available, and will display them in the Photoshop.com folder. The titles shown here are from the two themes added during Fall 2008, Scary Halloween and Autumn Leaves.

Review questions

1 What are the three main panels in Adobe Premiere Elements, and what function does each serve?

2 Which workspace contains the controls for importing content from video cameras, other devices, and files already stored on your hard disk?

3 What are the two views of the My Project panel, and what are their respective strengths?

4 What are the three major benefits of the Plus Membership of Photoshop.com?

Review answers

1 The three main panels are the Monitor, Tasks, and My Project panels. You build your movies by adding clips to the My Project panel. The Monitor panel serves multiple roles, allowing you to preview your movies and create titles and other effects. The Tasks panel has four workspaces that allow you to organize your clips, create InstantMovies, and render your movies for sharing with others. It also contains content like effects, transitions, Themes, Titles, and Disc Menus.

2 You access capture and import controls from Get Media view in the Organize workspace.

3 Adobe Premiere Elements offers two views in the My Project Panel, Sceneline and Timeline. The Sceneline shows only the first frame of the clip, and is ideal for quickly arranging the order of your clips and performing basic edits. The Timeline displays clips on separate tracks, and is superior for advanced edits like picture-in-picture and other overlay effects, and for adding background music or narration to your productions.

4 Plus Members receive up to 20 GB of storage space (compared to 2 GB for the Basic Membership), access to tutorials, ideas, and additional content when released by Adobe.

2 GETTING READY TO EDIT

Now that you're familiar with the Adobe Premiere Elements interface, let's learn how to create a project, set relevant user preferences, and configure the interface to your liking. For those tempted to skip this chapter, understand that while Adobe Premiere Elements is a wonderfully flexible and customizable program, once you choose a project setting and start editing, you can't change the setting.

While often you can work around this issue, in some instances you may have to abandon the initial project and start again using a different setting to achieve the desired results. Invest a little time here to understand how Adobe Premiere Elements works with project settings so you can get your project done right the first time.

In this lesson, you'll learn to do the following:

- Create a new project
- Choose the optimal setting for your project
- Set preferences for Auto Save, Scratch Disks, and the user interface
- Customize window sizes and locations in the workspace
- Restore the workspace to its default configuration

 This lesson will take approximately 1 hour.

Collecting assets for your movie.

Setting up a new project

Adobe Premiere Elements can work with video from any source, from DV camcorders shooting 4:3 or 16:9 (widescreen) standard-definition (SD) video, to the latest AVCHD and HDV high-definition (HD) camcorders. For the best results, you should choose a project setting that matches your source footage, following the procedure described below.

After you choose a setting, Adobe Premiere Elements will automatically use the same setting for all future projects, which should work well if you use the same source video format for all subsequent projects. Should you change the format, however—for example, from DV to HDV—remember to change your project setting as well.

1   Launch Adobe Premiere Elements and click the New Project button in the Welcome screen. If Adobe Premiere Elements is already open, choose File > New > Project.

2   Check the Project Settings in the lower-left corner of the New Project screen. If the Project Settings match your source footage, proceed to step 4. If not, click the Change Settings button to open the Setup screen.

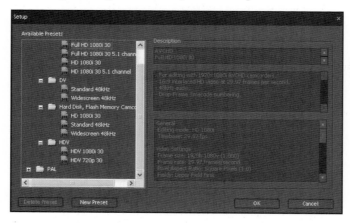

● **Note:** For more information on a Preset, click the setting, and Adobe Premiere Elements will display technical details in the Description field.

3   Click the Preset that matches your source footage.

4   After choosing a Preset, click OK to close the Setup dialog.

5   In the New Project panel, choose a name and storage location for the new project. Then click OK to save the new project file.

Diagnosing settings-related issues

If you've chosen the wrong project setting, the most common problem will relate to differences in the aspect ratio of your video, as evidenced by black bars across the sides or top and bottom of the video in the Monitor panel, which is a display technique called letterboxing. Adobe Premiere Elements will letterbox a 16:9 video displayed in a 4:3 window, producing the black bars on the top and bottom of the video in the Monitor panel below.

1   To view the current project setting, choose Edit > Project Settings > General. In this project, as you can see in the Project Settings screen, the Editing Mode is DV NTSC, but the Pixel Aspect Ratio is D1/DV NTSC (0.9), which is 4:3 video. Both fields are grayed out and inactive, indicating that you can't change their values. Click OK to close the Project Settings screen.

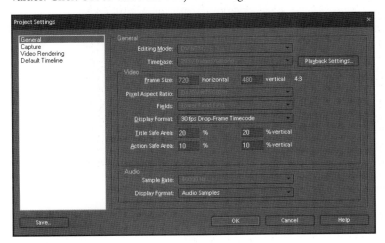

2 To view aspect ratio-related information about clips in the My Project panel, choose Window > Info. If you don't have any clips in the My Project panel, load Lesson12_Start.prel (see instructions in Lesson 1).

3 Click any clip in the Timeline or Sceneline. In the Video description line in the Info panel, you can see that the video has a frame rate of 29.97 frames per second (fps) and a resolution of 720x480, but that the aspect ratio is 1.2, which designates widescreen video.

To display the widescreen video in the 4:3 project, Adobe Premiere Elements inserts letterboxes on the top and bottom of the widescreen video. You can eliminate the letterboxes using the controls discussed in Working with Motion Controls in Lesson 6, which is a good solution when including one widescreen clip in a 4:3 movie. If all of your clips are widescreen, however, you should restart the project using a widescreen setting.

Choosing the correct setting

There are many different video formats, several with multiple flavors, which can make it challenging to choose the correct setting. This sidebar will identify and detail the most frequently used settings in Adobe Premiere Elements to simplify your selection. Note that you may have to consult the documentation that came with your camcorder for details on the video format captured by the camcorder.

Before beginning, understand that there are two aspect ratios that relate to camcorder video. The *display aspect ratio* is either 4:3 (standard) or 16:9, which is also called widescreen or sometimes anamorphic. These are the aspect ratios that you're most familiar with, as they're identical to the two common aspect ratios of TV sets.

The other aspect ratio is the *pixel aspect ratio*, which describes how the pixels that comprise the video must be adjusted during display. For example, all AVCHD video displays at 1920x1080. However, "HD" AVCHD video is stored by the camcorder at a resolution of 1440x1080, and each horizontal pixel must be stretched by a factor of 1.33 during display to achieve full resolution. For this reason, AVCHD video stored at a resolution of 1440x1080 has a pixel aspect ratio of 1.33.

In contrast, "Full HD" AVCHD video is captured at 1920x1080 resolution, so no stretching is required to produce the full1920x1080 display. Full HD video has a pixel aspect ratio of 1.0.

Adobe Premiere Elements can work with virtually any source of video, and once you choose the proper setting, you'll never have to worry about these aspect ratios again. However, to identify the setting that matches your source video, you may have to learn these highly technical details, especially if you're working with AVCHD.

AVCHD: There are four AVCHD presets, differentiated by the resolution of video stored by the camcorder and audio channels. The two "Full HD"

presets are for AVCHD video stored by the camcorder at 1920x1080 resolution (pixel aspect ratio of 1.0), while the "HD" presets are for AVCHD video captured and stored at 1440x1080 resolution (pixel aspect ratio of 1.33). Both formats have a display aspect ratio (as opposed to pixel aspect ratio) of 16:9, as do all HD formats. The two 5.1 channel presets are for video recorded with 5.1-surround sound, while the other two presets are for video recorded with stereo audio.

DV: There are two types of DV footage. Standard DV has a display aspect ratio of 4:3 and a pixel aspect ratio of .9, while widescreen DV has a display aspect ratio of 16:9 and a pixel aspect ratio of 1.2.

HDV: There are two varieties of HDV, 1080i 30 and 720p 30. (The "30" represents the number of frames per second in the video.) Unless you're shooting HDV with a first-generation JVC camcorder, you're almost certainly shooting 1080i, which displays at 1920x1080, and has a storage resolution of 1440x1080 and a display aspect ratio of 1.33. HDV 720p 30 has storage and display resolutions of 1280x720, and a display aspect ratio of 1.0.

Hard Disk and Flash Memory camcorders: Adobe Premiere Elements has three presets for hard disk and Flash Memory camcorders. Use HD 1080i for all HD camcorders, irrespective of the pixel aspect ratio. Use Standard 48 kilohertz (kHz) for standard-definition (720x480 resolution) video with a display aspect ratio of 4:3, irrespective of pixel aspect ratio. Use Widescreen 48 kHz for SD (720x480 resolution) video with a display aspect ratio of 16:9, irrespective of pixel aspect ratio.

Working with Project Preferences

For the most part, once you have the right project setting selected, you can jump in and begin editing with Adobe Premiere Elements. However, at some point you may want to adjust several program preferences that impact your editing experience. Here are the preferences that will prove relevant to most video editors.

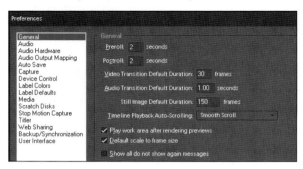

● **Note:** Adjusting these default durations will impact only edits made after the adjustment. For example, if you change the Still Image Default Duration to 120 frames, Adobe Premiere Elements will assign this duration to all still images added to the project thereafter, but won't change the duration of still images already inserted into the project.

1   To open the General Preferences panel, choose Edit > Preferences > General. There are multiple preferences in this panel; most important are the Video and Audio Transition Default Durations and the Still Image Default Duration, the latter of which controls the duration of all still images added to your project.

2   Click Auto Save to view Auto Save preferences.

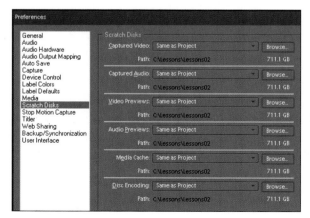

Better saved than sorry

With Auto Save enabled, Adobe Premiere Elements automatically saves a copy of your project at the specified duration, which you can customize. You can also change the number of separate projects that Adobe Premiere Elements saves.

Adobe Premiere Elements saves all Auto Save files in a separate sub-folder, entitled Adobe Premiere Elements Auto-Save, which is located in the folder containing your current project file.

It's good practice to manually save your project periodically during editing to preserve your work in the event of a power outage or other random crash. Should a crash occur, you may be able to recover some of the editing that you've done subsequent to your last manual save by loading the most recent project automatically saved by Adobe Premiere Elements.

You load these just like any other project: click File > Open Project, navigate to the Adobe Premiere Elements Auto-Save folder, and choose the newest project file.

3   Click Scratch Disks to view the Scratch Disk preferences. This preference identifies the folders used to store audio and video clips that Adobe Premiere Elements creates while producing your project. This includes clips captured from your camcorder, video and audio previews, and media encoded for recording onto DVD or Blu-ray Disc. By default, Adobe Premiere Elements stores this content in the same folder as the project file. If you run short of disk space, you can change the location of the scratch disk by clicking the Browse button next to each category of content, and choosing a different location on a separate disk.

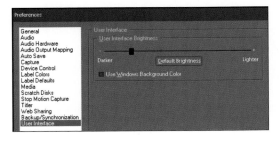

4   Click User Interface. Drag the User Interface Brightness slider to the right to make the interface brighter, and to the left to make it darker. These adjustments can be useful when editing under varying lighting conditions, like in a dark or extremely bright room.

5   Select the Use Windows Background Color checkbox to substitute the Windows default background color for Adobe Premiere Elements' background colors, and click OK to close the Preferences panel.

These are the most critical preferences to consider before starting your first project. With these configured, let's explore other options for customizing your workspace.

Customizing the workspace

Adobe Premiere Elements uses a docking system to fit all the panels into the available space of the application window. However, panels can be moved and resized so that you can create a workspace that best fits your needs.

With Adobe Premiere Elements open, notice that the Monitor panel, the Tasks panel, and the My Project panel are separated by solid vertical and horizontal dividing lines. These dividers can be quickly repositioned to give you more space to work in one of the panels when you need it.

1   To increase the height of the My Project panel, hover your pointer over the dividing line between the My Project and Monitor panels until it converts to a two-headed cursor and then drag it up toward the Monitor panel.

You can use a similar technique to expand the size of the Monitor panel by dragging it to the right, or expand the Tasks panel by dragging it to the left.

2   To reset the panels to their default layout, choose Window > Restore Workspace. Notice how everything snaps back to its original position. Consider restoring your workspace if you find your screen becomes cluttered.

To save some space on your screen, the docking headers of the panels, which contain title and sometimes palette menu and Close buttons, are hidden by default in Adobe Premiere Elements.

3 To show the docking headers, choose Window > Show Docking Headers. To hide them again, choose Window > Hide Docking Headers.

While the default workspace layout has every panel docked into a specific position, you may find it helpful from time to time to have a more flexible environment. To do this, you can undock, or float, your panels.

4 If the docking headers are not currently visible, choose Window > Show Docking Headers. Then, click the docking header of the My Project panel and drag it a short distance in any direction. As you drag the header, the panel becomes translucent. When you release the pointer, the My Project panel becomes a floating window, allowing the Monitor panel and the Tasks panel to expand toward the bottom of the main window.

● **Note:** The Tasks panel is the only panel that cannot be undocked.

▶ **Tip:** When you work with multiple monitors, you can choose to display the application window on the main monitor and place floating windows on the second monitor.

5 Close the My Project panel by clicking its Close button (✖) in the upper-right corner.

6 Reopen the panel by choosing Window > My Project. Notice that the panel opens where you have previously placed it. This is because Adobe Premiere Elements remembers the locations of the panels, and retains them as part of the customized workspace.

● **Note:** The Tasks panel is the only panel that cannot be closed.

7 Choose Window > Restore Workspace to return to the default workspace layout.

● **Note:** To learn more about customizing your workspace, choose Help > Adobe Premiere Elements Help, and then search for "Customizing the workspace" in the Adobe Help Center window.

Review questions

1 What's the most important factor to consider when choosing a project setting?

2 Why is it so important to choose the right setting at the start of the project?

3 What is letterboxing, and what's a common cause for having letterboxes appear in your project?

4 What is Auto Save, and where do you adjust the Auto Save defaults in Adobe Premiere Elements?

5 What command do you use for restoring your workspace to the default panel configuration?

Review answers

1 Choose a setting that matches the primary video that you will use in the project. For example, if you're shooting in widescreen DV, you should use a Widescreen DV project setting.

2 It's critical to choose the right setting when starting a project because unlike most Adobe Premiere Elements configuration items, you can't change the Project Setting after you create the project. In some instances, you may have to start the project over using the correct setting to produce optimal results.

3 Letterboxing is a display technique characterized by black bars on the sides, or on the top and on bottom of video in the Monitor panel. One of the most common causes of letterboxing is a discrepancy between the display aspect ratio of the project setting and the display aspect ratio of a video file imported into the project. For example, if you import 4:3 video into a 16:9 project, Adobe Premiere Elements will display letterboxes on both sides of the video in the Monitor panel.

4 Adobe Premiere Elements' Auto Save function automatically saves a copy of the project file at specified intervals, guarding against loss of work due to power outages or other random crashes. You can adjust the Auto Save defaults in the Preferences panel accessed by choosing Edit > Preferences.

5 Choose Window > Restore Workspace.

3 VIDEO CAPTURE AND IMPORT

This lesson describes how to capture and import video from your camcorder and other devices for editing in Adobe Premiere Elements and introduces the following key concepts:

- Connecting a camcorder to your PC

- Capturing video from a camcorder

- Using the Media Downloader to import video from an AVCHD camcorder, digital still camera, DVD, or DVD-based camcorder or other similar devices

- Importing audio, video, or still images already on your hard drive into an Adobe Premiere Elements project

 This lesson will take approximately 1.5 hours.

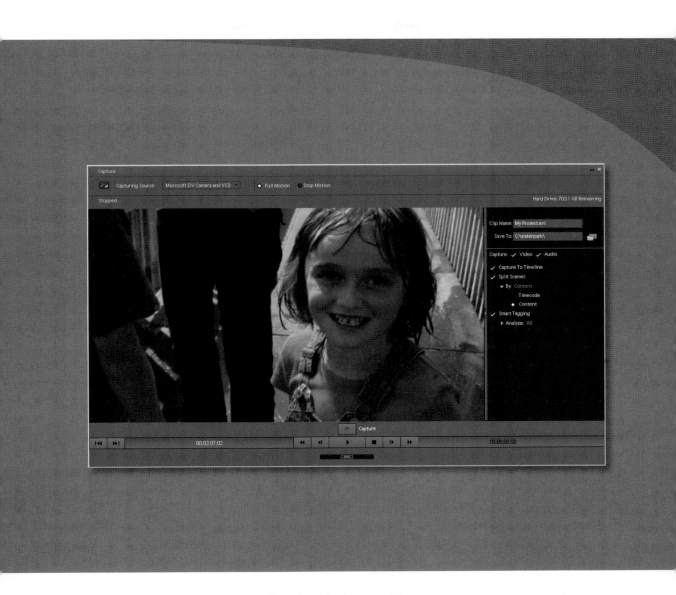

Capturing video from your DV camera.

Capturing video with Adobe Premiere Elements

When videographers started editing video on computers, the typical source was an analog camcorder. Today, while some Adobe Premiere Elements users still shoot analog video, most will start with DV or HDV source footage, or AVCHD, or video shot with a digital still camera, or even video imported from a previously created DVD.

Whatever the source, Adobe Premiere Elements includes all the tools necessary to capture or import your footage so you can begin producing movies. Though the specific technique will vary depending upon the source, Adobe Premiere Elements guides your efforts with device-specific interfaces. All you have to do is connect the device to your computer as described below, and choose the appropriate icon from Get Media view in the Edit workspace.

Note: Adobe Premiere Elements lets you add video, audio, graphics, and still images to your project from numerous sources. In addition to capturing footage, you can import image, video, and audio files stored on your computer's hard disk, card readers, mobile phones, DVDs, Blu-ray Discs, CDs, digital cameras, other devices, or the Internet.

Adobe Premiere Elements has two basic interfaces for capturing or importing video. After a quick overview of these interfaces, this lesson will detail how to capture video from a tape-based camcorder, and then how to import content from an AVCHD camcorder or any other device that stores video on a hard disk, SD card, or optical media. All the concepts in this section and the specific Adobe Premiere Elements features that support them are described in more detail in Adobe Premiere Elements User Guide.

Capture interfaces

When you shoot video, it's stored locally on your camcorder, either on tape, SD media, a hard drive, or even an optical disc like a DVD. Before you can edit your movie in Adobe Premiere Elements, you have to transfer these clips to a local hard disk. In addition to capturing or importing video from a device, you may have content on your hard disk to import into the project.

Tape and live capture vs. clip-based import

Adobe Premiere Elements provides three interfaces for accomplishing these tasks. If you're capturing video footage from a tape-based camcorder, such as DV or HDV, or live from a webcam or WDM (Windows Device Model) device, you use the Capture panel.

If you're importing video clips from a hard disk, SD media, or optical media, you use the Media Downloader. Again, to open the appropriate interface, just connect your device and click the correct icon in Get Media view in the Organize workspace; Adobe Premiere Elements will do the rest.

If the audio, video, or still image files are already on your hard drive, click the PC Files and Folders icon in Get Media view in the Organize workspace and navigate to and select the files as normal. This lesson details this procedure at the end of the chapter.

Capturing tape-based or live video

If you're capturing from a DV or HDV camcorder, or webcam, you'll use the Capture panel. This lesson will discuss some preliminary concepts relating to these devices and then detail the procedure.

Connecting your device

The simplest way to capture DV or HDV video is to connect the camcorder to a computer with an IEEE 1394 port. Adobe Premiere Elements supports a wide range of DV devices and capture cards, making it easy to capture DV source files.

Some DV and HDV camcorders also have USB 2.0 ports. USB 2.0 is a high-speed transfer protocol similar to IEEE 1394. When present on a DV/HDV camcorder, the USB 2.0 connector is typically used only for transferring digital still images, rather then tape-based video, shot by the camcorder to the computer. When both connectors are present, use the IEEE 1394 connector for video capture.

● **Note:** Though it's extremely rare, sometimes when connecting your computer to your camcorder via an IEEE 1394 connector, an electrical charge from the computer can damage the camcorder. To minimize this risk, always turn off both devices before capture, then connect the IEEE 1394 cable, then turn on your computer, and, finally, turn on the camcorder.

Capture Video
How to connect your DV camcorder to your computer

DV
4 pin
DV connector

FireWire
* 6 or 4 pin
DV connector   DV

* DV = i.LINK =   FireWire = IEEE1394a = 1394

Most DV/HDV camcorders have a four-pin IEEE 1394 connector, while most computers have a larger, six-pin connector. Note, however, that some computers, particularly notebooks, may also have a four-pin IEEE 1394 connector. When purchasing an IEEE 1394 cable, make sure that it has the appropriate connectors.

If capturing from a webcam or WDM device, Adobe Premiere Elements will capture the video from the USB 2.0 connector used to connect the device with your computer.

System setup

Before you attempt video capture, make sure that your system is set up appropriately for working with digital video. The following are some general guidelines for ensuring that you have a DV-capable system:

- Make sure that your computer has an IEEE 1394 port. This port may either be built into your computer, or available on a PCI or PC card (often referred to as *capture cards*) that you install yourself. The majority of computers manufactured now include onboard IEEE 1394 cards.

- Make sure that your hard disk is fast enough to capture and play back digital video. The speed at which digital video files transfer information, called the *data transfer rate* (often shortened to *data rate*), is 3.6 megabytes per second (MB/sec). The sustained (not peak) data transfer rate of your hard disk should meet or exceed this rate. To confirm the data transfer rate of your hard disk, see your computer or hard disk documentation.

- Consider using a secondary hard drive for capture and production for extra capacity and to enhance capture performance. In general, most internal hard disks should be sufficiently fast for capture and editing. However, external drives that connect via USB 2.0 and IEEE 1394, though excellent for data backup chores, may be too slow for video capture. If you're looking for an external drive for video production, a newer technology called eSATA offers the best mix of performance and affordability, though you may have to purchase an internal eSATA adapter for your computer or notebook.

- Make sure that you have sufficient disk space for the captured footage. Five minutes of digital video occupies about 1 gigabyte (GB) of hard disk space. The Capture panel in Adobe Premiere Elements indicates the duration of footage that you can capture based on the remaining space on your hard disk. Be certain beforehand that you will have sufficient space for the intended length of video capture. Also, some capture cards have size limits on digital video files from 2 GB and up. See your capture card documentation for information on file size limitations.

- Make sure that you periodically defragment your hard disk. Writing to a fragmented disk can cause disruptions in your hard disk's transfer speed, causing you to lose, or drop, frames as you capture. You can use the defragmentation utility included with Windows or purchase a third-party utility.

- The state of high-end video hardware changes rapidly; consult the manufacturer of your video-capture card for suggestions about appropriate video storage hardware.

Capture options

When you capture video from a tape or live source, you have multiple capture options, including whether to capture audio and video, whether to capture to the Timeline, to split scenes, and to apply Smart Tagging. Let's briefly discuss each option before working through the capture process.

The Capture settings dialog

Capturing video or audio only

By default, Adobe Premiere Elements captures both audio and video when capturing a clip. You can change this default in the Capture Settings dialog that appears in the Capture panel that opens after you select your video source. In the top line of the dialog, both Video and Audio are selected by default. To capture only audio, deselect the Video checkbox. To capture only video, deselect the Audio checkbox.

Note that you can easily remove either the audio or video portion of the captured clip during editing. Unless you're absolutely certain that you won't use either the audio or the video, capture both and remove the undesired media during editing.

Capture to Timeline

The Capture to Timeline option automatically inserts all captured clips into the My Project panel. By default, this option is selected. If you'd prefer to manually drag all clips to the My Project panel, deselect this option.

Capturing video clips with Scene Detect

During capture, Adobe Premiere Elements can split the captured video into scenes, which makes it much easier to find and edit the desired content. Adobe Premiere Elements can use one of two scene-detection techniques to detect scenes: Timecode-based and Content-based.

Timecode-based scene detection is available only when capturing DV source video. As the name suggests, this technique uses timecodes in the video itself to break the capture clips into scenes. Specifically, when you record DV, your camcorder automatically records a time/date stamp when you press Stop or Record. During capture, Adobe Premiere Elements creates a new scene each time it detects a new time/date stamp, and creates a separate video file on your hard drive for each scene.

Content-based scene detection, which is your only option for HDV or webcam videos, analyzes the content after capture to identify scene changes. For example, if you shot one scene indoors and the next outdoors, Adobe Premiere Elements would analyze the video frames and detect the new scene.

When detecting scenes using Content-based scene detection, Adobe Premiere Elements stores only one video file on your hard drive, and designates the scenes in the Organize and Edit workspaces. After capture, while scanning the captured video for scene changes, Adobe Premiere Elements displays a status panel describing the operation and apprising you of its progress.

During capture, Adobe Premiere Elements will default to Timecode-based scene detection for DV source video, and Content-based scene detection for HDV and webcam-based videos. We suggest leaving Scene Detect enabled during video capture and using these defaults. To change these defaults in the Capture panel (which you'll learn how to open below), do the following:

1   To disable Scene Detect entirely, deselect the Split Scenes checkbox in the Capture settings on the right of the Capture panel.

2   If capturing DV video, you can opt for either the Timecode or Content-based scene detection. In most instances, the former will be faster and more accurate. To change from Timecode- to Content-based scene detection, select the Split Scenes checkbox, twirl the By: triangle if necessary to view both options, and click the Content radio button.

Capturing video clips with Smart Tagging

Smart Tagging is a feature that analyzes captured video clips and adds quality tags, such as shaky or bright; or interest tags, such as faces or motion. You can use these tags to quickly find your highest-quality video. In addition, the InstantMovie feature uses Smart Tags when arranging clips for movies.

The roles that Smart Tagging plays in video production are detailed in the section entitled Smart Tagging your clips in Lesson 4. In general, Smart Tagging takes relatively little time and produces a wealth of useful information about your clips. We suggest leaving Smart Tagging enabled during capture, as this is the default setting.

To change this default, deselect the Smart Tagging checkbox in the Capture settings on the right of the Capture panel.

With Smart Tagging enabled, Adobe Premiere Elements will scan the video after capture and display a status window describing the operation and apprising you of its progress.

With these options covered, let's discuss one more capture-related feature and then capture video.

Capturing clips with device control

When capturing clips, device control refers to the ability to control the operation of a connected video deck or camcorder using controls within the Adobe Premiere Elements interface, rather than using the controls on the connected device. This mode of operation is more convenient because Adobe Premiere Elements offers controls like Next Scene or Shuttle that may not be available on your camcorder's controls.

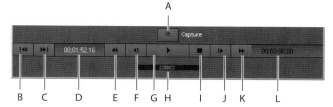

Capture panel controls:
A. Capture. **B.** Previous Scene. **C.** Next Scene. **D.** Current Position – Timecode Display.
E. Rewind. **F.** Step Back (Left). **G.** Play/Pause. **H.** Shuttle. **I.** Step Forward (Right). **J.** Fast-Forward.
K. Stop. **L.** Capture Duration (active only during capture)

You probably know most of these controls because they're similar to your camcorder or VCR. You may not be familiar with the Shuttle control, which you can drag with your pointer to the left or right to rewind or fast-forward the video. This control is position-sensitive; the further you drag the shuttle widget from the center, the faster the tape fast-forwards or rewinds. The Previous Scene and Next Scene controls use Timecode-based scene detection to advance backwards or forwards to the previous or next scenes.

Adobe Premiere Elements should be able to establish device control with all DV and HDV camcorders, but it's not available when capturing from webcams, WDM devices, or analog camcorders. You can still capture video from these sources without device control, though the capture procedure is slightly different. Procedures for capturing both with and without device control are detailed in the following section.

Debugging device control issues

As mentioned, Adobe Premiere Elements should be able to establish device control with all DV and HDV camcorders. If you see the error message "No DV camera detected," or "No HDV camera detected," Adobe Premiere Elements can't detect your camcorder. In this case, you won't be able to establish device control, and may not be able to capture video. Here are some steps you can take to attempt to remedy this situation.

1   First, exit Adobe Premiere Elements and make sure that your camcorder is turned on and running (and hasn't timed out due to inactivity) in VCR, Play, or other similar mode. Also check to see that your IEEE 1394 cable is firmly connected to both the camcorder's and computer's IEEE 1394 ports. Then run Adobe Premiere Elements again and see if the program detects the camcorder.

2   If not, check your Project Settings and make sure that they match your camcorder (DV project if DV camcorder, HDV project if HDV camcorder).

3   If Adobe Premiere Elements still doesn't detect your camcorder, determine if Windows detects your camcorder, which is necessary for Adobe Premiere Elements to detect the device. When you turn your camcorder on and off, Windows should respond, usually with an audible alert, and often by opening a Digital Video Device dialog.

In addition, check to see if your camcorder is identified in Windows Explorer. If Windows doesn't respond when you turn your camcorder on and off, if your camcorder isn't identified in Windows Explorer, or both, it's likely that there's a hardware issue, like a defective cable, or faulty IEEE 1394 port on your camcorder or computer. Try substituting new devices (cable, camcorder, computer) until you identify the faulty component.

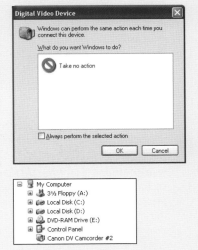

(continues on page 42)

Debugging device control issues (*continued*)

4   If Windows does recognize your camcorder, you may have a configuration problem within Adobe Premiere Elements. In the Capture panel, choose Capture Settings, which opens the Project Settings dialog to the Capture Format.

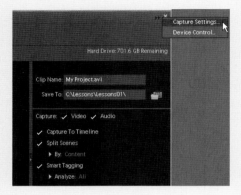

5   In this dialog, choose the correct capture device, either DV or HDV. Close and reopen the Capture panel. If Adobe Premiere Elements still doesn't detect your camcorder, try step 6.

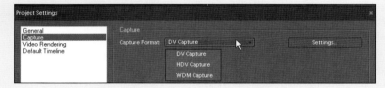

6   In the Capture panel menu, choose Device Control, which opens the Preferences dialog with the Device Control view visible.

7   In this dialog, choose the format that matches your connection, DV/HDV for IEEE 1394, and USB Video Class 1.0 for USB. Close and reopen the Capture panel. If Adobe Premiere Elements still doesn't detect your camcorder, try step 7.

8   Most HDV camcorders can also record and play DV video. However, if you are capturing DV video and your camcorder is set to record HDV, Adobe Premiere Elements may detect an HDV camcorder rather than DV (or vice versa). For example, if you shot HDV in your last shoot, but were capturing DV video from a previous shoot, Adobe Premiere Elements may detect an HDV camcorder rather than a DV camcorder. In this situation, set the camcorder to record DV video, and once you return to VCR or Play mode, play a few seconds of DV video, which may enable Adobe Premiere Elements to detect the DV camcorder.

Capturing stop-motion and time-lapse video

Using stop-motion and time-lapse video, you can make inanimate objects appear to move, or show a flower grow and bloom in seconds. In this mode, you capture single video frames at widely spaced time intervals for later playback at normal frame rates.

You create stop-motion animations or time-lapse videos by using the Stop Motion button in the Capture panel. You can capture frames either from pre-recorded tape or from a live camera feed. Stop-motion capture lets you manually select the frames you want to capture; Time Lapse capture automatically captures frames at set intervals. Using Time Lapse mode you can reduce a lengthy event, such as a sunset or a flower blooming, to a very short span.

Note: You cannot capture stop-motion video from an HDV source.

—From Adobe Premiere Elements Help

To capture stop-motion from a tape-based device, do the following:

1   Connect your tape device to your computer and turn it on. Then do one of the following:

  • If capturing live from a camcorder, place the camcorder in Camera mode.

  • If capturing from videotape, place the device in Play, VTR, or VCR mode.

2   In the Capture panel, click the Stop Motion button.

3   Click the Create New Stop Motion button in the middle of the Capture panel preview pane.

4   If capturing from videotape, use the camcorder's controls to move to the desired frame. If capturing live, adjust your scene as desired. Click Grab Frame whenever the Capture panel displays a frame that you want to save to the hard disk. Each frame you grab will appear as a .bmp file in Project view with a sequential number in its filename.

5   Close the Capture panel and in the dialog that appears, save the still images as a movie file.

See "Capture stop-motion and time-lapse video" in Adobe Premiere Elements Help for more information.

Capturing with the Capture panel

With this information as prologue, let's look at the process for capturing video via Adobe Premiere Elements' Capture panel.

1   Connect the DV camcorder to your computer via an IEEE 1394 cable.

2   Turn the camera on and set it to the playback mode, which may be labeled VTR, VCR, or Play.

3   Launch Adobe Premiere Elements.

● **Note:** This exercise assumes that a DV camera has been successfully connected to your computer and that you have footage available to capture. If this is not the case, you can still open the Capture panel in order to review the interface; however, you will not be able to access all the controls.

4 In the Organize workspace, click Get Media.

5 In Get Media view, select DV Camcorder ( ) to follow along with this procedure. Selecting HDV Camcorder ( ), or Webcam or WDM Device ( ) will also open the Capture panel, though some settings will be different from this example.

The Capture panel appears. Note that if you're capturing from videotape, your preview screen will be black until you actually start to play the video.

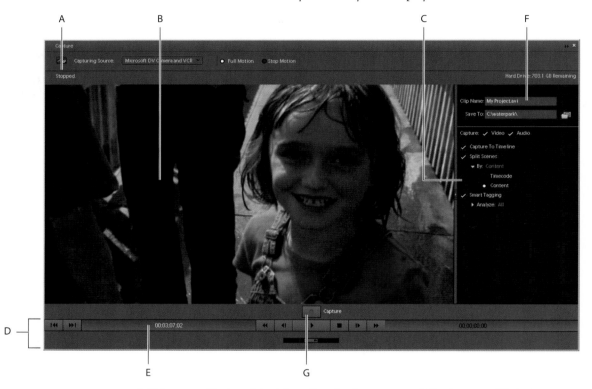

A. Status area—Displays status information about your camera. **B.** Preview area—Displays your current video as played through your camera. **C.** Capture settings—Enables you to change the capture settings. **D.** Device controls—Contains buttons used to directly control your camera. **E.** Current position—Timecode display. Shows you the current frame of your video, measured in the format of hours;minutes;seconds;frames. **F.** Clip name—By default, Adobe Premiere Elements uses the project name to name the AVI movie clips. **G.** Capture/Pause button

6 On the upper-right area of the Capture panel, choose the desired Clip Name and Save To location for the captured files. Note that Adobe Premiere Elements defaults to the project name for Clip Name, and uses the folder where you stored your project file for the default Save To location. If desired, change any of the default Capture settings.

7 At the bottom of the Capture panel, use the navigation controls to navigate to the first scene you'd like to capture.

● **Note:** If your DV camera is connected but not turned on, your Capture panel will display Capture Device Offline in the status area. Although it is preferable to turn on your camera before launching Adobe Premiere Elements, in most cases turning on your camera at any point will bring it online.

8   Click the Capture button ( ), and Adobe Premiere Elements automatically starts playing video on the DV camcorder, captures each scene as an individual movie clip, and adds it to your project.

● **Note:** To stop capturing video at any point, click the Pause button or press Esc on your keyboard to end the capture process. If enabled, the Smart Tagging window will appear as Adobe Premiere Elements analyzes the clip, and then close. Any clips you have captured already remain in your project.

9   After clicking the Capture button, it converts into the Pause button ( ). To stop capturing video, either click the Pause button, or press the Esc key on your keyboard.

● **Note:** When capturing without device control, use the camcorder's playback controls to navigate to a position about 20 seconds before the first scene you wish to capture. Then click Play, and about 10 seconds before that scene appears, click the Capture button ( ). Adobe Premiere Elements will start capturing the video. Capture the desired scenes, and about 10 seconds after the last target frame, click the Stop button ( ) to stop capture.

● **Note:** If you receive the error message "Recorder Error - frames are dropped during capture," or if you're having problems with the device control, it's likely that your hard disk is not keeping up with the transfer of video. Make sure you're capturing your video to the fastest hard disk available; for example, an external IEEE 1394 drive rather than a hard disk inside a laptop computer.

10 After you've completed capturing your video, close the Capture panel by clicking the Close button ( ) in the upper-right corner. Your captured clips appear in the Organize workspace, as well as in Project view in the Edit workspace. If you enabled Capture to Timeline, Adobe Premiere Elements will also place each clip into your Sceneline in sequential order.

● **Note:** When capturing DV and webcam footage, you will see video in the Preview area of the Capture panel. When capturing HDV, you won't see any video in the Preview area, and will have to watch the LCD screen on your camcorder to determine when to stop capture.

Converting analog video to digital video

Before DV camcorders were widely manufactured, most people used camcorders that recorded analog video onto VHS, 8mm, or other analog tape formats. To use video from analog sources in your Adobe Premiere Elements project, you must first convert (digitize) the footage to digital data, because Adobe Premiere Elements only accepts direct input from digital sources. To digitize your footage, you can use either your digital camcorder or a standalone device that performs analog-to-digital (AV DV) conversion.

You can perform a successful conversion using the following methods:

- Use your digital camcorder to output a digital signal from an analog input. Connect the analog source to input jacks on your digital camcorder and connect the digital camcorder to the computer. Not all digital camcorders support this method. See your camcorder documentation for more information.

- Use your digital camcorder to record footage from your analog source. Connect your analog source's output to the analog inputs on your digital camcorder. Then, record your analog footage to digital tape. When you are finished recording, Adobe Premiere Elements can then capture the footage from the digital camcorder. This is a very common procedure. See your camcorder documentation for more details on recording from analog sources.

- Use your computer's sound card, if it has a microphone (mic) input, to capture sound from a microphone.

- Use an AV DV converter to bridge the connection between your analog source and the computer. Connect the analog source to the converter and connect the converter to your computer. Adobe Premiere Elements then captures the digitized footage. AV DV converters are available in many larger consumer electronics stores.

Note: If you capture using an AV DV converter, you might need to capture without using device control.

—*From Adobe Premiere Elements Help*

Using the Media Downloader

As mentioned at the start of this lesson, you will use Adobe Premiere Elements' Media Downloader to import clips from DVDs, DVD-based camcorders, AVCHD camcorders, digital still cameras, and mobile phones and players. In essence, if the video is stored on a hard disk, SD card, optical disc, or other storage media other than tape, you'll import it with the Media Downloader.

In this exercise we'll use the Media Downloader to import video from an AVCHD camcorder. If you don't have an AVCHD camcorder, you can follow along using video captured on a digital still camera, DVD camcorder, or mobile phone, or even a non-encrypted DVD, such as one that you've previously produced with Adobe Premiere Elements. Note that Adobe Premiere Elements will not import video from DVDs that are encrypted, such as most Hollywood DVD titles.

1   Connect your AVCHD camcorder to your computer via the USB 2.0 port.

2   Turn the camcorder on and set it to PC mode, or whichever mode is used to transfer video from camcorder to computer.

3   Launch Adobe Premiere Elements.

4   In the Organize workspace, click Get Media.

5   In Get Media view, select AVCHD Camcorder ( ) to follow along with this procedure. Selecting DVD Camcorder or PC DVD Drive ( ), or Digital Still Camera ( ), or Mobile Phones and Players ( ) will also open Media Downloader, though some settings will be different from this example.

The Media Downloader opens using the Advanced dialog. (If the Advanced dialog isn't showing, click Advanced Dialog in the lower left of the Adobe Premiere Elements - Media Downloader window.)

● **Note:** This connection procedure will vary by device; some AVCHD camcorders require that you set the camcorder into PC Mode before connecting the USB 2.0 cable, others the reverse. Please check the documentation that came with your camcorder for additional details.

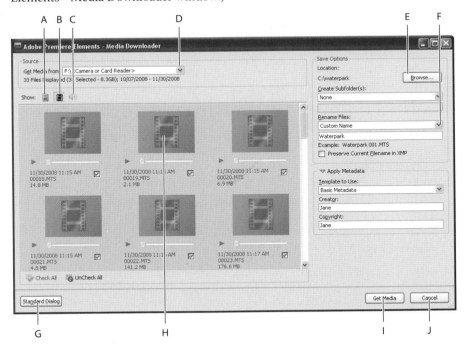

Adobe Premiere Elements Media Downloader (Advanced dialog): **A.** Show/hide image files. **B.** Show/hide video files. **C.** Show/hide audio files. **D.** Available drives and devices. **E.** Location for saved files. **F.** Naming convention. **G.** Standard Dialog button. **H.** Importable files. **I.** Get Media button. **J.** Cancel button.

Note: When you import a DVD using the Media Downloader, files for menus are distinguished from video files by the word *Menu*, as in Menu_Epgc_Esf_938876809.psd.

6 Under Source, choose the drive or device from the Get Media view menu.

Once you choose the drive or device, Adobe Premiere Elements will populate the Media Downloader. When importing video from most devices, including DVDs and most digital still cameras, thumbnails of all available video and still image files will appear in the dialog. When importing video from an AVCHD camcorder in the current version of Adobe Premiere Elements, no video thumbnail will be shown, though the Media Downloader will display thumbnails of digital still images captured by the AVCHD camcorder.

7 To show or hide specific file types, click the Show/Hide Images button ( ), Show/Hide Video button ( ), or Show/Hide Audio button ( ), located above the thumbnail area.

Note: You cannot preview AVCHD video in the current version of Adobe Premiere Elements.

8 To preview a video file, click the black triangle in the lower-left corner of the video thumbnail image.

9 To specify a location for the saved files, do one of the following:

- To save files to the default location—which is the location where you previously stored files captured by the Media Downloader—leave the location unchanged.

- To specify a new location for saving the files, click Browse and choose a folder, or click Make New Folder to create a new folder.

- Optionally, Adobe Premiere Elements saves imported files to one or more subfolders. Select Today's Date (yyyy mm dd) from the Create Subfolder(s) menu to save imported files in a subfolder—using today's date as name—in the location you have chosen.

- To create a single folder with a name of your choice, select Custom Name from the Create Subfolder(s) menu and enter the name of the folder in the text box that appears.

10 To rename the files using a consistent name within the folder, select an option other than Do Not Rename Files from the Rename Files menu. When the files are added to the folder and to the Media panel, the file numbers are incremented by 001. For example, if you enter *Waterpark* as Custom Name under Rename Files, Adobe Premiere Elements will change the filenames to Waterpark 001.MTS, Waterpark 002.MTS, and so on.

11 In the thumbnail area, select individual files to add to the Media panel. A checkmark below a file's thumbnail indicates that the file is selected. By default, all files are selected. Only selected files are imported. Click a checkbox to deselect it, thus excluding the related file from being imported.

12 Click Get Media. This transfers the media to the destination location, which is typically your hard disk. You can click Stop in the Copying dialog at any time to stop the process.

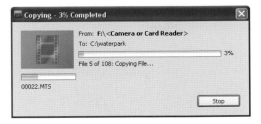

Files that you import using the Media Downloader appear in the Organize workspace, as well as Project view in the Edit workspace.

Importing content from your hard disk

Follow this procedure to import audio, video, or still-image content that's already on your hard disk.

1 In the Organize workspace, click Get Media.

2 Click PC Files and Folders ( ).

Adobe Premiere Elements opens the Add Media panel.

3 To change to a new disk or folder, click the Look In list box and navigate to a new location.

4 To display only certain files types in the dialog, click the Supported Files of type list box, and choose the desired file type. The dialog displays only files of the selected type.

5 To change the file view in the dialog, click the View menu.

6 To import files, choose them in the dialog as you normally would, and click Open.

Files that you import using the Add Media dialog appear in the Organize workspace, as well as in Project view in the Edit workspace.

Review questions

1 How do you access the Capture panel in Adobe Premiere Elements?

2 Why is having a separate hard disk dedicated to video a good idea?

3 What is Scene Detect and how would you turn it on or off if you wanted to?

4 What is the Media Downloader and when would you use it?

5 What is device control?

Review answers

1 Click Get Media from the Organize Workspace, and then click the DV Camcorder, HDV Camcorder, or Webcam or WDM Device buttons.

2 Video files take up large amounts of space compared to standard office and image files. A hard disk stores the video clips you capture and must be fast enough to store your video frames. Additionally, the more free defragmented space you have on a hard disk, the better the performance of real-time capture will be.

3 Scene Detect is Adobe Premiere Elements' ability to detect scene changes in your video (based on timecode or by content) during video capture and save each scene as an individual clip in your project. You can select or deselect Scene Detect by Timecode and Scene Detect by Content in the Capture panel menu.

4 The Media Downloader is a feature of Adobe Premiere Elements that enables you to import media from AVCHD camcorders, digital still cameras, mobile phones and players, and DVDs, whether from a camcorder or PC DVD driver.

5 Device control is the ability of Adobe Premiere Elements to control the basic functions of your digital video camera (such as play, stop, and rewind) through the interface in the Capture panel. It's available on most DV and HDV camcorders.

4 ORGANIZING YOUR CONTENT

Once you've captured or imported your content, you can drag it to the My Project panel from either the Organizer or Project view in the Edit workspace. Why two locations? Because as you'll read in this chapter, each has its own unique strengths.

For example, the Organizer is ideal for tagging your clips for easy search and retrieval, for creating Instant Movies, and for creating albums to back up to Photoshop.com. Project view works well when you'd like to sort and trim your clips before adding them to the Sceneline or Timeline.

Fast and efficient movie production is all about organization. In this lesson, you'll learn how to do the following:

- Manually tag your clips in the Organizer

- Apply Smart Tagging in the Organizer

- Create an Album for backing up your projects to Photoshop.com

- Create an InstantMovie using manual and Smart Tagging

- Create a "rough cut" of your movie in Project view

- Trim clips using the Preview window in Project view

- Drag clips to the My Project panel from either the Organizer or Project view

 This lesson will take approximately 2 hours.

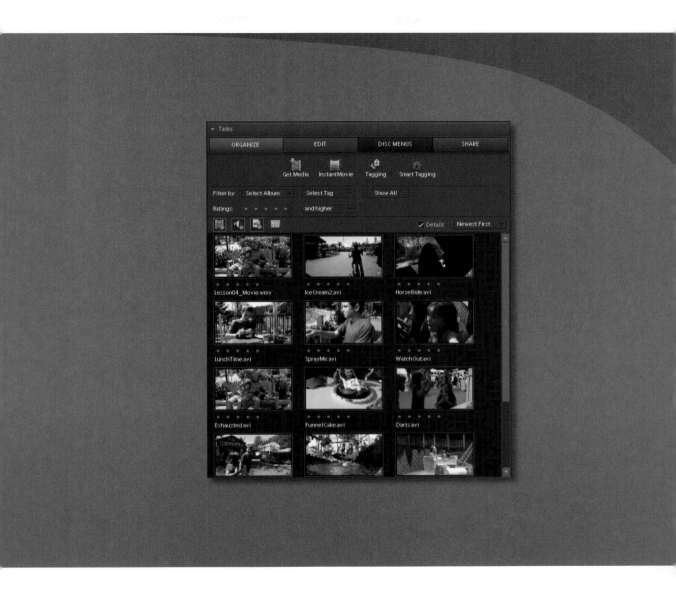

Collecting assets in the Organizer.

Getting started

To begin, let's review a final version of the movie you'll be creating.

1 Before you begin, make sure that you have correctly copied the Lesson04 and 05 folder from the DVD in the back of this book onto your computer's hard disk. See "Copying the Classroom in a Book files" in the Getting Started section at the beginning of this book.

2 Launch Adobe Premiere Elements.

3 In the Welcome screen, click the Open Project button. If necessary, click Open in the pop-up menu. The Open Project dialog opens.

4 In the Open Project dialog, navigate to the Lesson04 and 05 folder you copied to your hard disk. Within that folder, select the file Lesson04_Start.prel, and then click Open. Make sure that you don't select the Lesson05_Start.prel file, which is in the same folder. If a dialog appears asking for the location of rendered files, click the Skip Previews button.

Your project file opens with the Monitor, Tasks, and My Project panels open.

5 Choose Window > Restore Workspace to ensure that you start the lesson with the default window layout.

Viewing the completed movie before you start

To see what you'll be creating in this lesson, you can take a look at the completed movie.

1 In the Edit workspace of the Tasks panel, click the Project button. In Project view, locate the file Lesson04_Movie.wmv (which should be the only file), and then double-click it to open the video into the Preview window.

2 In the Preview window, click the Play button ( ) to watch the video about a visit to a water park, which you'll be building in this lesson.

3   When finished, close the Preview window by clicking the Close button (✖) in the upper-right corner of the window.

Working in the Organizer and Project views

The Organizer in Adobe Premiere Elements is a customized view of the Organizer used in Adobe Photoshop Elements. If you are familiar with the Organizer in Photoshop Elements, you will feel right at home using the Organizer in Adobe Premiere Elements. The Organizer helps you find and sort material for your projects from among all the media files available on your computer. Use it to find all clips, for example, that you've placed into a Photoshop Elements Album or Adobe Premiere Elements project, and then sort the clips using a range of tools.

The Organizer is the default view in the Tasks panel and should be open when you run Adobe Premiere Elements for the first time. If it's not showing now, click Organize in the Tasks panel, or choose Window > Organizer.

There are several points you should understand about the Organizer and Project view.

First, when you first run Adobe Premiere Elements, either loading an existing project or starting with a new project, the Organizer will display all files that you've imported into all previous Adobe Premiere Elements projects so you can easily reuse this content if desired. In contrast, Project view contains only files that you have captured or imported into that project.

For the sake of discussion, let's look at the current contents of Project view in the Edit workspace. In the Tasks panel, click the Edit tab, and then the Project button (). Assuming that you haven't imported any additional files into the project, Project view should contain only one file, Lesson04_Movie.wmv, which you just played.

As you'll learn in exercises below, the Organizer is for browsing through files, tagging them, creating albums for backup to Photoshop.com, and creating InstantMovies. In contrast, Project view is a repository for content that you've already included in the project. Clips appearing in the Organizer when you first run the program have not been imported into the project, and won't appear in Project view until you either import them or drag them to the My Project panel. Let's load some files from the lesson folder to reinforce this point.

Follow this procedure to import audio and video clips from the Lesson04 and 05 folder.

1   In the Organizer, click the Get Media button ( ).

2   Click PC Files and Folders ( ).

    Adobe Premiere Elements opens the Add Media panel.

3   Navigate to the Lesson04 folder. In the "Files of type" pop-up menu, choose "AVI Movie (*.avi)" and select all the visible files (and not the .wmv, .wav, or .png files). Click Open to import the clips.

After importing the clips, your Organizer should display only the clips you just imported. Project view, which previously contained only one file, should also contain all files that you just imported.

If you compare the two panels, you will see the same files in both. However, if you closed the project file and later reopened it, the Organizer will again contain *all* files previously imported into *all* previous Adobe Premiere Elements projects, while Project view will contain only those files imported into *that specific* Adobe Premiere Elements project.

With this as background, let's take a deeper look into both workspaces, starting with the Organizer.

Finding clips in the Organizer

The role of the Organizer is to help you find files using different search methods. Some basic search methods are available without any action on your part, while advanced methods are available after you've rated the clips, or applied keyword or Smart Tags to your clips, all discussed below. In this short section, you'll learn how to use the basic tools in the Organizer to find the desired file.

1   To find files in the Organizer, *do any or all of the following*:

  •   Browse through the entire catalog by using the scroll bar at the right side of the Organizer.

  •   Select either Newest First or Oldest First from the Media Arrangement According to Date menu located in the upper-right corner of the Organizer to sort the files in chronological or reverse-chronological order.

  •   Select which media type to show—or not to show—using the icons just below the Ratings field.

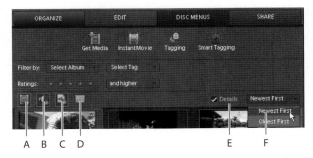

A. Show/Hide Video. **B.** Show/Hide Audio. **C.** Show/Hide Still Image.
D. Set Date Range. **E.** Details checkbox. **F.** Media Arrangement according to date.

- Restrict your search to files created within a period of time by choosing Set Date Range and then entering a start and end date in the Set Date Range dialog.

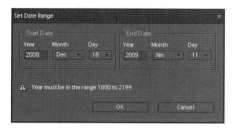

- Select the Details checkbox to show star ratings, filename, and other details in the Organizer.

- Use the Media Arrangement according to date list box to display the newest clips first, or the oldest clips first.

- Click the Filter By: List box and choose either an Album () or Project ( ). The Organizer will display content from that Album or Project.

- To show all content in the Organizer, click the Show All button.

2 To add a still image, video, or audio file from the Organizer to your project, drag the file from the Organizer into the Timeline or Sceneline of the My Project panel. This will also automatically add the file to Project view.

The Organizer and Tagging panel

The Organizer has two panels, the Organizer shown in the previous section, and the Tagging panel, which you can open by double-clicking a clip in the Organizer, or by clicking the Tagging button () in the Organizer. You can perform many activities in both panels, but the Tagging panel is generally better for manually tagging and applying Smart Tagging to clips. The Organizer is better for finding clips to include in a project. For this reason, this exercise will detail how to perform manual and Smart Tagging in the Tagging panel, then search for clips using those tags in the Organizer.

Let's start with a brief description of tagging, which you perform in one or more of three ways, via star ratings (1–5), applying keyword tags, and using Smart Tags. At a high level, all tags allow you to more easily find the clips to include in a particular movie. For example, if you review and rate all of your clips on a scale of 1–5, you can later search for only clips that you rated 4 or above, an easy way to find high-quality clips and eliminate poor-quality clips.

Keyword tags allow you to tag a clip by person, location, event, or other tag, with customizable categories. For example, in this exercise, you'll apply several keyword tags to the clips from this project, and then search for clips containing these keyword tags.

Finally, when you perform Smart Tagging on a clip, Adobe Premiere Elements analyzes the video to detect scenes based upon content; hunt for scenes with faces; and identify scenes that are out of focus, shaky, underexposed, or overexposed. Using this qualitative data, Adobe Premiere Elements then categorizes all clips as high-, medium-, or low-quality. This serves a valuable triage function that you can later use to search for the best clips for your movie.

For example, if you shot an hour of video on your last vacation, Smart Tagging allows you to identify medium-quality and higher clips containing faces (presumably family members), and produce a movie containing only these clips. What would literally take you hours to accomplish manually, Smart Tagging can produce in a few moments.

Using all these tags in any combination, you can hunt for clips to manually produce into a movie, or create an InstantMovie, which is a professional-looking edited movie, complete with titles, soundtrack, effects, and transitions, that you'll create using a fast and simple step-by-step process.

Tagging clips in the Tagging panel

Let's open and explore operations in the Tagging panel.

1   In the Organizer, double-click the clip LunchTime.avi. Adobe Premiere Elements opens the Tagging panel. In this view, you can preview the clip using the playback controls.

A. Back to Grid View. **B.** Preview area. **C.** Rewind. **D.** Step back (left arrow key).
E. Play/Pause Toggle (spacebar). **F.** Step forward (right arrow key).
G. Fast-Forward **H.** Current-time indicator. **I.** Docking header.

2 Click Play to play the video file, and use the playback controls to fast-forward, rewind, and otherwise experiment with these controls.

● **Note:** Three keyboard shortcuts apply to all Adobe Premiere Elements preview and playback panels: Click the spacebar to start and stop clip playback, and use the arrow keys to navigate frame by frame forwards (right arrow) and backwards (left arrow).

3 In the upper left of the Tagging panel, click the Back to Grid View button. Adobe Premiere Elements displays all clips currently in the Organizer in a Browser panel. This is the view that's most convenient for creating and applying keyword tags, applying Smart Tags, and creating Albums for backing up your clips.

● **Note:** Double-clicking any clip in Browser view will return the Tagging panel to Preview view where you can play the clip.

Browser panel

● **Note:** You can position the Tagging panel anywhere on screen by grabbing the Docking header and moving the panel to the new location. You can also resize the panel by grabbing and dragging any edge to the desired size.

Working with star ratings

Follow these procedures to apply and delete star ratings, and to search for clips based upon the star ratings. Ratings range from 1 (on the extreme left) to 5 (on the extreme right).

1   In the upper-right corner of the Tagging panel (or Organizer), select the Details checkbox.

2   Hover your pointer over the star ratings beneath any clip, and click the star that corresponds with the desired rating for that clip. Go ahead and rate a few clips so you can sort by rating in Step 5.

3   To change a rating, use the same procedure and choose a different rating.

4   To delete the star rating, click and drag the pointer from right to left, starting at the rating and extending to the left of the first star.

5   To find clips based upon their assigned ratings in the Organizer (or the Tagging panel), click the number of target stars and adjust the list box as desired. Adobe Premiere Elements displays only those files that meet the selected criteria.

6   Click the Show All button to view all clips in the Organizer. If working in the Tagging window, click the Close button on the upper right to close the window.

Working with keyword tags

Adobe Premiere Elements includes general categories of keyword tags that you can apply as is, or customize with your own categories or subcategories. In this lesson, you'll create and apply two custom categories in the Tagging panel, and then search for clips based on those keywords in the Organizer.

1   Click the Tagging button in the Organizer to open the Tagging panel in Grid view.

2 Under Keyword Tags in the Tagging panel, click the twirl-down triangle next to People to expose Family and Friends, and select Family.

3 Under Keyword Tags, click the Create New button () and choose New Sub-Category.

4 In the Create Sub-Category panel, type *Kids* in the Sub-Category Name field.

Adobe Premiere Elements creates the new sub-category.

5 Repeat steps 2–4 to create the sub-category Water Park under Places.

6 In the Browser panel, click to select a clip with a child. Then press and hold the Ctrl key, and click all other kid clips to select them, too. You should have multiple clips selected.

7 Drag the Kids keyword tag to any of the selected kid clips. When you release the pointer, Adobe Premiere Elements applies the keyword tag to all selected clips.

8 Use the same procedure to apply the Water Park tag to *all* clips in the Tagging panel except for Lesson04_Movie.wmv. You'll use the Water Park tag to produce the InstantMovie in the next clip.

9 In the Organizer or Tagging panel, or both, select the box next to the keyword tags to show only those files tagged with the selected keyword tags. In both panels, Adobe Premiere Elements will show only the clips containing kids that were shot at the water park.

Working with Smart Tagging

When you apply Smart Tagging to a clip, Adobe Premiere Elements analyzes the clip to detect scenes based upon content, hunt for certain content types like faces, and rank the quality of your clips. Then you can use this information just like keyword tags to include or exclude clips from the Organizer or Tagging panel. Follow these steps to apply Smart Tags to the project clips.

1   If necessary, click the Tagging button in the Organizer to open the Tagging panel in Grid view.

2   Click to select all clips and then right-click and choose Perform Smart Tagging.

3   Alternatively, in the Organizer, click to select the target clips and click the Smart Tagging () button.

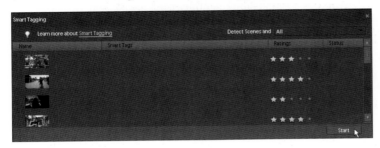

4   Either way, Adobe Premiere Elements opens the Smart Tagging panel. Click Start on the bottom right to start Smart Tagging.

5 Adobe Premiere Elements starts Smart Tagging and reports its progress in the Smart Tagging panel. The duration of the process will vary by clip length, clip format, and the speed of your computer.

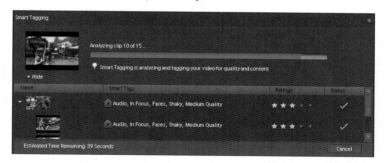

► **Tip:** As with keyword tagging, you can use the tags created via Smart Tagging in either the Organizer or Tagging panel. You can use these tags by themselves or in conjunction with keyword tags or even star ratings. For example, in the Tagging panel, click Two Stars and Higher in the top toolbar, click the Water Park tag in the Keyword tags, and click Faces and Medium Quality in Smart Tags. Adobe Premiere Elements will display only those clips that meet these criteria.

6 When the tagging process is complete, click Done to close the Smart Tagging panel.

7 Make sure the Details checkbox on the upper right of the Tagging panel Browser (and Organizer) is selected. In both panels, a purple tag ( ) beneath the clip's thumbnail indicates that Smart Tagging has been applied. A yellow tag ( ) indicates that keyword tags have been applied. To view which tags have been applied, double-click the clip in either the Organizer or Tagging panel. Tagging details will appear beneath the Preview window.

8 To remove a tag, right-click the tag in the Tagging panel (in Preview view) and delete the tag, or right-click the thumbnail in the Tagging panel's Grid view or in the Organizer, and choose the tag to remove.

9 Close the Tagging panel by clicking the Close button () in the upper-right corner of the panel.

Note: When you close the Tagging panel, the search criteria from that panel are applied to the Organizer, so that only the clips appearing in the Tagging panel before you closed it will appear in the Organizer.

Working with clips after Smart Tagging

Let's take a moment to understand what happens to clips
after Smart Tagging. To review, during Smart Tagging, Adobe
Premiere Elements breaks the clip into different scenes based
upon content changes (as opposed to timecode, like DV files);
finds different types of content like faces; and rates the quality
of each clip based upon factors like exposure, focus, and stability.

In the Organizer, you'll know that the clip has been split into multiple scenes if
there is a Step Forward icon (⏭) on the right of the clip. Click that icon, and
Adobe Premiere Elements displays all scenes separately in the Organizer, surrounded by a border that's a lighter gray than the rest of the Organizer. This lets
you know that all of the scenes are part of a single clip.

In this view, you can treat each scene as a separate clip, for example, dragging it to
the My Project panel to include it in a project, or double-clicking it to play it in the
Tagging panel and view the tags applied to the clip. You can consolidate all scenes
back into a single frame by clicking the Step Backward icon to the right of the final
scene (⏮).

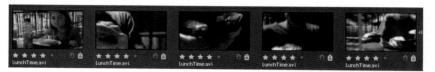

Smart Tagging also changes the presentation in Project view. Click the Edit tab and
the Project icon to view files in Project view. Scroll down until you see the folder
labeled LunchTime.avi01. Note that the separate scenes shown in the Organizer are
also available in Project view. However, none of the tagging, either keyword tags or
Smart Tags, are shown in Project view.

Again, use the Organizer to find tags and clips to include in the project. Once
included, you can manage these files in Project view.

Creating an InstantMovie

In this lesson, you'll create an InstantMovie from the clips that you tagged for the water park in a previous lesson. Again, an InstantMovie is a professional-looking edited movie, complete with titles, soundtrack, effects, and transitions that you'll create by following a simple wizard.

1   In the Organizer, click the Show All button (if showing) to display all clips available in the Organizer. If the button is not visible, it's already been selected.

2   Click the second Filter By: List box, click the twirl-down arrow next to Places, and then and select the checkbox next to Water Park. The Organizer will display only those clips previously tagged with the Water Park tag.

3   Click to select all clips in the Organizer, and then click the InstantMovie ( ) button. Adobe Premiere Elements opens the InstantMovie Wizard. You can preview any Style by clicking it, and stop the preview by clicking it again.

4   Choose Kid's Channel and click Next. If this theme is not available, choose another.

5 Customize the Theme as desired. *Accept the options as is, or do any or all of the following*:

- Customize the Opening and Closing Titles.

- Select the Auto Edit checkbox to have Adobe Premiere Elements analyze your clips, and edit them to fit the selected theme, which is recommended. If you don't check Auto Edit, Adobe Premiere Elements uses the clips as is and doesn't edit them.

- In the Music box, choose the Theme Music radio button to use the background music from the selected Theme, or the No Music radio button. To use your own background music, click the My Music radio button and then click the Browse button to choose the target song. Then drag the Music/Sound FX slider to the desired setting, dragging to the right to prioritize audio captured with the video clips, and to the left to prioritize the selected background music.

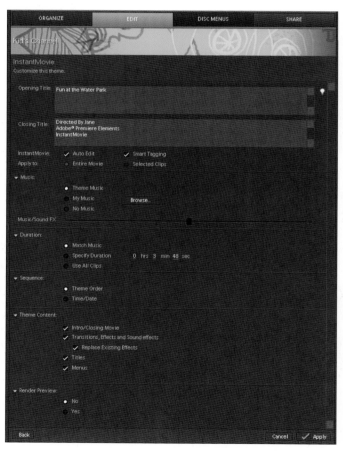

● **Note:** The Apply to: radio buttons only become active when you apply a Theme to clips already inserted into the My Project panel, not when you create an InstantMovie from the Organizer.

- In the Duration box, choose the desired option. Match Music produces a movie that matches the duration of the selected music, and is recommended. Or, you can specify a duration, or choose Use All Clips, which uses all clips at their original duration with no background music.

- In the Sequence box, choose Theme Order (recommended), which allows Adobe Premiere Elements to use clips as they best match the theme, or Time/Date, which uses the clips in the order that they were shot.

- In the Theme Content box, choose the content to incorporate into the InstantMovie, and whether to replace any existing content with theme-based content.

- In the Render Preview box, choose Yes to render a preview of the InstantMovie after completion, or No to preview in real time from the My Project panel (recommended).

6   After selecting your options, click Apply to create the InstantMovie. Click No when the InstantMovie dialog opens and asks if you want to select more clips. Adobe Premiere Elements creates the InstantMovie and inserts it into the My Project panel.

7   Use the playback controls in the Monitor panel to preview the InstantMovie.

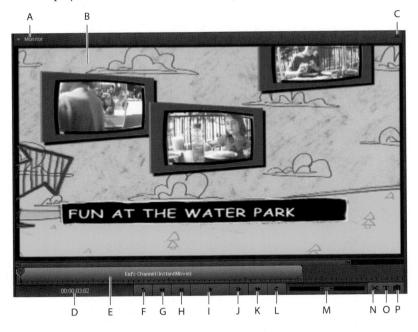

A. Docking header.
B. Preview area.
C. Panel menu.
D. Current Time.
E. Clip Representation in Mini-Timeline. **F.** Go to Previous Edit Point.
G. Rewind. **H.** Step Back (Left). **I.** Play/Pause (Spacebar). **J.** Step Forward (Right). **K.** Fast-Forward. **L.** Go to Next Edit Point. **M.** Shuttle.
N. Split Clip (Ctrl+K).
O. Add Default Text.
P. Freeze Frame.

8 Adobe Premiere Elements adds the InstantMovie to the My Project panel (either Timeline or Sceneline, whichever was selected) in consolidated form. To break apart the InstantMovie into its components to edit them, click to select the new InstantMovie, right-click, and choose Breakapart InstantMovie.

Uploading files to Photoshop.com

Depending upon your membership level in Photoshop.com, you can back up as much as 2 gigabytes (GB) of video files to the site. To upload video files, you must first create an Album and then add the video file to that Album.

Follow this procedure to back up video files to Photoshop.com.

● **Note:**
Photoshop.com services are currently available only for Adobe Premiere Elements users in the United States.

1 In the Organizer, click the Tagging button ( ). Adobe Premiere Elements opens the Tagging panel.

2 Under Album in the Tagging panel, click the Create New Album or Album Group button ( ), and choose New Album. Adobe Premiere Elements opens the Create Album panel.

3 Type *Water Park - 2008*, and make sure that Backup/Synchronize is selected. Then click OK to close the panel.

4 In the Keyword tags box, select the checkbox next to the Water Park tag. The Tagging panel will display only those clips previously tagged with the Water Park tag.

5 Select all clips.

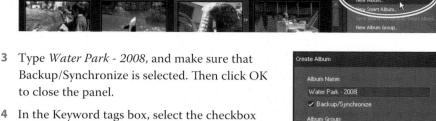

6 Drag the Water Park album tag to any of the selected clips. When you release the pointer, the album tag is applied to all selected clips.

● **Note:** Once you create the Album, you may be prompted to log into www.Photoshop.com. If you haven't created an account, you can do so by clicking Join Now on the www.Photoshop.com homepage. If you don't have an account, or aren't currently logged in, you'll get an error message in your Preferences panel.

7 Under Album in the Tagging panel, Click the Launch Backup/Synchronization Preferences (   ) button. Adobe Premiere Elements opens the Preferences panel, open to the Backup/Synchronization preferences. In this panel, if not already selected, do the following:

- Select the Backup/Sync checkbox.
- Select the New Albums will Backup/Sync Automatically checkbox.
- Select the Sync checkbox for Water Park – 2008.

● **Note:** You must be logged into Photoshop. com to view this screen.

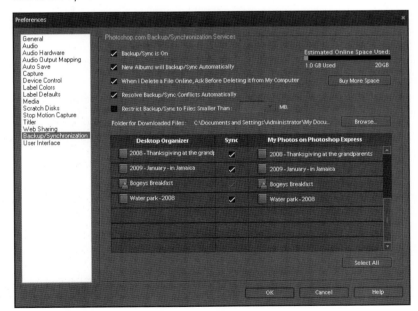

● **Note:** Much of Adobe Premiere Elements' tagging and album-related functionality is very similar to features in Photoshop Elements. If you have any questions about these features, check Chapters 2 and 3 in *Adobe Photoshop Elements 7 Classroom in a Book*.

8   Unless you have a burning desire to store random videos of another family on your Photoshop.com site, under Album in the Tagging panel, click the Water park – 2008 album, then the Delete Album button (🗑). Adobe Premiere Elements will delete the Album and remove any files from that Album previously uploaded to Photoshop.com.

Working with Project view

As discussed previously, Project view is where Photoshop Elements stores all clips captured or imported into a project. The filenames in Project view identify the files imported into the project.

● **Note:** By clicking the column headers, you can choose to sort by other attributes, or toggle between ascending and descending order. You can customize which columns you want shown in Project view by choosing Edit Columns from the panel menu in the docking header of the Tasks panel.

It's important to note that files listed in Project view are simply references to the clips you import, not the clips themselves. The original clips you import are on your hard disk and are untouched by Adobe Premiere Elements. Cutting or editing a clip in Adobe Premiere Elements does not affect the original file. Adobe Premiere Elements records your modifications along with the reference to the original file in Project view. This means that a 20 MB clip takes up 20 MB of space on your hard disk whether you use only a portion of the clip—by trimming away unwanted sections—or whether you use this clip in its full length (or even two or more times) in a project.

1   To show Project view, select the Edit tab and then click Project. Or, choose Window > Available Media. Project view lists all the source clips imported to your Adobe Premiere Elements project. When you capture video or import files, the individual clips are automatically placed in Project view in alphabetical order, as shown here.

2   If necessary, use the scroll bar on the right side of Project view to scroll down toward the bottom of the list.

3   If the docking headers are not currently visible, choose Window > Show Docking Headers. Then, choose View > Icon from the panel menu located at the right end of the Tasks panel docking header, or click the Icon View button () in the lower-left corner of Project view. This will change your view from the default List view to Icon view, which offers a larger thumbnail preview and an ability to sort files in Project view that you'll explore in a future lesson.

4 Return to List view by choosing View > List from the panel menu, or by clicking the List View button (▦) in the lower-left corner of Project view.

● **Note:** You may need to expand the size of the Tasks panel to be able to see all the information provided.

5 Choose View > Preview Area from the panel menu. The preview area opens at the top of Project view. Click the clip labeled LunchTime.avi (not the LunchTime folder) in Project view to select it. Important information about the clip appears in the preview area, including the duration of the clip and how many times it is used in the project.

6 Click the Play button (▶) to the left of the thumbnail to begin playing the clip in the preview area. The Play button turns to a Stop button (■). Click the Play/Stop button after about 5 or 6 seconds into the clip. The clip will pan from a young girl to a young boy. Use the slider below the thumbnail to move forwards or backwards in the clip, if necessary.

7 Click the Poster Frame button (▣) just above the Play button to assign the current frame as the new poster frame for this clip.

A poster frame is the image used to identify a video clip in Project view. By default, Adobe Premiere Elements assigns the first frame of a video clip as the poster frame. Oftentimes, the first frame is not a good indicator of the clip's content. In such a case, selecting a different poster frame can make the clip easier to recognize.

8 Choose View > Preview Area from the panel menu to close the preview area. In Project view, notice the new poster frame that you assigned for the LunchTime.avi clip.

Trimming a clip in the Preview window

One of the most important editing tasks is removing unwanted footage from the beginning and end of your clips. Adobe Premiere Elements has multiple ways of accomplishing this task, but you can access one of the simplest techniques in Project view.

● **Note:** Trimming a clip in the Preview window does not change the In and Out points of instances of that clip already included in the My Project panel. It only sets the In and Out points for all subsequent instances of that clip placed in the My Project panel.

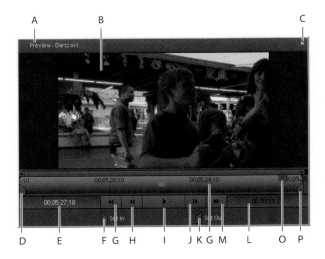

A B C

D E F G H I J K G M L O P

A. Docking header.
B. Preview area. **C.** Close window. **D.** In point handle.
E. Current time in movie.
F. Set In point.
G. Rewind. **H.** Step Back (Left). **I.** Play/Pause (spacebar). **J.** Step Forward (Right).
K. Set Out point
L. Clip Representation in Mini-Timeline. **M.** Fast-Forward. **N.** Clip duration.
O. Current-time indicator.
P. Out point handle.

1   Locate the Darts.avi clip in Project view. Double-click the clip to open it in the Preview window. Note that the name of the clip is displayed in the title bar of the Preview window.

2   Click the Play button ( ) and play this clip from beginning to end. You'll note a few moments of black at the end of the clip. You'll trim that out below.

The timecode in the lower-left corner of the Preview window displays the timecode of that clip on the original DV tape, while the timecode in the lower-right corner shows clip duration. You can navigate through this clip by clicking the timecode in the lower-left corner of the Preview window, and then dragging left or right.

3   Place your pointer over the current-time indicator in the lower-left corner of the Preview window, and then click and drag to scrub through the clip.

4   Drag the current-time indicator in the mini-timeline to reposition it.

5   Trim the clip. To begin, set a new In point by clicking and dragging the In point handle ( ) to the desired location on the mini-timeline in the Preview window. Or, position the current-time indicator ( ) at the desired position, and then click the Set In Point button ( ).

6   Next, trim out the black frames at the end of the clip. To set a new Out point, click and drag the Out point handle ( ) to the desired location on the mini-timeline in the Preview window (about 00;05;27;18 as shown in the lower-left corner). Or, position the current-time indicator ( ) at the desired position (00;05;27;18), and then click the Set Out Point button ( ).

7   Click the Close button ( ) to close the Preview window.

● **Note:** In and Out points specified in the Preview window are automatically applied to all instances of the clip subsequently added to the Sceneline. Use the Monitor panel to change the In and Out points of specific instances of clips already included in the Sceneline.

8 Repeat the same procedure with the Elephant.avi clip, removing the black frames at the end by setting a new Out point at about 00;05;06;03.

9 Click the Close button (⊠) to close the Preview window.

Creating a rough cut in the Project view

After trimming your clips, it's often convenient to arrange them in the desired order before dragging them to the My Project panel, which is called a *rough cut* of your movie. This is very easy to accomplish in Project view using the Icon view discussed above. In this exercise you will create a rough cut and then drag it to the My Project panel.

1 If you still have the InstantMovie in your MyProject panel, delete it by right clicking the movie, and in the Sceneline choosing Delete Scene and its objects, or in the Timeline by right-clicking and choosing Clear.

2 In the lower-left corner of Project view, click the Icon View button (▣).

3 Drag the clips into the order shown in the screenshot shown in the previous figure, leaving out Lesson04_Movie.wmv.

▶ **Tip:** To increase the workspace, you can drag the horizontal dividing line between the Tasks panel and the Monitor panel to the left. To snap all clips back into view and to close any gaps between the clips, choose Clean Up from the panel menu. Or choose Window > Restore Workspace to restore your workspace to its default layout.

4 Click to select all clips and then drag them to the first clip target in the Sceneline in the My Project panel. When you release the pointer, Adobe Premiere Elements will insert the clips into the Sceneline.

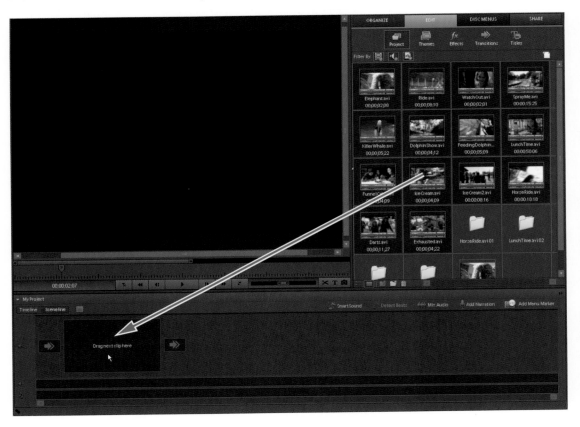

5 Click Play to watch the rough cut that you just created.

Review questions

1 What's the difference between the Organizer and Project view?

2 What is Smart Tagging? Are there any situations in which you wouldn't you want to apply Smart Tagging?

3 After creating an InstantMovie, how do you break up the movie to edit it further?

4 What is a rough cut and where would you create one?

5 How do you upload your clips to Photoshop.com?

Review answers

1 The Organizer is used for tagging and finding clips that you've imported into all projects. Project view contains only those clips that you've imported into the project.

2 When you apply Smart Tagging to a clip, Adobe Premiere Elements analyzes the clip to detect scenes based upon content, hunt for certain content types like faces, and rank the quality of your clips. Other than processing time, there's very little downside to applying Smart Tagging. Your video clips will be divided into useful scenes, and you can find high-quality clips much faster than you could manually.

3 Click the clip with your pointer to select it, then right-click and choose Break apart Instant Movie.

4 A rough cut is a collection of clips in the desired order. You can create a rough cut using the Icon view in Project view.

5 To upload clips to Photoshop.com, create an Album in the Tagging panel, then drag the new Album tag onto the target clips.

5 EDITING VIDEO

In the last lesson, you learned to organize your video in the Organizer and Project views. In this lesson, you'll learn how to take that footage and shape it into a refined final version. You'll use these basic editing techniques:

- Insert, delete, and rearrange clips in the Sceneline and Timeline

- Trim and split clips

- Use Clip and Timeline markers

- Add a Frame Hold to your movie

Over the course of this lesson, you will work on a short home movie. You'll be working with video and audio clips provided on the DVD-ROM included with this *Adobe Premiere Elements 7 Classroom in a Book.* If you were producing an actual project of your own, you would be working with your own source videos.

 This lesson will take approximately 2 hours.

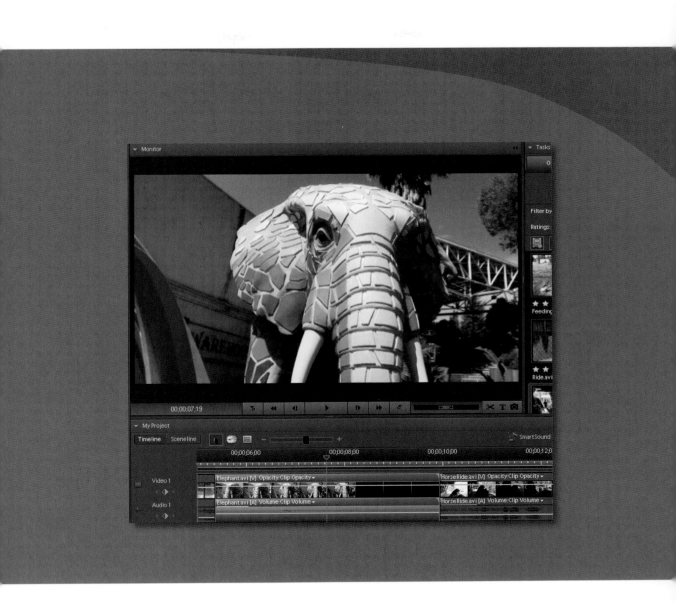

Trimming a clip in the Timeline.

Getting started

To begin, launch Adobe Premiere Elements, open the Lesson05 project, and review a final version of the movie you'll be creating.

1 Before you begin, make sure that you have correctly copied the Lesson04 and 05 folder from the DVD in the back of this book onto your computer's hard disk. See "Copying the Classroom in a Book files" in the Getting Started section at the start of this book.

2 Launch Adobe Premiere Elements.

3 In the Welcome screen, click the Open Project button, and then the Open project folder.

4 In the Open Project dialog, navigate to the Lesson04 and 05 folder you copied to your hard disk.

5 Within that folder, select the file Lesson05_Start.prel, and then click Open. Be sure not to select Lesson04_Start.prel. If a dialog appears asking for the location of rendered files, click the Skip Previews button.

Your project file opens with the Monitor, Tasks, and My Project panels open.

6 Choose Window > Restore Workspace to ensure that you start the lesson with the default panel layout.

Viewing the completed movie before you start

To see what you'll be creating in this lesson, you can take a look at the completed movie.

1 In the Edit tab of the Tasks panel, click Project ( ). In Project view, locate the file Lesson05_Movie.wmv, and then double-click it to open the video in the Preview window.

2 In the Preview window, click the Play button ( ) to watch the video about a visit to the water park , which you will build in this lesson.

3 When done, close the Preview window by clicking the Close button () in the upper-right corner of the window.

Setting up your DV hardware

If you're working with a DV camcorder, you can preview your work on an external monitor. Note that this procedure is optional; it's not required to complete any of the lessons in this Classroom in a Book.

Sending video/audio output from Adobe Premiere Elements to an external monitor takes a bit of setup but is often worthwhile. Computer monitors and TV monitors use two different methods for displaying video; therefore, the color and brightness levels you see on your computer monitor often do not match those on a standard TV set. Previewing your video on a TV will allow you to spot earlier in a project potential issues such as the length of shots, transitions, titles, etc.

To connect your computer to your VCR and TV, do the following:

1 Connect your DV camcorder to the IEEE 1394 port or a USB (Universal Serial Bus) port on your PC.

2 Using an AV connector (which should have come with your DV camcorder), connect your camcorder to your TV set.

(continues)

Working with the Monitor panel

After you organize your clips, drag them into either the Timeline or Sceneline of the My Project panel. Regardless of which view you choose, you'll preview your work in the Monitor panel. The Timeline and Sceneline are different panels for arranging clips and applying effects, and can show different views of the project.

In contrast, the Monitor panel shows one frame of the project, and one frame only. The displayed frame is at the location of the current-time indicator ( ). In the Sceneline, the current-time indicator is in the mini-timeline just below the preview area. In the Timeline, the current-time indicator is positioned on the Timeline itself. More on that when you learn about editing in the Timeline below.

Now let's explore the functions of the Monitor panel.

1 Select the first clip in the Sceneline, and then click the Play button ( ) in the Monitor panel to begin playback. As the movie is playing, notice that the timecode in the lower-left corner of the Monitor panel is advancing. To pause playback, press the spacebar. Or once again click the Play button, which becomes the Pause button ( ) during playback.

Previewing in Adobe Premiere Elements

Adobe Premiere Elements attempts to preview all movies at full frame rate. While working with the sample DV clips provided in these lessons, you should be able to preview at full frame rate with any computer that meets the system requirements as specified on the retail box, Adobe website, and elsewhere.

However, with high-definition formats such as AVCHD and HDV and more advanced effects, preview may slow down considerably, especially on older computers. If this occurs, check the Adobe Premiere Elements Help file, in particular a section entitled "Render an area for preview."

A. Docking header **B.** Preview area **C.** Panel menu **D.** Current Time **E.** Clip Representation in Mini-Timeline **F.** Playback controls **G.** Current-Time Indicator.

2   You can locate a specific frame in your movie by changing your position in time. Place your pointer over the timecode in the lower-left corner of the Monitor panel, and your Selection tool (⬚) will change to a hand with two arrows (⬚).

3   Click and drag the hand with two arrows icon to the right, advancing your video. The pointer will disappear while you are dragging and reappear when you stop. As long as you keep holding down the mouse button you can move backwards and forwards through the video. This is known as *scrubbing* through your video.

About timecode

Timecode represents the location of the frames in a video. Cameras record time-code onto the video. The timecode is based on the number of frames per second (fps) that the camera records, and the number of frames per second that the video displays upon playback. Digital video has a standard framerate that is either 29.97 fps for NTSC video (the North American broadcast video standard) or 25 fps for PAL (the European broadcast video standard). Timecode describes location in the format of hours;minutes;seconds;frames. For example, 01;20;15;10 specifies that the displayed frame is located 1 hour, 20 minutes, 15 seconds, and 10 frames into the scene.

—*From Adobe Premiere Elements Help*

4   The Shuttle control located in the lower-right corner of the Monitor panel lets you navigate through the movie in a similar fashion. To move forward through your video, click, and then drag the Shuttle control to the right. The further to the right you move the Shuttle control, the faster you move through the video. This method is useful for quickly scanning a project for edit points.

A. Go to Previous Edit Point. **B.** Rewind. **C.** Step Back. **D.** Play/Pause.
E. Step Forward. **F.** Fast-Forward. **G.** Go to Next Edit Point. **H.** Shuttle.
I. Split Clip (Ctrl+K). **J.** Add default text. **K.** Freeze Frame.

● **Note:** To move to a specific frame in the movie—say, 9 seconds, 15 frames in—type the number *915*. This tells Adobe Premiere Elements to move to the ninth second and fifteenth frame of the movie.

5   You can move to a specific point in your movie by entering the time in the Timecode control. Click the timecode in the lower-left corner of the Monitor panel and it will change to an editable text field. Type the number *900* and then press Enter to move to the 9-second point of your project.

6   Click the Step Forward button () repeatedly to advance your video one frame at a time. Video is simply a series of frames shown at a rate of approximately thirty frames per second. Using the Step Forward () or Step Back () button enables you to locate moments in time very precisely. You also can use the right and left arrow keys on the keyboard to accomplish the same functions.

7   Click the Go to Next Edit Point button () to jump to the first frame of the next clip. Notice in the mini-timeline that the current-time indicator () jumps to the beginning of the next clip representation. Click the Go to Previous Edit Point () to jump to the previous edit. Or, you can use the Page Up and Page Dn keys on your keyboard to accomplish the same functions.

● **Note:** You can export a single frame of video as a still image using the File > Export > Frame menu command. To avoid video interlace artifacts in the still image, click Settings in the Export Frame dialog, and then choose Deinterlace Video Footage in the Keyframe and Rendering section.

8   Reposition the current-time indicator in the mini-timeline by clicking and dragging it to the left or to the right.

9   The Zoom control, located just above the mini-timeline in the Monitor panel, lets you zoom in to get a more detailed view of the clips, zoom out to see more of the entire movie in the mini-timeline, or scroll through the mini-timeline to find a clip. To work with the Zoom control, *do any of the following:*

   •   To zoom in, drag the left Zoom Claw () to the right, or drag the right Zoom Claw to the left.

- To zoom out, drag the left Zoom Claw to the left, or drag the right Zoom Claw to the right.

- Scroll through the mini-timeline by clicking and dragging the gray center bar of the Zoom control.

10 Press the Home key on your keyboard to position the current-time indicator at the beginning of the movie. The KillerWhale.avi clip shown in a small window in the first scene has one video above it, the FamilyFun_Frame title clip.

11 To select and edit the FamilyFun_Frame title in the Monitor panel, right-click the image in the Preview window, and then choose Select > familyfun_frame from the context menu.

● **Note:** Generally, when you're working with multiple clips at the same position in the project, you'll find it easier to work in the Timeline than in the Sceneline.

In the mini-timeline, a bluish-gray-colored clip representation for the Title 01 clip appears above the lavender-colored clip representation for the KillerWhale.avi clip. Now you can edit that clip directly using the techniques shown here.

Working with the My Project panel in the Sceneline

As mentioned, the My Project panel has two views: A Sceneline for basic movie editing, and a Timeline for more advanced techniques. You can switch between the two views by clicking either the Sceneline or the Timeline button in the upper-left corner of the My Project panel.

Adding clips in the Sceneline

In the Sceneline, each clip is represented by its first frame. This display makes it easy to arrange clips into coherent sequences without regard for clip length. This technique is referred to as *storyboard-style* editing.

1   If the My Project panel is not already in the Sceneline, click the Sceneline button.

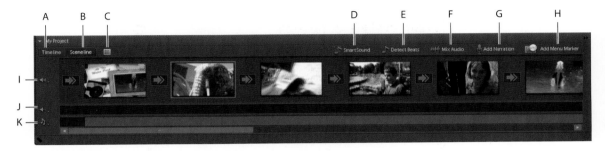

The Sceneline:
A. Switch to Timeline. **B.** Sceneline (selected). **C.** Properties. **D.** SmartSound. **E.** Detect Beats in Music. **F.** Mix Audio. **G.** Add Audio Narration. **H.** Set Marker for Disc Menu. **I.** Change Track Volume (Scenes). **J.** Change Track Volume (Narration). **K.** Change Track Volume (Soundtrack).

2   To add clips in the Sceneline, do *any of the following*:

   • To add a clip at the end of the movie: Use the scroll bar at the bottom of the My Project panel to scroll to the end of the movie. In Project view, click a clip, and then drag it onto the empty clip target at the end of the movie.

- To add a clip before another: In Project view, click a clip, and then drag it onto an existing clip in the Sceneline. The new clip will be inserted before the clip it was dropped onto.

- To add a clip after another: In the Sceneline, select the clip after which you want to add the new clip. In Project view, click the clip you want, and then drag it onto the Monitor panel. The new clip will be inserted after the clip currently selected in the Sceneline.

▶ **Tip:** Press the Shift key while dropping to get more options.

3   Choose Edit > Undo to undo the changes you made in the last step.

Moving clips in the Sceneline

Working in the Sceneline makes it easy to move around clips in your movie. Here's how it works.

1   To move a clip to a new position in the movie, click the clip in the Sceneline, and then drag it to a position before or after another clip. Release the pointer when a vertical blue line appears at the desired position.

2   To move several adjacent clips to a new position in the movie, Ctrl-click to select multiple clips in the Sceneline, and then drag them before or after another clip. Release the pointer when a vertical blue line appears at the desired position.

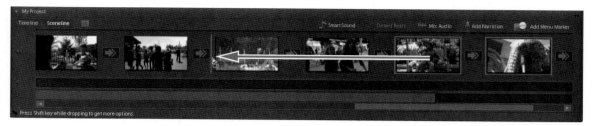

Note: A transition following a scene moves with the scene.

3   If a scene consists of multiple objects like the first scene in this movie with the superimposed title images, you can choose to move just the scene, or the scene and all its objects. Shift-drag the first scene, and position the vertical blue line after the second scene, and then release the pointer.

4   Choose Move just Scene from the menu that appears.

4   Choose Edit > Undo to undo the changes you made in the last step.

Deleting clips in the Sceneline

You may find, as your project develops, that you want to remove scenes you've imported into the Sceneline.

1   To delete a scene, right-click it in the Sceneline, and then choose one of the following from the context menu:

*   Delete Scene and its objects: This option deletes the clip and any overlays it might have.

*   Delete just Scene: This deletes the clip but leaves the overlays in place.

The clips following the deleted clip move to the left to close the gap. This is the default behavior when deleting clips in Adobe Premiere Elements and is called a *ripple deletion*.

2 Choose Edit > Undo to undo the changes you made in the last step.

Trimming clips in the Sceneline

Although deleting unnecessary clips and thoughtfully rearranging the order of clips will make a better video, you will inevitably want to shorten the length of some clips to create a more compelling movie. Here's how you'll accomplish this task.

Every clip has a beginning and an end. In editing terminology these are referred to as the *In points* and *Out points*. Setting In and Out points does not actually delete frames from the hard disk, but instead isolates a portion of the clip for use in your movie. When you trim a clip in Adobe Premiere Elements you are simply changing the In and Out points.

1 Click Elephant.avi, the second clip in the Sceneline, and then press the spacebar to play the clip. As you'll see, about halfway through the clip, the video goes black. These are the frames you'll trim away.

2 Watching the current timecode in the bottom left of the Monitor panel, drag the current-time indicator to the 00;00;07;19 mark.

● **Note:** When a clip is deleted from the Sceneline, the transition following the clip is also deleted; when a clip is deleted from the Timeline, the preceding and following transitions are deleted.

3   Click the Out point handle ( ), located on the right side of the current clip representation in the mini-timeline, and then drag it to the left until you reach the current-time indicator. Notice that your Monitor panel has changed to a split screen.

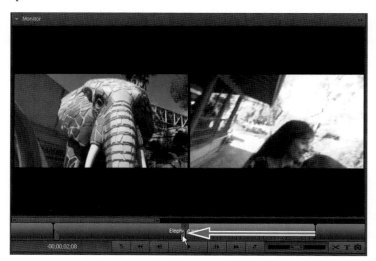

4   Release the pointer when the Out point handle you are dragging is aligned with the current-time indicator at 00;00;07;19.

5   Click the Elephant.avi clip again in the Sceneline, and then press the spacebar to play. Notice your new edit point at the end of the first clip, and that you've trimmed away the black frames.

Using the Split Clip tool

The Split Clip tool allows you to cut single clips into multiple clips. This can come in handy when you want to split a long captured clip into separate clips, as you'll do in this exercise.

1   Click LunchTime.avi, which is the ninth clip in the Sceneline, and then press the spacebar to play the clip. There are some interesting sections in here, but it's clearly too long to leave as is.

2   Position the current-time indicator at the 00;00;59;59 mark, which marks the end of the first usable portion.

3 To split the clip at the position of the current-time indicator, click the Split Clip button ( ), located near the right end of the Monitor panel just below the mini-timeline. You might have to resize the Monitor panel to its full width in order to see this icon. Or, choose Timeline > Split Clip.

4 Next, drag the current-time indicator to, and split the clip, at the following points:

- 00;01;23;00 (close-up of burger)
- 00;01;25;15 (end burger close-up)
- 00;01;37;00 (about to put top on burger bun)

LunchTime.avi is divided into five clips.

5 Now delete the second and fourth clips. Click the second clip to select it, then right-click the clip representation and choose Delete.

6 Repeat this procedure for the fourth clip.

7 Click the first LunchTime.avi clip and then press the spacebar to play the movie. Notice how deleting sections of the longer clip improves the overall flow of the movie.

8 When you are finished reviewing the movie, choose File > Save As.

9 In the Save Project dialog, name the file *Lesson05_Work* and save it in your Lesson04 and 05 folder.

● **Note:** Once you split a clip, Adobe Premiere Elements treats each subclip as a completely separate clip, which you can trim or re-order, just as with any other clip.

Working with the My Project panel in the Timeline

While most basic editing tasks can be performed in the Sceneline together with the Monitor panel, you'll use the Timeline for many advanced editing tasks, especially those that involve *layering*, which means having multiple clips in the project at the same location. For example, creating a Picture-in-Picture (PiP) overlay with one video over another, as you have in the title of the Lesson 5 project, is easier in the Timeline.

Briefly, the Timeline graphically represents your movie as video and audio clips arranged in vertically stacked tracks. Before working with the Timeline, follow the instructions at the start of this lesson to load Lesson05_Start.prel.

1 In the My Project panel, click the Timeline button to switch to the Timeline. Depending on your monitor size, you might want to increase the height of the My Project panel to have more space to display additional video and audio tracks.

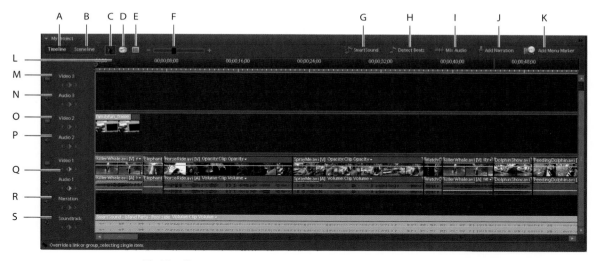

The Timeline:
A. Timeline (selected). **B.** Switch to Sceneline. **C.** Selection tool. **D.** Time Stretch tool. **E.** Properties. **F.** Zoom slider. **G.** Detect Beats in Music. **H.** Mix Audio. **I.** Add Audio Narration. **J.** Set Marker for Disc Menu. **K.** Add Menu Marker. **L.** Time ruler. **M.** Video track. **N.** Audio track. **O.** Set Video Track Display Style. **P.** Set Audio Track Display Style. **Q.** Add/Remove Keyframe. **R.** Narration. **S.** Soundtrack.

The Timeline displays time horizontally. Clips that fall earlier in time appear to the left, and clips that come later in time appear to the right. Time is indicated by the time ruler near the top of the Timeline.

The Zoom controls in the Timeline let you change the time scale, allowing you to zoom out to see your entire video or zoom in to see time in more detail.

2   Click the Zoom In button (■), once to zoom into the Timeline. Click and drag the Zoom slider to the right to zoom in further.

Zooming in enables you to make precise edits in the Timeline. In doing so, however, you cannot see the entire Timeline at once.

3   To see other parts of your project, click and drag the scroll bar at the bottom of the Timeline to scroll through the Timeline.

4   Adobe Premiere Elements has keyboard shortcuts that enable you to quickly zoom in and out. Press the equals sign (=) to zoom in one step per keystroke; press the minus sign (-) to zoom out one step per keystroke. Press the backslash (\) key to fit the entire video into the Timeline.

Working with tracks

The Timeline consists of vertical tracks where you arrange media clips. Tracks let you layer video or audio and add compositing effects, Picture-in-Picture effects, overlay titles, soundtracks, and more.

You'll perform most of your editing in the Video 1 and the Audio 1 tracks. Directly above these are the Video 2 and Audio 2 tracks. Note that the stacking order of video tracks is important. The Monitor panel displays (and Adobe Premiere Elements produces) the tracks from the top down. Accordingly, any opaque areas of the clip in the Video 2 track will cover the view on the clip in the Video 1 track.

Conversely, the clip in the Video 1 track will show through any transparent areas of the clip in the Video 2 track. This is how the clips are combined for the title that starts the movie in this lesson. The title is on the Video 2 track, and like many Adobe Premiere Elements title templates, it has a transparent frame through which the clip on the Video 1 track, KillerWhale.avi, shows through. Note that in Lesson 6 you'll learn how to shrink and tilt the clip, as was necessary here.

Below the Video 1 and Audio 1 tracks are two more audio tracks, Narration and Soundtrack. Audio tracks are combined in playback, and their stacking order is not relevant.

Adobe Premiere Elements starts with three open video tracks (Video 1, 2, and 3) and five open audio tracks (Soundtrack; Narration; and Audio 1, 2, and 3), which should be sufficient for most projects. Should you need additional video or audio tracks, you can add them by choosing Timeline > Add Tracks. You can delete any empty tracks by choosing Timeline > Delete Empty Tracks.

1 Drag the current-time indicator in the time ruler of the Timeline as far to the left as it will go. Or, press the Home key to position the current-time indicator at the beginning of the movie.

2 Depending on the height chosen for the My Project view, you may need to scroll up using the scroll bar at the right end of the Timeline view to locate the Video 2 track.

3 There is a Title image in the Video 2 track. Titles usually have some form of transparency, allowing you to view parts of video in the track below them.

4 Click the Zoom In button (![button]) at the top of the Timeline to magnify your view. As you zoom into the Timeline, you will see the full name of the title image, familyfun_frame.

5   Place your pointer over the yellow line running horizontally through the clip, the clip's Opacity graph. Your pointer will change to a white arrow with small double black arrows (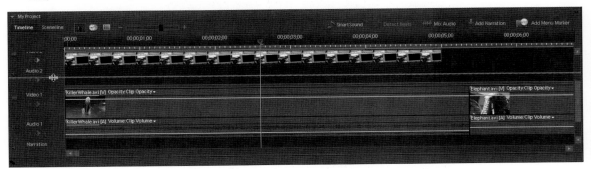).

6   Click and drag the Opacity graph all the way to the bottom. This changes the Opacity of this clip to 0%, which makes it completely transparent. Notice the effect in the Monitor panel. Click and drag the Opacity graph back up to 100% to restore the clip's opacity.

● **Note:** Located next to the name of each video clip in Adobe Premiere Elements, the Opacity property is always enabled by default. There are additional properties you can control by clicking the Opacity menu and choosing a different option. You will learn these techniques in Lesson 6, "Working with Effects."

Changing the height of tracks

You can change the height of each track in the Timeline for better viewing and easier editing of your projects. As a track enlarges, it displays more information. You will now adjust the height of the Video 1 track.

1   If necessary, scroll down in the Timeline to see the Video 1 track.

2   At the left side of the Timeline, place your pointer between the Audio 2 and the Video 1 tracks; your pointer should change to two parallel lines with two arrows ( ). Click and drag up to expand the height of this track.

3   Choose Window > Show Docking Headers if the docking headers are not currently visible. From the My Project panel menu, choose Track Size > Small, Track Size > Medium, or Track Size > Large, to change the track size for all tracks in the Timeline at the same time.

Customizing track views

You can display clips in the Timeline in different ways, depending on your preference or the task at hand. You can choose to display a thumbnail image at just the beginning of the clip; at the head and tail of the clip; or along the entire duration of the clip, as seen in the previous illustration. For an audio track, you can choose to display or hide the audio waveform of the audio contents.

1   By default, Adobe Premiere Elements displays all the frames in a video clip. However, at times you may find you would like to work with fewer visual distractions in your clip. Click the Set Display Style button ( ) to the left of the Video 1 track to set the display style to Show Head and Tail. This will show you the first frame and last frame of all the clips in Video 1.

2   Click the Display Style button again to view the Head Only of the clip.

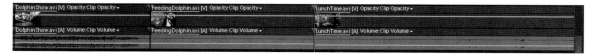

3   Click the Display Style button again to view the clip by its name only. No thumbnails will be displayed on the clip.

4   Click the Display Style button one more time to view the default style all of the frames.

Editing in the Timeline

Editing in the Timeline is very similar to editing in the Sceneline, although several controls are in different places. Most notably, the mini-timeline beneath the Monitor panel moves to the Timeline itself, as does the current-time indicator. Other than that, all playback controls are identical.

A. Docking header.
B. Preview area.
C. Panel menu.
D. Current Time.
E. Time ruler.
F. Playback controls.
G. Current-Time Indicator.

Beyond the interface issues, most of the basic clip-related operations are also identical. For example, you add clips to the Timeline the same way you add them to the Sceneline. You move clips around the same way, and you delete clips the same way. If you repeat the exercises you've already completed in this chapter using the Timeline rather than Sceneline, you'll quickly become adept at all of these operations.

Trimming and splitting clips is also very similar, but because these operations are so critical to everyday editing, let's run through them again in the Timeline.

Trimming clips in the Timeline

Every clip has a beginning and an end. In editing terminology these are referred to as the *In points* and *Out points*, as described earlier in this lesson. Setting In and Out points does not actually delete frames from the hard disk, but instead isolates a portion of the clip for use in your movie. When you trim a clip in Adobe Premiere Elements you are simply changing the In and Out points.

1   Press the Home key to move the current-time indicator to the first frame of the project.

2   Press the Page Dn key to move to the start of Elephant.avi, the second clip in the Timeline, and then press the spacebar to play the clip. As you'll see, about halfway through the clip, the video goes black. These are the frames you'll trim away.

3   Click the Zoom In button (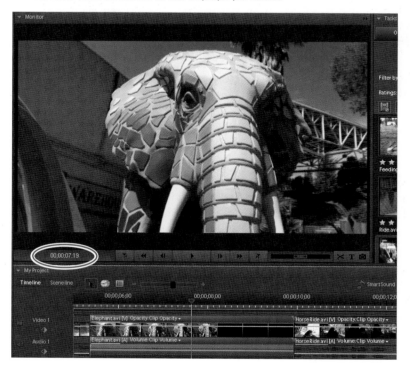) at the top of the Timeline to magnify your view. Trimming in the Timeline is easier when you're zoomed into the clip. Zooming in and out to make these adjustments will feel awkward at first, but will quickly become second nature.

4   Click and drag the scroll bar at the bottom of the Timeline to move the elephant.avi clip beneath the Monitor panel.

5   Watching the current timecode in the bottom left of the Monitor panel, drag the current-time indicator to the 00;00;07;19 mark.

6   Hover the pointer over the right edge of Elephant.avi in the Timeline. The pointer changes to a two-headed drag pointer (). Drag the pointer to the left until you reach the current-time indicator. Notice that your Monitor panel has changed to a split screen.

● **Note:** This is an Adobe Premiere Elements behavior worth understanding. The left side of the screen is showing the last frame of the clip you are shortening. It will start out black and then show the elephant statue once you're reached the current-time indicator. The right side of the split screen shows the first frame of the next clip. This frame will not change because you're not trimming this clip. Essentially, this split screen is a preview of what your edit line will look like after you've trimmed the first clip.

7   Release the pointer when the drag pointer is aligned with the current-time indicator at 00;00;07;19. Click the Elephant.avi clip again in the Timeline, and then press the spacebar to play. Notice your new edit point at the end of the first clip, and that you've trimmed away the black frames.

Using the Split Clip tool

The Split Clip tool allows you to cut single clips into multiple clips. This can come in handy when you want to split a long captured clip into separate clips, as you'll do in this exercise.

1   Press the Home key, then press the Page Dn key eight times, which should take you to the start of LunchTime.avi, and then press the spacebar to play the clip. There are some interesting sections in here, but it's clearly too long to leave as is.

2   Use the Zoom In button () at the top of the Timeline to magnify your view, and then click and drag the scroll bar at the bottom of the Timeline to roughly center LunchTime.avi in the Timeline.

3   Drag the current-time indicator to the 00;00;59;59 mark, which marks the end of the first usable portion.

4   To split the clip at the position of the current-time indicator, click the Split Clip button ( ), located near the right end of the Monitor panel, just below the mini-timeline. You might have to expand the Monitor panel to its full width in order to see this icon. Or, choose Timeline > Split Clip.

5   Next, drag the current-time indicator to the following points and and split the clip at each point as you reach it in turn:

   • 00;01;23;00 (close-up of burger)

   • 00;01;25;15 (end burger close-up)

   • 00;01;37;00 (about to put top on burger bun)

6   You've now divided LunchTime.avi into five clips. Let's delete the second and fourth clips.

7 Click the second clip to select it, then right-click the clip representation and choose Delete and Close Gap. This closes the gap between the clip immediately preceding the deleted clip, and the clip after it. Repeat this procedure for the fourth clip.

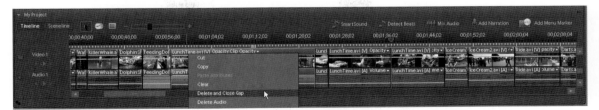

8 Drag the current-time indicator to the start of the first LunchTime.avi clip and then press the spacebar to play the movie. Notice how deleting sections of the longer clip improves the overall flow of your video.

Note: Once you split a clip, Adobe Premiere Elements treats each sub-clip as a completely separate clip, which you can trim or re-order just as with any other clip.

Using Clip and Timeline markers

As the video projects you work on become longer and longer, you will find the need to identify various sections of your movies. Adobe Premiere Elements provides two main methods of marking important points in a project. Clip markers are used within an individual clip for several purposes—for example, to identify a particular action or sound. Timeline markers are placed on the time ruler in the Timeline to mark scenes, locations for titles, or other significant points within the entire movie. Timeline markers can include comments and even URLs to link to web pages.

Markers can be numbered or unnumbered. You should use numbered markers if you plan to use many markers, allowing you to jump quickly to a specific marker number. In the next exercise, you will add an unnumbered clip marker to identify a specific point in a clip, and Timeline markers to identify where you would like to add titles.

Note: Adobe Premiere Elements also lets you add menu markers to the Timeline to designate chapter points used for DVD navigation. You'll learn how to create menu markers in Chapter 11.

Adding a clip marker

1 Click the Edit tab of the Tasks panel, and then click the Project button to enter Project view.

2 Next, double-click FeedingDolphin.avi to open it in the Preview window.

3 In the Preview window, click and drag the current-time indicator to the 00;05;18;16 mark. This marks the point in the scene where the boy is about to say "awesome."

Note: If you're having trouble positioning the current-time indicator at the exact timecode that you are looking for, you can always use the left and right arrow keys on your keyboard to move backwards or forwards one frame at a time.

4 Right-click the clip and choose Clip > Set Clip Marker > Unnumbered. This adds a Clip marker to the FeedingDolphin.avi clip, identified by a little triangle in the mini-timeline.

5 In the Preview window, drag the current-time indicator toward the beginning of the clip.

● **Note:** Markers you add to a source clip (opened from Project view of the Tasks panel) appear in each instance of the clip that you subsequently add to the movie. You need to switch to Timeline view to work with clip markers in your movie.

6 Right-click the mini-timeline in the Preview window, and then choose Go to Clip Marker > Next from the context menu. This will position the current-time indicator at the next clip marker—in this case, the 00;05;18;16 mark of the clip.

7 Click the Close button to close the Preview window.

Adding a Timeline marker

Unlike a Clip marker, which is attached to an individual clip, Timeline markers are placed in the Timeline and are used to mark specific points in your movie. Additionally, you can add comments to a Timeline marker to help yourself or others identify the purpose of a marker.

1 Click the Timeline button in the My Project panel. Press the Home key on your keyboard to place the current-time indicator at the beginning of your Timeline.

2 Press the Page Dn key on your keyboard to advance to the beginning of the fourth clip in your Timeline, the SprayMe.avi clip.

3 Right-click the time ruler at the top of the Timeline, and choose Set Timeline Marker > Unnumbered. A Timeline marker appears at the top of the Timeline in the time ruler. The newly added marker may be difficult to see, as it is partly hidden beneath the current-time indicator handle.

4 Press the Page Dn key five times to advance the current-time indicator to the beginning of the LunchTime.avi clip. You should now be able to see clearly the first marker you added. If necessary, reduce the Timeline magnification by clicking the Zoom Out ( ) button.

5 Right-click the time ruler at the top of the Timeline, and choose Set Timeline Marker > Unnumbered to add another marker at the position of your current-time indicator.

6 Press the Page Dn key five more times to advance the current-time indicator to the beginning of the Ride.avi clip.

7 Right-click the time ruler at the top of the Timeline, and choose Set Timeline Marker > Unnumbered to add another marker at the position of your current-time indicator. You'll use these three markers to indicate where you would like to later add titles.

8 Double-click the first marker you added to the Timeline at the beginning of the SprayMe.avi clip to open the Marker dialog. Under Comments, type *Add Meet the Dolphins title here.* Click OK to close the Marker dialog.

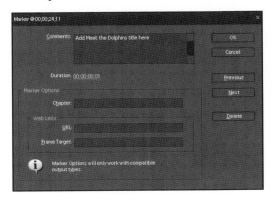

9 Right-click in the time ruler, and choose Go to Timeline Marker > Next to move to the second marker you added to the Timeline (at the beginning of the LunchTime. avi clip). Double-click the marker to open the Marker dialog. In the Comments field, type *Add Lunch Time title here.* Click OK to close the Marker dialog.

10 Right-click in the time ruler and choose Go to Timeline Marker > Next to move to the second marker you added to the Timeline (at the beginning of the Ride. avi clip). Double-click the marker to open the Marker dialog. In the Comments field, type *Add Afternoon Fun title here.* Click OK to close the Marker dialog.

● **Note:** To move markers, simply click and drag them to the new location. To delete markers, right-click and choose Clear Timeline Marker.

Adding a Frame Hold

Occasionally during a video, there may be a moment that you would like to freeze, or hold, the video. An example might be during a football game when a player catches the ball. Adobe Premiere Elements gives you the ability to display a single frame for the duration of a clip, while letting its soundtrack play unaltered. To do this, use the Frame Hold feature.

1 In the Timeline, drag your current-time indicator to 00;01;44;17, where the girl runs across the screen chased by the boy.

2 In the Monitor panel, click the Split Clip button.

3 In the Timeline, right-click the second clip section and choose Frame Hold from the context menu to open the Frame Hold Options dialog.

Insert comments, chapter information, or URL links in a Timeline marker

In addition to indicating important frames of a movie, Timeline markers can contain comments, chapter numbers, or URLs. You can include comments, chapter numbers, or web links only in Timeline markers, not Clip markers.

If you intend to import your movie into Adobe® Encore®, you can use Timeline markers to specify chapter links. Adobe Encore automatically converts Timeline markers with text or numbers in the Chapter field to chapter points. It also places the contents of the Comment field into the Description field of the chapter point.

If your movie is intended for the web and you are comfortable designing frame-based web pages, you can use Timeline markers to change what appears in other parts of the web page. Timeline markers can specify a URL and web page frame. When you include the movie in a frame-based web page, the browser displays each specified link in the specified frame. So, as the movie plays, your web page can change as each marker is reached. For example, in a family web page, as your vacation movie plays, you can populate the other frames of the web page with commentary and still images about the vacation. This advanced technique requires careful planning to coordinate the frames and content. You must export the movie using a file type that supports web markers: QuickTime or Windows Media.

You can set the markers to be longer than one frame in duration. In the Timeline, the right side of a Timeline marker's icon extends to indicate its duration.

1   In the time ruler in the Timeline, double-click a Timeline marker to open the Marker dialog.

2   Do *any of the following*:

  - To create a comment, type a message in the Comments field.

  - To change the duration of the marker, drag the duration value or click the value to select it, type a new value, and press Enter.

  - To create a chapter point for Encore, enter the chapter name or number in the Chapter box.

  - To create a web link, enter the web address and frame number in the URL and Frame Target boxes. The frame number must match a frame in the web page that contains the movie.

3   To enter comments or specify options for other Timeline markers, click Previous or Next.

4   Repeat steps 1–3 until you are finished modifying Timeline markers, and click OK.

—*From Adobe Premiere Elements Help*

4   In the Frame Hold Options dialog, select the Hold On checkbox and choose In Point from the menu next to it. Click OK.

5   Drag the current-time indicator to the beginning of the first IceCream.avi clip section, and then press the spacebar to play the movie. When the current-time indicator reaches the second IceCream.avi clip section, the image freezes for the duration of this clip section, although the sound continues normally.

6   When finished reviewing, save your project as *Lesson05_End.prel*.

Wonderful! You've finished another lesson and learned about editing your movie by trimming, splitting, deleting, and rearranging clips in the Sceneline and Timeline as well as in the Monitor and Preview panels. You've worked with clip and Timeline markers and added a Frame Hold to your movie.

Review questions

1   What are the key differences between the Timeline and Sceneline?

2   What is an In point and what is an Out point, and what can you do with each?

3   What are two methods of shortening your video clips?

4   How does Adobe Premiere Elements combine video tracks at the same position on the Timeline?

5   What are the most common uses of markers?

Review answers

1   Adobe Premiere Elements offers two views in the My Project Panel, Sceneline and Timeline. The Sceneline shows each clip as a separate thumbnail, without regard to duration, and doesn't show all available video tracks. The Timeline graphically represents your movie project as video and audio clips arranged in vertically stacked tracks, with clip duration represented by the length. There are many common activities that you can perform in both views, including arranging clips, trimming frames from the beginning or end of a clip, splitting and deleting clips, and adding titles and effects. Many producers use both views in the course of a project: for example, adding and sequencing content in the Sceneline, then switching over to the Timeline to add background music, titles, and other clips. Once you start working with multiple video clips at the same location, the Timeline becomes the superior view.

2   The In point is the first frame of your clip as seen in the Sceneline or Timeline, and the Out point is the last frame. Both the In and Out points can be moved to create a shorter or longer clip.

3   You can shorten your clips by trimming their In points and Out points, or by splitting the clip and deleted unwanted portions.

4   Adobe Premiere Elements renders the tracks from the top down. Any opaque areas of the clip in the Video 2 track will cover the view on the clip in the Video 1 track. Conversely, the clip in the Video 1 track will show through any transparent areas of the clip in the Video 2 track, or if you reduce the Opacity of the clip in the Video 2 track.

5   Clip markers are used to specify points in a clip that you'll later use in editing, such as a specific occurrence. For example, if a dolphin jumped and splashed the crowd, you might want to add a sound effect at that location. Timeline markers are used to specify points in the project where you want to add project elements, such as titles.

6 WORKING WITH EFFECTS

In this lesson, you'll learn how to apply effects to the water park clips that you already know from previous lessons, and you'll also apply these effects to two new clips. Specifically, you'll learn how to do the following:

- Apply video effects
- Change effects and settings
- Copy effects and settings from one clip to another
- Create a pan over a still image with preset effects
- Control visual effects with keyframes
- Create a Picture-in-Picture effect
- Composite one video over another with Videomerge

 This lesson will take approximately 2 hours.

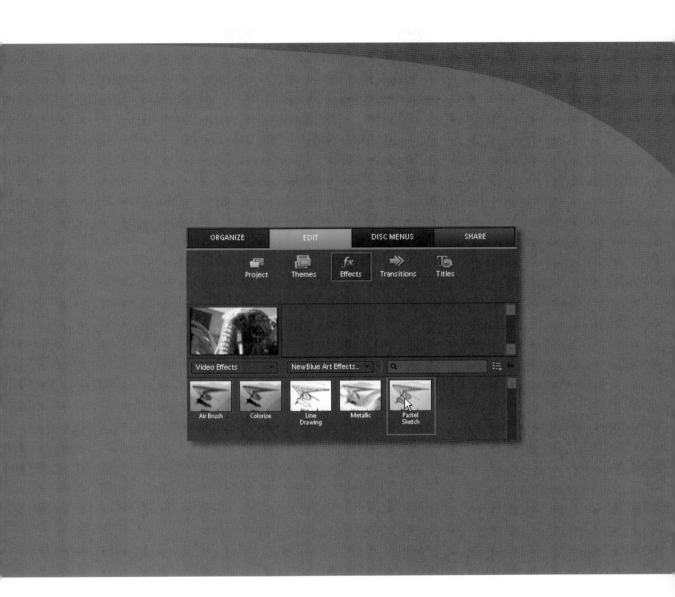

Selecting and applying effects to your video.

Getting started

To begin, launch Adobe Premiere Elements, open the Lesson06 project, and review a final version of the movie you'll be creating.

1 Before you begin, make sure that you have correctly copied the Lesson06 folder from the DVD in the back of this book onto your computer's hard disk. For more information, see "Copying the Classroom in a Book files" in the Getting Started section at the start of this book.

2 Launch Adobe Premiere Elements.

3 In the Welcome screen, click the Open Project button, and then Open folder.

4 In the Open Project dialog, navigate to the Lesson06 folder you copied to your hard disk. Within that folder, select the file Lesson06_Start.prel, and then click Open. If a dialog appears asking for the location of rendered files, click the Skip Previews button.

Your project file opens with the Monitor, Tasks, and My Project panels open.

5 Choose Window > Restore Workspace to ensure that you start the lesson with the default panel layout.

Viewing the completed movie before you start

To see what you'll be creating in this lesson, you can play the completed movie.

1 In the Edit tab of the Tasks panel, click Project ( ).

2 In Project view, locate the file Lesson06_Movie.wmv, and then double-click it to open the video into the Preview window.

3 In the Preview window, click the Play button ( ) to watch the video about a visit to the water park, which you will build in this lesson.

4 When done, close the Preview window by clicking the Close button ( ) in the upper-right corner of the window.

Using effects

● **Note:** Adobe Premiere Elements offers a large selection of diversified effects. It's a good idea to look up the gallery of video effects in your Adobe Premiere Elements Help file, which gives you a quick overview of all those effects actually applied to an image.

Effects ( ) are located in the Edit tab of the Tasks panel. All effects are stored in either the Audio Effects folder or the Video Effects folder, and are organized by type. For example, all video effects that create a blur are grouped within the Blur & Sharpen folder inside the Video Effects folder.

It's helpful to think about effects in the following categories:

- *Curative effects*: Curative effects correct problems in your video footage, including footage that's too bright or too dark, backlighted video, video that's too shaky because it was shot without a tripod, and even video that's a bit blurry. You can find corrective effects in the Adjust folder (including the Auto Color, Auto Contrast, Auto Levels, and Shadow Highlight effects), Blur Sharpen folder (Sharpen), Image Control folder (Black & White, Color Balance HLS, Color Balance RGB), Gamma Correction folder (Tint), and Video Stabilizer folder (Stabilizer).

- *Overlay effects*: Overlay effects allow you to composite one image over another. You can find overlay effects in the Keying and Videomerge folders.

- *Artistic effects*: Most other effects are artistic effects that let you create a different look or feel from the original clip. These artistic effects can be quite powerful, like the Old Film effect in the New Blue Film Look folder that can make your video look like an aged video by adding details like scratches and graininess. Other artistic effects let you add lightning to a clip (Lightning effect in Render folder), add earthquake-like effects (Earthquake effect in the NewBlue Motion Effects Elements folder), place a spotlight on a subject (Lighting effects in the Adjust folder), and do many other things.

- *Speed controls*: You can speed up or slow down your clips in the Timeline of the My Project panel by right-clicking the clip and choosing Time Stretch, or by choosing Clip > Time Stretch in the Adobe Premiere Elements menu.

Note: You can view fixed effects by clicking the clip in the My Project panel to select it, and then clicking the Properties ( ) button in the upper left of the My Project panel. This opens the Edit workspace in Properties view. Here are the functions of all fixed effects, which you open by clicking the twirl-down triangles to the left of each effect.

- *Motion effects*: Motion effects allow you to zoom into and around your original video clip or still image, and are used to adjust the framing of a video or create a pan-and-zoom effect. You adjust these parameters using the Motion controls found in the fixed effects that are automatically applied to every clip in the My Project panel.

- *Image control*: Lets you control the brightness, contrast, hue, and saturation of clips.

- *Motion*: Lets you reposition, scale, anchor, and rotate video clips, and remove flicker from them.

- *Opacity*: Lets you make a clip transparent, and by using keyframes, create fades and dissolves.

- *Volume*: Lets you control the volume of audio clips.

- *Balance*: Lets you adjust the balance of audio clips.

A. Properties button. **B.** Fixed effects. **C.** Properties view.

Note that once you apply an effect from the Effects panel to a clip, you can also adjust its parameters and set keyframes in the Effects Properties view. All effects that you add to a clip appear in the order in which you add them.

Though you can apply any and all of these effects at any time during the course of a project, the recommended workflow is to apply curative filters first, then speed and motion, then other artistic effects. You can add an effect to any clip in the My Project panel, and even apply the same effect numerous times to the same clip, but with different settings. By default, when you add an effect to a clip, it is active for the duration of the clip.

Perfecting your clips

All projects are unique and all source clips present their own unique issues. The project that you're working on was shot outside on a bright, sunny day, so the lighting was generally good. Colors are also bright and accurate because the auto-white balance functions on most camcorders work extremely well in sunlight. To perfect the video in this shoot, you'll correct backlighting in several clips, boost the color saturation in another, apply the Sharpen and Stabilizer effects, and reframe a shot using the Motion controls.

However, indoor shoots typically present a completely different range of problems since lighting is often inadequate and camcorders sometimes have problems producing accurate colors when shooting under fluorescent or incandescent lighting. When your personal projects include indoor shoots, you should experiment with the Brightness, Contrast, Hue, and Saturation adjustments in the Image Control fixed effect, and the Auto Color, Auto Contrast, and Auto Levels controls in the Adjust folder. Often applying the latter three—either individually or concert—can produce quite remarkable improvements in minimal time and with little effort.

Applying and resetting fixed effects

It's usually most convenient to start by adjusting the Brightness, Contrast, and Saturation of a clip using the Image Control adjustments. Here's the procedure:

1   In either the Sceneline or Timeline, click DolphinShow.avi, which is the seventh clip in the movie.

    Shot under a roof, this clip is dark and a bit drab. Let's fix that.

2   Click the Properties button on the upper left of the My Project panel.

3   In Properties view, click the twirl-down triangle to the left of the Image Control effect to open the parameter settings.

4   Drag the Brightness slider to the right until it reaches the value of 5 (or click the numeric entry to make it active and type *5*, then press Enter).

5   Drag the Contrast slider to the right until it reaches the value of 104 (or click the numeric entry to make it active and type *104*, then press Enter).

6   Drag the Saturation slider to the right until it reaches the value of 200 (or click the numeric entry to make it active and type *200*, then press Enter).

7   In Properties view, to the left of the twirl-down triangle, find the Eyeball icon (■) to the left of the Image Control effect. The eyeball toggles the effect on or off so you can compare the clip with and without the adjustments. Toggle the eyeball on and off a few times.

8   Click the Eyeball icon again to toggle the effect on. Note that the Eyeball icon isn't simply for preview; if you don't toggle the effect back on, Adobe Premiere Elements will ignore the effect when rendering the final movie.

9 If you're satisfied with the results, click Done in the lower right of Properties view to return to the Organize workspace.

10 To reset the Image Control parameters to their default values, click the Image Control effect to select it, and then click Reset in the lower right of Properties view. This technique works for any effect, whether embedded or otherwise. Choose Edit > Undo to undo the reset and keep the adjusted values.

● **Note:** You don't have to click Done to "set" the effect; you could have simply clicked another clip and continued to edit. Once you apply and configure an effect, it remains applied until you reset or delete the effect.

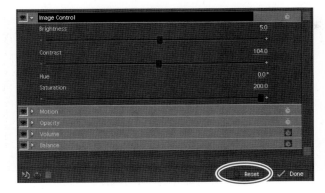

11 Choose File > Save As and save your project as *Lesson06_Work.prel*.

Reframing a clip using Motion controls

The other fixed effect that you'll frequently use are the Motion controls. In this exercise, you'll learn how to use the effect to reframe a shot; later in the lesson you'll learn how to use these controls to create a pan-and-zoom effect within an image.

The clip you'll edit is the final clip of the project, Exhausted.avi, a shot of children and a parent worn out after a day at the water park. Unfortunately, it's a fairly long shot, and we'd prefer to use a close-up in our project. In this lesson, you'll use Motion controls to zoom reframe the shot to a close-up.

1 In either the Sceneline or Timeline, click Exhausted.avi, which is the final clip in the movie.

2 Click the Properties button in the upper left of the My Project panel.

3 In Properties view, click the twirl-down triangle to the left of the Motion effect to open the parameter settings.

4 Drag the Scale slider to the right until it reaches the value of 135 (or click the numeric entry to make it active and type *135*, then press Enter).

5   In the Monitor panel, click the frame to make the center crosshair active. Then drag the frame around until the subjects are positioned to your liking. As you drag the frame around, note that the numeric Position parameters on the right are updated as you move it. You can position the frame either by dragging it directly as you just did, or by typing in new numeric parameters.

6   In the Monitor panel, right-click the frame, and choose Magnification > 100%. This sets your preview at a pixel for pixel preview, which is helpful when previewing Motion control adjustments.

7   Click the Play button in the Monitor panel to preview the effect.

You may notice that the frame looks fuzzy while it's playing, and then gets sharper once it stops. That's because Adobe Premiere Elements shows an approximation of the applied effect during preview to maximize preview smoothness. Zooming in too far with motion controls can cause a slight blurriness, which you want to assess before finalizing the effect. To accomplish this, you'll render the effect and then preview again. Before doing this, however, let's learn how to use the Position, Scale, and Rotation controls to fit a killer whale into a small box.

Using the Position, Scale, and Rotation controls

This refers, of course, to the start of the movie, where Motion controls fit the KillerWhale.avi clip into the frame in the title above it. To view how this worked, position the current-time indicator around 00;00;03;00 into the movie, then click KillerWhale.avi on the Video 1 track, and then click the Properties button on the top left of the My Project panel.

As an exercise, click the Motion bar in Properties view, and then click the Reset button to reset the Motion controls to their default setting. Then, experiment with the individual Motion controls to get the killer whale back in the box. As a last resort, you can click the numerical value for each control and type *578.3* and *283.4* (Position), *58.0* (Scale), and *-4.0* (Rotation), as shown here.

Frame   KillerWhale.avi

Rendering effects

Now, back to the Exhausted.avi clip and the rendering process. Note that you don't have to render your effects to preview them, since Adobe Premiere Elements will show a very close approximation of the effect when you preview in the Monitor panel without rendering. If you render the effect, however, you'll see exactly what the final video will look like in your final project, which is valuable in some instances, such as when you use the Motion controls to reframe and zoom into the video.

Adobe Premiere Elements lets you know when you need to render for an accurate preview by placing a red line in the time ruler of the Timeline. After you render, that line turns green. Rendering an effect is a two-step process: first you designate the work area to render, then you press the Enter key to render the work area , which is a small bar below the Timeline that you can position to render only the clips beneath the bar.

A. Red line in time ruler.
B. Work area bar.

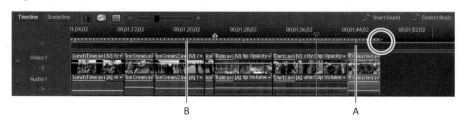

B   A

Note that you must be in the Timeline to render an effect. Here's how it works.

1   Click the Timeline button to make sure you are in the Timeline.

2   Position the work area bar over Exhaused.avi. Because it's the last clip in the movie, the end of the work area bar (highlighted in the figure above) is positioned correctly.

3   Unless you previously moved it to a different position, the start of the work area bar is positioned at the start of the movie. To set the beginning of the work area bar to the first frame of Exhausted.avi, press the backslash (\) key on your keyboard to display the entire Timeline, and then drag the beginning of the work area bar to the first frame of Exhausted.avi.

4   Or, to set the start of the work area bar to the first frame of Exhausted.avi, move the current-time indicator ( ) to the start of the clip, then press Alt+[on your keyboard.

5 To render the preview, press Enter on your keyboard. Adobe Premiere Elements renders the preview, and then plays the rendered work area.

The reframing looks good, but the movie looks slightly blurry, which can happen when you zoom into a movie clip. Next, you'll learn to fix that using the Sharpen effect.

▶ **Tip:** If you see only one red line in the Timeline, press the Enter key on your keyboard, and Adobe Premiere Elements will render only the frames beneath that red line, but then will start playing the video at the start of the movie. This procedure not only directs Adobe Premiere Elements to render just the selected frames; it also starts the preview at the start of the defined work area.

▶ **Tip:** Once you've added multiple effects, you may want to preview the entire movie. To position the work area bar over the entire movie, press the backslash key to display the entire Timeline, then double-click anywhere in the work area bar. This will position the work area bar over the entire movie; press Enter on your keyboard to render all sections of the Timeline that require rendering.

Choosing and applying effects

You've finished working with the fixed effects for the moment; now you'll select and apply a standard effect from the Effects view. You can apply standard effects in either the Sceneline or Timeline; use the view that you feel most comfortable using.

1 Select Effects ([fx Effects]) in the Edit tab of the Tasks panel.

2 In the list box next to Video Effects, click and select Blur & Sharpen.

3 To apply the effect, drag the Sharpen effect from Effects view and drop it onto the last clip in your Sceneline, Exhausted.avi. Adobe Premiere Elements applies the effect immediately, and you should see a slight sharpening in the clip.

4 Click the Properties button in the upper left of the My Project panel or the Edit Effects button in Effects view to open Properties view.

5 In Properties view, click the twirl-down triangle to the left of the Sharpen effect to open the parameter settings.

6 Drag the Sharpen Amount slider to the right until it reaches the value of 20. Or, click the numeric entry to make it active and type *20*, then press Enter.

7 In the Properties panel, toggle the effect on and off using the Eyeball icon to gauge the impact of the effect. Make sure that you leave the eyeball showing so that the effect is engaged.

8 Press the Enter key on your keyboard to render the effect and preview again.

● **Note:** If you zoom in too far using the Motion controls, your image won't be sharp even if you apply the Sharpen effect. In that case, you have to find the best balance between image position and sharpness.

9 If you're satisfied with the results, click Done in the lower right of Properties view to return to the Organize workspace. If not, repeat the process described in this exercise to apply additional sharpening to the clip.

10 Save your project.

Deleting effects

You can't delete fixed effects, but to delete any other effect, right-click to select it, and then choose either Delete Selected Effect or Delete All Effects from Clip.

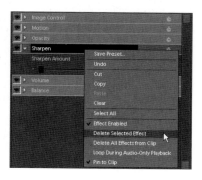

Fixing backlighted video

If you shoot video against a bright background with automatic exposure set on your camcorder, the background will usually be bright, but the subject's faces may be very dark. This is a very common condition called *backlighting*. In this exercise, you'll learn to apply and configure Adobe Premiere Elements' Shadow Highlight filter to correct this problem.

1 In either the Timeline or Sceneline, click the third clip (HorseRide.avi) to select it, and then drag the current-time indicator to 00;00;12;00.

2 Click the Properties button in the upper left of the My Project panel.

3 In Properties view, click the twirl-down triangle to the left of the Image Control adjustments to open the parameter settings. Using the Brightness and Contrast sliders, try to find parameters that brighten the woman's face without fading the entire frame. You won't be able to; the Brightness adjustment brightens all pixels in the frame, but you need to brighten only the darker pixels.

4 Reset the Image Control parameters by clicking the Image Control effect, and then the Reset button.

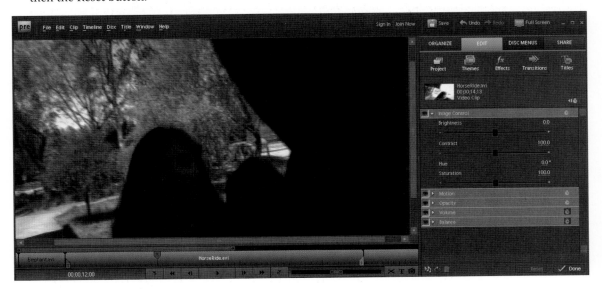

5 In the list box next to Video Effects, click and select Adjust.

6 Drag the Shadow Highlight effect from the Effects view onto the third clip in the project, HorseRide.avi.

7 Use the playback controls to preview the effect and then drag the current-time indicator back to 00;00;12;00.

8 Click the Properties button on the top left of the My Project panel or the Edit Effects button in Effects view to open the Effects Properties view.

9   In Properties view, click the twirl-down triangle to the left of the Shadow/ Highlight effect to open the parameter settings.

● **Note:** The Shadow Highlight effect divides each video frame into three regions based upon the original brightness of the pixels in the frame, Shadows (darkest regions), Highlights (brightest regions), and Midtones (all other regions). The Shadow and Highlight sliders let you customize the adjustments to these respective regions, while the effect doesn't modify Midtone values at all.

10 The default parameters work well with this clip. To adjust the effect manually, deselect the Auto Amounts checkbox.

11 To adjust the darker regions, drag the Shadow Amount to the right to increase the brightness of pixels in the Shadows (including the faces in this clip) and to the left to decrease the brightness.

12 To adjust the brightest regions, drag the Highlight Amount slider to the right to darken the brightness of Highlight pixels.

These are the most important manual controls; to learn about the others, check the Adobe Premiere Elements Help file.

13 Following steps 5 and 6, apply the Shadow Highlight effect to WatchOut.avi (the 5th clip), IceCream2.avi (the 13th clip), and Darts.avi (the 16th clip).

14 Save your project as *Lesson06_Work.prel*.

Stabilizing shaky footage

One common problem with home video footage is excessive shakiness, which can occur when you walk while shooting, or if you shoot from a moving car or bus. Most clips in this project are stable, but the 12th clip in the Project, IceCream.avi, could use some improvement. Play the clip and you'll notice excessive shakiness. In this exercise, you'll apply the Adobe Premiere Elements Stabilize filter to correct this problem.

1 In the list box next to Video Effects, click Video Stabilizer.

2 Drag the Stabilizer effect from Effects view and drop it onto the 12th clip in the project, IceCream.avi.

3 Click the Properties button in the upper left of the My Project panel or the Edit Effects button in Effects view to open the Effects Properties view.

4 In Properties view, click the twirl-down triangle to the left of the Stabilizer effect to open the parameter settings.

5 Drag the current-time indicator to 00;01;11;21. You will notice a small black bar on the bottom of the video frame on this and surrounding frames.

6 In Properties view, drag the Zoom slider to the right until the bar disappears.

7 Drag through the rest of the clip to see if any other bars appear. If not, click Done on the lower right in Properties view to return to the Organizer or move on to your next edit.

Play the clip, using the eyeball to the left of the Stabilizer effect to toggle it on and off. Definitely easier to watch with the Stabilizer effect applied.

● **Note:** As you've seen, the Stabilize effect works, in part, by zooming into the video, which can cause some softness. Consider applying the Sharpen effect to counteract this softness.

Changing playback speed

Speed changes are a commonly used effect, and Adobe Premiere Elements has two techniques for speeding up or slowing down your video. In this exercise, you'll learn how to adjust the speed of clips bounded by others in the Timeline. In a subsequent exercise, you'll learn how to adjust the speed of a clip positioned on a separate track from the other content.

Specifically, in this exercise, you'll adjust the speed of the second clip in the project, Elephant.avi, which is a signature structure in the water park. The current clip is only about 2 seconds long—almost too quick to recognize—so you'll increase that to about 4.5 seconds. Note that you can only implement this effect in the Timeline, so step 1 will send your clip to the Timeline of the My Project panel.

1 In the My Project panel, click the Timeline button to switch to Timeline. If necessary, zoom into the Timeline so you can easily see the individual clips.

2 Right-click Elephant.avi, the second clip in the project, and choose Time Stretch. Adobe Premiere Elements opens the Time Stretch panel.

3 Type *50* in the Speed box (where it will appear as 50.00%), and select the Maintain Audio Pitch checkbox.

4 Click OK to close the panel. Nothing changes in the Timeline because Adobe Premiere Elements doesn't automatically move any clips when you change the speed of an adjacent clip. In other words, though you've slowed down the frames visible on the Timeline, you haven't extended the duration of the clip.

5 To extend the duration of the clip, hover the pointer over the right edge of Elephant.avi in the Timeline. The pointer changes to a two-headed pointer ( ) with the bracket pointing to the left. Make sure that you're grabbing the Elephant.avi clip, not the next clip in the timeline, HorseRide.avi.. Drag the pointer to the right until the pop-up box on the Timeline, or the timecode on the bottom left of the split-screen monitor reads +00;00;02;10. If you drag too far, the black frames that you trimmed out of the clip in Chapter 5 will start to appear.

6 Save your project as *Lesson06_Work.prel*.

Working with keyframes

Every clip in the Timeline, and most effects, can be modified over time. This involves a concept called *keyframing*. Essentially, a keyframe is a location in the Timeline where you specify a value for a specific property. When you set two keyframes, Adobe Premiere Elements interpolates the value of that property over all frames between the two keyframes, essentially creating an animated effect.

For example, in the next exercise, you'll use keyframes to create an image pan, essentially simulating the movement of a camera over a still image. Or you can use keyframes to animate the appearance of an effect, which you'll do in a subsequent exercise.

Understanding how to use keyframes enables significant flexibility and creativity in your projects. Although they sound foreign at first, if you work through the next few exercises, you'll quickly grasp their operation and utility.

Creating an image pan with keyframes

The image pan is a popular device in many documentaries and films. An image pan is defined as a movement of the camera, usually from left to right, although it can be from top to bottom. In traditional production, an image pan would actually involve the physical movement of a camcorder over an image; however, if you're working with footage from a stationary camera, Adobe Premiere Elements enables you to simulate the camera movement using the Motion controls.

In this exercise, you'll use a horizontal image pan to end your water park project.

1   Choose File > Get Media from > Files and Folders. Navigate to the Lesson06 folder and select the 06_imagepan.jpg image. Then, click Open to import it.

● **Note:** In Properties view, note that this image is 2,277 pixels wide and 1,280 pixels high. Though it's not critical that image resolution exceed that of the project (720x480 in this instance), when it does, it indicates that you can zoom into regions in the video without causing blurriness. In general, when adding still images to a project, it's best to use images with a resolution larger than that of the project.

2   In Project view, right-click the 06_imagepan.jpg image and choose Properties. Properties view enables you to—among other things—identify the size of the digital image you have imported.

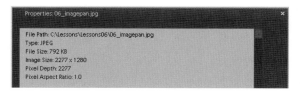

3   Click the Timeline button to switch to the Timeline in the My Project panel.

4   Click and drag the 06_imagepan.jpg image onto the Video 2 track in your Timeline so that it extends by about 1 second over the end of the last clip in the Video 1 track. Position the current-time indicator so that you can see the superimposed image in the Monitor panel.

5   The image has been automatically scaled to fit entirely into the Monitor panel. Although the original image was 1,280 pixels high, Adobe Premiere Elements automatically scaled the image down to 480 pixels high. To return the image to its original size, right-click the image and choose Scale to Frame Size to deselect this option.

6   Click the Properties button in the upper left of the My Project panel or the Edit Effects button in Effects view to open the Effects Properties view.

7   In Properties view, click the twirl-down triangle to the left of the Motion effect to open the parameter settings.

8   In the upper right of Properties view, click the Show keyframes (◀◉) button. You may need to expand the size of Properties view to better view the keyframes.

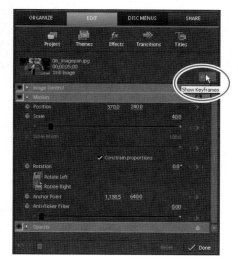

9 Note the mini-timeline at the top of Properties view, which has the exact same values as the Timeline in the My Project panel for the selected clip, and has a matching current-time indicator. In the mini-timeline, drag this to the extreme left, to the start of the clip.

10 To the right of the Motion property is a small stopwatch. Click it and notice that a small diamond appears in the mini-timeline within Properties view to the right of each property in the Motion control. Each of these is a keyframe; next, you'll adjust the top two.

11 Click the Position values to make them active and type *370* and *240,* as shown here.

12 Drag the Scale slider to the left until it reaches the value of 40. Or click the numeric entry to make it active and type *40,* then press Enter.

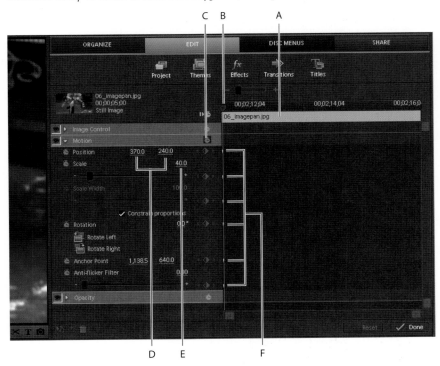

A. Mini-timeline. **B.** Current-Time Indicator. **C.** Toggle Animation button (enables keyframes). **D.** Horizontal and vertical position values. **E.** Scale values (as a percentage of total size). **F.** Keyframes.

You've set the keyframes for the initial position to the desired values. Now you'll create and set the values for the second keyframe.

13 Drag the current-time indicator all the way to the right of the mini-timeline until the Monitor goes black. Then press the left arrow key one time to move one frame to the left. The final frame of the image should appear in the Monitor.

14 Click the Position values to make them active and type *400* and *255,* as shown. After you change the values, Adobe Premiere Elements automatically inserts a keyframe.

15 Drag the Scale slider to the left until it reaches the value of 50; or click the numeric entry to make it active and type *50,* then press Enter. After you change the values, Adobe Premiere Elements automatically inserts a keyframe.

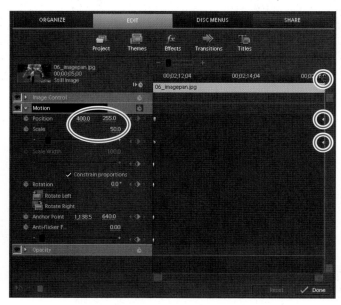

● **Note:** The current-time indicators in Properties view and in the Timeline of the My Project panel are actually the same. You can use either one to navigate through your clip. However, the Timeline in Properties view enables you to navigate through only the currently selected clip and is used primarily for working with keyframes.

16 Drag the current-time indicator to the beginning of the 06_imagepan.jpg clip, and then press the spacebar to play the clip. You'll see a slow zoom into the picture and text. Press the spacebar again to stop playback.

17 Save your project as *Lesson06_Work.prel*.

Creating a fade-in using keyframes

You can control keyframes in two locations in Adobe Premiere Elements: Properties view and the Timeline. In this exercise, you will control the opacity keyframes of a video clip in the Timeline.

1 Click to select the 06_imagepan.jpg clip in the Video 2 track. You may need to scroll to the right in the Timeline to fully see the clip.

2 Place the current-time indicator shortly before the end of the Exhausted.avi clip (this is the last clip in the Video 1 track). Click the Zoom In tool (■) in the Timeline to increase your view of the clip. When working with clip keyframes, it is often helpful to increase the magnification. The orange line spanning horizontally across the clip is the connector line (or graph) between keyframes. By default, all clips have the Opacity property enabled.

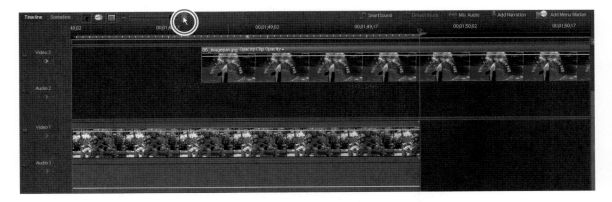

3   Working with the top clip (06_imagepan.jpg), place your pointer over the orange connector line at the location of the current-time indicator. The pointer changes to a double-arrow icon (↕).

4   Click and drag the connector line down toward the bottom of the clip. As you drag, you will see a small window with changing numbers. The numbers represent the opacity values. Drag the connector line down to approximately the 50% level. Don't worry if you can't get an exact number. When you release the pointer, you will see that the clip is now semi-translucent, enabling you to catch a glimpse of the video clip below.

5 Click and drag the connector line back up towards the top of the clip to restore the clip's opacity to 100%.

Now you'll add keyframes to help Adobe Premiere Elements create a cross-dissolve between the two clips.

6 Position your pointer over the orange connector line at the beginning of the top clip, 06_imagepan.jpg. You need the pointer to change to the double-arrow icon (⤢). This can be a little tricky because your pointer changes to the Trim Out tool if you position it too far to the left. With the double-arrow icon as pointer, hold down the Ctrl key on your keyboard, and then click the connector line once. You should see a small yellow diamond added to the orange connector line at the beginning of the clip, representing your first keyframe.

7 Then, using the same procedure, create a keyframe on the clip beneath 06_imagepan.jpg at the same location in the Timeline. This clip should be Exhausted.avi.

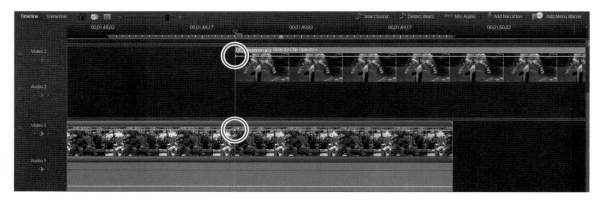

8 Press the Page Dn key on your keyboard to move the current-time indicator to the end of Exhausted.avi. Position your pointer over the orange connector line at the end of Exhausted.avi, hold down the Ctrl key, and then click to add a second keyframe.

9 Next, using the same procedure as in step 8 (Ctrl-click), create a keyframe in the top clip, 06_imagepan.jpg, at the same location in the Timeline.

You should now have four keyframes, two in 06_imagepan.jpg and two in Exhausted.avi, as indicated by the two diamonds on their respective connector lines.

10 Click the keyframe at the start of the 06_imagepan.jpg clip and drag it down to the bottom of the track. The number on the right of the yellow box next to the pointer is the Opacity value; drag until that value equals 0.00.

11 Click the keyframe at the end of the Exhausted.avi clip and drag it down to the bottom of the track. The number on the right of the yellow box next to the pointer is the Opacity value; drag until that value equals 0.00.

12 To view the Opacity fade-in and fade-out, move your current-time indicator to the beginning of the 06_imagepan.jpg clip, and then press the spacebar.

13 Save your project as *Lesson06_Work.prel*.

In Lesson 7, you'll learn how to create a similar effect using the Cross Dissolve transition. Though the visual effect is similar, working with keyframes lets you customize the effect to a much greater degree.

Working with keyframes

Once you've set a keyframe, you can modify it by clicking and dragging it to a new location or value. To delete a keyframe, right-click it and choose Delete.

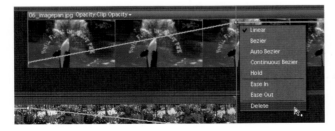

The other keyframe-related controls shown in the right-click menu are advanced options that control the rate and smoothness of change applied by Adobe Premiere Elements. For more on these options, check the Help file for a section titled "Controlling change between keyframes."

Finally, you can access all keyframes inserted on the Timeline in Properties view. Select the clip 06_imagepan.jpg, and then click the Properties (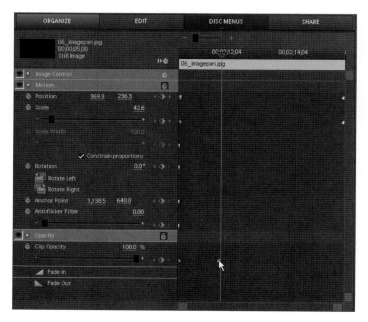) button in the upper left of the My Project panel. This opens Properties view.

If necessary, click the Show Keyframes ( ) button on the top right in Properties view to view the keyframes. Then, click the twirl-down triangle to the left of the Clip Opacity effect to open the parameter settings and view the keyframes that you created in the Timeline.

You can set and modify opacity-related keyframes in either or both locations. In general, the Timeline is best for fast and simple adjustments, like the fade-in that you just applied, while Properties view is superior for complicated, more precise adjustments.

Using keyframes to animate effects

You've learned how to apply effects and how to create and modify keyframes. Now you'll learn how to animate an effect using keyframes. This is a very powerful capability; essentially, it lets you create your own custom transition using any Adobe Premiere Elements effect.

One word of caution: this section is more advanced than some users of Adobe Premiere Elements may need, so feel free to skip to the next lesson if you wish.

However, you should know that such keyframing is the basis of animation in programs such as Adobe Premiere Pro and Adobe After Effects—which means this could be a useful introduction to using those tools—and this exercise is not difficult to complete. If you do choose to skip it, you can always revisit this exercise later if you wish.

In this exercise, you will be animating the NewBlue Pastel Sketch effect to create a unique transition that you'll apply to the start of each major section of the water park project.

1 To begin, select Effects ( ) in the Edit tab of the Tasks panel, and in the list box next to Video Effects, click and select NewBlue Art Effects Elements.

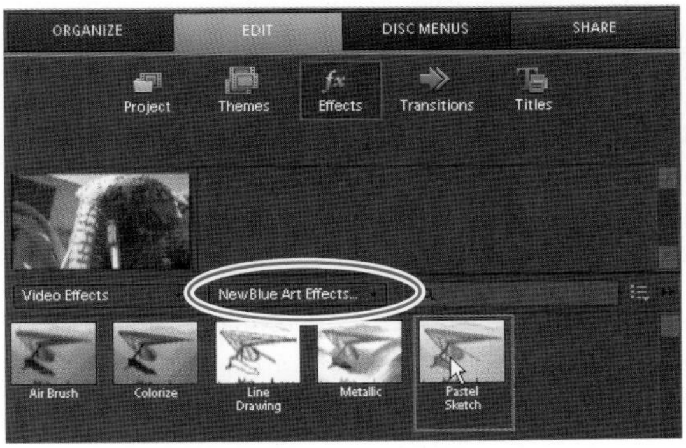

2 Locate the Elephant.avi clip (the second clip in the Timeline) and click the clip to select it.

3 Place your current-time indicator on the first frame of the Elephant.avi clip. Increase the magnification of the Timeline if needed.

4 Drag the Pastel Sketch effect from Effects view and drop it onto the Elephant.avi clip to apply it. You will see the effect applied in the Monitor panel.

5 Click the Edit Effects button in Effects view, and then click the twirl-down triangle next to Pastel Sketch to reveal the controls.

6 If keyframes are not showing, in the top right of Properties view, click the Show keyframes ( ) button. You may need to expand the size of Properties view to better view the keyframes.

7 With the current-time indicator at the start of the clip, click the small stopwatch to the right of the Pastel Sketch controls to enable animation for this property. After you click the stopwatch, a small diamond appears in the mini-timeline within the Properties view to the right of the Density and Blend properties in the Pastel Sketch control. These are the initial keyframes.

8 Let's modify the initial keyframe for Pastel Sketch Density. To do this, drag the Pastel Sketch Density slider to the right until it reaches a value of 100; or, click the numeric entry to make it active and type *100*, then press Enter. You've now set and customized the initial keyframes to your liking.

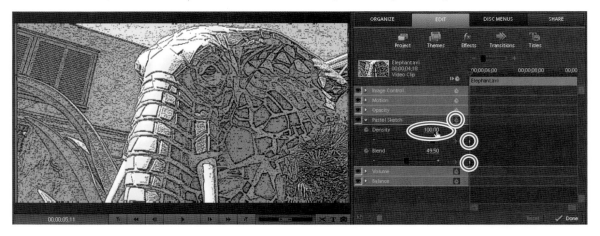

9 Now you'll set the second set of keyframes. In the mini-timeline in Properties view, click and drag the current-time indicator to the right to 00;00;06;11 (which you can see on the bottom left of the Monitor panel).

10 Drag the Pastel Sketch Blend slider to the right until it reaches the value of 100; or, click the numeric entry to make it active and type *100*, then click Enter. This tells Adobe Premiere Elements to show 100% of the original clip (and 0% of the effect) at that location, which essentially turns the effect off.

Changing the value automatically adds a second keyframe, which is represented as a second diamond in the Timeline in Properties view. Once animation has been turned on, Adobe Premiere Elements will automatically animate the effect between the two values.

11 Drag the current-time indicator to the beginning of the clip, and then press the spacebar to play the clip and the effect.-current-time indicator to the beginning of the clip, and then press the spacebar to play the clip and the effect. to the beginning of the clip, and then press the spacebar to play the clip and the effect. The clip starts out with the Pastel Sketch in full effect, and returns to normal appearance at the 00;00;06;11 mark. Press the spacebar again to stop playback.

12 Save your project as *Lesson06_Work.prel*.

Copying effects from one clip to another

Because effects are added to a single clip at a time, it would be quite time-consuming to place the same effect across numerous clips, especially if you had to drag and drop the effect on each clip. Fortunately, Adobe Premiere Elements provides a simple way to copy effects and their settings from one clip to another.

1 Click the second clip, Elephant.avi, in either the Sceneline or Timeline to select it.

2 Click the Properties button in the upper left of the My Project panel to open the Effects Properties view.

3 Click the Pastel Sketch effect in Properties view.

4 Choose Edit > Copy.

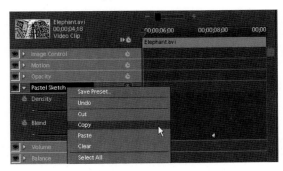

Note: You could also have right-clicked in Properties view and chosen Copy, or used the keyboard command Ctrl+C to copy the selected effects.

5 In either the Sceneline or Timeline, click to select the SprayMe.avi clip (the fourth clip from the start of the movie), and click the Properties button on the upper left of the My Project panel to open the Properties view.

6 Right-click in the blank gray area beneath the fixed and standard effects in Properties view, and then choose Paste. Adobe Premiere Elements applies the Pastel Effect to this clip with the same properties and keyframes.

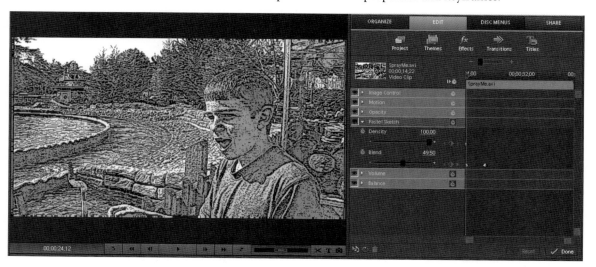

7 Repeat this procedure and paste the effect (you shouldn't have to copy again; just continue to paste) onto the first instance of LunchTime.avi (9th clip) and onto Ride.avi (15th clip).

8 Click the top of the My Project panel to make it active. Press the Home key to place the current-time indicator at the beginning of the project, and then press the spacebar to begin playback. When reviewing the movie, note the effects you have applied to the clips.

9 Choose File > Save As and save your project as *Lesson06_End.prel*.

This concludes the main lesson; next, you'll learn how to implement two additional effects using other source clips in a separate project file.

Creating a Picture-in-Picture overlay

Adobe Premiere Elements can superimpose multiple tracks of video. In this exercise, you will superimpose one video clip in a small frame over your pre-existing background clip that covers the entire screen. This effect is called a Picture-in-Picture (PiP) overlay.

1 To load the project file containing the new content, click File > Open Project, then navigate to the Lesson06 folder you copied to your hard disk.

2 Within that folder, select the file Greenscreen.prel, and then click Open. If a dialog appears asking for the location of rendered files, click the Skip Previews button.

3 Choose Window > Restore Workspace to ensure that you start the lesson with the default panel layout.

4 In the Timelime, click Rockshow.avi, the only clip. The selected clip appears in the Monitor panel.

5 In the Edit tab of the Tasks panel, click the Project button.

6 In Project view, locate the Gina_guitar.avi clip. Click once to select the clip, then hold down the Shift key and drag the clip towards the upper-left corner of Rockshow.avi clip in the Monitor panel.

7 Release the pointer and choose Picture-in-Picture from the menu that appears. Click No in the Videomerge panel.

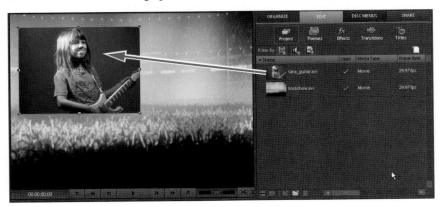

8 Click to select the superimposed clip and notice that the clip changes appearance. There are now handles on the edges, indicating that the clip is active.

9 Select Window > Properties to open Properties view.

10 In Properties view, click the arrow to the left of Motion to reveal its properties. Make sure the Constrain Proportions checkbox is selected.

11 Place your pointer over the value for Scale, and then click and drag to change the value to 40. As you change the scale, the Gina_guitar.avi clip shrinks to 40% of its original size.

● **Note:** If the superimposed clip is longer than the background clip, it appears over successive clips in the Sceneline for its entire duration, and appears superimposed over those clips during playback.

12 If necessary, you can reposition the clip using the Position controls. Or simply click and drag the clip to the desired position in the Monitor panel.

13 Click the Home button on your keyboard to go to the start of your project, and then press the Play button (▶) to review your work.

14 Save your project as *Lesson06_pip.prel*.

Compositing two clips using Videomerge

Compositing is the process of merging two clips together, one atop the other, while removing the background color of the top clip to reveal the second. This allows you to place your subject in a variety of environments, both real and simulated.

Adobe Premiere Elements' Videomerge effect makes compositing as easy as drag and drop. Videomerge automatically determines the background of the top clip and makes it transparent. Video or image clips on the tracks below it become visible through the transparent areas. You'll get the best results with Videomerge if you shoot the clip to be composited using the following rules:

• Create a strong (preferably dark or saturated), solid, uniform color background to shoot against.

• Make sure that the background is brightly and uniformly lit to avoid shadows.

• When choosing a background color, avoid skin tones and colors that are similar to the subject's clothing or hair color. (Otherwise, the skin, clothes, or hair will become transparent, too). Bright green and blue are the best choices.

With this as background, reload the Greenscreen.prel project file (you should have already saved the first project as Lesson06_pip.prel), and follow this procedure.

1   In the Timeline, click Rockshow.avi, the only clip. The selected clip appears in your Monitor panel.

2   In the Edit tab of the Tasks panel, click the Project button.

3   In Project view, locate the Gina_guitar.avi clip. Click once to select the clip, then hold down the Shift key and drag the clip onto the Rockshow.avi clip in the Monitor panel.

4   Release the pointer and choose Place on Top and Apply Videomerge. Adobe Premiere Elements inserts Gina_guitar.avi in the Video 2 track over Rockshow. avi, automatically detects the blue background, and makes it transparent.

● **Note:** If the superimposed clip is longer than the background clip, it appears over successive clips in the Sceneline for its entire duration, and appears superimposed over those clips during playback.

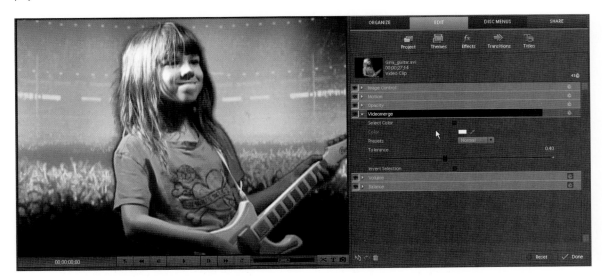

5   In the Timeline, click Gina_guitar.avi to select it, and then click the Properties (▤) button on the upper left of the My Project panel.

6   In Properties view, click the twirl-down triangle to the left of the Videomerge effect to open the parameter settings.

Most of the time, Videomerge will automatically produce optimal results without adjustment. Should you need to customize your Videomerge settings, check the Videomerge section in the Adobe Premiere Elements Help file.

Changing speed using the Time Stretch tool

Previously, you learned how to change the speed of clips bounded in the Timeline by other clips on both sides. Now, you'll learn how to use the Time Stretch tool to accomplish the same task, but in a more visual way.

Here's the problem you'll solve. The Rockshow.avi clip used as a background in the last two exercises is 31 seconds long, and the Gina_guitar.avi clip is about 27 seconds long. You could just trim the Rockshow clip to the same duration, but that would delete content at the end of that clip.

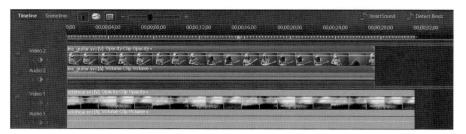

A more elegant solution is to use Adobe Premiere Elements' Time Stretch feature to speed up the Rockshow.avi clip so that it's the same duration as Gina_guitar.avi. Follow this procedure:

1 In the Timeline, click the Time Stretch icon (⬛) on the upper left of the My Project panel.

2 Hover your pointer over the right edge of the Rockshow.avi clip until the Time Stretch icon (⬛) appears.

3 Click and drag the right edge of the Rockshow.avi clip to the left until it aligns with the end of the Gina_guitar.avi clip.

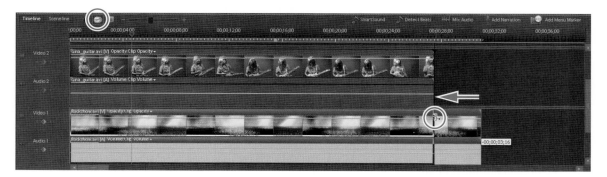

4 Click the Selection Tool icon (⬛) on the upper left of the My Project panel to restore the normal pointer.

5. Right-click Rockshow.avi and choose Time Stretch. Adobe Premiere Elements opens the Time Stretch panel. Note that the speed should have increased to 112.86, which is precisely the correction needed to make Rockshow.avi the same duration as Gina_guitar.avi. In most instances, you would click Maintain Audio Pitch to maintain the pitch of the clip, but since Rockshow.avi has no audio, this isn't necessary in this case.

6. Save your project as *Lesson06_videomerge.prel*.

Exploring on your own

Congratulations! Now you understand how to apply video settings, change effects and settings, copy effects from one clip to another, create an image pan, animate an effect with keyframes, create a Picture-in-Picture effect, and composite one video over another with Videomerge. Here are some effects that you can experiment with on your own.

1. Create a PiP effect using two or more clips on the same screen.

2. Experiment with alternative effects such as Adjust > Brightness & Contrast, or Distort > Bend. To get a sense of the different effects available in Adobe Premiere Elements, choose Help > Premiere Elements Help, or press F1 to access the Help guide. Listed in the Applying Effects section is a gallery of video effects.

3. Experiment with the various effects presets located in the Effects panel, specifically, the Horizontal and Vertical image pans.

Review questions

1 What are curative effects and when should you apply them?

2 What is the quickest way to apply identical effects and settings to multiple clips?

3 What are fixed effects, and what is their purpose?

4 What is a keyframe and what does it contain?

5 How do you modify keyframes once they have been added to a clip?

Review answers

1 Curative effects are effects that improve one or more aspects of a clip, such as exposure, backlighting, or excessive shakiness. You should apply curative effects to a clip before applying artistic and other effects.

2 After selecting the clip that contains the effect or effects that you wish to copy, click an effect to select it in the Properties panel, or Shift-click to select multiple effects. Copy your selection by choosing Edit > Copy. Then select the clip to which you wish to transfer the effects and choose Edit > Paste.

3 Fixed effects are the Property parameters that every clip in Adobe Premiere Elements has enabled by default. These effects are Motion, Opacity, and Volume. Within the Motion effect, Scale, Position, Rotation, and Anchor Point are all properties that can be adjusted to create, for example, a PiP effect.

4 A keyframe contains the values for all the controls in the effect and applies those values to the clip at the specific time.

5 Once keyframes have been added to a clip, they can be adjusted by clicking and dragging them along the connector line. If there are two keyframes, moving one keyframe farther away from the other extends the duration of the effect; moving a keyframe closer to another keyframe shortens the effect.

7 CREATING TRANSITIONS

If you've followed the lessons in this book in order, you should now feel comfortable adding and deleting footage in your project, and trimming clips to improve the pacing of the movie you're producing. In this lesson, you'll learn how to take a project in which your clips have already been sequenced and trimmed and add nuance and dimension using transitions between the clips. You'll learn how to do the following:

- Apply a transition using Transitions view
- Preview transitions
- Modify transition settings
- Create fade-ins and fade-outs
- Render transitions

 This lesson will take approximately 1 hour.

Inserting a transition between two clips in Sceneline view.

Getting started

You will modify scenes in this lesson's project by adding transitions in stages. But first you'll review a final version of the project you'll be creating.

1   Before you begin, make sure that you have correctly copied the Lesson07 folder from the DVD in the back of this book onto your computer's hard disk. See "Copying the Classroom in a Book files" in the Getting Started section at the start of this book.

2   Launch Adobe Premiere Elements.

3   In the Welcome screen, click the Open Project button, and then Open folder.

4   In the Open Project dialog, navigate to the Lesson07 folder you copied to your hard disk.

5   Within that folder, select the file Lesson07_Start.prel, and then click Open. If a dialog appears asking for the location of rendered files, click the Skip Previews button.

   Your project file opens with the Monitor, Tasks, and My Project panels open.

6   Choose Window > Restore Workspace to ensure that you start the lesson in the default panel layout.

Viewing the completed movie before you start

To see what you'll be creating in this lesson, you can play the completed movie.

1   In the Edit tab of the Tasks panel, click Project (![Project]). In the Project view, locate the file Lesson07_Movie.wmv, and then double-click it to open the video in the Preview window.

2   In the Preview window, click the Play button (![Play]) to watch the video about a visit to the water park, which you will build in this lesson.

3   When done, close the Preview window by clicking the Close button (![Close]) in the upper-right corner of the window.

About transitions

Transitions phase out one clip while phasing in the next. The simplest form of a transition is the cut. A cut occurs when the last frame of one clip is followed by the first frame of the next. The cut is the most frequently used transition in video and film, and the one you will use most of the time. However, you can also use other types of transitions to achieve effects between scenes.

Transitions

Using transitions, you can phase out one clip while phasing in the next, or you can stylize the beginning or end of a single clip. A transition can be as subtle as a cross dissolve, or emphatic, such as a page turn or spinning pinwheel. You generally place transitions on a cut between two clips, creating a double-sided transition. However, you can also apply a transition to just the beginning or end of a clip, creating a single-sided transition, such as a fade to black.

When a transition shifts from one clip to the next, it overlaps frames from both clips. The overlapped frames can be either frames previously trimmed from the clips (frames just past the In or Out point at the cut) or existing frames repeated on either side of the cut. It's important to remember that when you trim a clip, you don't delete frames; instead, the resulting In and Out points frame a window over the original clip. A transition uses the trimmed frames to create the transition effect or, if the clips don't have trimmed frames, the transition repeats frames.

—From Adobe Premiere Elements Help

Using Transitions view in the Tasks panel

Adobe Premiere Elements includes a wide range of transitions, including 3D motion, dissolves, wipes, and zooms. The animated thumbnail view that appears when you click on a specific transition gives you a good idea of how it might be applied to your project. Transitions are grouped into two main folders in Transitions view: Audio Transitions and Video Transitions.

1   To access Adobe Premiere Elements transitions, click the Transitions button ( ) in the Edit tab of the Tasks panel. Hover over or select a transition to see an animated preview.

2   Select Video Transitions (if it's not already selected) from the category menu in the upper-left corner of Transitions view. Then select NewBlue 3D Transformations Elements from the menu next to it to see only the different types of transitions in Transitions view.

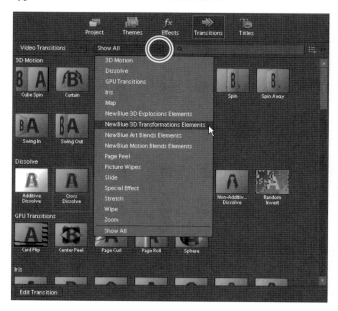

3   Adobe Premiere Elements 7 includes a Favorites category to which you can add your most frequently used transitions. Right-click the Checker Board transition in Transitions view, and then select Add to Favorites from the context menu.

4   To view the content of your Favorites category, select Favorites from the category menu in the upper-left corner of Transitions view. You'll see the Checker Board transition added to the Favorites category.

Applying a transition

Understanding how transitions work is essential to using them successfully. For a transition to shift from one clip to another, the transition must overlap frames from both clips for a certain amount of time.

1   In the Monitor panel, position your current-time indicator at the 00;00;24;12 mark, the edit point between the HorseRide.avi clip and the SprayMe.avi clip. You will be placing a transition between these two clips.

2   If Sceneline is not already selected in the My Project panel, switch to it now.

3   From Transitions view, which should still be showing the content of the Favorites category, drag the Checker Board transition to the rectangle between the HorseRide.avi clip and the SprayMe.avi clip in the Sceneline. You will know the transition has been added because its icon is visible in the rectangle between the two clips in the Sceneline.

> ● **Note:** You do not have to reposition the current-time indicator to place transitions between clips. However, it is often helpful in locating the correct point in your project.

4   In the Sceneline, double-click the rectangle between the two clips to preview the Checker Board transition. After the transition ends, press the spacebar to stop playback.

> ● **Note:** To delete a transition, right-click it and choose Delete.

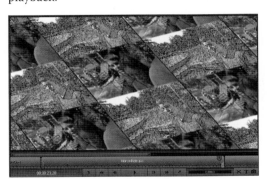

Viewing transition properties

When you add a transition to a clip, the default length of the transition is determined by your preferences. You can change the length of transitions after applying them. Additionally, there are several other attributes of transitions that you can adjust. These include alignment, start and end values, border, and softness.

In this exercise, you will add a Push transition that pushes one image off screen to replace it with the next clip. You will then modify the various attributes of the transition in Properties view.

1 In Transitions view of the Edit tab, choose Video Transitions from the category menu. Make sure Show All is selected in the menu next to it. Then, click in the text search box to the right of the magnifying glass icon (🔍) and type the word *push*. Adobe Premiere Elements automatically searches the list of video transitions and locates the Push transition.

2 If necessary, scroll to the right in the My Project panel until you can see the fourth and fifth clips of the movie, SprayMe.avi and WatchOut.avi. Drag the Push transition from Transitions view to the rectangle between these two clips in the Sceneline.

3 In the Monitor panel, position the current-time indicator a few frames before the transition. Press the spacebar to view the transition. The Push transition will push the first clip off to the side. After the transition ends, press the spacebar to stop playback.

4 Select the Push transition in the Sceneline, and then click the Edit Transition button in the lower-left corner of Transitions view. This will load the transition's parameters into Properties view where you can edit them.

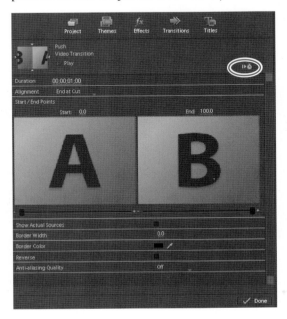

5 Click the Show Keyframes button (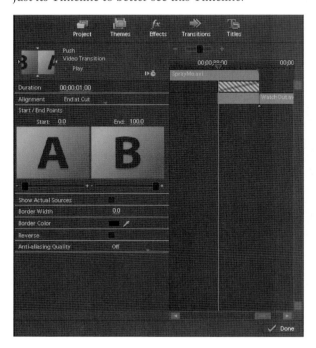) at the top of Properties view to view a magnified version of your Timeline. This enables you to view the transition as it is applied between your two clips. If necessary, resize the Properties panel or just its Timeline to better see this Timeline.

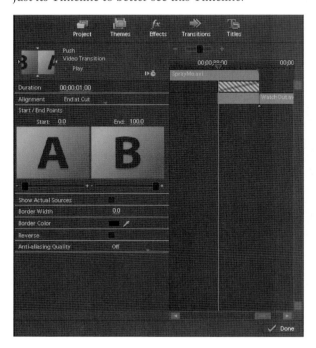

6 In the Timeline of Properties view, drag the current-time indicator back and forth over the transition to preview your transition effect.

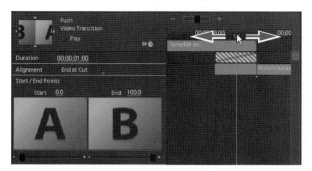

You will now modify the settings of the transition.

Modifying transition settings

All transitions have default settings. To achieve specific results, you can customize the settings in Properties view. Modifying the length of a transition is easy, as you will see in this exercise.

1   To change the length of a transition in Properties view, place your pointer over the Duration value, and then drag to the left to change the Duration to 00;00;00;15 (15 frames). Remember that there are 30 frames in 1 second of NTSC video; therefore, 15 frames represent a half-second of time.

2   Drag the current-time indicator—in either the Monitor panel or Properties view—to a position before the Push transition and press the spacebar to preview the transition. After the transition ends, press the spacebar to stop playback. If you should accidentally click the track area of your Sceneline, you will deselect the transition and its parameters will vanish from Properties view. Don't worry; just click the transition in your Sceneline to select it again and display its parameters in Properties view.

3   In Properties view, select the checkbox marked Reverse. This reverses the transition so that the second clip now pushes the first clip to the left. Depending on the size of your monitor, you may need to scroll down and resize Properties view or its Timeline to be able to see this checkbox.

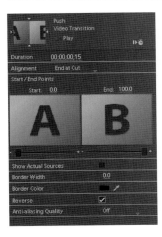

4   Drag your current-time indicator to approximately halfway through the transition; we used the 00;00;38;26 mark. Because you're in the middle of the transition, your screen will be split in half. This makes it easier to preview the modifications you will apply in the next steps.

5   If necessary, scroll down Properties view to view the additional controls. Click the value for Border Width, type the number *30*, and then press Enter. This creates a 30-pixel border on the edge of your transition. The default color of the border is black; but you can modify this as well.

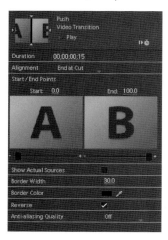

6   Click the black color swatch, next to the Border Color. This opens the Color Picker dialog.

7   In the color slider, which displays the spectrum of colors in a vertical strip, click in the blue hues.

8   Then, inside the larger color spectrum, click in the lower-right corner to select a medium blue.

9   Click OK to close the Color Picker dialog. The border of your transition is now 30 pixels wide and blue.

10 Drag your current-time indicator to a position before the transition, and then press the spacebar to play your modified transition. After the transition ends, press the spacebar to stop playback.

11 Choose File > Save As, name the file *Lesson07_Work* in the Save Project dialog, and then click Save to save it in your Lesson07 folder.

Replacing a transition

Replacing an existing transition between two clips is done in essentially the same way as adding a new transition: simply drag the transition from the Media panel onto the existing transition in the Sceneline. You can do this repeatedly to compare the effects of different transitions.

To practice adding and replacing transitions—this time using the Timeline—you will now apply an Iris Box transition between clips nine and ten of the movie (the first and second instances of the LunchTime.avi clip that you split and trimmed in Lesson 5), and then replace it with an Iris Round transition.

1   In the My Project panel, click the Timeline button. If necessary, use the zoom controls and scroll your view so that the second and third LunchTime.avi clips are visible in the Timeline. Press the Page Up and Page Dn keys to position the current-time indicator at the edit line between the two clips. You might want to click the Zoom In tool ( ) to magnify the view at this edit line.

2   If necessary, click the Transitions button to open Transitions view in the Edit tab, then click in the text search box to the right of the magnifying glass icon (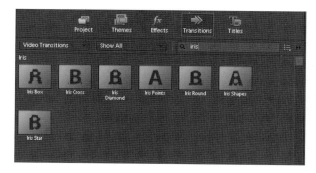), select the word "push," and then type *iris* to automatically list all of the Iris transitions.

3   In the following steps, do not release the pointer until instructed. Drag the Iris Box transition over the Edit line between the first and second LunchTime.avi clips in the Timeline; do not release the pointer. Pay careful attention to the appearance of your pointer.

▶ **Tip:** For more information about transition alignment, search for "transition alignment options" in Adobe Premiere Elements Help.

4   Move your pointer on top of the edit line between the two clips. Notice how your pointer changes to the Center at Cut icon ( ), and then release the pointer. This will center the transition over the cut.

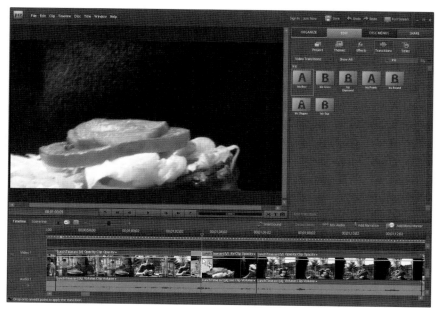

5 Preview the Iris Box transition by dragging your current-time indicator before the transition, and then pressing the spacebar. When the transition is over, press the spacebar to stop playback. Notice how the transition is represented by a gray box with two arrows above the cut between the clips in the Timeline.

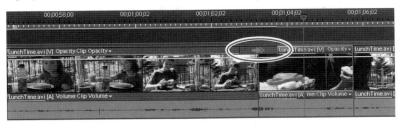

6 In Transitions view, click the Iris Round transition and drag it on top of the Iris Box transition in the Timeline to replace it. You may have only one transition between two clips at a time.

7 Preview the new transition by dragging the current-time indicator before the transition and pressing the spacebar to start playback. After the transition ends, press the spacebar to stop playback.

● **Note:** The "slicing" artifacts that you see in this preview appear because this project uses an interlaced preset. Once this video is rendered onto a DVD, these interlacing artifacts will disappear.

Adding a single-sided transition to create a fade-in

Transitions do not necessarily need to be located between two clips. For example, you can quickly add a fade-in and fade-out to the beginning and end of your movie.

1 If you're not already in Timeline view, in the My Project panel, click the Timeline button. Press the Home key to position the current-time indicator at the beginning of the first clip. Arrange the Timeline so that the Video 1 and Video 2 tracks are showing.

2 In the Transitions view of the Edit tab, select the word "iris" in the text search box to the right of the magnifying glass icon (), and then type the word *dip*. Two Dip transitions will automatically be located in the Dissolve folder.

3 Drag the Dip to Black transition from Transitions view to the beginning of the familyfun_frame clip on the Video 2 track.

4 Drag the Dip to Black transition from the Transitions view to the beginning of the KillerWhale.avi clip on Video 1 track.

5 Press the spacebar to play the transition. The beginning of the transition starts at black, and then fades in to the video. After the transition ends, press the spacebar to stop playback.

6 To extend the duration of these transitions by a half-second, grab the right edge of each transition box one at a time, and drag it to the right until the text box next to the drag pointer indicates that you've added 00;00;00;15. Release the pointer.

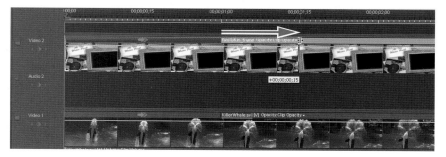

7   Press the End button to move the current-time indicator to the end of the movie. Then drag a Dip to Black transition to the end of 06_imagepan.jpg on the Video 2 track at the end of the movie to fade to black at the end of the movie.

8   Save your project as *Lesson07_End.prel*.

GPU (Graphics Processing Unit) transition effects

Adobe Premiere Elements comes with many GPU-accelerated transitions including Card Flip, Center Peel, Page Curl, Page Roll, and Sphere. These transitions take advantage of the added video processing capabilities offered by video display cards that have Graphics Processing Unit (GPU) chips. These display cards help with graphics acceleration, so transitions can be previewed and rendered more quickly than by the CPU alone. If you have a display card that supports DirectX 9.x, Pixel Shader (PS) 1.3 or later, and Vertex Shader 1.1 or later, you can use the GPU-accelerated transitions. They are visible only if you have a card with a GPU and they reside in the Video Transitions view.

—*From Adobe Premiere Elements Help*

Making transitions work in your movie

Now that you know the "how" of transitions, let's spend a bit of time discussing the "when" and "why." While there are few absolutes about the art of transitions, your productions will benefit by incorporating these two concepts into your creative decisions.

First, recognize that you don't need to include a transition between each and every clip in your movies. If you watch a Hollywood movie, for example, you'll notice that transitions are seldom used between clips *within a scene*, but are often used *between scenes*.

Why? Because the transition lets the viewer know that there's been a change in time or location. That is, if a scene jumped from a kitchen at night to the back yard the next day, simply jumping from scene to scene would confuse the viewer. You can imagine the viewer thinking, "Hey, what happened here? One second they were in the kitchen drinking milkshakes at night, and the next second they were playing dodge ball in the yard in sunlight." However, if the editor had inserted a fade to black between the two scenes, the viewer would understand that a change is coming.

Within the context of the Water Park project, there are three distinct scenes that follow the opening, which you identified with Clip Markers in Chapter 5 and with an animated pastel sketch in Chapter 6. First are the scenes in which the dolphins and killer whales perform, starting with the SprayMe.avi clip. Second is lunch, which starts with LunchTime.avi; third is Afternoon fun, starting with Ride.avi.

These would be the natural locations for transitions within this project. In fact, in the project going forward, you'll notice that the Checker Board transition has been inserted at these locations. The Push transition located between clips four and five, and the Iris Round transitions between clips nine and ten have been deleted.

Of course, with family videos, your goal is to produce smiles, not to win an Academy Award. If you'd like to use transitions as content, rather than in their traditional role, feel free to add as many as you'd like, anywhere you'd like. Just be sure to at least consider the following rule.

When using transitions, you should match the tone of the transition to the tone of the movie. In a fun, family video like the water park project, you could use any transition that Adobe Premiere Elements offers—often the zanier, the better. This is why highly noticeable transitions are used frequently in children's shows like *Barney & Friends* or *The Wiggles*. In fact, for some events, tone trumps rule number 1.

On the other hand, when shooting a solemn event–say, a wedding or graduation–the tone is much more serious. In these instances, you'd probably want to use only Cross Dissolves or the occasional Fade to Black transition to maintain that tone.

Exploring on your own

Our compliments, that's another lesson well done! You've discovered how transitions can make your projects more professional-looking by adding continuity between clips. You've learned about placing, previewing, modifying, and rendering different transitions.

As you continue to edit with transitions, you'll get a better idea of how to use them to enhance the tone or style of your project. The best way to develop that style is through trying out different transitions and discovering how they affect your movie.

1 Make the changes to your project discussed in the immediately preceding section.

2 Experiment with different transitions; preview their animated icons in Transitions view. Remember that dragging a transition onto an existing transition will replace it.

3 Be sure that you are comfortable with modifying the default parameters of your transitions. One by one, select the transitions you have added and explore their settings in Properties view.

Review questions

1   Where are Video Transitions located and what are two ways to locate specific transitions?

2   How do you modify transitions?

3   How can you extend the duration of a transition?

Review answers

1   Video transitions are located in Transitions view, which can be accessed at any time from your Edit workspace. You can browse for individual transitions, which are organized in categories and by transition type. Additionally, you can find a specific transition by typing its name or part of its name into the search field in Transitions view.

2   Click the transition to select it and choose Edit Transition in Properties view.

3   One method of extending the duration of a transition is to change its length in Properties view. Select the transition in the Sceneline to access its properties in Properties view. You can also change the duration of a transition by dragging its edges in the Timeline of the My Project panel.

8 WORKING WITH SOUND

The sound you use has a big impact on your movies. Adobe Premiere Elements provides you with the tools to narrate clips while previewing them in real time; create, add, and modify soundtracks; and control the volume levels within clips. The project in this lesson helps you explore the basics of working with audio. You will create a background music track, adjust the volume of an audio clip, add sound effects, add a narration clip, and mix the audio for maximum effect. Specifically, you'll learn how to do the following:

- Create a custom-length background music track with SmartSound

- Add an audio track and match it to the length of the video

- Use the Audio Mixer

- Adjust the volume of an audio track with keyframes

- Add narration

- Use audio effects

 This lesson will take approximately 1.5 hours.

Mixing your soundtrack in Adobe Premiere Elements.

Getting started

To begin, you'll launch Adobe Premiere Elements and open the project used for this lesson. Then you'll review a final version of the project you'll be creating.

1   Before you begin, make sure that you have correctly copied the Lesson08 folder from the DVD in the back of this book onto your computer's hard disk. For more information, see "Copying the Classroom in a Book files" in the Getting Started section at the beginning of this book.

2   Launch Adobe Premiere Elements and click the Open Project button in the Welcome screen. If Adobe Premiere Elements is already open, choose File > Open Project, and click the Open folder.

3   Navigate to your Lesson08 folder and select the project file Lesson08_Start.prel. Click the Open button to open your project. If a dialog appears asking for the location of rendered files, click the Skip Previews button. The Adobe Premiere Elements work area appears, with the Organize workspace selected in the Tasks panel.

4   The project file opens with the Properties view and the Media, Monitor, and My Project panels. Choose Window > Restore Workspace to ensure that you start the lesson with the default panel layout.

Viewing the completed movie for the first exercise

To see what you'll be creating as your first project in this lesson, a video about a visit to the water park, you can play the completed movie.

1   In the Edit tab of the Tasks panel, click Project ( ). In Project view, locate the file Lesson08_Movie.wmv, and then double-click it to open the video into the Preview window.

2   In the Preview window, click the Play button ( ) to watch the video about a visit to the water park, which you will build in this lesson.

3   When you're finished watching the completed video, close the Preview window by clicking the Close button ( ) in the upper-right corner of the window.

Creating background music with SmartSound

Adobe has partnered with SmartSound to provide you with a library of musical soundtracks to match your project, as well as easy access to a complete library of background music that you can purchase directly from SmartSound (www.smartsound.com). As you'll learn in this exercise, using SmartSound Quicktracks for Adobe Premiere Elements you can quickly choose and create a custom-length soundtrack that matches the mood of your production. In fact, the background track you've been hearing in previous exercises was built in SmartSound; now you'll learn how it was created.

You can create SmartSound Music tracks in either the Sceneline or Timeline of the My Project panel; in this exercise, you'll work in the Timeline.

1   If necessary, switch to the Timeline by clicking the Timeline button in the upper-left corner of the My Project panel.

2   Press the End key on your keyboard to move the current-time indicator to the end of the project. Note the timecode in the bottom left of the Monitor panel, which should be 00;01;53;22. You'll use this duration in a later step to choose the duration of the background music track.

3   Press the Home key on your keyboard to return the current-time indicator to the start of the project.

4   In the upper-right corner of the My Project panel, click the SmartSound (SmartSound) button. Adobe Premiere Elements opens the SmartSound Quicktracks for Adobe Premiere Elements panel.

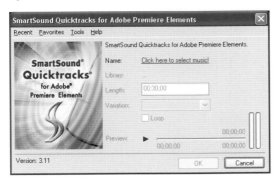

5   Click the Click here to select music! link. Adobe Premiere Elements opens SmartSound Maestro. As you can see in the Find Music column, you can select On My Computer to search for tracks you already own, or select All to search for music on the SmartSound website. Once you choose the library, you can further search by style and intensity to narrow your choices in the Results area.

6   In the Find Music column, choose On My Computer.

7   In the Style list box, choose World.

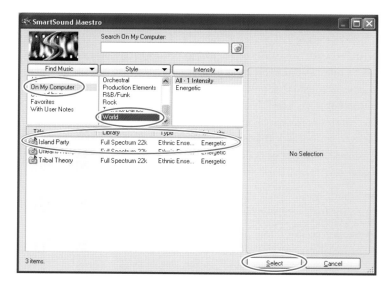

8 In the results area that displays the tracks your search criteria returned, choose Island Party, which is the track you will add to this project. Click the Select button, and SmartSound Maestro closes and the SmartSound Quicktracks for Adobe Premiere Elements dialog opens.

9 In the Length box, type *01;53;22*. Note that you'll have to enter each two-digit number separately into the Length duration box, starting with those on the left, which is different from other similar numeric fields within Adobe Premiere Elements.

10 Click the Preview button to preview the song; you may also choose another variation from the Variation list box and preview again.

11 When you're satisfied with your selection, click OK, and Adobe Premiere Elements opens the Exporting SmartSound Soundtrack dialog.

12 Make sure that you'll be saving the background music track to the Lesson08 folder.

13 Delete the timecode originally appended to the filename and name the file *SmartSound – Island Party – Pool side*, then click Save. You don't have to add the .wav extension; SmartSound will do this automatically.

14 SmartSound saves the file, briefly displaying an export window, and inserts it into the Soundtrack track in the project starting at the location of the current-time indicator.

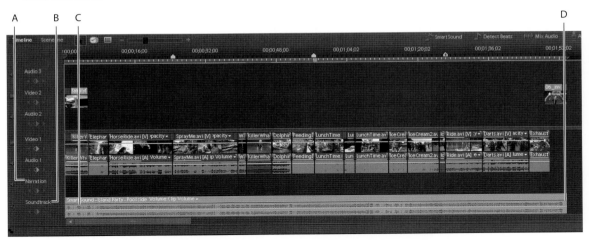

A. Narration track. **B.** Soundtrack track. **C.** New SmartSound audio track. **D.** Ending of SmartSound audio track.

15 Choose File > Save As, name the file *Lesson08_Work* in the Save As dialog, and then save it in your Lesson08 folder.

You can play the new sound file by clicking the spacebar. Again, you'll note that the song is the one that we've used in previous chapters to help the flow of the movie. If you drag your current-time indicator to a few seconds before the end of the movie, and then press the spacebar again to play the last few bars, you'll note that the soundtrack ends naturally, not abruptly, demonstrating that SmartSound really does deliver theme-specific, custom-length soundtracks.

If you play the movie through, you'll also note that the audio included with the original video files is much louder in this project than in previous chapters. That's because in previous chapters, the volume on these files was reduced to mix more effectively with the background music, a skill you'll learn in the next exercise.

Adjusting the volume of an audio track

Background tracks are great, but for maximum impact, you have to mix the background music or narration, or both, with the audio contained in the video clips. As you'll learn, there are multiple techniques that you can use to adjust the volume of your audio components to achieve the optimal mix.

There are no hard and fast rules regarding how to mix background music tracks and ambient audio, or the audio included with the video. In general, the background music carries this production, so you never want the ambient sounds to completely drown it out. Conversely, when ambient sounds are significant, particularly when subjects are speaking, you want to reduce the background music so that the speech is clearly audible.

Adjusting clip volume with the volume graph

In Lesson 6, you learned how to adjust clip opacity on the Timeline by dragging the Opacity graph upwards and downwards. You can adjust the volume of any audio clip the exact same way. Let's mute the volume of the background music clip using this technique so you can adjust the ambient audio of several video clips.

Note: Adjusting the volume line doesn't change the waveform display. However, as you'll see in the next exercise, adjusting gain directly does change the waveform. Though adjusting the volume line is easier and more accessible than adjusting gain directly, if you overboost volume, you can produce distortion without being able to view the clipping itself in the waveform. For an explanation of waveform and clipping, see the sidebar "About waveforms."

1   Working with the SmartSound-Island Party-Pool side clip on the Soundtrack track, place your pointer over the yellow volume graph line. You can do this at any location in the clip. The pointer changes to a double-arrow icon ( ).

2   Drag the volume graph down until the text box changes to negative infinity dB (-oodB). This effectively mutes the clip.

As you'll see, you can also mute a track in the Audio Mixer, which is more efficient when you have multiple clips on a track. With just one clip, however, it's faster and easier to simply drag down the volume line in the track itself.

About waveforms

By default, Adobe Premiere Elements' audio tracks display the file as a waveform, which is a graphic representation of the volume of audio in the file. When volume is low, the bushy line representing the waveform narrowly surrounds the centerline. As volume increases, the bushy line extends farther away from the centerline. Volume is optimal when the peaks in the individual waveform approach, but just barely touch, the outer edges of the graph area.

Once you understand what the waveform represents, it's much simpler to diagnose and resolve problems with your audio files. For example, on the left in this figure, the WatchOut.avi waveform indicates that volume levels are close to optimal. Though you may want to adjust them upwards slightly, overall, this is a very good starting point. The volume on the KillerWhale.avi clip is similarly very close to optimal.

Problems appear in the next two clips. In DolphinShow.avi, where the volume was boosted too far using the gain controls, you see the top of the waveform pressing against the outer border of the graph area. This is a condition called "clipping," where the outer edges of the waveform are truncated because volume is too high. In severe cases, clipping causes noticeable distortion that can make the clip unusable.

In this case, since the clipping occurred after making a gain adjustment, you would simply undo the gain adjustment and boost volume again using a lower level. If there was clipping in your audio source file, there's nothing you can do except hope that the clipping isn't accompanied by distortion. If distortion is present, you can't really fix it; you can only reduce the volume so that your viewers can't hear it.

In the fourth clip, the volume is simply too low. While you can boost the volume using different techniques, this can also increase the background noise present in the clip. In these instances, you can try Adobe Premiere Elements' DeNoiser filter, but like all noise reduction filters, this isn't a panacea, and may not resolve the problem.

Note that several of these waveforms were adjusted for demonstration purposes and won't look the same on your project timeline.

Adjusting clip volume with gain controls

You've learned how to adjust volume using the volume graph; now let's learn how to use the gain controls. First, let's discuss the concept of normalization. In the sidebar "About waveforms," you learned that increasing audio volume too much can cause clipping, which is often accompanied by distortion.

Normalization boosts the volume of the entire audio file to a level just below that which would produce distortion at any point in the clip. The fastest and surest way to boost audio volume to the maximum without introducing distortion is via normalization.

The only problem with normalization comes when you have a clip with extreme low and high volumes. Say you were shooting a wedding, and didn't get close enough (or outfit the bride and groom with microphones) to capture the vows at sufficient volume. So the levels are very low when the bride and groom are speaking. However, when the crowd starts applauding, the levels are quite high. If you apply normalization to this clip, Adobe Premiere Elements won't boost the volume of the applause beyond the point of causing distortion, which often means that it won't boost the volume of the vows at all. Your best option in this case is to split the audio clip into low- and high-volume regions—say, vows in one, applause in another—and apply normalization separately, or only to the vows audio. Here's the procedure.

1 Drag the current-time indicator to the first LunchTime.avi clip, the ninth clip in the My Project panel. Click the spacebar to play the video. As you can see (and hear), the low volume matches the anemic levels in the waveform itself.

2 Click the first LunchTime.avi clip to select it.

3 If working in the Timeline, right-click and choose Audio Gain. If working in the Sceneline, choose Clip > Audio Options > Audio Gain. Adobe Premiere Elements opens the Clip Gain panel.

4 Click the Normalize button. Adobe Premiere Elements calculates the maximum volume increase possible without producing distortion, which in this case is a volume boost of 12.7. If desired, you can modify this value by dragging over the number or clicking the field to make it active and inserting the desired gain adjustment, either positive or negative.

5 Click OK to apply the gain adjustment and close the Clip Gain panel. You'll see the levels in the waveform on the Audio 1 track increase substantially.

6 Shift the current-time indicator to the start of the clip, and press the spacebar to play the clip again. The volume should be much higher, and you will hear more of the background noise of the water park, though the levels aren't distracting. If you study the waveform in the Timeline, you'll also notice that Adobe Premiere Elements boosted the volume of the entire clip only at the point where the sharp peak on the right touched the edges of the graph area. Note that we had to increase the height of the audio tracks to make this easily visible. We describe how in Chapter 5, *Changing the height of tracks*.

How does normalization relate to manual adjustments to the volume graph? It's completely separate, so if you normalize your audio files and then increase the volume using the volume graph, you'll very likely cause clipping and produce distortion. In general, when mixing your audio, you should consider normalizing all clips first, then adjusting volume only downward using either the volume graph or the Audio Mixer, which are essentially different options for accessing the same controls.

7 Take a moment now and normalize the volume of other clips in the Timeline, and then move to the next exercise.

Resetting clip volume

Before working with the Audio Mixer, you should reset the clip volume graph you adjusted in a previous exercise. You can do this by grabbing the volume graph with your pointer and dragging it upwards to the original zero value. However, often it's difficult to reset the value exactly to the original value.

Alternatively, follow this procedure to reset the audio volume in Properties view.

1 Click SmartSound – Island Party – Pool side.avi on the Soundtrack.

2 Click the Properties button on the upper left of the My Project panel.

3   In Properties view, click the twirl-down triangle to the left of the Volume control to open the parameter settings. You should see clip volume set to negative infinity.

4   Click the Volume effect, and then, on the lower right of Properties view, click the Reset button to reset the volume to its default level. Adobe Premiere Elements sets the volume back to 0.0 decibels (dB).

Note: This procedure highlights that the volume graph on the Timeline is essentially the same control as the Volume control in Properties view. This means that you can create keyframes for volume adjustments, either in the Timeline or in Properties view. Conversely, you can neither control clip gain adjustments in Properties view nor set keyframes.

Working with the Audio Mixer

When you have multiple tracks of audio playing at once, the audio you want to hear can get lost. Using the Audio Mixer, you can adjust the volume and balance of the different audio tracks as the audio plays, so you can make sure your audience hears what you want them to hear. For example, you can lower the volume for the Soundtrack while people are talking, and increase it again when they are silent.

1   Press the Home key to place the current-time indicator at the beginning of the movie. Press the spacebar to begin playing your video.

You will hear the steel drums of the SmartSound clip, as well as the audio part of the video clips, background noise, and voices of the family.

2   When you're finished previewing the movie, press the Home key again to set the current-time indicator right at the beginning of the video, which is where you want to start mixing audio.

3   Click the Mix Audio button (Mix Audio) or choose Window > Audio Mixer. Adobe Premiere Elements opens the Audio Mixer.

178   LESSON 8   Working with Sound

4   In the Audio Mixer panel, choose Show/Hide Tracks from the Audio Mixer panel menu on the upper right of the panel, and then deselect all but the Audio 1, Narration, and Soundtrack tracks.

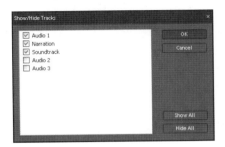

● **Note:** In Adobe Premiere Elements, volume is measured in decibels. A level of 0.0 dB is a track's original volume, not silence. Changing the levels to a negative number reduces the volume (but not necessarily to silence), and changing the volume to a positive number increases the volume.

5   Click OK. Your Audio Mixer panel shows only the three audio channels you will work with: Audio 1 and Soundtrack in this exercise; Audio 1, Soundtrack, and Narration in a future exercise.

6   Press the Home key to place the current-time indicator at the beginning of the project, and then press the spacebar to begin playback.

7   Grab the levels handles for Audio 1 and the Soundtrack and adjust them as desired. Note that all adjustments made via the Audio Mixer will be reflected as keyframes on the audio track itself and in its respective Properties view, but will become visible only after you stop playback.

Some thoughts on mixing strategies

Mixing strategies vary from project to project. In this project, using background music, one approach would be to lower the volume of the background track and maximize ambient sound, especially when a family member is speaking. Following this approach, you would reduce the volume of the Audio 1 track only when the sound is overbearing (like the KillerWhale.avi clip) or distracting.

Another approach would be to maintain the level of the background music track, and reduce the Audio 1 track except when family members are speaking. As editor, producer, and chief creative officer, it's up to you to select the best approach for the project.

Workflows also vary by project and editor. Probably the fastest approach is to consider the work performed in real time with the Audio Mixer as a "first draft," which you can fine tune via the keyframes inserted by the Audio Mixer. Don't interrupt your workflow by stopping to make changes; get through the movie first in real time, and then adjust the keyframes in the Timeline.

Raising and lowering volume with keyframes

You learned about working with keyframes in video in Lesson 6 in a section titled (appropriately enough) "Working with keyframes." Audio keyframes operate identically to the video-related keyframes discussed in that lesson. To refresh your memory, a keyframe is a point in the Timeline where you specify a value for a specific property—in this case, audio volume. When you set two keyframes, Adobe Premiere Elements interpolates the value of that property over all frames between the two keyframes.

For some properties, including opacity for video and volume for audio, you can create keyframes in the Timeline by pressing the Ctrl key, and clicking the associated graph with your pointer. Next, drag the keyframe upwards or downwards to adjust its value, or to the left or right to adjust its location. To delete keyframes in the Timeline, click to select them, then right-click and choose Delete.

Alternatively, you can create and modify keyframes in Properties view. This exercise will review these procedures and reinforce the relationship between keyframes in the Timeline and keyframes in Properties view. Specifically, in this exercise, you will add keyframes to fade in the volume of the music track at the beginning of your movie.

1   Using the My Project panel in the Timeline, place the current-time indicator near the start of the clip—we used the 00;00;01;00 mark.

2   Click to select the SmartSound – Island Party - Pool side clip in the Timeline's Soundtrack.

3   Select Window > Properties, and then click the Show Keyframes button ( ) in the upper-right corner of Properties view.

4   Use the Zoom Slider to zoom into the mini-timeline until you can see the 00;00;01;00 timecode in the mini-timeline.

5   Click the Toggle Animation button ( ) for the Volume effect to activate keyframes. This will set the first keyframe at the current-time indicator. If the Toggle Animation button is already activated, click to disable it (and delete all keyframes), then click again to activate keyframes.

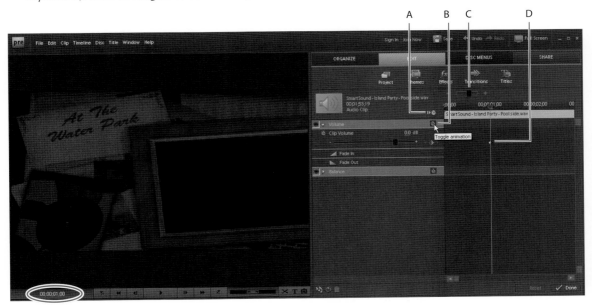

A. Show Keyframes button. **B.** Toggle Animation button. **C.** Zoom Slider. **D.** Keyframe.

You'll set the next keyframe in the Timeline.

6   Press the Page Up key to move the current-time indicator to the beginning of the movie. If necessary, use the Zoom Slider on top of the Timeline to zoom in for more detail.

7 In the Timeline of the My Project panel, position the pointer over the orange volume graph of the SmartSound – Island Party - Pool side.wav clip at the current-time indicator. Make sure not to position the pointer too far to the left. The pointer needs to change to a white arrow with double arrows ( ) and not the Trim Out tool ( ). Press the Ctrl key on your keyboard, and then click the volume graph to add a second keyframe.

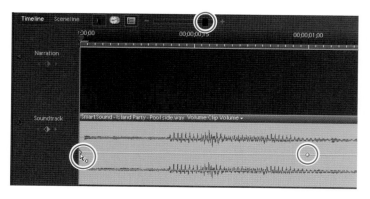

8 Drag the new keyframe all the way down to create a fade out. You can check Properties view: the Clip Volume reads -oo to resemble the mathematical symbol $-\infty$ for negative infinity.

● **Note:** This exercise was designed to help show the relationship between audio keyframes in the Timeline and Properties view. However, this lesson learned, a faster way to produce a fade-in effect is to click the Fade In icon (Fade In) for the audio clip in the Properties view as shown above.

9 To hear this change, press the Page Up key, and then press the spacebar to play. You'll hear the soundtrack fade in over the first second of the production rather than starting at full strength.

10 Save your project as *Lesson08_work.prel*.

Edit to the beat of your favorite song

Click Detect Beats in the Sceneline or Timeline to automatically add markers at the beats of your musical soundtrack. Beat detection makes it easy to synchronize slide shows or video edits to your music.

1   Add an audio clip or a video clip that includes audio to the soundtrack in the Timeline or Sceneline.

2   Click the Detect Beats button (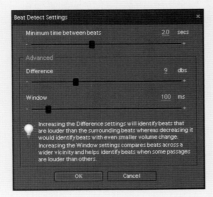) at the top of the Timeline or Sceneline.

3   In the Beat Detect Settings dialog, specify settings as desired and click OK.

4   Markers appear in the Timeline corresponding to the beats in the soundtrack.

Creating a split edit

At times, you may want the audio to begin before the video or to extend after the video into the next clip (or vice versa). Trimming linked audio and video separately is called a split edit. Usually, when you create a split edit in one clip, you must create one in the adjacent clip so they don't overlap each other. You can create two kinds of split edits:

- A J-cut, or audio lead, in which audio starts before linked video, or video continues after the audio.

- An L-cut, or video lead, in which video starts before linked audio, or audio continues after the video.

—From Adobe Premiere Elements Help

Adding narration

Now let's add narration to the project.

1 Make sure you have Timeline selected in the My Project panel.

2 Choose File > Get Media from > PC Files and Folders, select the file Lesson08_ Narration.wav, and click Open.

3 Press the Home key to move the current-time indicator to the start of the clip. Then drag the Lesson08_Narration.wav clip from Project view and drop it onto the Narration track in the Timeline.

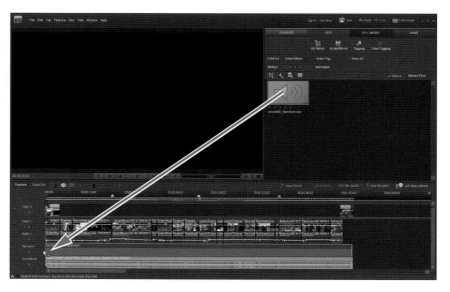

4 Click the Play button () to hear the voiceover added to the project. Note that you need to lower the volume of the background music to make the narration more audible.

5 Click the Mix Audio button (Mix Audio), and in the Audio Mixer panel that opens, drag the handle in the Soundtrack channel down to -6.0 dB.

6 Click the Play button ( ) and listen to the improved audio mix.

While the overall sound is better, the narration is still a bit indistinct. You'll fix that by applying the Dynamics sound effect in the next exercise.

Narrating a clip

In this exercise, you're working with a narration that we supplied, but at some point, you may want to create your own narration. For best results, confirm that your microphone is working correctly with your computer and Adobe Premiere Elements before narrating a clip.

Using your computer's microphone, you can narrate clips while previewing them in the Monitor panel. Your narration is then added to the Narration soundtrack visible in either the Timeline or Sceneline.

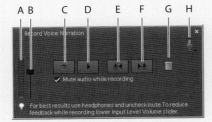

Record voice narration: **A.** Volume indicator. **B.** Input Volume Level slider. **C.** Record. **D.** Play. **E.** Go To Previous Narration Clip. **F.** Go To Next Narration Clip. **G.** Delete. **H.** Microphone source.

(continues)

Narrating a clip (*continued*)

1   If you're working in the Timeline, drag the current-time indicator to the point where you want the narration to begin. If you're working in the Sceneline, select the clip you want to narrate. Then, in the Monitor panel, drag the current-time indicator to the point where you want the narration to begin.

2   In the Timeline or Sceneline, click the Add Narration button ( Add Narration). The Record Voice Narration panel opens.

3   In the Record Voice Narration panel, click the Mic Source button and select your sound device from the menu.

4   For best results, turn off your computer speakers to prevent feedback. To monitor sound while you narrate, plug headphones into your computer and deselect Mute Audio While Recording. If your speakers are turned on, move as close to the microphone as possible, and keep the microphone as far away from the speakers as possible to prevent feedback.

5   Speak into the microphone at a conversational volume, and raise or lower the Input Volume Level slider until your loudest words light up the orange part of the meters.

6   Click the Record Narration button.

7   Near the top of the Record Voice Narration panel, a timer appears next to Start Recording In. When Start Recording In changes to Recording, speak your narration as the selected clip plays.

8   When you finish narrating, click the Stop button. (If you don't click the Stop button, recording automatically stops at the beginning of the next file in the Narration track, or 30 seconds past the end of the last clip in the Timeline or Sceneline.)

9   To preview your recording, click the Go To Previous Narration button. Then click the Play Present Narration button.

10 To continue recording from the point at which you stopped, click the Record button again to overwrite any narrations that are already in the Narration track.

11 Click the Pause button at any time to stop the preview.

An audio clip containing your narration is added to the Media panel and to the Narration track in the Timeline or Sceneline (below the selected clip). In the Sceneline, a microphone icon appears in the upper-right corner of the clip you've narrated.

—*From Adobe Premiere Elements Help*

Adding a sound effect

Adobe Premiere Elements includes a wide variety of audio effects to improve or enhance the audio portion of your video projects. These effects include controlling volumes and frequencies of the different channels, detecting and removing tape noise, or eliminating background noise, and inverting channels or adding the reverberation of sounds to give ambience and warmth to the audio clip. You can find the audio effects in Effects view.

In this exercise, you'll add the Dynamics sound effect to Lesson08_Narrration.wav. As you'll see, one component of the Dynamics effect, called compression, boosts the softer sounds in an audio file without increasing the higher levels. However, unlike normalization, which simply boosts audio volume, compression actually changes the tone of the audio file as well, so applying too much compression can add a noticeable harshness to the audio.

Used in moderation, however, compression is a great tool for improving the legibility of narration, or voices contained in videos, especially when used in conjunction with background music or loud, ambient sounds.

1 Click Edit in the Tasks panel, and then click Effects (![fx Effects]) to open Effects view.

2 Choose Audio Effects from the menu at the top of the panel.

3 Drag the Dynamics effect onto Lesson08_Narration.wav located in the Narration track.

4 To refine the effect setting, click the Edit Effects button at the bottom of the Tasks panel, and expand the effect by clicking the twirl-down triangle next to Dynamics, then the twirl-down triangle next to Custom Setup. You might need to scroll down in order to see all effect properties.

5 In the Custom Setup box, *do the following*:

- Make sure that Compressor is selected.

- Deselect Auto

- Type *12.00* into the MakeUp text box. Note that we've used a relatively high level to make sure you hear the effect. If you think the result sounds slightly distorted, you can always enter a lower number to use a lower level.

6 Press the Home key, and then press the spacebar to again play the video.

7 Choose File > Save As, and save the file as *Lesson08_ End.prel*.

Exploring on your own

Great news: You've finished another lesson and learned the basics of working with sound. Specifically, you learned to create a custom-length soundtrack with SmartSound, how to use the Audio Mixer, how to adjust audio gain directly, how to create and adjust keyframes in the Timeline and Properties view, how to add narration to your projects, and how to boost the legibility of that narration.

But you're not finished yet. The best way to master the audio tools in Adobe Premiere Elements is to continue to explore them until you're really comfortable with all of its soundtrack creation capabilities.

1 Experiment with different songs available in SmartSound. Think of some projects you have upcoming (birthdays, holidays, vacations) and try to find the appropriate tracks for those videos.

2 Experiment with various audio effects such as Delay and Dynamics. A description of Adobe Premiere Elements audio effects can be found in the "Audio Effects" section of Adobe Premiere Elements Help.

3 As you did for the fade-in of the soundtrack, try to create a fade-out for the end of your project.

Review questions

1 What is the Audio Mixer and how do you access it?

2 How would you change the volume of a clip over time using keyframes?

3 How do you change the presets of an audio effect?

4 How is compression different from normalization and when would you use each technique?

Review answers

1 Using the Audio Mixer, you can easily adjust the audio balance and volume for different tracks in your project. You can refine the settings while listening to audio tracks and viewing video tracks. Each track in the Audio Mixer corresponds to an audio track in the Timeline or Sceneline, and is named accordingly. You can access the Audio Mixer by clicking the Mix Audio button or choosing Window > Audio Mixer.

2 Each clip in the Adobe Premiere Elements Timeline has a yellow volume graph that controls the keyframes of the clip. To add keyframes, you Ctrl-click the line. You must have at least two keyframes with different values to automatically change the volume level of an audio clip. You can also use the Audio Mixer to set keyframes to change the volume of your audio clip over time.

3 First, select the clip that contains the effect you want to adjust in the Timeline. Then, in the Effects view, click the Edit Effects button. In Properties view, expand the property by clicking the triangle next to the property name (if available), and then drag the slider or angle control.

4 Normalization boosts the audio volume of all samples of an audio clip the same amount, stopping when further volume increases would produce distortion in the loudest sections of the clip. Compression increases the volume of lower-volume regions while ignoring the loudest regions. Normalization is a tool that can be used nearly universally to boost volume, while compression should be used only when necessary to make a specific audio track more distinct.

9 TITLES AND CREDITS

In this lesson, you'll learn how to create original titles and rolling credits for a home movie about a trip to the water park. You'll be adding still titles and rolling titles, placing images, and using the drawing tools in the Monitor panel. Specifically, you'll learn how to do the following:

- Add and stylize text
- Superimpose titles and graphics over video
- Create and customize rolling titles
- Use title templates

 This lesson will take approximately 2 hours.

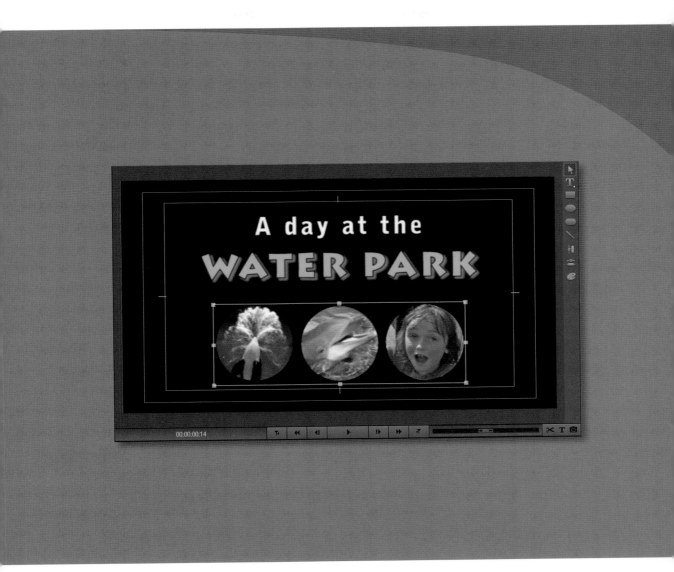

Creating a full-screen opening title in Adobe
Premiere Elements.

Working with titles and the title-editing mode

Within Adobe Premiere Elements, you can create custom graphics and titles. When you add a title over one of your video clips, it is also added to your Project view as a new clip. As such, it is treated much like any other clip in your project. It can be edited, moved, deleted, and have transitions and effects applied to it.

Adobe Premiere Elements allows you to create original titles using text, drawing tools, and imported graphics. However, to help you quickly and easily add high-quality titles to your project, Adobe Premiere Elements also provides a number of templates based on common themes such as Sports, Travel, and Weddings.

Getting started

To begin, you'll launch Adobe Premiere Elements and open the Lesson09 project file. Then you'll review a final version of the project you'll be creating.

1 Before you begin, make sure that you have correctly copied the Lesson09 folder from the DVD in the back of this book onto your computer's hard disk. See "Copying the Classroom in a Book files" in the Getting Started section at the beginning of this book.

2 Launch Adobe Premiere Elements and click the Open Project button in the Welcome screen. If necessary, click Open in the menu that appears. If Adobe Premiere Elements is already open, choose File > Open Project.

3 Navigate to your Lesson09 folder and select the project file Lesson09_Start.prel. Click the Open button to open your project. If a dialog appears asking for the location of rendered files, click the Skip Previews button. The Adobe Premiere Elements work area appears, with the Edit workspace selected in the Tasks panel.

4 The project file opens with the Properties view and the Media, Monitor, and My Project panels in view. Choose Window > Restore Workspace to ensure that you start the lesson with the default panel layout.

Viewing the completed movie before you start

To see what you'll be creating as your first project in this lesson, a video about the water park, you can play the completed movie.

1   In the Edit tab of the Tasks panel, click the Project button (▣). In Project view, locate the file Lesson09_Movie.wmv, and then double-click it to open the video into the Preview window.

2   In the Preview window, click the Play button (▶) to watch the video about a visit to the water park, which you will build in this lesson.

3   When done, close the Preview window by clicking the Close button (✖) in the upper-right corner of the window.

Creating a simple title

You can add titles to your movie—whether simple still titles, advanced titles with added graphics, or styled text scrolling across the screen horizontally or vertically—directly in the Monitor panel of Adobe Premiere Elements. To begin, you will create a basic still title. You will work with the water park project, starting by adding a title clip at the beginning of the movie. First you will add a few seconds of black video, over which you can then type the title text.

1   In the Sceneline of the My Project panel, click the first clip to select it. In the upper-right corner of Project view, click the New Item button (▣), and then choose Black Video from the menu that appears.

2   Adobe Premiere Elements inserts a 5-second black video clip after the first clip in the Sceneline. To move the black video clip to the beginning of the movie, click and drag it to the left of the first clip in the Sceneline.

3 With the black video still selected in the Sceneline, choose Title > New Title > Default Still. Adobe Premiere Elements places the default title text over the black video in the Monitor panel and switches to title-editing mode. In the mini-timeline of the Monitor panel, notice the bluish gray-colored clip representation for the new title clip that is placed on top of the lavender-colored clip representation for the black video clip. Also notice the text and drawing tools now visible on the right side of the Monitor panel, and the text options, text styles, and text animation choices accessible from Properties view.

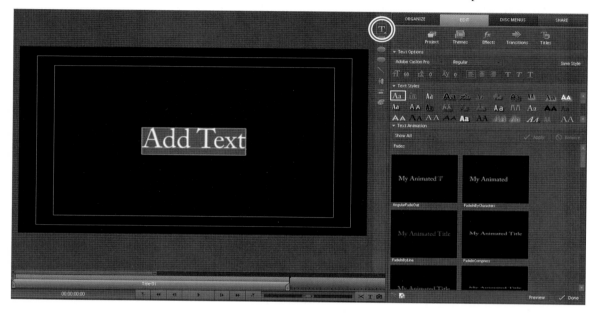

● **Note:** The Horizontal Type tool is grouped with the Vertical Type tool. To switch between the two, click and hold the Tool button, and then choose from the menu that appears.

4 The Horizontal Type tool should be selected by default. If not, click the Horizontal Type tool button (⊤) to the right of the Monitor panel to select it now.

5 Click in the text box and drag your pointer over the default text to select it, type the words *A day at the*, and then press the Return key to create a new line. Next, type the words *WATER PARK*.

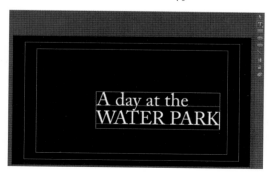

6   To reposition your text, click the Selection tool (⬉) in the upper-right corner of the Monitor panel, and then click anywhere inside the text to select the text block. Drag to reposition the text so it appears centered in the upper third of your title window. There are two white margins in the title window; these are referred to as the title-safe and action-safe margins. Stay within the inner margin (title-safe) while repositioning your text. Don't worry about the exact position for now; you'll reposition the text later in this lesson.

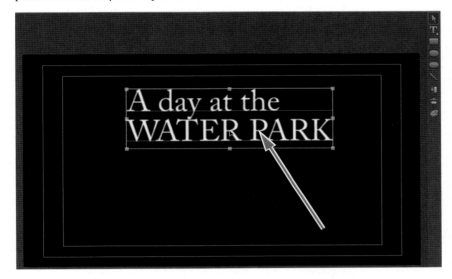

7   Choose File > Save As, name the file *Lesson09_Work* in the Save As dialog, and then click Save to save it in your Lesson09 folder.

▶ **Tip:** You can add multiple text entries to a single title, or create multiple titles, each containing unique text strings.

Adobe Premiere Elements treats basic titles, such as the one you just created, like still image files. Once you have created a title, an image file is automatically added to your Project view. In this case, the new title was superimposed over the black video clip at the beginning of the movie, but as you will see, you can also place it over any other clip in your movie. After creating and adding a title to the project, you can change text or appearance at any time.

Modifying text

After entering your title text, you can adjust text appearance, much like in a word processor or page layout program. In this exercise, you will learn how to adjust the alignment of your type as well as its style, size, and color.

Title-safe and action-safe margins

The title-safe and action-safe margins visible in the Monitor panel when in title-editing mode designate the title's visible safe zones. These margins are visible by default.

Safe zones are useful when producing DVDs or other video that will be viewed on a traditional TV set, rather than on your computer. That's because when displaying video, most consumer TV sets cut off a portion of the outer edges of the picture, which is called *overscan*. The amount of overscan is not consistent across TVs, so to ensure that everything fits within the area that most TVs display, keep text within the title-safe margins and keep all other important elements within the action-safe margins.

If you are creating content for computer-screen viewing only, the title-safe and action-safe margins are irrelevant because computer screens display the entire image.

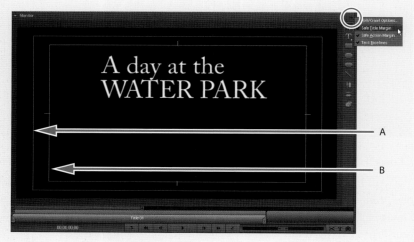

A. Safe Action margin. **B**. Safe Title margin.

To turn title-safe and action-safe margins on or off, choose Window > Show Docking Headers if the docking headers are not currently visible, and then choose Safe Title Margin or Safe Action Margin from the Monitor panel menu. Or right-click in the Monitor panel, and then choose View > Safe Title Margin or View > Safe Action Margin from the context menu. The margin is visible if a checkmark appears beside its name.

Changing the text alignment, style, and size

To begin, let's switch over to the Timeline, so you can see how Adobe Premiere Elements displays titles in that view.

1 Click Timeline in the upper-left portion of the My Project panel. In the Timeline, double-click the new title (Title 01), which should be on the Video 2 track.

2 To center the text in its text box, use the Selection tool ( ) to select the title text box, and then click the Center Text button ( ) located under Text Options in Properties view.

3 In the Monitor panel, choose the Type tool and drag it in the text box to select the first line of text. Under Text Options in Properties view, choose Bell Gothic Std from the font menu and Black from the style menu next to it.

4 With the first line of text still selected, to change the font size, *do the following*:

• Under Text Options in Properties view, place the pointer over the Size value ( ). The pointer will change to a hand with two black arrows ( ).

- Drag to change the Size value to 50. If you have difficulties getting a precise value by dragging, click the size value once, and then type *50* into the text field.

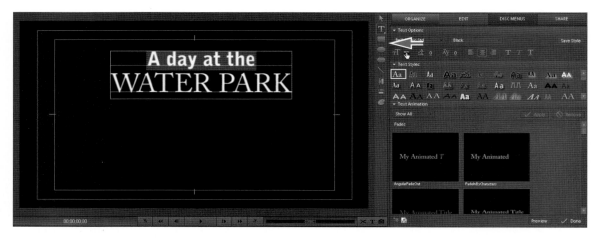

5 Select the second line of text—the words "WATER PARK"—with the Type tool, and choose Lithos Pro White 94 from the list of predefined text styles under Text Styles in Properties view. This changes the text font and applies a drop shadow.

▶ **Tip:** You can also change the size of text by selecting its text box, and then clicking and dragging one of the anchor points. Hold down the Shift key as you are dragging to maintain a proportional height and width of the text box and the type therein.

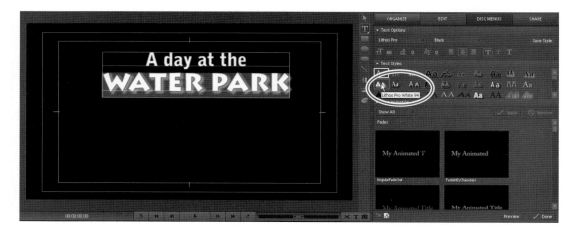

6   Next, we'll spread the letters in the bottom line of text. Select the bottom line of text with the Text tool, and *do the following*:

- Under Text Options in Properties view, locate the Kerning value next to the Kerning icon (). Position the pointer over the numerical value and it will change to a hand with two black arrows ( ).

- Next, drag the size value to 5. If you have difficulties getting a precise value by dragging, click the size value once, and then type 5 into the text field.

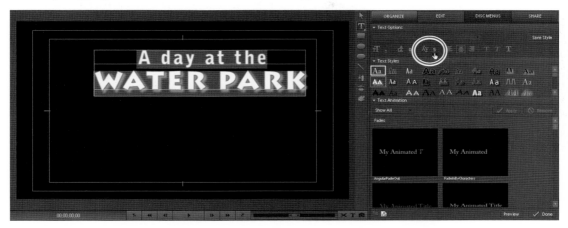

7   Now we'll increase the spacing between the two lines of text. To begin, select both lines of text with the Text tool, and *do the following*:

- Under Text Options in Properties view, place the pointer over the Leading value ( ). The pointer changes to a hand with two black arrows ( ).

- Drag the size value to 20. If you have difficulties getting a precise value by dragging, click the size value once, and then type *20* into the text field.

8   Choose File > Save to save your work.

Centering elements in the Monitor panel

At this point, your title probably isn't precisely centered horizontally within the frame. You can fix this manually, or you can let Adobe Premiere Elements do the work for you.

1 Using the Selection tool, click the text box to select it.

2 Choose Title > Position > Horizontal Center. Or, right-click the text box, and then choose Position > Horizontal Center. Adobe Premiere Elements centers the text box horizontally within the frame. Depending on how you positioned the box earlier in this lesson, you might see little or no change.

3 Choose File > Save to save your work.

Changing the color of your type

As you have seen, changing the style and size of your type is easy. You can change all text within a text box equally by first selecting the text box using the Selection tool, and then applying the change. Or, you can restrict the change to portions of the text by selecting them using the Type tool. You will now change the color of the words "WATER PARK."

1 Select the Horizontal Type tool (T), and then click and drag over the words "WATER PARK" to highlight the text.

Next, you'll change the color of the type from white to an orange-yellow. Note that any changes you make will apply to only the selected type.

2 Click the Color Properties button (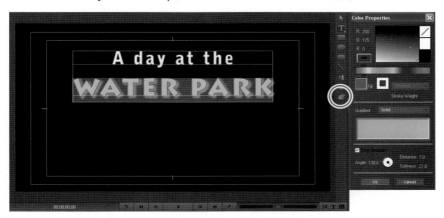) at the bottom of the tool buttons in the Monitor panel to open the Color Properties dialog. Set the RGB values to R: *255*, G: *175*, and B: *0*. Notice that Drop Shadow is selected. This is part of the definition of the predefined style Lithos Pro White 94.

3 Click OK to close the Color Properties dialog. Use the Selection tool and click outside the text box in the Monitor panel to deselect the text and review your work.

4 Choose File > Save to save your work.

Adding an image to your title files

To add an extra element of depth and fun to your titles, you can import and insert images from any number of sources. For instance, you can use photos from your digital still camera as elements in your title file. In this exercise, you will use an arrangement of still images taken from the video clips and place it in the lower half of the title image.

1 With the Monitor panel still in title-editing mode, choose Title > Image > Add Image, or right-click the Monitor panel, and then choose Image > Add Image from the context menu. Or, click the Add Image button ( ) located in the lower-left corner of Properties view.

The file Open dialog appears. By default, the dialog may point you to the list of files in Adobe Premiere Elements Logos folder. These are the default images that were installed with the application. Feel free to use these in your other projects, whether from this book or otherwise.

2 In the Import Image as Logo dialog , navigate to the Lesson09 folder. Within that folder, select the file title_waterpark.psd, and then click Open to import the image into your title.

3 The image of three circles appears stacked in front of the text box in your title. Use the Selection tool to drag the placed image towards the bottom of the title screen, making sure that the bottom of the image stays above the title-safe area.

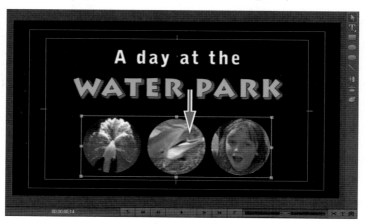

▶ **Tip:** If you have overlapping frames, you can change the stacking order by right-clicking on a selected frame, and then using one of the Arrange commands from the context menu. To align multiple frames, select the frames you wish to align, and then right-click and choose any of the Align Objects commands from the context menu.

4 If you're unhappy with the size of the image you've inserted, drag any anchor point to resize the placed image. Hold down the Shift key while dragging to maintain the height and width proportions of the image.

5 Right-click the image and choose Position > Horizontal Center from the context menu.

6 Choose File > Save to save your work.

Creating Fade In and Fade Out effects

Any transition that you use on video clips can also be added to title clips. In this exercise, you will add a Fade In and Fade Out effect to the title clip.

1 In the Timeline view of the My Project panel, click Title 01, which should be on the Video 2 track.

2 On the upper left of the My Project panel, click the Properties button (▦).

3 In Properties view, click the triangle next to Opacity to see the Opacity controls.

4 Under Opacity in Properties view, click the Fade In button once. The title image seems to disappear from the Monitor panel. Drag the current-time indicator in the Timeline to the right to see the image slowly fade in. After 1 second (30 frames for NTSC) the clip's opacity is at 100% and fully visible again. In the Timeline, you can see the keyframes that Adobe Premiere Elements added to effectuate the fade-in transition.

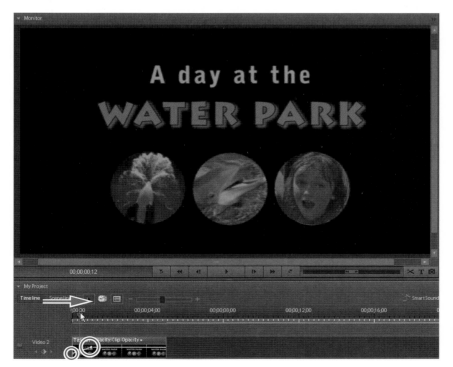

Animate a still title

You can easily apply a preset animation to any still title that contains only a single line of text. Text animation presets quickly and easily animate the characters in your title so that they fade or pop characters into view, or fly in from the top or bottom of the screen. For example, using the Fade In Characters preset instantly makes each separate character in your title fade into view until the title is complete.

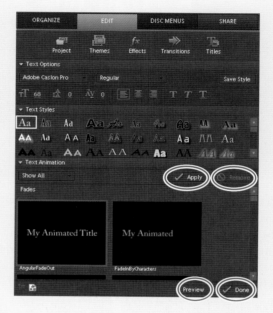

To preview an animation, position the pointer on the animation thumbnail in the Text Animation section of the Tasks panel. (To see the Text Animation section, you must select a title so that the Tasks panel is in title-editing mode.)

1   To begin, do *one of the following*:

  • Create a new still title.

  • In the Timeline, double-click the title clip.

  • In the Sceneline, select the superimposed clip. In the Monitor panel, click the clip, and then double-click the title text.

  The Tasks panel changes to Title Editor view, displaying the text options.

2   Under Text Animation, select an animation preset. Click the Preview button in the lower-right corner of the Tasks panel to see how the animation looks on your title text.

3   To apply the animation to the title, *do one of the following*:

  • Click the Apply button in the upper-right corner of the Text Animation section in the Tasks panel.

  • Drag the animation preset to the Monitor panel and drop it on top of the title text.

4   Click Done at the bottom of the Tasks panel to close out of Title Editor view.

Note: To remove an animation from a title, select the title text and click the Remove button in the upper-right corner of the Text Animation section in the Tasks panel.

—*From Adobe Premiere Elements Help*

5 Back in Properties view, click the Fade Out button once to add a Fade Out effect for the clip.

6 Review your work by playing the movie from the beginning, and then choose File > Save to save your project.

Superimposing a title over video clips

Inserting titles over a black background video works well for opening titles, but Adobe Premiere Elements lets you superimpose titles directly over video clips to give them a look that's more suitable for titles that appear in the middle of a video. Though you can add titles in both the Timeline and Sceneline, in this exercise, you'll work in the former, adding titles at the locations where you inserted markers back in Lesson 5.

1 With Timeline selected in the My Project panel, press the Home key on your keyboard to move to the start of the movie.

2 Right-click the time ruler in the first few seconds of the project and choose Go to Timeline Marker > Next. Adobe Premiere Elements will jump to the first timeline marker, which is located at 00;00;24;01.

3 Double-click the marker which is located behind the current-time indicator. You'll see the comment "Add Meet the Dolphins here." That's the title you'll add at this location. Click OK to close the Properties dialog.

4 Choose Title > New Title > Default Still. With the Text tool, select the default text and type *Meet the Dolphins*.

5   Use the Selection tool to position the title in the lower-left corner of the title-safe area.

To improve the readability of the text, you can try to change the text color or apply a style with a drop shadow. Or, you can add a colored rectangle behind the text, as explained in the following steps.

6   Select the Rectangle tool (■) from the tools on the right side of the Monitor panel. Drag to create a rectangle over the text you just created. Don't worry about obscuring the text; in a moment, you'll position the rectangle behind the text.

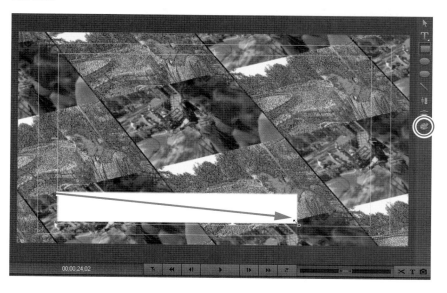

7 Click the Color Properties button (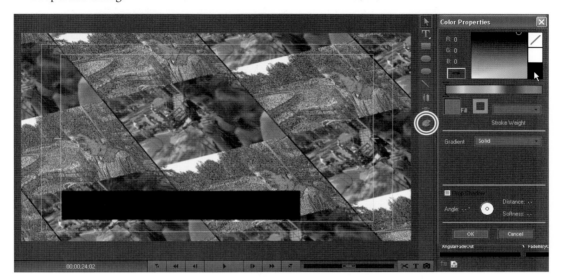) at the bottom of the tool buttons in the Monitor panel to open the Color Properties dialog. Set the color to black by clicking the large black rectangle near the upper-right corner of the dialog. Click OK to to apply the color to the rectangle you created and close the Color Properties dialog.

8 Let's soften the black color by making the background slightly transparent. Right-click the rectangle, and choose Transform > Opacity. Adobe Premiere Elements opens the Opacity panel. Type *60.00* into the Opacity % field and click OK to close the panel.

9 Now you'll shift the new rectangle behind the text. Right-click the rectangle and choose Arrange > Send to Back to place your rectangle behind your white type. The white text is now clearly visible over the rectangle. If necessary, you can edit the size of the rectangle by clicking it to make it active and then dragging any edge to a new location.

When you add multiple elements such as text, squares, or circles to a title, you create a stacking order. The most recent items added (in this case, the rectangle) are placed at the top of the stacking order. You can control the stacking order—as you did here—using the Arrange commands from the Context menu or the Title menu.

To quickly add matching titles at the same position in other clips, you can use the Copy and Paste commands.

10 Using the Selection tool, click to select the rectangle, and then shift-click to also select the text frame. Choose Edit > Copy.

11 Right-click the time ruler and choose Go to Timeline Marker > Next. Adobe Premiere Elements will jump to the second timeline marker located at about 00;00;56;07.

12 Choose Title > New Title > Default Still to switch to title-editing mode. Use the Selection tool to select the default text which was added, and then choose Edit > Clear.

13 Choose Edit > Paste to add the black rectangle with the words "Meet the Dolphins" at the same position as in the original clip. Using the Type tool, select the words "Meet the Dolphins" and replace them by typing *Lunch Time*.

14 Use the Selection tool to select the black rectangle, and adjust its width to the new text length by dragging the right-center anchor point to the left.

15 Use the same procedure to add the title *Afternoon Fun* at the third marker, which should be at about 00;01;25;24, and then adjust the size of the rectangle.

16 Following the procedure discussed earlier in the "Creating Fade In and Fade Out effects" section of this lesson, fade each title in and out.

17 Review your movie, and then save your project.

Creating a rolling credit

The titles you have created to this point have been static, but Adobe Premiere Elements can create animated titles as well. There are two types of animated titles: rolls and crawls. A rolling credit is defined as text that moves vertically up the screen, like the end credits of a movie. A crawl is defined as text that moves horizontally across the screen, like a news ticker. In this exercise you will create a rolling credit at the end of the project.

1 Press Page Down on your keyboard repeatedly until the current-time indicator moves to the end of the last clip on the Video 2 track, which should be 06_imagepan.jpg.

2 Choose Title > New Title > Default Roll. Adobe Premiere Elements switches to title-editing mode and inserts a new Rolling title.

3 Using the Type tool, select the text Main Title at the top of the Monitor panel, and then type *The End*.

4 Right-click the title text box, and choose Position > Horizontal Center.

5 Click the other text box, and press Ctrl+A on your keyboard to select all text. Then type *Starring:* and press Enter to move to the next line. On the next line, type *Gina*, press Enter, type *Peter*, press Enter, type *Mommy*, press Enter, type *Daddy*, and press Enter once more.

6 Press Enter to move to the next line, then type *Filmed by:*. Press Enter, type *Daddy*, press Enter twice, type *Produced by:*, press Enter, and type *Mommy*.

7 To center the text, click the Center Text button ( ) under Text Options in Properties view.

8 Right-click the text box and choose Position > Horizontal Center from the context menu.

<span></span>**9** Choose Title > Roll/Crawl Options.

Note: The Roll/ Crawls Options command is also accessible from the Monitor panel menu.

10 In the Roll/Crawl Options dialog, make sure Roll is selected for Title type, and that both Start Off Screen and End Off Screen options are also selected. Finally, make sure that Preroll, Ease-In, Ease-Out, and Postroll values are all set to 0. Click OK to close the dialog.

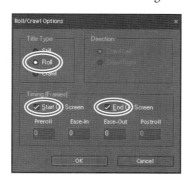

When you play the clip, the text box with the credits will move—in the 5-second default length of the title—from bottom to top across the monitor.

11 Place your current-time indicator just before the beginning of the rolling credits. Press the spacebar to play the rolling credits clip, and then save your project.

Changing the speed of a rolling title

When Adobe Premiere Elements creates a rolling title, it spreads the text evenly over the duration of the title. The only way to change the speed of a rolling title is to increase or decrease the length of the title clip. The default duration for titles is 5 seconds. If you want to have the text move more slowly across the screen, you need to increase the clip length.

1 In the Timeline, place your pointer over the end of the Title 06 rolling title clip. When the pointer changes to a red bracket pointing to the left (![icon]), drag the clip to the right. Note that as you drag there is a small yellow context menu that shows you how much time you are adding to the clip. Add 5 seconds to the length of the clip, and then release the pointer.

2 Place your current-time indicator just before the beginning of the rolling credits. Press the spacebar to play the rolling credits clip. Notice how your titles are now moving more slowly on the monitor.

3 Save your project as *Lesson09_End.prel*.

● **Note:** If your titles do not display smoothly, they may need to be rendered. Pressing the Enter key on your keyboard will render all effects, transitions, and titles in a project.

Using title templates

Creating your own titles, as you have done in the exercises in this lesson, will give you the most flexibility and options when it comes to customized titles. However, this involves performing a considerable number of steps from start to finish. To help you get started designing your titles, Adobe Premiere Elements ships with numerous templates for different types of projects. All you need to do is customize the text, replace an image, or do both to create a great-looking title.

1   Select Titles () in the Edit tab of the Tasks panel. Choose a category of title templates from the menu on the left, and then choose a template name from the menu on the right. If necessary, scroll down to see all available templates within the chosen theme, such as rolling titles and alternative title graphics.

2   To superimpose a title template over a video clip, select the clip in the Sceneline, and then drag the template from Titles view onto the Monitor panel. If you're working in the Timeline, drag it to a track above the target video clip.

3   Use the Type tool to select the default text and replace it with your own text. Use the Selection tool to reposition or resize text and image frames. Add or delete text and image frames as necessary.

Exploring on your own

Experiment with the different templates Adobe Premiere Elements provides. Keep in mind that elements like the color of text and the position of graphics can be modified. Here are a few steps to follow as you discover what's available:

1   Replace the custom title you created with a title created from a template.

2   Explore the drawing tools available to you when in title-editing mode.

3   Create an animated title, choosing from the available options under Text Animation in Properties view.

4   Place different transitions between your title clips and your video clips to view the different effects you can achieve.

Congratulations, you have completed the lesson. You've learned how to create a simple still title with text and graphics. You changed the style, size, alignment, and color of text. You've positioned and aligned text and graphic frames in the Monitor panel, and you've used one of the Arrange commands to change the stacking order of overlapping frames. You added black video to your project and applied Fade In and Fade Out effects to your title clip. You know now how to create rolling credits and how to use and customize title templates. It's time for a well-earned break. But before you stop, review the questions and answers on the next page.

Review questions

1 How do you create a new title?

2 How do you exit title-editing mode, and how can you re-enter it to make adjustments to a title clip?

3 How do you change the color of title text?

4 How do you add a Fade In or Fade Out effect to a superimposed title clip?

5 What is a rolling credit, and how do you speed it up or slow it down?

Review answers

1 With a video clip selected in the My Project panel, choose Title > New Title > Default Still. A title clip will be created and superimposed over the selected video clip.

2 To exit title-editing mode, click Done in the lower-right corner of Properties view, or click to select any clip in the My Project panel. To re-enter title-editing mode, click to select the superimposed title text image in the Monitor panel, and then double-click it.

3 Switch to title-editing mode in the Monitor panel. Select the text using the Type tool. Then click the Color Properties button, and pick a new color in the Color Properties dialog.

4 In the Monitor panel, right-click the scene, and then select the title clip from the context menu. Under Opacity in Properties, click the Fade In or Fade Out button.

5 A rolling credit is text that scrolls vertically across your screen. The only way to make a rolling credit change speed is by selecting the clip in the Timeline of the My Project panel, and then extending the length of the clip to slow it down, or shorten the length of the clip to speed it up.

10 WORKING WITH MOVIE THEMES

Over the last six chapters, you learned how to produce a completely customized movie from your source clips. In this chapter, you'll learn how to apply a Movie theme to your source clips to produce an engaging, stylized movie in a matter of moments.

Movie themes are collections of professionally created theme-specific titles, effects, transitions, and background music. Before applying a theme, Adobe Premiere Elements analyzes your video footage for content, and then edits your content to best fit the tone of the theme.

As with InstantMovies, you can apply an entire theme or just parts of it to perfectly fit your creative concept. In this lesson, you'll learn how to do the following:

- Select a Movie theme
- Choose some Movie theme properties and apply them to your clip
- Edit your movie after applying a Movie theme

 This lesson will take approximately 30 minutes.

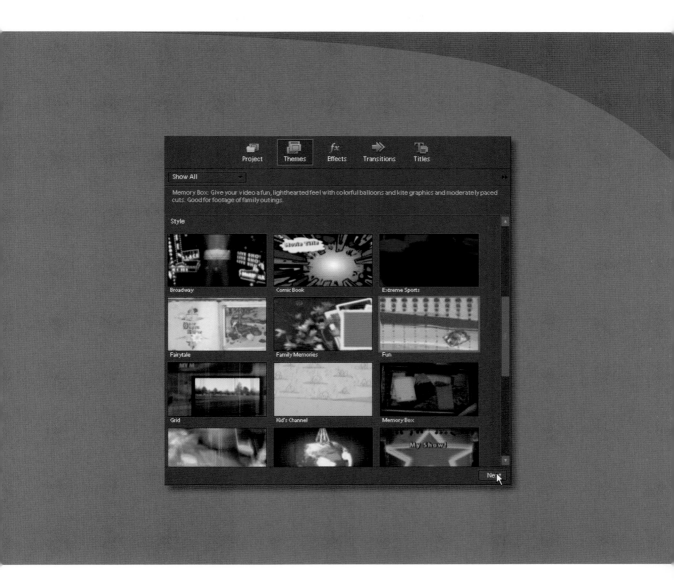

Choosing a movie theme.

Getting started

To begin, launch Adobe Premiere Elements, open the Lesson10 project, and review a final version of the movie you'll be creating.

1   Before you begin, make sure that you have correctly copied the Lesson10 folder from the DVD in the back of this book onto your computer's hard disk. See "Copying the Classroom in a Book files" in the Getting Started section at the beginning of this book.

2   Launch Adobe Premiere Elements.

3   In the Welcome screen, click the Open Project button. If necessary, click Open in the pop-up menu. The Open Project dialog opens.

4   In the Open Project dialog, navigate to the Lesson10 folder you copied to your hard disk. Within that folder, select the file Lesson10_Start.prel, and then click Open. If a dialog appears asking for the location of rendered files, click the Skip Previews button.

    Your project file opens with the Monitor, Tasks, and My Project panels open.

5   Choose Window > Restore Workspace to ensure that you start the lesson with the default panel layout.

Viewing the completed movie before you start

To see what you'll be creating in this lesson, take a look at the completed movie.

1   In the Edit workspace of the Tasks panel, click the Project button. In Project view, locate the file Lesson10_Movie.wmv, and then double-click it to open the video into the Preview window.

2   In the Preview window, click the Play button (![Play button]) to watch the video about a visit to a water park, which you'll be building in this lesson.

3   When finished, close the Preview window by clicking the Close button (![Close button]) in the upper-right corner of the window.

About Movie themes

You first had a glimpse of Movie themes back in Lesson 4, when you learned how to create an InstantMovie from the Organizer. As you recall, an InstantMovie is a Movie theme applied to clips in the Organizer. In this chapter, you'll learn how to apply a Movie theme to clips in the Timeline.

When should you use each approach? When you create an InstantMovie, you can choose your content via tagging and apply Smart Tagging to your source clips, which is fast and effective when attempting to identify the best 3 or 4 minutes of video from a mass of source clips.

Note that creating an InstantMovie in the Organizer differs from working in the Timeline in one fundamental way: you can't edit source clips before applying the InstantMovie. This makes applying Movie themes in the Timeline a better option if there's source footage that you don't want included in the final movie.

Movie themes enable you to quickly create videos with a specific look and feel. The Wedding Doves theme, for example, adds an elegant, animated introduction, an overlay of flying white doves, wedding background music, and closing credits for a wedding video. In contrast, the Comic Book theme provides more funky effects and fonts along with Picture-in-Picture overlays that might be more appropriate for a kids' party video.

You can apply all the properties in a theme, choose to add only a subset, or even just modify some parts. Likewise, you can add a theme to an entire movie or to only a single clip.

You access Movie themes via the Themes button (![Themes]) in the Edit tab of the Tasks panel. The different themes use animated thumbnails that give you a good idea of the overall feel of the theme.

● **Note:** When you apply a theme, all of the effects and transitions that you've previously applied to a project are deleted and replaced by the theme. Before applying a theme, choose File > Save to save your project. If you apply a theme, and then decide you don't like it, choose Edit > Undo to return to your original version.

Applying a Movie theme

In the exercises that follow, you'll apply a Movie theme to the water park clips that you've edited throughout the book. You'll apply the theme to clips in the My Project panel, using either the Timeline or Sceneline, so you should edit out any undesired scenes before applying a theme.

However, don't spend a lot of time ordering the clips on the Timeline; if you choose, Adobe Premiere Elements will either arrange the clips to best fit the Movie theme, or display them in chronological order. In addition, don't correct brightness, contrast, or stabilization issues before applying a theme, because in order for Adobe Premiere Elements to apply the theme-specific effects, it will have to remove all the effects you've previously applied. Don't worry; as with InstantMovies, you can edit your movie after applying the Movie theme, and correct any color, brightness, or stabilization issues then.

Once you've got all desired clips in the Timeline, here's the procedure for applying a Movie theme.

1   Click the Themes button ( ) in the Edit tab of the Tasks panel.

2   Click the Fun Style to select it, and then click Next.

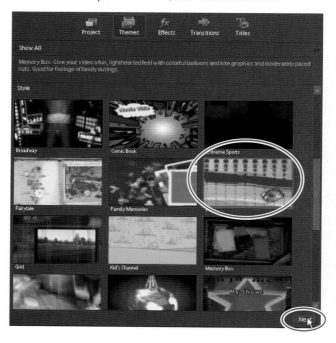

3 Customize the Theme as described here. *Do the following*:

- Select the Auto Edit checkbox to have Adobe Premiere Elements analyze your clips, and edit them to fit the selected theme. If you don't select Auto Edit, Adobe Premiere Elements uses the clips as is and doesn't edit them.

- In the Music box, check the My Music radio button, then click the Browse button to choose the target song. Navigate to the Lesson10 folder and choose SmartSound – Island Party – Pool side.wav.

- Leave the Music/Sound FX slider at the default setting, which evenly mixes audio captured with the video clips and background music.

● **Note:** The Smart Tagging checkbox is only active when applying an InstantMovie in the Organizer panel.

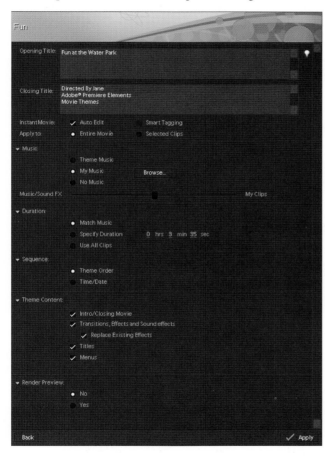

- In the Duration box, choose Match Music, which produces a movie that matches the duration of the selected music. Note that alternatively, you can specify a duration, or choose Use All Clips, which uses all clips at their original duration with no background music.

- In the Sequence box, choose Theme Order, which allows Adobe Premiere Elements to use clips as they best match the theme. Your other option, Time/Date, uses the clips in the order that they were shot.

- In the Theme Content box, leave all checkboxes selected.

- In the Render Preview box, leave No selected.

4 After selecting your options, click Apply to create the InstantMovie. Adobe Premiere Elements opens a warning dialog letting you know that user-applied effects will be replaced or removed. Click OK to apply the theme.

5 Adobe Premiere Elements creates the InstantMovie and inserts it into the My Project panel.

6 Use the playback controls in the Monitor panel to preview the InstantMovie.

7 Adobe Premiere Elements adds the InstantMovie to the My Project panel in consolidated form. To break apart the InstantMovie into its components to edit them, click to select the new InstantMovie, right-click, and choose Break Apart InstantMovie.

8 Choose File > Save As, name the file *Lesson10_End* in the Save As dialog, and then save it in your Lesson 10 folder.

Exploring on your own

Experiment with the different Movie themes provided with your copy of Adobe Premiere Elements. Keep in mind that you can apply an entire theme or pick and choose parts of it.

Apply a Movie theme to selected clips in the My Project panel to get familiar with this option.

Well done, you have completed this lesson. You've learned how to apply a Movie theme and how to customize its properties.

Review questions

1 What is a Movie theme?

2 How is a Movie theme different from an InstantMovie?

3 When are InstantMovies a better option than applying Movie themes to clips in the Timeline?

4 How do you edit a movie after applying a Movie theme?

Review answers

1 Movie themes are templates that enable you to quickly turn your clips into a more professional-looking movie. You can choose from event-based themes like Birthday or more style-based themes like Silent Film. A Movie theme includes coordinated transitions, effects, and music, as well as layouts for titles and credits. You can apply an entire theme or choose to select only parts of it.

2 InstantMovies are Movie themes applied to clips in the Organizer.

3 InstantMovies are a better option when you'd like to use tagging and Smart Tagging to help choose videos included in the movie. Applying Movie themes in the My Project panel is preferred when you have to edit content before applying the Movie theme.

4 Right-click the finished movie and choose Break Apart InstantMovie.

11

CREATING MENUS

In this lesson you'll create a menu for a movie to be recorded on a DVD or Blu-ray Disc. You can follow along with most of this lesson even if your system does not have a DVD or Blu-ray Disc burner, although it will be helpful if it does. You will learn how to add menu markers that allow your viewers direct access to scenes in your movies, and how to create and customize disc menus. You will also learn how to preview a menu and then burn a DVD or Blu-ray Disc for playback on a standard DVD or Blu-ray Disc player. Specifically, you'll learn how to do the following:

- Add menu markers to your movie
- Create an auto-play disc
- Use Templates to create disc menus
- Customize the look of the menus
- Preview a disc menu
- Record a DVD or Blu-ray Disc

 This lesson will take approximately 2.5 hours.

Creating a DVD with menus.

Getting started

To begin, you'll launch Adobe Premiere Elements, open the Lesson11 project, and review a final version of that project.

1 Before you begin, make sure that you have correctly copied the Lesson11 folder from the DVD in the back of this book onto your computer's hard disk. See "Copying the Classroom in a Book files" in the Getting Started section at the beginning of this book.

2 Launch Adobe Premiere Elements.

3 In the Welcome screen, click the Open Project button and then click Open in the pop-up menu. In the Open Project dialog, navigate to the Lesson11 folder, select the file Lesson11_End.prel, and then click Open. If a dialog appears asking for the location of rendered files, click the Skip All Previews button.

A finished version of the project file you will create in this lesson opens with the Monitor, Tasks, and My Project panels open. You may review it now or at any point during the lesson to get a sense of what your project should look like.

4 Select Disc Menus in the Tasks panel to switch to the Disc Menus workspace. In the Disc Layout panel, click Preview to open the Preview Disc window.

The Preview Disc window allows you to view and test your menus as they will appear when played on a DVD or Blu-ray player.

5 In the Preview Disc window, click the Scenes button in the main menu to switch to the Scene Selection menu. Click the Dolphins button to begin playing this section.

6   Press the spacebar on your keyboard to stop the playback, and then close the Preview Disc window by clicking the Close button (⊠) in the upper-right corner of the window.

7   After reviewing the finished file, choose File > Close. In the dialog, click No so that you do not save any changes made to the project. Then, click the Open Project button, click Open, select the file Lesson11_Start.prel, and click Open. If a dialog appears asking for the location of rendered files, click the Skip Previews button.

8   Choose Window > Restore Workspace to ensure that you start the lesson with the default panel layout.

Understanding DVDs and Blu-ray Discs

DVD is an optical disc storage medium similar to a compact disc but capable of storing much more data. For example, a CD stores about 700 megabytes (MB) of data. A DVD stores up to 4.7 gigabytes (GB) of data on a single layer, or up to 8.4 GB on a dual layer disc. DVD is actually a generic term that encompasses a few different formats. The format you will be working with in Adobe Premiere Elements is commonly referred to as DVD-Video. In terms of disc content and playability, this is the same type of DVD that you can purchase or rent and play on a DVD player connected to your TV set or on a computer fitted with the appropriate drive.

A Blu-ray Disc—often abbreviated as BD—is an optical disc format that can store 25 GB on a single-layer disc or 50 GB on a dual-layer disc. It gets its name from the blue-violet laser a Blu-ray player uses to read it (as opposed to the red laser used by CD and DVD players and drives).

To make a DVD or Blu-ray Disc in Adobe Premiere Elements, you must have a compatible DVD or Blu-ray Disc burner. It is important to note that although your system may have a DVD or Blu-ray Disc player it may not be a recordable drive, also known as a DVD or Blu-ray Disc writer or burner. A computer drive that's described as "DVD-ROM" or "BD-ROM" will only play DVDs or Blu-ray Discs, not record them. (But a "BD-ROM/DVD-R/CD-R drive" will play Blu-ray Discs, play and record DVDs, and play and record CDs.) Check the system specifications of your computer to see which drive (if any) you have. Drives capable of recording DVDs and Blu-ray Discs are also available as external hardware. Often such external recordable drives are connected through your system's IEEE 1394 port, although some drives connect through the USB port.

Note that the process of authoring your projects, or creating menus and menu markers, is identical for Blu-ray Discs and DVDs. You'll designate which type of disc to record just before you burn the disc itself in the final exercise in this lesson.

Physical media

The type of disc onto which you will record your video is important. There are two basic formats you should be aware of: Recordable (DVD-R and DVD+R for DVDs, BD-R for Blu-ray Discs) and Rewritable (DVD-RW and DVD+RW for DVDs, BD-RE for Blu-ray Discs). Recordable discs are single-use discs; once you record data onto a recordable disc you cannot erase the data. Rewritable discs can be used multiple times, much like the floppy disks of old.

There are also dual-layer DVD-Recordable discs (DVD-R DL and DVD+R DL) that offer 8.5 GB of storage space instead of the 4.7 GB of standard DVD-R, DVD+R, DVD-RW, and DVD+RW discs. Dual-layer BD-R discs, featuring 50 GB of storage space, will come to market soon, but you don't need to be concerned with them at this point.

So which format should you choose? Compatibility is one of the major issues with these formats. On the DVD side, there are many older DVD players that may not recognize some rewritable discs created on a newer DVD burner, for example. Compatibility is also more of a concern with dual-layer media than with single-layer discs. Another issue is that, as of this writing, the media for recordable discs is less expensive than the media for rewritable discs. However, if you make a mistake with a recordable disc, you must use another disc, whereas with a rewritable disc you can erase the content and use the disc again. For this reason, we suggest using rewritable discs for making your test discs, and then using recordable discs for final or extra copies.

On the Blu-ray Disc side, the technology is still fairly new and playback compatibility is at least a minor issue with all media. But because the BD-R and BD-RE formats were developed at the same time, BD-RE discs are just as likely to play in a given player as their BD-R counterparts. Generally, the cost of BD-R and BD-RE media is about the same, but because it is so high for both ($10–$15 per disc), you're better off using BD-RE discs for your projects so you can re-record if you make a mistake.

Manually adding scene markers

When watching a DVD or Blu-ray Disc movie, you normally have the option to jump to the beginning of the next chapter by clicking a button on the remote control. To specify the start of chapters or sections in your project, you must add scene markers.

1   Scroll through the entire movie in the Timeline of the My Project panel.

This project consists of three main sections, labeled Meet the Dolphins, Lunch Time, and Afternoon Fun. Each section has a title superimposed for the first 5 seconds, and a marker that you inserted back in Chapter 5. You will place scene markers at the beginning of each section so your viewers can access these sections more easily during playback. You'll start by adding the marker for the Meet the Dolphins section.

2   Click the Home key on your keyboard to move the current-time indicator to the start of the movie.

3   Right-click the time ruler within the first few seconds of the project and choose Go to Timeline Marker > Next. Adobe Premiere Elements will jump to the first timeline marker located at 00;00;24;01.

4   Click the Add Menu Marker button (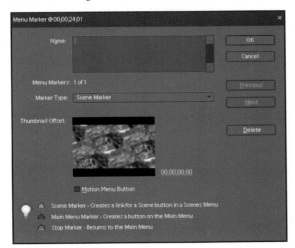) located near the upper-right corner of the My Project panel to open the Menu Marker dialog. You will work more with this dialog later in this lesson; for now, just click OK to close the dialog.

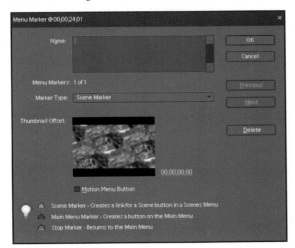

5   Notice the green scene marker icon added just below the previous marker on the time ruler.

● **Note:** This project is only about 2 minutes long due to necessary limitations on the file size. Most projects would likely be longer, but the basic principles remain the same.

● **Note:** You may have to move the current-time indicator to better see the green scene marker beneath.

6   In the My Project panel, click the Sceneline button to switch to Sceneline. If necessary, scroll to the right to view the SprayMe.avi clip. Notice the scene marker icon added to the clip in the Sceneline.

7   Click the Timeline button in the My Project panel to return to the Timeline.

8   Right-click the time ruler and choose Go to Timeline Marker > Next. Adobe Premiere Elements will jump to the second timeline marker located at about 00;00;56;07.

9   Again click the Add Menu Marker button () in the My Project panel to add a second scene marker at the position of the current-time indicator. In the Menu Marker dialog, click OK to create the scene marker and to close the dialog.

10 Right-click the time ruler and choose Go to Timeline Marker > Next. Adobe Premiere Elements will jump to the third timeline marker located at about 00;01;26;05. Add another scene marker. You should now have three markers in your project, one for each section of this short movie.

Creating an auto-play disc

Most professional DVDs or Blu-ray Discs have menus to help viewers navigate through the disc content. You will work with menus shortly, but there is a quick and easy way to produce a disc without menus: creating an auto-play disc. An auto-play disc is similar to videotape; when you place the disc into a player it will begin playing automatically. There is no navigation, although viewers can jump from scene to scene—defined by the markers you just added—using a remote control.

Auto-play discs are convenient for shorter projects that don't require a menu, or as a mechanism to share unfinished projects for review. For most longer or finished projects, you'll probably prefer to create a menu.

Note: The Auto-Play button should be dimmed and no template selected. Click the Auto-Play button if your Disc Layout panel looks different from the one shown here.

1   Select Disc Menus in the Tasks panel to switch to the Disc Menus workspace. The Disc Layout panel replaces the Monitor panel, and Templates view opens in the Disc Menus tab of the Tasks panel. If you want to see the panel names, choose Window > Show Docking Headers.

2   In the Disc Layout panel, click the Preview button to open the Preview Disc window. The Preview Disc window allows you to view and test your disc as it will appear when viewed on a DVD or Blu-ray Disc player.

3   In the Preview Disc window, click the Play button ( ) to begin playing your project. Once the first video clip begins playing, press the Next Scene button ( ) and the video jumps to the next scene. The scenes are defined by the scene markers you added to your project. When viewing this disc on a TV set, viewers can use a remote control to advance through the scenes.

4   Click the Close button ( ) in the upper-right corner of the Preview Disc window to close it.

5   Choose File > Save As and save this project file into your Lesson11 folder as *Lesson11_Work.prel*.

Automatically generating scene markers

Manually placing markers in the Timeline gives you ultimate control over the placement of your markers. For longer videos however, you may not wish to place all the markers by hand. To make the process of placing markers easier, Adobe Premiere Elements can create markers automatically based on several configurable parameters.

1 Choose File > Save As and save this project file into your Lesson11 folder as *Lesson11_Markers.prel.* You will return to the original project file after you finish exploring the automatic generation of scene markers.

2 In the Disc Layout panel, choose Auto-Generate Menu Markers from the panel menu. Or, right-click in the preview area of the Disc Layout panel, and then choose Auto-Generate Menu Markers from the context menu.

3 The Automatically Set Menu Scene Markers dialog appears. Keep the default option selected to set a scene marker At Each Scene, or, to be more specific, at the beginning of every clip on the Video 1 track. The Clear Existing Menu Markers checkbox should remain deselected unless you wish to erase existing markers. Click OK to close the dialog. Adobe Premiere Elements will insert scene markers at the beginning of every clip.

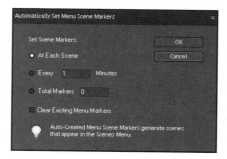

4 If you're not in the Timeline already, switch to the Timeline in the My Project panel to review the position of all the markers in your project.

5 Click the Preview button in the Disc Layout panel.

6 In the Preview Disc window, click the Play button (▶) to begin playing your project. Once the first video clip begins playing, click the Next Scene button (▶▶▏) repeatedly and notice how the video jumps from scene to scene.

7 Click the Close button (✖) in the upper-right corner of the Preview Disc window to close it.

8 Right-click in the preview area of the Disc Layout panel, and then choose Auto-Generate Menu Markers to again open the Automatically Set Menu Scene Markers dialog. Choose the Total Markers option and type *4* into the number field. Select the Clear Existing Menu Markers checkbox, and then click OK.

● **Note:** You can reposition markers in the Timeline by clicking and dragging them to the left or right.

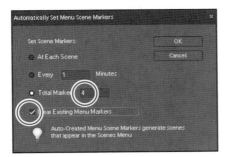

There are now four markers evenly spread out across the Timeline.

Using the Total Markers option may be preferable to creating a marker for every clip in order to cut down on the number of scenes in your movie. As you will see in the next exercise, when creating a disc with menus, Adobe Premiere Elements will automatically create buttons and menus based on the markers in your project. Too many markers might result in too many navigation buttons and screens for your movie.

9 Choose File > Save. Then choose File > Open Recent Project > Lesson11_Work.prel to return to the project file from the previous exercise.

Creating a disc with menus

The auto-play disc you created in the last exercise is the quickest way to go from an Adobe Premiere Elements project to an optical disc you can watch in your living room. However, auto-play discs lack the ability to jump directly to different scenes, as well as other navigational features that most users expect when watching a DVD or Blu-ray Disc. You can quickly create such navigation menus in Adobe Premiere Elements using a variety of templates designed for this purpose.

1 If you are not currently in the Disc Menus workspace, select Disc Menus in the Tasks panel to switch to it now.

2 Adobe Premiere Elements ships with many distinctive menu templates—pre-designed and customizable menus that come in a variety of themes and styles. Select General from the category menu, and then select the template called Fun from the menu next to it.

● **Note:** To replace the selected template, simply click another to select it, and then click Apply to apply it to the project, or simply drop it onto the Disc Layout panel. To delete all menus, right-click within the Disc Layout window and choose Change to Auto-Play.

3 To apply the Fun template to your project, click to select the template in Templates view, and then click the Apply button (✔ Apply) in the lower-right corner of Templates view. Or, drop the template from Templates view onto the Disc Layout panel.

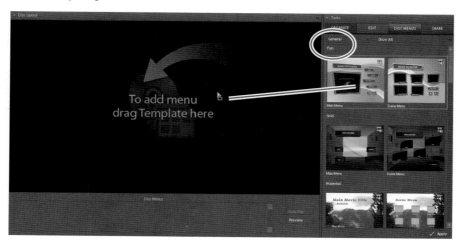

Each template contains a main menu and a scenes menu. The main menu is the first screen that the viewer sees when the disc is played. The Scenes menu is a secondary panel accessed when the viewer clicks the Scene Selection button in the main menu.

4   Under Disc Menus at the bottom of the Disc Layout panel, click to select Main Menu 1.

There are two buttons currently visible in this menu: Play and Scenes. Additionally, there is a generic text button called Movie Title Here. You will now change the text of this generic button to something more appropriate for your project.

5   In the preview area of the Disc Layout panel, click the Movie Title Here text once. A thin, white rectangle appears around the button indicating that it is selected. Now double-click the Movie Title Here text to open the Change Text dialog. If the text under Change Text is not already highlighted, select it now, and then type *At the Water Park*. Click the OK button to close the Change Text dialog and to commit the change.

6   Click the Preview button to preview the main menu. Place your pointer over the Play and Scenes buttons, but do not click them yet. Notice the orange circles that appear in the text box when the pointer passes over them. This rollover effect is part of the menu template, and shows the viewer which button they're selecting. Click the Play button and the movie begins to play.

The preview feature shows how your DVD will look after recording the project to disc. Note, however, that the quality of the previewed video may not be indicative of the final video. As mentioned in previous chapters, because of the differences between computer monitors and TV sets, you may see noticeable horizontal lines as the video is playing on the computer monitor. These lines are referred to as interlacing, and will not be visible in the final movie when played on a TV.

7 As the movie is playing, click the Main Menu button () at the bottom of the Preview Disc window. Clicking this button at any point during playback returns you to the main menu, so you don't have to watch the whole movie if you're just testing your menus.

8 Click the Close button (✱) in the upper-right corner of the Preview Disc window to close it.

9 Choose File > Save to save your project file.

Modifying Scene Marker buttons

One of the benefits of DVDs or Blu-ray Discs is the ability to jump quickly to specific scenes in the movie. For each scene marker you add in the Timeline, Adobe Premiere Elements automatically generates a Scene Marker button on the Scenes menu. If the template has image thumbnails on the Scenes menu, as the menu you're working with does, Adobe Premiere Elements automatically assigns an image thumbnail to it. You can customize the appearance of a Scene Marker button by providing a name for the label and changing the image thumbnail used to identify the scene. Note that if you have more scene markers than scenes on a Scene menu, Adobe Premiere Elements creates additional Scenes menu pages and navigational buttons to jump back and forth between the pages.

Changing button labels and image thumbnails

1 Click the Scenes Menu 1 thumbnail under Disc Menus in the Disc Layout panel to view the Scenes menu.

Adobe Premiere Elements has generated the three Scene Marker buttons and their image thumbnails based on the scene markers you added in the first exercise. By default, Adobe Premiere Elements named the Scene Marker buttons Scene One, Scene Two, and Scene Three. You'll customize these for your content shortly.

In addition, by default, the thumbnail in the Scene Marker button is the first frame of the clip the button links to. This doesn't work well in this case because the clips are obscured either by a transition or the animated pastel sketch effect, so viewers can't easily discern the content of the scene. You'll change these thumbnails to more appropriate frames.

2   Press Home on your keyboard to shift the current-time indicator to the start of the movie. Then, right-click the time ruler within the first few seconds of the project and choose Go to Menu Marker > Next. The current-time indicator jumps to the first menu marker.

● **Note:** When using menu templates, one- or two-word titles fit best into the text boxes.

3   Double-click the first marker to open the Menu Marker dialog for the first marker. In the Name field, type *Dolphins*.

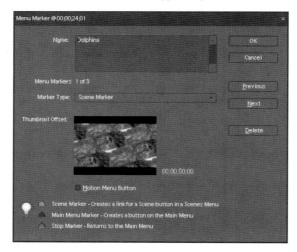

4   In the Thumbnail Offset section, notice that the time counter is set to 00;00;00;00. Place your pointer over the time counter, and then drag to the right. Navigate to about 00;00;27;01, and then release the pointer to freeze the movie at that location. Or, click the time counter and enter the timecode directly. Click OK, and Adobe Premiere Elements updates the button name and image thumbnail in the Scenes menu.

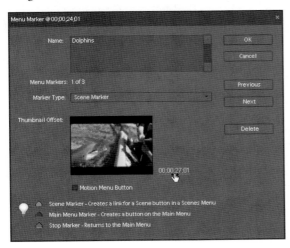

You will now change the names of the remaining two buttons and their respective image thumbnails.

5   Right-click the time ruler and choose Go to Menu Marker > Next. The current-time indicator jumps to the second menu marker.

6   Double-click the second marker to open the Menu Marker dialog. In the Name field, type *Lunch Time*. Place your pointer over the time counter, click and drag to the right to about 00;00;07;02, and then release the pointer to freeze the movie at that location. Click OK, and Adobe Premiere Elements updates the button name and image thumbnail in the Scenes menu.

7   Repeat steps 5 and 6, moving to the third marker, typing *Afternoon Fun* into the name field, and dragging the time counter to about 00;00;11;04. Click OK, and Adobe Premiere Elements updates the button name and image thumbnail in the Scenes menu.

8   When finished, click the Preview button to open the Preview Disc window. Click the Scenes button to navigate to the Scenes menu. Notice that Adobe Premiere Elements has updated button names and thumbnails.

9 At the bottom of the Preview Disc window you can see a group of navigation buttons, which simulate the controls on a DVD remote control. Click any of the arrows to advance through the Scene Menu buttons, and click the center circle (the Enter button) to play that scene. Adobe Premiere Elements automatically controls the navigation of all menu buttons, so you should preview all scenes on the disc to ensure that you placed your markers logically. When done, close the Preview Disc window.

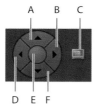

A. Up. **B**. Right. **C**. Main Menu button.
D. Left. **E**. Enter. **F**. Down.

10 Choose File > Save to save your project file.

Working with submenus

Before you start customizing menu appearance, there are some other navigation and button placement options that you should be aware of. For example, many Hollywood movies have a link on the main menu to bonus or deleted clips sections. Adobe Premiere Elements lets you create a submenu button on your main menu by adding a special menu marker.

In addition, by default, once a viewer starts watching any portion of the movie, the video will continue on to the end, even if there are intervening scene markers. In the project you've been working on this isn't a problem, but with other projects you may wish to stop playback after a scene completes and return the viewer to the menu. You can accomplish this using the stop marker discussed below.

In this exercise you will add a button on the main menu linking to a bonus video clip.

1   Under Disc Menus in the Disc Layout panel, click to select Main Menu 1. There are currently two buttons in this menu: the Play and Scenes buttons. The template design leaves space for more buttons below these two buttons, if needed.

2   Select the Timeline in the My Project panel. Press the End key on your keyboard to navigate to the end of the last clip.

    You will now add a special marker to the end of your movie.

3   Click the Add Menu Marker button (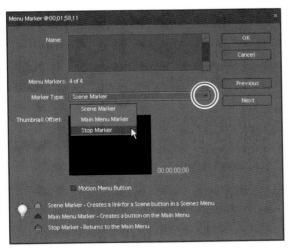) located near the upper-right corner of the My Project panel to open the Menu Marker dialog.

4   Choose Stop Marker from the Marker Type menu. When a stop marker is reached during playback, the viewer will return to the main menu.

5   Click OK to add the stop marker. In the Timeline, stop markers are colored red to help you differentiate them from the green scene markers and the blue main menu markers. You will learn more about main menu markers later in this lesson.

    You will now add an additional clip named FunnelCakeFast.avi to the end of your Timeline. This clip will be a bonus clip that users can access from the main menu, but is not part of the main movie.

Three types of menu markers

Scene Markers (⌂): Adding a scene marker to your Timeline will automatically add a scene button to the scene menu of your disc. Scenes menus are secondary to the main menu, and there should be a Scenes button on the main menu that links to the Scenes menu.

Main Menu Markers (⌂): Adding a main menu marker to your Timeline will automatically add a button to the main menu of your disc. Most templates have space for either three or four buttons on the first menu page. The Play Movie button and the Scenes button are present by default. This will leave you with space for one or two more buttons, depending on the template you have chosen. If you add additional main menu markers to your movie, Adobe Premiere Elements will create a secondary main menu.

Stop Markers (⌂): Adding a stop marker to your Timeline will force Adobe Premiere Elements to stop the playback of your Timeline and return the viewer to the main menu. Use stop markers to control the viewer's flow through the movie. For example, if you want the viewer to return to the main menu after each scene, insert a stop marker at the end of each scene. You can also use stop markers to add bonus or deleted scenes after the main movie, linking to this content using either scene or main menu markers.

6 Select the Edit tab of the Tasks panel, and then click Project. From Project view, click and drag the FunnelCakeFast.avi clip into the Video 1 track, after the Credit sequence at the end of your Timeline. Be sure to place the clip a few seconds from the last clip, leaving a gap between the clips.

7 Press the Page Dn key to advance the current-time indicator to the beginning of the added FunnelCakeFast.avi clip, and then click the Add Menu Marker button ( ) to open the Menu Marker dialog.

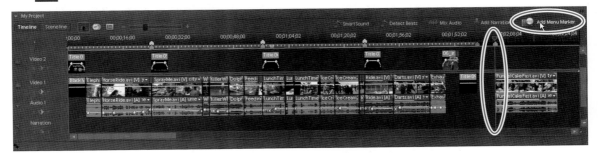

8 In the Menu Marker dialog, choose Main Menu Marker from the Marker Type menu. In the name field, type *Bonus Clip*, and then click OK to close the Menu Marker dialog.

Adobe Premiere Elements adds a button named Bonus Clip to the Main Menu 1 in the Disc Layout panel.

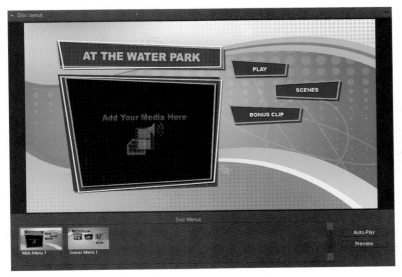

9 Click the Disc Menus tab and then the Preview button, and then click the Bonus Clip button to play the video associated with it. When the bonus clip has finished playing, the main menu appears. If you play the main movie from start to finish, you will not see the bonus clip because of the stop marker you added at the end of the last clip in the main movie.

● **Note:** You do not have to add a stop marker at the end of the bonus clip. When Adobe Premiere Elements reaches the end of the Timeline, it will automatically return the viewer to the main menu.

10 Close the Preview Disc window.

11 Choose File > Save to save your project file.

Customizing menus in Properties view

When you produce a disc in Adobe Premiere Elements, you have multiple customization options for your menu, including the ability to change fonts and font colors, to add a still image or video background, to add background music to the menu, and to animate the button thumbnails on your menus. You accomplish all these tasks in Properties view, which displays different options depending upon the object you select. Let's take a quick tour.

1   Make sure you are in the Disc Menus workspace, and then choose Window > Restore Workspace to reset the location of your panels.

2   Under Disc Menus in the Disc Layout panel, click the Scenes Menu 1 thumbnail to make sure the Scenes Menu 1 menu is loaded.

3   Click in the Scenes Menu 1 menu near the bottom of the menu, being careful not to select any navigational or thumbnail buttons.

Properties view displays two sections: Menu Background and Motion Menu Buttons. You can expand and collapse these two sections by clicking the arrows to the left of the section. In the Menu Background section there are subsections for Video or Still backgrounds and Audio backgrounds.

4   Click the Dolphins marker button. Adobe Premiere Elements displays a rectangle, referred to as the *bounding box*, around the button. There are eight selection points around the box that you'll work with in a moment.

Note that Properties view now displays two sections: Menu options on top, and Text options on the bottom. The Menu options are very similar to those selected in the Menu Marker panel. Some, such as the Poster Frame In Point, you can change directly in Properties view; others, such as the Button Type, you have to return to the Menu Marker panel to modify.

5 Click the Scene Selection title in Scenes Menu 1. Adobe Premiere Elements displays a bounding box around the title and displays only the Text options in Properties view.

Those are three control sets of Properties view. Click the menu component you'd like to edit, and Adobe Premiere Elements automatically opens the necessary controls. As always, in addition to clicking the menu to open Properties view, you can also choose Window > Properties from the Adobe Premiere Elements main menu to open Properties view.

Customizing menus with video, still images, and audio

You can customize your menus in Adobe Premiere Elements by adding a still image, video, or audio to the menu. You can also combine multiple items, such as a still photo and an audio clip. Alternatively, you can add a video clip and replace the audio track with a separate audio clip.

Note that your customization options differ based upon the selected menu template. If the menu has a drop zone, like the template you're working with in this lesson, still images or video inserted into the menu will display in the drop zone.

Otherwise, with templates that lack drop zones, the inserted still image or video will appear full-screen in the menu background. You'll see an example of that in a moment.

Although Adobe Premiere Elements allows you to customize a disc menu, keep in mind that changes made will not be saved back to the template; they apply to only the current project. If you would like to create custom templates to be used in multiple projects, you can create one in Adobe Photoshop Elements, and then add the template to Adobe Premiere Elements.

Adding a still image or video clip to your menu

You'll use the same procedure to add a still image or video clip to a menu. In this exercise, you'll insert a video clip into a menu. By default, when you insert a video, the audio plays with the video as well, though you can change this by inserting a separate audio file, as you will do later.

Follow this procedure to add a video clip to your menu.

1   Under Disc Menus in the Disc Layout panel, click to select Main Menu 1. Click in the main menu, being careful not to click one of the active buttons.

2   In Properties view, in the Menu Background box click the Browse button and navigate to the Lesson11 folder and choose the Menu.avi clip. Press Open to close the dialog and insert the clip into the menu panel. Note that you'd follow this same procedure to select a still image to either fit into the drop zone or use as a full-screen background image.

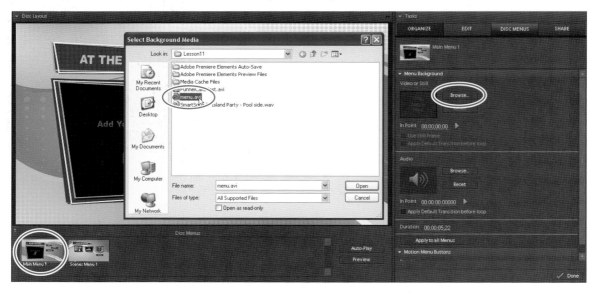

3 Note the options available in the Menu Background box in Properties view. Specifically, you can do the following:

- Play the video by clicking the green play triangle ().

- Choose an In Point for the video to start, either by dragging the time counter or by typing in the timecode for the desired starting point.

- After choosing an In Point, you can select the Use Still Frame checkbox to use the current frame as the background or within the drop zone.

- Note that the maximum duration for video menus is 30 seconds, and that the menu will loop indefinitely after that time. You can apply the default transition to the video clip before it starts to loop by selecting the Apply Default Transition before loop checkbox.

Leave the options at their default settings, and click Preview to preview the menu. When finished, close the Preview window and return to the Disc Layout panel.

4 Choose File > Save to save your project file.

As mentioned, when you add a video to a menu with a drop zone, the video plays within that drop zone. When you add a video to a menu without a drop zone, the video plays in the background. You can see that in the following figure, which you can reproduce by dragging the Camera menu from the General category onto the Disc Layout panel.

Accordingly, to create a menu with your own full-screen still image or video in the background, choose a template without a drop zone. If you opt to customize a menu with a full-screen background image or video, you'll have to manually insert it into each menu created by Adobe Premiere Elements. Note that you can insert a different still image or video clip as a background in each menu, or use the background image that came with the menu template.

Adding an audio clip to the background

Let's substitute a separate audio clip for the audio included with the menu.avi video clip. Use this same procedure to add audio to any menu template, whether modified with a still image background or used as is.

1 Click Main Menu 1 in the Disc Layout panel to open its Properties view. If necessary, scroll down the Properties view to locate the Audio section.

2 Click the Browse button, select the soundtrack.wav clip in the Lesson11 folder, and then click Open.

3 If you'd like to add a fade-out so the audio loops nicely, select the Apply Default Transition before loop checkbox.

4 In the Disc Layout panel, click the Preview button. You can see the video or video frame and hear the audio track you selected for the Main menu background.

5 Close the Preview window.

6   If you'd like to remove the audio portion from the menu background, click the Reset button next to the speaker icon in the Audio section of Properties view.

7   Following this same procedure, select Scene Menu 1 from the Disc Layout panel and add the soundtrack.wav clip as the background audio file, making sure to enable the default transition.

8   Save your project.

Animating buttons

If the menu template that you select uses thumbnail scene buttons, you can elect to animate the buttons. With an animated button, a designated duration of video from the linked scene will play within the thumbnail while the menu displays. The main menu for this project does not include any buttons with image thumbnails. However, the scene menu does have image thumbnails. You will now animate these thumbnails.

1   Select the Scenes Menu 1 thumbnail under Disc Menus in the Disc Layout panel.

2   Click the Dolphins button to select it. Currently this button is displaying a still frame extracted from the video clip at the 00;00;27;01 mark.

3   In Properties view, in the Menu box scroll down, if necessary, to see all of the Poster Frame section, and then select the Motion Menu Button checkbox. To animate all marker buttons, click the Apply to all Marker Buttons button.

4   If you'd like to change the In Point of the video clip and play a different segment in the animated thumbnail, drag the time counter (currently reading the 00;00;27;01) to the desired spot.

5   Click an empty area of your background menu. This deselects the current scene button, and Properties view switches to the Menu Background properties. Scroll down to the bottom of Properties view, if necessary, to locate the Motion Menu Buttons box.

● **Note:** You cannot set the Out Point, or the end of clips, in Properties view, but you can set all your motion menu buttons to be the same duration, as explained below.

6 Note that the default duration for the Motion Menu Buttons is 00;00;29;29, or just under 30 seconds. Leave this value at the default.

7 Click the Preview button in the Disc Layout panel. In the Main menu, click the Scenes button to access the Scenes menu. All of the buttons should now be animated.

8 Close the Preview Disc window.

9 If you'd like to pick a different In point for your thumbnail video, select the Motion Menu Button option and choose suitable In Points for the two other scene buttons. If you didn't click the Apply to all Marker Buttons button above, you must individually activate scene buttons to animate them. All animated buttons share the same duration.

10 Save your project.

Customizing button size, location, and text attributes

Beyond adding still images, video, and audio to your menu, you can also change the size, appearance, and location of buttons and text on your menus. In this exercise you will make changes to your menu appearance and buttons.

1 Make sure you are in the Disc Menus workspace, and then choose Window > Restore Workspace to reset the location of your panels.

2 Under Disc Menus in the Disc Layout panel, click the Main Menu 1 thumbnail to make sure the main menu is loaded.

3 Click the Play button to select it. Adobe Premiere Elements opens the eight-point bounding box. Place your pointer on the upper-right corner, and then drag upward and outward to enlarge the text box.

Scaling text boxes in this manner can be tricky because the width and height do not scale proportionally. Text can easily become distorted.

Overlapping buttons

Buttons on a disc menu should not overlap each other. If two or more buttons overlap, there is a potential for confusion. Someone who is using a pointer to navigate and click the menu may not be able to access the correct button if another one is overlapping it. This can easily happen if button text is too long or if two buttons are placed too close to each other.

Overlapping buttons can sometimes be fixed by shortening the button name or, in general, by simply repositioning the buttons. By default, overlapping buttons in Adobe Premiere Elements are outlined in red in the Disc Layout panel. This feature can be turned off or on by choosing Show Overlapping Menu Buttons from the Disc Layout panel menu at the right side of the docking header.

4   Press Ctrl+Z on your keyboard to undo the changes. Adobe Premiere Elements allows you to undo multiple steps, so you can backtrack through your changes.

5   With the Play Movie button still selected, press the equals sign (=) on your keyboard and the text box size increases proportionally. Press the minus sign (-) on your keyboard to reduce the size of your text box proportionally. Using the keyboard commands to change the size avoids the risk of distorting the text.

6   Click the Scenes button in the Disc Layout panel to select it, and then press the left arrow key on your keyboard to move it. Pressing the arrow keys on your keyboard allows you to move a button one pixel at a time in the direction of the arrow. Press the right arrow key to move the button back to its original location.

7   Save your project.

Note: All buttons and titles within Adobe Premiere Elements templates are within the title-safe zone. If you plan to resize or move buttons or text on the menu, you should enable Show Safe Margins in the Disc Layout panel menu at the right side of the docking header menu as shown below and make sure that all content is within the title-safe zone before recording your disc.

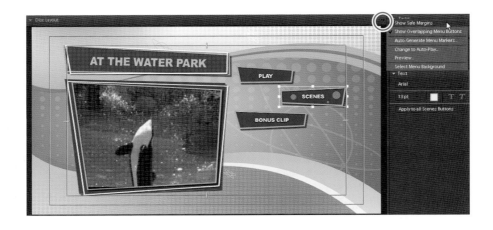

Changing menu button text properties

Properties view lets you modify the font, size, color, and style of your menu buttons, and you can automatically apply changes made to one button to similar buttons.

You can modify the text attributes of five types of objects: Menu Titles, which are objects that are text-only and are not linked to clips or movies; Play buttons, which link to the beginning of your main movie; Scene Marker buttons, which link to the Scenes menu; Marker buttons, which directly link to a menu marker on the Timeline; and Navigational buttons, such as the link back to the main menu in the Scenes menu.

A. Menu Title. **B.** Play button.
C. Scene button. **D.** Marker button.
E. Navigational button.

1. Under Disc Menus in the Disc Layout panel, click the Scenes Menu 1 thumbnail.

2. Click the Dolphins marker button. Properties view updates automatically and shows that this is a marker button—specifically, a Scene Marker button. The Text subsection allows you to change the properties of the text. If necessary, scroll down in Properties view to see all of the Text subsection.

3. In the Text subsection, click the font menu, and then choose Adobe Garamond Pro from the list of available fonts. (Notice that this font is located under the Garamond font, not sorted with the fonts whose names start with the letter A.) The marker text appearance changes.

4. Click the style menu, currently set at Regular, and change the style to Bold.

5. The next menu, the Text Size menu, allows you to change the text size to any of the preset sizes. Change the text size to 18 pt.

6. Click the white color swatch next to the Text Size menu to open the Color Picker dialog. You will now change the color of your text to orange. Click once in the vertical color spectrum in the general range of orange. Then, click in the lower-right corner of the large color field to choose a bright orange. We selected a color with R: 222, G: 159, B: 13. Click OK to apply the color.

A. Click here to pick the specific shade within the selected range of colors. **B.** Click here to change the general range of colors.

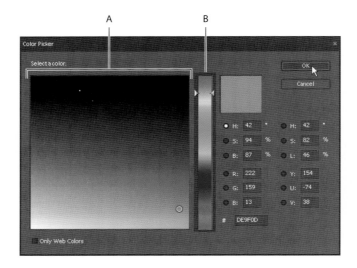

Notice that the other scene marker buttons have retained their original formatting. Normally, changes affect only the selected object. But Adobe Premiere Elements also gives you the option to change the text attributes of all buttons of the same type simultaneously.

7 In the Text subsection of Properties view, click the Apply to all Marker Buttons button. This applies the same text attributes to all three Scenes Marker buttons.

Note: You can override any single button by returning to Properties view and making changes for just the selected button.

8 Under Disc Menus in the Disc Layout panel, click the Main Menu 1 thumbnail. Notice that the Bonus Clip marker has also changed its appearance. This is because the Marker Button category encompasses both Scene Marker and Main Menu Maker buttons.

9 Note that the text for the third marker button, Afternoon Fun, is now too big for its background box. To fix that, choose Edit > Undo, select the Bonus Clip marker button in Main Menu 1, and then click the Apply to all Marker Buttons button in the Text subsection of Properties view. This first resets the text attributes of the Bonus Clip marker button, and then applies them to all three Scene Marker buttons as well.

10 Choose File > Save As and save this project file into your Lesson11 folder as *Lesson11_Final.prel*.

Burning DVDs or Blu-ray Discs

After you have previewed your disc and have checked the menus and button names, you are now ready to record the project to a DVD or Blu-ray Disc. As noted at the beginning of the chapter, you must have either a DVD or a Blu-ray Disc writer to record a respective disc.

When making a DVD or Blu-ray Disc, Adobe Premiere Elements converts your video and audio files into a compressed format. Briefly, compression shrinks your original video and audio files to fit it on a disc. For example, a 60-minute video in DV format requires approximately 13 GB of hard disk space. However, a DVD-video holds only 4.7 GB of space. So how do you fit 13 GB of video into a 4.7 GB disc? Through compression!

The process of compression can be quite lengthy. In essence, Adobe Premiere Elements evaluates every frame of video in your project and attempts to lower the file size without sacrificing the image quality. You should allow quite a bit of time for this process. For example, 60 minutes of video may take 4 to 6 hours of time to compress and record onto a DVD, and compressing and recording HD video onto a Blu-ray Disc can take even longer. For this reason, it may be a good idea to initiate the disc-burning process (which begins with compressing the video) at a time when you will not need your computer.

To maintain maximum quality, Adobe Premiere Elements compresses the movie only as much as is necessary to fit it on the disc. The shorter your movie, the less compression required and the higher the quality of the video on the disc.

Note: This exercise ends with the burning of a DVD. If you do not wish to create a DVD, you may follow the steps of the exercise up to the point of writing the disc. If you will be creating a DVD, we suggest using a DVD-RW (Rewritable) disc, if you have one available, so that you can reuse the disc later.

1   Select the Share workspace by clicking the Share tab in the Tasks panel.

2   Save your current project. It is always a good idea to save your Adobe Premiere Elements project file before burning a disc.

3   Click the Disc button ( ) in the How would you like to share? box to open the Disc view. Choose DVD from the list at the top of Disc view. To burn a Blu-ray Disc, select Blu-ray from that list.

4   Make sure Burn to Disc is selected in the "Burn to" menu. You would select the option to burn to a folder on your hard disk if you prefer to use an alternative program to burn your discs.

5   In the Disc Name field, type *Water Park*. Software playing DVDs or Blu-ray Discs on a personal computer may display this disc name.

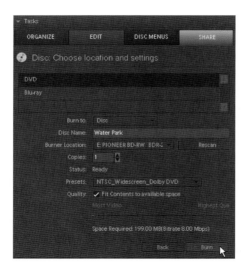

6 Select the desired DVD or Blu-ray Disc burner from the Burner Location menu. If you don't have a compatible disc burner connected to your computer, the Burner Location menu is disabled and the Status line reads "No burner detected."

● **Note:** Adobe Premiere Elements detects only burners that are connected and turned on at the time you started Adobe Premiere Elements. If you connected and turned on any burners after that point, they are not recognized until you restart Adobe Premiere Elements.

7 If you wish to create a DVD or Blu-ray Disc, make sure that a compatible blank disc is inserted in the disc burner. If you insert a disc after you start this process, click Rescan to have Adobe Premiere Elements recheck all connected burners for valid media.

8 Next to Copies, select the number of discs you want to burn during this session. For this exercise, choose 1. When you select multiple copies, Adobe Premiere Elements asks you to insert another disc after the writing of each disc is completed, until all the discs you specified have been burned.

9 Select the "Fit Contents to available space" checkbox. This will ensure that Adobe Premiere Elements maximizes the quality of your video based on disc capacity.

10 From the Presets menu, select the NTSC_Widescreen_Dolby DVD option. Adobe Premiere Elements is also capable of burning a project to the PAL standard (used in Europe, parts of Africa, South America, and the Middle East, Australia, New Zealand, some Pacific Islands, and certain Asian countries), in both normal or widescreen format.

11 If you wish to burn a disc at this point, click the Burn button. If you do not wish to burn a disc, click the Back button.

Choosing Blu-ray Disc quality options

When burning to Blu-ray Disc, you have multiple compression and resolution options. In general, recording to MPEG-2 is much faster than H.264 and quality is very similar at high to moderate data rates. Unless you're recording 2 or more hours to a Blu-ray Disc, MPEG-2 should deliver equal quality in much less time.

When choosing a target resolution, use the native resolution of your source footage. For example, HDV has a native resolution of 1440x1080, so if you recorded in HDV, you should produce your disc at that resolution. If you have a recent AVCHD camcorder, you may be recording in native 1920x1080, so use that resolution for your Blu-ray Disc. If you're not sure what resolution you're recording in, check the documentation that came with your camcorder.

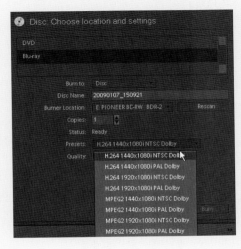

Congratulations, you have successfully completed this lesson. You learned how to manually and automatically add scene markers to your movie, and then created an auto-play disc and—by applying a menu template—a disc with menus. You added a submenu for a bonus clip and learned about stop and main menu makers. You customized the disc menus by changing text attributes, background images, button labels, and image thumbnails. You added sound and video clips to the menu background, and activated motion menu buttons. Finally, you learned how to burn your movie onto a DVD or Blu-ray Disc.

Review questions

1. What is an auto-play disc? What is the benefit of creating one? The disadvantage?

2. How would you identify separate scenes for use in your disc menu?

3. What is a submenu, and how would you add one to your disc menu?

4. Which menu button text properties can you change, and how are these properties modified?

5. Which type of menu template should you choose if you want to insert a still image or video file as a full-screen background for your disc menus?

Review answers

1. An auto-play disc allows you to create a DVD or Blu-ray Disc quickly from the main movie of your project. The advantage of an auto-play disc is that it can be quickly and easily created, while the disadvantage is that it does not have a menu for navigation during playback.

2. Separate scenes can be defined by placing a scene marker on a specific frame in the Timeline. Scene markers are set in the Timeline using the Add Menu Marker button.

3. A submenu is a button on your main disc menu that points to a specific section of your project, such as a credit sequence or a bonus clip. Submenus are created by adding a main menu marker to your Timeline.

4. You can change the font, size, color, and style of your text buttons. Changing the properties of your text is done inside Properties view for objects selected in the Disc Layout panel.

5. You should choose a template that does not include a drop zone. If you insert a still image or video into a menu template with a drop zone, it will display that content within the drop zone.

12 SHARING MOVIES

This lesson is based on a project that you finished in a previous chapter, which you'll now share using multiple techniques. In this lesson, you'll learn how to send your completed video project to the digital media or device of choice, for example a DV camera. You will also learn the different ways you can export movies to view online or on a personal computer. Specifically, you'll learn how to do the following:

- Upload a video file to YouTube

- Export a video file for subsequent viewing from a hard disk

- Export a video file for viewing on an iPod or other mobile device

- Record your video file back to DV/HDV tape

- Export a single frame as a still image

- Use the Quick Share feature to save and reuse your favorite sharing methods

 This lesson will take approximately 2 hours.

Sharing a video on YouTube.

About sharing and exporting

Apart from creating DVDs or Blu-ray Discs, you can export and share movies, still images, and audio in a variety of file types for the web, computer playback, mobile devices, and even videotape. The Share workspace in the Tasks panel is your starting point for exporting your finished project. Here you choose your target and configuration options.

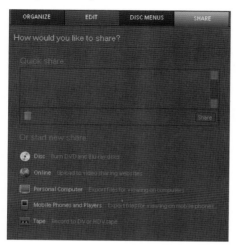

Selecting any of the options listed under How would you like to share? opens a view in the Tasks panel that provides output-specific options and settings. Share view simplifies sharing and exporting by providing presets of the most commonly used formats and settings. If you want to specify unique settings for any format, you can click Advanced options and make changes.

When exporting using the Share workspace, you can create a Quick Share preset to save and reuse your favorite sharing method for future projects, along with all the settings. Whenever you want to share a project using those settings, just select that preset and click the Share button.

The first step for all sharing is choosing your desired target. The exercises in this chapter walk through examples of the available targets in the Share workspace.

Getting started

To begin, you'll launch Adobe Premiere Elements and open the project used for this lesson. Then you'll review a final version of the project you'll be creating.

1   Before you begin, make sure that you have correctly copied the Lesson12 folder from the DVD in the back of this book onto your computer's hard disk. See "Copying the Classroom in a Book files" in the Getting Started section of this book.

2   Start Adobe Premiere Elements and click the Open Project button in the Welcome screen and then click Open. If Adobe Premiere Elements is already open, choose File > Open Project.

3   Navigate to the Lesson12 folder and select the project file Lesson12_Start.prel. Click the Open button to open your project. If a dialog appears asking for the location of rendered files, click the Skip Previews button. The Adobe Premiere Elements work area appears, with the Edit workspace selected in the Tasks panel.

4   The project file opens with Properties view and the Media, Monitor, and My Project panels visible. Choose Window > Restore Workspace to ensure that you start the lesson with the default panel layout.

Viewing the completed movie for the first exercise

To see what you'll be exporting in this lesson, play the completed movie.

1   In the Edit tab of the Tasks panel, click Project ( ). In Project view, locate the file Lesson12_Movie.wmv, and then double-click it to open the video into the Preview window.

2   In the Preview window, click the Play button ( ) to watch the video about a visit to the water park, which you will build in this lesson.

3   When done, close the Preview window by clicking the Close button ( ) in the upper-right corner of the window.

If the movie looks familiar, that's because it's the project you finished back in Chapter 8 after adding a soundtrack and narration. Now it's time to share the fruits of your hard work with the world!

Sharing online

Let's start by uploading the project to YouTube. It's faster if you already have an account with YouTube, but if not, you can sign up as part of the process. Follow these steps to upload your project to YouTube:

1   Click Share in the Tasks panel, and then click Online ( ).

2   Choose YouTube from the list at the top. Adobe Premiere Elements uses the Flash preset for YouTube for all files produced to upload to YouTube.

● **Note:** The other option available when sharing online is to upload a video to your website via FTP.

3 Choose a quality level from the Quality menu. In the first release of Adobe Premiere Elements 7, Medium quality is your only option, but this may change as YouTube adds higher-quality features to its service.

4 If desired, click the Share WorkArea Bar Only to upload only the work area bar.

5 Click Next.

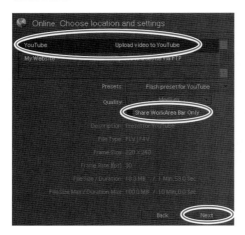

6 Log in to YouTube. If this is your first time uploading to YouTube, click Sign Up Now and register. Then log in.

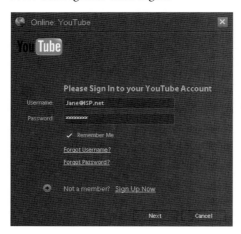

7 Click Next.

8 Enter the required information about your project: Title, Description, Tags, and Category. Choose a language, and then click Next.

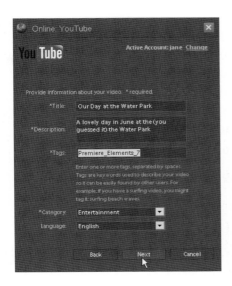

9 Choose whether you want to allow the public to view your project, or to keep it private, and then click Share. Adobe Premiere Elements renders the project and starts uploading to YouTube.

10 When the share is complete, the URL appears in the Share workspace and you can choose View My Shared Video to open YouTube and watch your video, or Send an E-mail to alert friends to your new posting.

● **Note:** We're pretty sure that there will be (at least) dozens, if not hundreds of copies of this video on YouTube by sometime in late 2009. It might be a better idea if you follow these latter steps to upload your own video to YouTube, or, if you do upload this sample movie, that you later delete it.

11 Do *one of the following:*

- To save your workflow as a Quick Share preset, click Save Workflow, and follow the instructions in the next lesson.

- To return to the main Share workspace without saving a Quick Share preset, click Finish.

Adding a Quick Share preset

Let's add that YouTube workflow to your Quick Share presets so you can access it more easily in the future. You can add a Quick Share preset any time you've completed a sharing action. Here's the procedure.

1 After sharing your project via YouTube, click Save Workflow. Adobe Premiere Elements opens the Save As Quick Share dialog.

2 Type a name and description, and click Save.

3 Adobe Premiere Elements saves the output preset in the Quick Share dialog. To share using this preset in the future, click the Share tab in the Tasks panel, then the desired Quick Share preset, and then the Share button. Adobe Premiere Elements will share the project using the selected Quick Share option.

Sharing on Your Personal Computer

In the previous exercise, you exported an Adobe Premiere Elements project to YouTube. In this exercise, you will export your project as a standalone video file to play on your own system, upload to a website, email to friends or family, or archive on DVD or external hard disk.

As you'll see in a moment, Adobe Premiere Elements lets you output in multiple formats for all these activities. Each file format comes with its own set of presets available from the Presets menu. You can also customize a preset and save it for later reuse, which you'll do in this lesson.

See the sidebar, "Choosing an output format" for more information on which preset to choose. In this exercise, you'll output a file using the Windows Media format.

1 In Share view, click the Personal Computer button (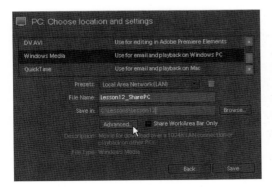).

2 In the list at the top of Share view, choose Windows Media.

3 In the Presets list box, choose Local Area Network (LAN).

4 Next to File Name:, enter *Lesson12_SharePC*, and then click Browse to select the Lesson12 folder as the Save in folder.

5 Click the Advanced button to open the Export Settings dialog. Here you can review the settings used for the chosen file format and preset. If necessary, you can make adjustments to the export settings, which will vary by format. Because the Water Park project is a 16:9 project, you'll have to modify the Frame Height to achieve this aspect ratio in your output file; otherwise, Adobe Premiere Elements will produce a 640x480 file with black bars on the top and bottom of your file. Click the Frame Height text box, and type *360*.

6 Click OK to close the Export Settings dialog. Since you modified the export settings, Adobe Premiere Elements lets you save the preset for later reuse, and opens the Choose Name dialog with all text highlighted, so you can simply type in a new name.

Formats

- **Adobe Flash Video**—Adobe Flash Video is a very high-quality format that's used by the majority of sites on the Internet for playback via the ubiquitous Adobe Flash Player. Use this format if producing files to be distributed from a website. However, the FLV files produced by this format require a standalone player like the Adobe Media Player to play back from a hard drive outside of the browser environment. Though the Adobe Media Player is rapidly gaining in popularity, many viewers still don't have this program, or a different standalone FLV player installed on their computers, so this format is not appropriate for creating files to send to other computers, whether by email, file transfer protocol (FTP), or via a Universal Serial Bus (USB) drive.

- **MPEG**—MPEG is a very widely supported playback format, though it is used almost exclusively for desktop or disc-based playback rather than for streaming. Use MPEG to create files for inserting into Blu-ray or DVD projects produced in other programs. For most casual disk-based playback, however, either QuickTime or Windows Media offer better quality at lower data rates, making them better options for files shared via email or FTP.

- **DV AVI**—This is the format used by DV camcorders. DV AVI is an excellent archival format for standard-definition (SD) productions, and a good choice for producing files to be further edited in other programs. However, DV AVI files are too large for casually distributing via email or FTP.

- **Windows Media**—Windows Media files, whether distributed via a website or by email or FTP, can be played by virtually all Windows computers via the Windows Media Player. Quality is good at lower bitrates, making Windows Media a good choice for producing files to be distributed via email to other Windows users. However, Macintosh compatibility may be a problem because Microsoft hasn't released a Windows Media Player for OS X, forcing users to download a third-party solution from Flip4Mac. When producing files for viewing on Macintosh computers, use the QuickTime format.

- **QuickTime**—QuickTime is the best choice for files intended for viewing on both Macintosh and Windows computers, whether distributed via the web, email, or other technique. All presets use the H.264 codec, which offers very good quality but can take a long time to render.

When producing a file for uploading to a website like Yahoo Video, Facebook, or Blip.tv, check the required file specifications published by each site before producing your file.

7   Type *640x360 widescreen preset*, then click OK to return to the Share
    workspace. When sharing future projects, you can access this preset from the
    Presets list box.

8   Check the File Name text box, and if changed, re-enter *Lesson12_SharePC*.

9   If desired, select the Share WorkArea Bar Only checkbox.

10 To start exporting your movie, click Save.

    Adobe Premiere Elements begins rendering the video, and displays a progress
    bar in Share view and an estimated time to complete each phase of the
    rendering process. Click Cancel at any time to stop the exporting process.
    Otherwise, you will see a Save Complete! message in Share view, once the
    rendering is complete.

11 Click Save As Quick Share to save the preset, or click Done to return to the
    Share workspace.

Exporting to mobile phones and players

Use this option to produce a file for a mobile phone or player like the Apple iPod
or iPhone, the Creative Zen or the Microsoft Zune. Note that most of these devices
have very specific and inflexible file requirements, so you shouldn't change any
parameters in the Export Settings window, since you may produce a file that's
unplayable on the target device.

In this lesson, you'll learn how to create a file for the iPod; if producing for a different device, just choose that device and preset in the appropriate steps.

1   In Share view, click the Mobile Phones and Players button ( ).

2   In the list at the top of Share view choose "Apple iPod and iPhone."

3   In the Presets list box, choose iPod and iPhone – High Quality to produce a
    high-quality file compatible with iPods, iPhones, the iPod touch, and similar,
    newerMP3 devices, keeping in mind that this file won't play on some older MP3

devices. Choose iPod and iPhone – Medium Quality for a lower-quality file that should be play on all MP3 devices, past and present. For the purposes of this exercise, choose iPod and iPhone - High Quality.

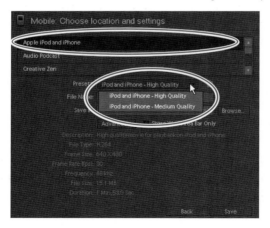

4   Next to File Name, enter *Lesson12_iPod*, then click Browse to select your Lesson12 folder as the Save in folder.

5   If desired, select the Share WorkArea Bar Only checkbox.

6   To start exporting your movie, click Save.

   Adobe Premiere Elements starts rendering the video, and displays a progress bar in Share view and an estimated time to complete each phase of the rendering process. Click Cancel at any time to stop the exporting process. Otherwise, you will see a Save Complete! message in Share view once the rendering is complete.

7   Click Save As Quick Share to save the preset, or click Done to return to the Share workspace.

After producing the file, transfer it to your device as normal. For example, use iTunes to upload the file to your iPod or iPhone.

Preparing to export to tape

The final Share option is Tape, and if you have access to a DV camera, you may want to use it for this exercise. We will proceed as if a DV camera is connected to your system, but if not, you may follow this exercise anyway.

To begin, connect your DV camera to your personal computer and turn it on, then open Adobe Premiere Elements. In most cases, if Adobe Premiere Elements is already open, it will recognize a DV camera as it is attached and turned on; however, we've found this happens more reliably if the DV camera is connected first.

When writing videos to tape, it's good practice to add some excess video to the start of the project to prevent your recording device from accidentally cutting off the first few seconds of your project. In this regard, Adobe Premiere Elements lets you create either a 5 second black video file, or a universal counting leader, which looks like the countdown video that preceded older movies you may have viewed in the theater. In this exercise, you'll add a universal counting leader to your project before writing it to tape.

1   Connect your DV camera to your computer. For help, refer to your owner's manual or the diagram located in Lesson 3, "Connecting your device."

2   Turn on your DV device and switch it to the VTR (or VCR) mode. If a Digital Video Device dialog appears, click the Cancel button to close it.

3   Start Adobe Premiere Elements and open the project file Lesson12_Start.prel in the Lesson12 folder. If a dialog appears asking for the location of rendered files, click the Skip Previews button.

4   In the Timeline of the My Project panel, press Home to move the current-time indicator to the start of the project.

5   In the upper-right corner of Project view, click the New Item button ( ), and then choose Universal Counting Leader from the menu that appears.

6   Adobe Premiere Elements opens the Universal Counting Leader Setup dialog. Leave all items at their default settings and click OK to close the dialog.

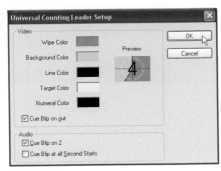

A new item called Universal Counting Leader appears in your Media panel, and Adobe Premiere Elements adds it to your Timeline after the first scene.

7   In the Timeline, drag the newly added Universal Counting Leader to the beginning of the movie, waiting for about 2 seconds for the 2 clips that comprise the opening title, KillerWhale.avi and familyfun_frame, to shift to the right. Then release the pointer, and Adobe Premiere Elements will move the Universal Counting Leader to the beginning of the movie, and shift the audio files to the right.

8   There's now a gap where the Universal Counting Leader had been. To close the gap, right-click the gap and choose Delete and Close Gap.

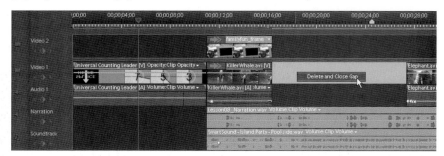

Adobe Premiere Elements deletes the gap and shifts all files after the gap to the left. You're now ready to write the project to tape.

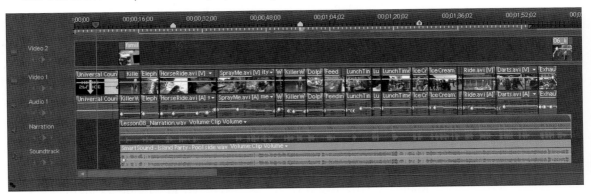

9   Choose File > Save As. Rename this file *Lesson12_DV.prel*.

Exporting to tape

Let's write the project to DV tape. If you connected an analog device such as a VCR to your DV camcorder, you can follow these steps as well to dub the video through your DV camcorder to the VCR.

1   Make sure your DV camcorder is turned on and in VTR (or VCR or Play) mode, and that you have enough blank tape to record your project.

When writing video to tape, Adobe Premiere Elements records only the video within the work area, not the entire project. So before starting, make sure that the work area includes the entire project.

2   In the Timeline of the My Project panel, press the backslash key (\) on your keyboard to display the entire project.

3   Double-click the WorkArea bar beneath the time ruler to make sure it extends to the end of the project.

● **Note:** The Delete and Close Gap command doesn't shift Menu markers in the time ruler. By adding the Universal Counting Leader at the start, all scene markers are now out of sync with their respective clips. This is of no consequence when exporting to a DV camera. For export to DVD or Blu-ray Disc, however, you would set markers only after you have finished editing your movie. If you make further changes, menu markers may become out of sync and need to be updated.

Work area bar   Work area end

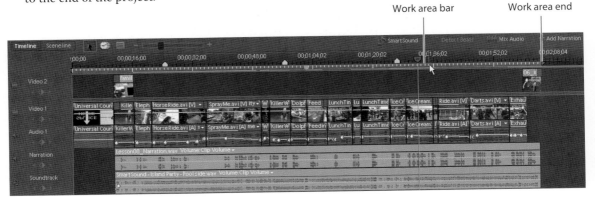

4 Select the Share tab in the Tasks panel, and then click the Tape button () at the bottom of Share view.

If your recording device is properly connected to your computer, the Export to Tape dialog opens.

Note: If you are recording to a DV device and Device Control is unavailable, click Cancel, choose Edit > Preferences > Device Control, make sure that your device is set up properly in the Device Control options, and then try recording to tape again.

5 If you're recording to a DV device, make sure the Activate Recording Device checkbox under Device Control is selected. This ensures that Adobe Premiere Elements can communicate with the device.

6 If you are using a DV device, click the Record button. After rendering project components as necessary, your DV device will begin to record as Adobe Premiere Elements begins to play the Timeline from

Export to Tape options

- **Activate Recording Device**—This option lets Adobe Premiere Elements control your DV device.

- **Assemble at timecode**—This option indicates the place on your DV tape that you want the recording to begin, if you have a tape that already has timecode recorded, or striped, on it. You stripe a tape by first recording only black video before you record your footage. You usually record black video by recording with the lens cap on. If your tape is not striped, leave this option deselected to have recording begin at the location where you have cued the tape.

- **Delay movie start by n frames**—Here you specify the number of frames that you want to delay the start of the movie so that you can synchronize it with the DV device recording start time. Some devices need a delay between the time they receive the Record command and the time the movie starts playing from the computer. Experiment with this setting if you are experiencing delays between the time you enable record and the time your DV device begins recording.

- **Preroll by n frames**—The number you enter here specifies the number of frames that you want Adobe Premiere Elements to back up on the recording deck before the specified timecode. Specify enough frames for the deck to reach a constant tape speed. For many decks, 5 seconds or 150 frames is sufficient.

- **Abort after n dropped frames**—Here you type the maximum number of dropped frames you want to allow before Adobe Premiere Elements aborts the recording. If you choose this option, you generally want to type a very low number because dropped frames will cause jerky playback, and are indicative of a hard disk or transfer problem.

- **Report dropped frames**—This specifies that Adobe Premiere Elements displays the number of dropped frames.

—*From Adobe Premiere Elements Help*

the beginning. If you are recording with an analog device, you must manually press the Record button on your device when Adobe Premiere Elements starts playing the Timeline.

7   Once the end of the project has been reached, the recording will stop automatically if you are using a DV device. If you're recording to an analog device, you must manually press its Stop button to stop recording.

8   Click the Cancel button to close the Export to Tape dialog.

Exporting a frame of video as a still image

Occasionally, you may wish to grab frames from your video footage to email to friends and family, include in a slide show, or for other purposes. In this exercise, you will learn to export a frame from the project and to create a preset to use when exporting frames in the future.

1   In the Timeline, drag the current-time indicator to timecode 00;00;52;20, or click the current timecode box on the lower left of the Monitor panel and type in *5220* and press Enter.

2   Click the Freeze Frame button (⬛) in the lower-right corner of the Monitor panel, and then click Export in the Freeze Frame dialog. You might have to enlarge the Monitor panel in order to see the Freeze Frame button.

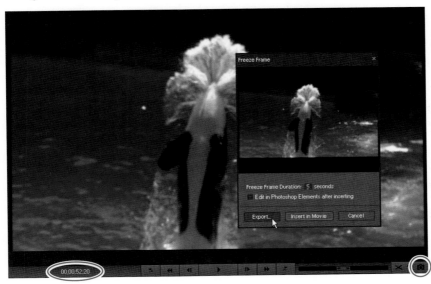

3 In the Export Frame dialog, click the Settings button to open the Export Frame Settings dialog. Don't worry about naming the file; you'll do that in a moment

4 In the General section of the Export Frame Settings dialog, choose JPEG from the File Type menu and select the Add to Project When Finished checkbox.

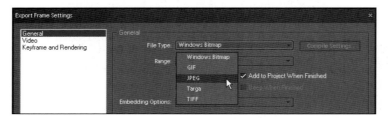

5 Click Video in the left column to access the Video control settings. Choose Square Pixels (1.0) from the Pixel Aspect Ratio menu, which optimizes the image for viewing on a computer monitor.

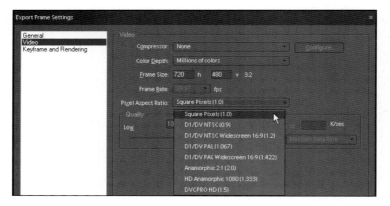

6 Click "Keyframe and Rendering" to access these controls. When working with interlaced source footage, as you are here, select the Deinterlace Video Footage checkbox to deinterlace the frame before storing the image. If working with progressive source footage, do not select Deinterlace Video Footage.

7 Click the Save button to open the Save Export Settings dialog.

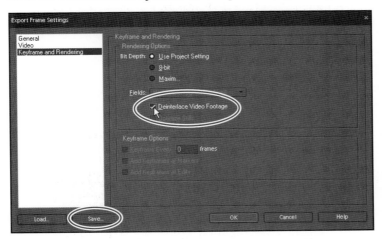

8 In the Name field of the Save Export Settings dialog, type *Still images for the Web*. In the Description field, type *Setting used to export still image for uploading to a blog or web site.*

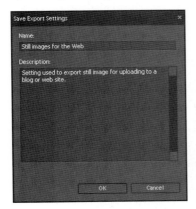

9 Click OK to save your setting and to close the Save Export Settings dialog, and then click OK to close the Export Frame Settings dialog. Back in the Export Frame dialog, locate the Lesson12 folder and name your file *killerwhale.jpg*. Click Save to save the still image onto your hard disk.

10 Click Cancel to close the Freeze Frame panel.

Because in step 4 you selected the Add to Project When Finished option, Adobe Premiere Elements has placed the still image you just saved in your Project view.

11 Double-click the killerwhale.jpg image to view it in the Preview window, and then close the Preview window and save your project.

12 In the Monitor panel, position the current-time indicator at another frame you wish to export as a still image, and then click the Freeze Frame button.

13 Click Export and then click Settings in the Export Frame dialog. Click Load in the Export Frame Settings dialog box. Select the Still images for the Web. prexport preset you have created in step 9. Click Open.

14 Click OK to establish the same export settings for this frame as used for the previous frame. Name the file *Lesson12_Frame.jpg*, and click Save to save it in the Lesson12 folder. Click Cancel to close the Freeze Frame window.

Congratulations, you've finished this lesson. You've learned how to use the Share workspace to upload a video file to YouTube, and export a video file for subsequent viewing from a hard disk. You've created a file for viewing on an iPod and exported a single frame to upload to a blog or website. You've also learned how to write your projects back to DV or HDV tape, and to use the Quick Share feature to save and reuse your favorite sharing methods.

Review questions

1   What's the best format to use for creating files to view on Windows computers or to share with other viewers with Windows computers?

2   Why shouldn't you change any encoding parameters for files produced for iPods or other devices?

3   Why should you add a universal counting leader to the beginning a file before writing it to DV or analog tape?

4   What's the easiest way to write a project to an analog tape format such as VHS?

5   What's the easiest way to upload your movie to a website such as YouTube?

Review answers

1   Windows Media is the best format for Windows because it combines small file size for easy transportability with high quality. Though virtually all computers can play MPEG-1 or MPEG-2 files, the files are usually too large for easy transport. QuickTime files may pose a problem because not all Windows computers support QuickTime, and Adobe Flash Video files with an FLV extension require a standalone player such as the Adobe Media Player, which not all computers have installed.

2   Devices have very specific playback requirements and if you change a file parameter and deviate from these requirements, the file may not load or play on the target device.

3   You should add a Universal Counting Leader or simply a black video file to the start of a project before writing it to tape to prevent the recording device from cutting off the initial frames of the video file.

4   Connect a VHS recorder to your DV camcorder via composite or S-Video connectors plus audio while writing your project to DV tape. Most DV camcorders will display the recorded signal out the analog ports while recording, which you can record on the VHS deck by clicking the record button on the deck.

5   Switch to Share view, and then click the Online button. Choose YouTube or My Website, and then follow the instructions in Share view to render and upload your movie.

13 WORKING WITH ADOBE PHOTOSHOP ELEMENTS

Adobe Photoshop Elements and Adobe Premiere Elements are designed to work together and let you seamlessly combine digital photography and video editing. You can spice up your video projects with title images or customized menu templates created in Photoshop Elements, or build slide show presentations in Photoshop Elements, and then use parts of them in Adobe Premiere Elements for further editing.

To work on the following exercises, you must have Photoshop Elements installed on your system. In this lesson, you will learn several techniques for using Photoshop Elements together with Adobe Premiere Elements. Specifically, you will learn how to do the following:

- Use the Send To command in Photoshop Elements to create a slide show in Adobe Premiere Elements

- Access Albums created in Photoshop Elements in Adobe Premiere Elements

- Paste images into Adobe Premiere Elements

- Create a Photoshop file optimized for video

- Edit a Photoshop image from Adobe Premiere Elements

 This lesson will take approximately 1.5 hours.

Working with Adobe Photoshop Elements still images in Adobe Premiere Elements.

Viewing the completed movie before you start

To see what you'll be creating, you can take a look at the completed movie.

1 Before you begin, make sure that you have correctly copied the Lesson13 folder from the DVD in the back of this book onto your computer's hard disk. See "Copying the Classroom in a Book files" in the Getting Started section of this book.

2 Navigate to the Lesson13 folder, and double-click Lesson13_Movie.wmv to play the movie in your default application for watching Windows Media Video files.

Getting started

You will now open Adobe Photoshop Elements 7 and import the files needed for the Lesson13 project.

1 Launch Photoshop Elements.

2 In the Welcome screen, click the Organize button to open the Photoshop Elements Organizer.

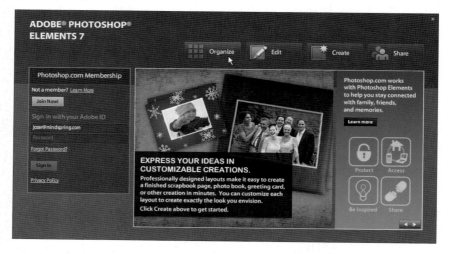

3 If you've previously used Photoshop Elements, your Organizer may be displaying the photos in your current catalog. If this is the first time you're launching Photoshop Elements, you may receive a message asking if you would like to designate a location to look for your image files. Click No, starting with an empty Organizer panel.

4 Choose File > Get Photos and Videos > From Files and Folders. Navigate to your Lesson13 folder and select—but do not open—the images subfolder. Then, click Get Photos.

5 Photoshop Elements will open the Import Attached Keyword Tags dialog. Click OK to import all keyword tags.

All the photos in this folder will be imported into Photoshop Elements.

6 If a message appears telling you that only the newly imported files will appear, click OK. In the Organizer, you should see 12 thumbnail images from a wedding. Thumbnail images are small versions of the full-size photos. You will be working with the full-size photos later in this lesson.

7 Under Albums in the Tagging window, click the Create new album or album group button (), and choose New Album. Adobe Premiere Elements opens the Album Details dialog.

8   In the Photoshop Elements menu, choose Edit > Select All to select the 12 new images. Then click on any one image and drag all the images into the Items window on the right and release the pointer.

9   In the Album Name field in the Album Details dialog, type *Wedding*.

10 On the lower left of the Album Details dialog, click Done to save the Album.

As you may recall from Lesson 4, the Organizer workspace in Adobe Premiere Elements can access albums created in Photoshop Elements. You'll learn how to access the newly created Wedding album from Adobe Premiere Elements in a later lesson.

Using the Send To command in Adobe Photoshop Elements

You can add images to an Adobe Premiere Elements 7 project using the File > Send To command in Adobe Photoshop Elements 7. Photoshop Elements will create a new project in Adobe Premiere Elements if none is currently open. Or, if there is a project currently open, Photoshop Elements will place the photos at the end of the current Sceneline or Timeline. In the following exercise you will create a new project and add images to it.

To sort images in the Organizer, Photoshop Elements uses the date and time information embedded in the image file by the digital camera. In the Organizer menu, choosing to show the oldest files first by selecting Date (Oldest First) enables you to create a slide show in chronological order when transferring the photos to Adobe Premiere Elements.

1   Right-click the first image (B0000022.jpg) and choose Show Properties from the context menu. Properties view opens to Properties-General view, which displays the name of the image and also details the file size, the date the photo was taken, and its location on your hard disk. The date the picture was taken is also displayed below the image thumbnail in the Photo Browser if you select the Details checkbox on the upper right of the Photo Browser. To show file names in the Photo Browser, choose View > Show File Names.

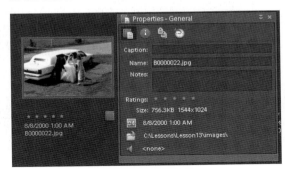

2   Press and hold the Ctrl key on your keyboard, and then in the Photo Browser click four images—B0000022.jpg, B0000025.jpg, B0000026.jpg, and B0000027.jpg—to select them. A blue outline appears around the thumbnail, as shown here, to indicate a selected image. In the next step, Photoshop Elements will process only the selected images.

● **Note:** Before performing the next step, make sure you do not have a project open in Adobe Premiere Elements. Otherwise the images will be placed in the open file.

3   Choose File > Send to Premiere Elements. A dialog may appear informing you that the files will be inserted at the end of your Timeline and that the Adobe Premiere Elements defaults will be used. Click OK. If Adobe Premiere Elements is not already open, it will launch automatically.

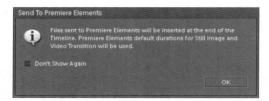

4   In the Adobe Premiere Elements New Project dialog, type *Lesson13_Start* in the name field. Click the Browse button. In the Browse For Folder dialog, navigate to the Lesson13 folder located on your hard disk and select it. Click OK to close the Browse For Folder dialog.

5   If necessary, click the Change Settings dialog and change the preset to NTSC-DV-Standard 48kHz. Click OK to close the Setup dialog, and then click OK to close the New Project dialog.

An Adobe Premiere Elements project is created, and the images you selected in Photoshop Elements are now visible in the Organizer view of the Tasks panel. They have also been added to Project view and placed in the Sceneline (and Timeline) of the My Project panel. The first image is displayed in the Monitor panel. In the Sceneline of the My Project panel you'll see all images as individual scenes.

6   With all scenes selected in the Sceneline, choose Clip > Group to place the entire group onto one target that can be moved as a single clip. Then, choose Clip > Ungroup to treat each still image as its own scene in the Sceneline.

7   Press the spacebar to play your project. Adobe Premiere Elements has used the default duration of 5 seconds for each still image and applied a cross dissolve as the default transition between each clip.

● **Note:** Although you might assume that the total length of the slide show is equal to the number of images multiplied by the default duration for still images, it's actually less than that. This is because Adobe Premiere Elements inserts the transition effect between the images by overlapping the clips by the default length of the transition effect. Note that you can change the default still image duration and transition duration in the Adobe Premiere Elements Preferences panel. See the section in Lesson 2 titled "Working with Project Preferences," for more details.

8   Return to Photoshop Elements by clicking the Adobe Photoshop Elements button at the bottom of your screen in the Windows taskbar (if it's visible), or by holding down the Alt key and pressing Tab until you see the icon for Adobe Premiere Elements. Then release the Alt key and Adobe Premiere Elements opens.

9 Click to select only one image, the one named B0000066.jpg, and then choose File > Send to Premiere Elements. Click OK to close the Send To Premiere Elements dialog if it appears. Your open application should switch to Adobe Premiere Elements and the image will be placed at the end of your Sceneline or Timeline.

10 Choose File > Save As and save this project file into your Lesson13 folder as *Lesson13_Work*.

Creating a slide show in Adobe Premiere Elements

You can create slide shows in Adobe Premiere Elements without stills being sent from Photoshop Elements.

1 In Lesson13_Work, click the Edit tab of the Tasks panel, and then click Project. You should see all the images added to the project in the previous lessons. In the Edit tab of the Tasks panel, select Media, and then click Project.

2 In the My Project panel, click the Sceneline button (if necessary) to enter the Sceneline.

3 Ctrl-click still images in the order in which you want them to appear in the slide show. Drag the selected group to a target area in the Sceneline and choose *one of the following*:

   • Add As Individual Stills (This option places each still image onto its own target area in the Sceneline).

   • Add As Grouped Slideshow (This option places the entire group onto one target that can be moved as a single clip).

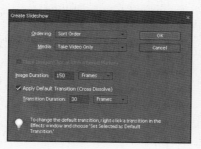

4 In the Create Slideshow dialog, select the required options and click OK.

A grouped slide show clip is created in the selected target area of the Sceneline. A slideshow icon appears to the upper right of the grouped slide show clip.

Moving images manually into Adobe Premiere Elements

Using the Send To Premiere Elements command in Photoshop Elements will not only add the images to Project view, but also place them in the Sceneline. At times you may prefer to add only the images to Project view so that you can manually place them in the My Project panel. To do this, you can copy images from the Photo Browser in Photoshop Elements and paste them into Adobe Premiere Elements, or open an Album created in Photoshop Elements in Adobe Premiere Elements. In this lesson, you will learn both these methods to transfer images from Photoshop Elements to Adobe Premiere Elements.

Using Copy and Paste to add images

The fastest way to move one or two images from Photoshop Elements to Adobe Premiere Elements is to use the copy and paste commands. Remember that you can press the Shift key to select sequential images to copy, or press the Ctrl key to select random images.

1 Make sure Photoshop Elements is your active application.

2 Press the Ctrl key, and then click to select B0000023.jpg, B0000024.jph and B0000028.jpg. Then choose Edit > Copy. Alternatively, you could use the keyboard shortcut Ctrl-C, or right-click the image thumbnail and choose Edit > Copy from the context menu.

3   Switch to Adobe Premiere Elements by clicking the Adobe Premiere Elements button at the bottom of your screen in the Windows taskbar, or holding down the Alt key and pressing Tab until you see the icon for Adobe Premiere Elements. Then release the Alt key, and Adobe Premiere Elements opens.

4   Select Project in the Edit tab of the Tasks panel to open Project view.

5   Choose Edit > Paste to add the images to Project view. You can also use the keyboard shortcut Ctrl-V, or right-click inside Project view and select Paste from the context menu. The files appear at the bottom of Project view.

After pasting the images into Project view, you can use the images just like any image that you imported into Adobe Premiere Elements.

Loading an album from Adobe Photoshop Elements

Copying and pasting images works well for small numbers of images, but sometimes you want to access the entire album. No problem, since as mentioned, Adobe Premiere Elements can open albums created in Photoshop Elements. Once open, you access the images just like content that you imported directly into Adobe Premiere Elements. You learned how to create and open albums back in Lesson 4; here's a brief refresher course.

1   In Adobe Premiere Elements, click the Organize tab to open the Organizer workspace.

2   In the Filter by: list box, scroll down and select the desired album—in this case, the Wedding album that you created earlier in the chapter.

Adobe Premiere Elements displays the Album's contents in Organizer view.

From Organize you can drop assets directly onto the Sceneline or the Monitor panel to add them to your project. Assets added from the Organizer will also be automatically added to Project view and tagged with a project-specific keyword tag. For more information on catalogs, keyword tags, and the Organizer view, see "The Organizer and Tagging panel" section of Lesson 4, "Organizing Your Content."

Creating a new Adobe Photoshop file optimized for video

The integration between Photoshop Elements and Adobe Premiere Elements works both ways. The first part of this lesson has focused on importing image files from Photoshop Elements into Adobe Premiere Elements. In this exercise, you will create a new still image in Adobe Premiere Elements, modify it in Photoshop Elements, and then use it in your Adobe Premiere Elements project.

1   Make sure you are in Adobe Premiere Elements. Choose File > New > Photoshop File. In the Save Photoshop File As dialog, navigate to your Lesson13 folder and name the file *Word_Balloon.psd*. Select the Add to Project (Merged Layers) checkbox, and then click Save. This will create a new Photoshop file in your Lesson13 folder and add a blank placeholder image in Project view.

2   Your application will automatically switch to Photoshop Elements. Click OK if you see a dialog notifying you that the file you are about to see was meant to be viewed on a TV screen. The file Word_Balloon.psd opens in the Photoshop Elements Editor.

Photoshop Elements has multiple components. The Organizer, which you used in the beginning of this lesson, enables you to sort and categorize your digital media files. The Editor, which you will use now, enables you to enhance and modify your digital images using a series of image-editing tools.

3   In the Editor, make sure Full Edit mode is selected. If necessary, click the Full Edit button under the Edit tab.

A. Full Edit button. **B.** Quick Fix button. **C.** Guided Edit. **D.** Tool options bar. **E.** Toolbox. **F.** Custom Shape tool. **G.** Color swatch.

The Word_Balloon image was automatically formatted for your digital video project using the dimensions 720 pixels wide by 480 pixels high. The checkerboard that you see indicates that the image is on a transparent background.

4 In the toolbox, select the Custom Shape tool () that is grouped with a range of other shape tools. The Custom shape menu offers a large selection of shapes ranging from ornaments, symbols, and arrows to frames, titles, characters, and much more.

5 In the tool options bar, which displays custom options for the selected tool, click the color swatch to open the Select color dialog. In the Select color dialog, enter the values R: *255*, G: *255*, and B: *255* to set the color to white, and then click OK.

6 Click the Shape menu in the tool options bar, and then select the Talk Bubbles category from the menu in the upper-right corner of the panel that appears.

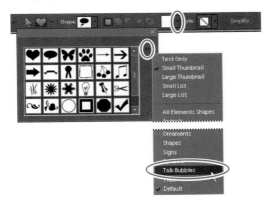

7 From within the Talk Bubbles category, double-click the last bubble on the bottom right to select the Thought 2 shape.

8 Now, place your pointer near the upper-left corner of the Word_Balloon document dialog. Drag down and to the right to create a word balloon, or thought bubble, shape. Release the pointer.

9 If necessary, use the Move tool (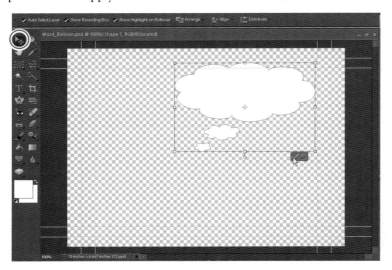) to reposition the bubble. Resize the bubble using the handles of the bounding box. Try to resize and position the shape as shown in the illustration below, and then click the green Commit button or press Enter to apply the transformation.

10 Choose File > Save. The Save As dialog should show the Lesson13 folder. If not, navigate there now. Make sure that the checkbox Save in Version Set with Original is deselected. The filename should default to Word_Balloon.psd. Click Save.

11 When the Alert dialog appears, notifying you that the file already exists, click OK. If an Adobe Photoshop Elements Format Options dialog appears, click OK to close it using the default settings. Then choose File > Close.

12 Switch to Adobe Premiere Elements by clicking the Adobe Premiere Elements button at the bottom of your screen in the Windows task bar, or by holding down the Alt key and pressing Tab until you see the icon for Adobe Premiere Elements. Then release the Alt key. Adobe Premiere Elements opens.

The Word_Balloon.psd file has automatically been updated in Project view. You can see a white thought bubble over a black background. But don't worry, the background that appears as black in Adobe Premiere Elements will be transparent once inserted into the Adobe Premiere Elements project.

13 In the Sceneline, select B0000027.jpg, the fourth clip with the newlyweds posing for a picture at the well. Hold down the Shift key on your keyboard and drag the Word_Balloon.psd file from Project view and onto the Monitor panel.

14 When you release the pointer, choose Place on Top from the menu that appears. Because the thought bubble was created on a transparent background, it is superimposed over the image below.

In the next exercise, you will add text to the thought bubble.

Hold down the Shift key while dropping the file from Project view onto the Monitor panel, and then choose Place on Top from the menu that appears.

15 If you don't like the placement of the thought bubble, you have three choices for changing it:

- Click to select the superimposed image in the Monitor panel, and then click and drag it to the desired location. Don't worry about the title-safe zone for this project.

- Use the Position parameters under Motion in Properties view (Window > Properties) to change the location of the superimposed clip. Check the small preview window above the Motion controls to make sure that Word_Balloon.psd is the active clip, and not B0000027.jpg.

- Jump back to Photoshop Elements by right-clicking the image in Project view and choosing Edit Original from the context menu. Adjust the position of the thought bubble, and save the changes. The appearance of the image will automatically update when you switch back to Adobe Premiere Elements.

16 Save your work.

Editing an Adobe Photoshop image in Adobe Premiere Elements

You can edit a Photoshop Elements image while you're working in Adobe Premiere Elements, using the Edit in Photoshop Elements command. Changes you make to the image will be updated automatically, even if the clip is already placed in your Sceneline or Timeline.

▶ **Tip:** When in the Timeline, pressing the equals sign (=) on your keyboard is a quick way to zoom in to better view the clips.

1 Switch to the Timeline in the My Project panel. If necessary, scroll to see the Video 2 track.

2 Click to select the Word_Balloon.psd clip, superimposed on Video 2 track in your Timeline. Notice that the duration of the superimposed image is slightly longer than the slide, which was shortened 15 frames by the transition that precedes it on the Timeline.

3   To adjust the duration of the superimposed thought bubble, position the pointer at the right edge of Word_Balloon.psd in the Video 2 track. When the pointer changes to Trim Out tool (), drag to the left until its right edge matches that of the B0000027.jpg clip. Then release the mouse button.

4   Right-click the Word_Balloon.psd clip in the Timeline and choose Edit in Adobe Photoshop Elements from the context menu. The Word_Balloon.psd file opens in Adobe Photoshop Elements.

● **Note:** If Photoshop Elements is closed, it will automatically launch and open the file.

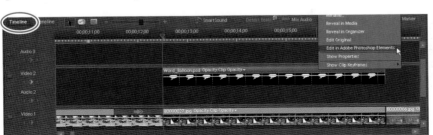

5   Select the Horizontal Type tool (), which is grouped with the Vertical Type tool in the toolbox.

6   Position your pointer inside the thought bubble near the left edge, and then click once to add an insertion point.

7   At the bottom of the toolbox, click the Default Foreground and Background Colors button. You will use the default black foreground color for your text.

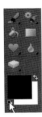

8   In the tool options bar, click the Font Family menu and choose Arial from the list of fonts. In the font size menu, select 36 pt.

9 Using the Type tool, enter the following phrase in the text layer: *Can we eat yet?*

10 Select the Move tool () in the toolbox and drag the text to center it properly in the thought bubble. If necessary, select the Shape 1 layer in the Layers panel, and then use the handles of the bounding box of the text bubble shape to adjust its size. When you're finished, click the green Commit button to commit the changes.

Can we eat yet?

11 Choose File > Save, overwriting the Word_Balloon.psd file in the Lesson13 folder. Close the file, and then switch to Adobe Premiere Elements. The changes made to the Word_Balloon.psd file in Adobe Photoshop Elements have automatically been updated in the Adobe Premiere Elements project. This is very useful because it removes the need to re-import an image file every time a change is made.

● **Note:** If your image looks grainy, click the B0000027.jpg clip to exit Title-editing mode. Then right-click the Monitor panel and choose Magnification > 100% from the menu.

12 If necessary, click the thought bubble in the Monitor panel to select it, and then drag to reposition it. Because the image is on a transparent layer, it can be easily repositioned.

13 Click the top of the Timeline to select it, and then press the Home key to place the current-time indicator at the beginning of the Timeline. Press the spacebar to play your project. When you're finished reviewing, save your work.

Microsoft Windows®
file associations

The Edit Original command can be very useful when there are changes to be made to an image. However, there are a few possible pitfalls to be aware of. When you use the Edit Original command on an image, Windows XP® opens the file in the application that is associated with the file name extension. For example, using the Edit Original command on the .jpg files used in this lesson may very well open them on your machine in another program such as a web browser. You can force Windows XP® to use Adobe Photoshop Elements as the associated application for your image files using the following steps. Be aware that you will need to perform these steps each time for different file types, .jpg, .gif, .tiff, etc. Additionally, if you happen to have both Adobe Photoshop and Adobe Photoshop Elements on the same machine, you will need to choose one to be the default application for opening image files.

To change file associations in Windows XP®, do the following:

1 Choose Start > My Computer.

2 Double-click a drive or folder.

3 Right-click the selected image file, and from the context menu that appears choose Open With > Choose Program.

4 In the Open With dialog, select Adobe Photoshop Elements (Editor) if it is in the list of Recommended Programs. If it's not in the list, click Browse and locate the application in your hard drive.

5 In the Open With dialog, make sure the checkbox Always Use the Selected Program to Open this Kind of File is selected.

For more information, see the help documentation that came with your copy of Microsoft Windows®.

Congratulations! You've finished the lesson on working with Photoshop Elements. You've discovered how to get photos from the Organizer and how to enhance them using the Editor. You also learned how to personalize a video clip with a speech bubble and text.

This is the last lesson in this book. We hope that you have gained confidence in using Adobe Premiere Elements 7, developed some new skills, and increased your knowledge of the product and the many creative things you can accomplish with it.. But this book is just the start. You can learn more by studying the Adobe Premiere Elements 7 Help system that is built into the application. Simply choose Help > Adobe Premiere Elements Help and browse or use the search functionality to find what you need. Also, don't forget to look for tutorials, tips, and expert advice on the Adobe website, www.adobe.com.

Review questions

1 Where can you find the command to place images from Adobe Photoshop Elements into Adobe Premiere Elements? Where are the images placed once they are sent to Adobe Premiere Elements?

2 What are additional ways to transfer images from Adobe Photoshop Elements in to Adobe Premiere Elements?

3 How do you create an Adobe Photoshop file in Adobe Premiere Elements? What are the advantages of doing so?

Review answers

1 In the Organizer of Adobe Photoshop Elements, choose the command File > Send to Premiere Elements. All files selected in the Photo Browser will be sent to Adobe Premiere Elements and added at the end of your Timeline. You can select individual images in the Adobe Photoshop Elements Photo Browser by Ctrl-clicking them.

2 You can transfer images from Photoshop Elements to Adobe Premiere Elements by by selecting them in Photoshop Elements, choosing Edit > Copy, switching to Adobe Premiere Elements, and then choosing Edit > Paste. From the Organizer view in Adobe Premiere Elements you can open a Photoshop Elements album, without having to open Adobe Photoshop Elements itself.

3 The command File > New > Photoshop File will create a blank Adobe Photoshop file that matches the dimensions and aspect ratio of the current project. This will enable you to use the various image editing tools in Photoshop Elements to modify or create images for use in your video project.

INDEX

Production Notes

Adobe Premiere Elements 7 Classroom in a Book was created electronically using Adobe InDesign CS3. Art was produced using Adobe InDesign, Adobe Illustrator, and Adobe Photoshop. The Myriad Pro and Warnock Pro OpenType families of typefaces were used throughout this book.

References to company names in the lessons are for demonstration purposes only and are not intended to refer to any actual organization or person.

Team Credits

The following individuals contributed to the development of this edition of *Adobe Premiere Elements 7 Classroom in a Book*:

Project Editor: Nancy Peterson
Production Editor: Tracey Croom
Development Editor: Stephen Nathans-Kelly
Copyeditor: Elizabeth Avery Merfeld
Tech Editor: Bob Lindstrom
Compositor: Kim Scott, Bumpy Design
Indexer: FireCrystal Communications
Interior design: Mimi Heft

Special thanks to Christine Yarrow.

Typefaces used

Adobe Myriad Pro and Adobe Warnock Pro are used throughout the lessons. For more information about OpenType and Adobe fonts, visit www.adobe.com/type/opentype/.

Photo credits

Photographic images, illustrations, and video supplied by Adobe Systems Incorporated. Photos and video are for use only with the lessons in the book.

Contributors

 Jan Ozer has worked in digital video since 1990, and since 1996, has served as a contributing editor to *PC Magazine* and *EventDV*. Jan's 14 books on digital video have been translated into seven languages, and include *Making a Movie in Premiere Elements: Visual QuickProject Guide*. When not chasing his two daughters around with a camcorder, Jan shoots and produces concert and training DVDs for local musicians in his adapted home of Galax, Virginia. Y'all come see us, y'hear!

 Elizabeth Whatley Ozer, the voice talent for Lesson 8, enjoys ballet dancing, singing, and acting, and plans to attend Julliard in the fall of 2016. Contributions, therefore, will be gladly accepted.

 Eleanor Rose Ozer, who generally directed the artistic components of this endeavor, enjoys cars, cats, and chocolate, not necessarily in that order. She plans to either be a Secret Service agent or an architect.

The fastest, easiest, most comprehensive way to learn
Adobe· Creative Suite· 4

Classroom in a Book®, the best-selling series of hands-on software training books, helps you learn the features of Adobe software quickly and easily.

The **Classroom in a Book** series offers what no other book or training program does—an official training series from Adobe Systems, developed with the support of Adobe product experts.

To see a complete list of our Adobe® Creative Suite® 4 titles go to www.peachpit.com/adobecs4

Adobe Press